Praise for *Will You Miss Me When I'm Gone?*

"[A] splendid new book that provides a definitive telling of the Carters' story. . . . Zwonitzer and Hirshberg . . . trace beautifully the Carters' music and their lives, which were intertwined in a way we rarely find with pop stars anymore. Along the way, the authors paint a detailed, fascinating picture of one more forgotten America that spawned an incredibly powerful voice in song."

—*Daily News* (New York)

"[An] enthralling, fact-filled, creatively conceived biography of the pioneer family of country music. . . . This is a must-read book for American music fans . . . by turns funny, serious, sad, happy, joyful, inspiring, and depressing. It will entertain you and inform you on every page."

—*The Courier-Journal* (Louisville)

"[An] absorbing and perceptive look at the original Carter Family's often troubled lives and their musical legacy."

—*Chicago Tribune*

"In *Will You Miss Me When I'm Gone?* authors Mark Zwonitzer and Charles Hirshberg fill a void in the five decade history of radio and country music. . . . This book is more than a biography of a family. It's an encyclopedia of great and near-great country music stars. . . . it's as American as apple pie and covers Dixie like the dew. You'll treasure it as a permanent part of your souvenirs."

—*The Roanoke Times*

"[T]horoughly researched. . . . This book is an essential work of musical Americana."

—*BookPage*

"This gem of a book brilliantly recounts the lives of three special people—A.P. and Sara Carter, plus Maybelle Carter, Sara's cousin and A.P.'s sister-in-law. . . . The authors . . . obviously grasp an essential point—that to understand the Carter Family's music, it is first necessary to understand their lives in the mountains of Virginia. . . . The music . . . —and the performers' lives that were shaped, then torn, by fame—is, in the hands of Zwonitzer and Hirshberg, nothing less than thrilling to read about. This is one of the best works of nonfiction in 2002."

—*Fort Worth Star-Telegram*

"Mark Zwonitzer and Charles Hirshberg's *Will You Miss Me When I'm Gone?* is a compassionate biography of the Carter Family that is by turns sweet and melancholy. The authors have captured the life and times of these remarkable people and made it read like one of the Carters' own epic mountain ballads. . . . Zwonitzer and Hirshberg bring to life a world long gone. The uncluttered grace of the Carters' music finds its way into the cadence of their prose. The stories are told with the relaxed good nature of someone sitting on a porch, talking about their neighbors. A.P. Carter's desolate loneliness and his wife's quiet desperation fuel this tale that has a soundtrack more evocative and poignant than *O Brother, Where Art Thou?*"

—*San Francisco Chronicle*

"I found myself moved and fascinated by *Will You Miss Me When I'm Gone?* . . . It is a superb history and an evocation of a purely American art form, practiced by three generations of a uniquely American family."

—*The Sun* (Baltimore)

"*Will You Miss Me When I'm Gone?*—the biography of the original Carter Family—rises above most music biographies. . . . It's a tragic tale of pride, success, and love—unrequited love, romantic love, love of family, and love of music."

—*The Charlotte Observer*

Will You Miss Me When I'm Gone?

The Carter Family and Their
Legacy in American Music

Mark Zwonitzer

with

Charles Hirshberg

Simon & Schuster
New York   London   Toronto   Sydney

Simon & Schuster
Rockefeller Center
1230 Avenue of the Americas
New York, NY 10020

First Simon & Schuster trade paperback edition 2004

SIMON & SCHUSTER and colophon are registered trademarks
of Simon & Schuster, Inc.

For information about special discounts for bulk purchases,
please contact Simon & Schuster Special Sales at
1-800-456-6798 or business@simonandschuster.com.

Designed by Paul Dippolito

Manufactured in the United States of America

1   3   5   7   9   10   8   6   4   2

Library of Congress Cataloging in Publication Data
Zwonitzer, Mark.
Will you miss me when I'm gone?: the Carter Family and their legacy in
American music / Mark Zwonitzer with Charles Hirshberg.
p.   cm.
Includes index.
1. Carter Family (Musical group). 2. Country musicians—United States—
Biography. I. Hirshberg, Charles. II. Title.

ML421.C33 Z86 2002
781.642'092'2—dc21
[B]   2002022395

ISBN 0-684-85763-4
0-7432-4382-X (Pbk)

For Gerri

Contents

Acknowledgments • ix

Prologue • 1

Pleasant • 13

Sara • 37

The Homeplace • 51

Maybelle • 65

Mr. Peer • 81

New Orthophonic Victor Southern Series • 97

Home Manufacture • 107

Fire on the Mountain • 127

Sara's Problem • 145

From a Business Standpoint • 163

Stuff • 183

XERA • 201

A New Act • 225

On the Road . . . • 245

. . . To Nashville • 259

Mama Maybelle • 283

Pleasant on the Porch • 315

On the Road Again • 335

Mother of Mine • 375

Index • 399

Acknowledgments

Over lunches, over and over, my friend Charles Hirshberg told me about this family down in Virginia, the Carters. It took me about five years to get cracking on the story. In the meantime, he was gathering facts. If not for his vision and enthusiasm, we would have missed out on the memories of dozens of people who have since died. Chuck's name is deservedly on the cover of this book. Chuck's wife, Annette Foglino, lived with this book as long as anyone, and her counsel was always wise.

The Original Carter Family left behind so much good music, it surely would have been greedy for a biographer to ask more of them. Still, the lack of primary written sources presented a problem. The original Carters—Sara, Maybelle, and A.P.—gave few interviews, kept no diaries, wrote few letters, and saved almost no correspondence. Whatever notebooks A.P. Carter saved were burned in a fire at a small tenant house where he stashed them near the end of his life. So determining the many, many sources of all that great music was a bit like detective work. And like an officer working a cold case should, I'd like to acknowledge those who gathered clues well in advance of me. At the top of that list is Ed Kahn, a scholar to be sure, but a gentleman above all. Beginning in the early '60s, Ed conducted a number of interviews with Maybelle and Sara. He went song by song, taking time to get their best recollections of where they'd heard each one (or how they came to find it or write it). He collected acetate transcription disks from Mexico, and stories from people who worked with the Carter Family at recording sessions in Camden or at the border radio stations in Texas. All this he made available to me, as well as material from the John Edwards Memorial Foundation. He also freely gave of his time, his wisdom, and his encouragement. And I thank him for it all. Mike Seeger, who was with Ed at many of those interview sessions, was another generous and thoughtful contributor. He has long been a champion of Carter Family music and has done more than anybody outside the family to keep it alive. Scholars whose work I benefited from include Charles Wolfe, who has uncovered so much of the original sheet music for songs that A.P. might have used for inspiration; Bill C. Malone, whose writing about early country music is the finest and most lucid available; and Nolan Porterfield, author of the seminal Jimmie Rodgers biography. Thanks also to the staff at the Southern Historic Folklife Collection at the University of North Carolina at Chapel Hill.

There were a number of people in the music business who spent hours telling their stories of life with the Carters. Chief among these were Chet Atkins, Becky Bowman Swearinger, John McEuen, and John Cohen. I would also like to thank Ralph Peer II for sharing his memories of his father.

Scores of friends and neighbors in Poor Valley (and Rich Valley and California) offered insights into the life and times of the Carters, including Clyde and Elsie Gardner, Minnie Curtis, Ruby Parker, Daphne Stapleton, Walter Meade, Gladys Greiner, and especially Peggy Hensley and her father, Chester Hensley, the finest tour guide in all of Scott County. I thank them all.

I am deeply indebted to Bill Clifton, who loved A.P. Carter and who helped me understand A.P.'s creative genius and his stubborn pride.

But in the end, the success of this enterprise depended on the family itself. Generations of Carters contributed to this book. It could not have been done without them; for me, their memories brought A.P., Sara, and Maybelle to life. Dale Carter and Barbara Powell (along with her husband, Glenn) are the sort of genealogists every family should have. They are diligent, exacting, and, best of all, always hunting a good story. Barbara, especially, shared her deep and human understanding of her aunt Sara. Vernon and F.M. Bays, Fern Salyers, Paul Hartsock, Lois Hensley, Bill Jett, and the irrepressible Theda Carter all shared their stories. And Stella Bayes Morris sat for days on end recalling the tale of her own parents and siblings. Her eye for detail knows no limits. Thanks to June Carter's daughters, Carlene and Rosie, and Anita Carter's daughter, Lorrie. And thanks also to Tom T. Hall and his wife, Dixie, and to Peggy Knight, each of whom the Carters count as family.

This book had two guardian angels. They were, of course, Carters. Rita Forrester and Flo Wolfe are granddaughters of A.P. and Sara, and truer testaments to the basic kindness of the family could not be found. They took time away from their own hectic lives to drive me all over Scott County, to make introductions to the people I should know, and to make sure those people answered my questions. They kept me well fed in all ways. Rita is an exemplary Poor Valley woman: always willing to do for others. Flo and her husband, John, opened their home to me on each and every visit I made. John laughed at me only on the occasions I most deserved it. A more stand-up man you will not meet.

Each of the children of Eck and Maybelle and of A.P. and Sara spent hours politely (and, it seemed, happily) answering insistent queries. Despite busy professional and personal lives and nagging illnesses, June Carter Cash and her husband, Johnny Cash, answered calls and letters for more than ten years. Joe Carter proved the finest breakfast companion a person could have and a gifted raconteur. Janette Carter, meanwhile, is the hero of this enterprise. Just before A.P. Carter died, he implored his youngest daughter to keep his music alive. She has done her level best to do that. For more than twenty-five years, with little help and less money, she has run a weekly music program at the Carter Fold and an annual festival. Her effort has been exhausting to both body and soul, and the last thing she needed was extra demands on her time. But she helped Charles and me with anything we asked. And I can never thank her enough.

Not all of the children lived to see the completion of this book. Gladys Carter Millard, Helen Carter Jones, and Anita Carter are gone now, so I hope a little piece of them lives on in these pages.

I would also like to thank my own friends and family. Thanks to editor Charles Adams, who saw potential in this book when few did and guided it to completion with an expert hand, and also to Simon & Schuster stalwart Cheryl Weinstein and copy editor Deirdre Hare, who saved me from myself. My friend and agent, Philippa Brophy, had to wait fifteen years to get a manuscript out of me. I thank her for her patience and her unflagging concern. Scott Yardley listened, as did Bruce Shaw, Yuka Nishino, and Curt Pesmen. Laura McKellar added research and good cheer. Richard Ben Cramer showed me what it takes.

To my in-laws—Rose Kukuc, Don Kukuc, Barbara and Robert Denninger—thanks for baby-sitting me and my children. My parents, Gary and Jean Zwonitzer, allowed me to find my own way. It's only now, watching my own children grow up, that I understand how hard that is. My brothers, Mike and Scot, showed me what it means to face down a challenge, and they are more heroic to me than they know.

Most important, thanks to Sam and Lila, who, despite all, love me best. So right back at ya. And finally, to my wife, Gerri, words will not do justice. I hope you know. And don't worry. It will get better.

Will You Miss Me When I'm Gone?

Above: The Original Carter Family. Maybelle (sitting) with A.P. and Sara (Flo Wolfe)

Opposite: Ezra "Eck" Carter and Maybelle, in Texas (Lorrie Davis Bennett)

Prologue

*My dear friends, my patients, my supplicants: Your many, many let-
ters—many hundreds of them since yesterday—lie here before me, touch-
ing testimony of your pain, your grief, the wretchedness that is visited
upon the innocent.*

It was 1939, the tenth year of the Great Depression. There were 20
million radio sets in American homes, and every day a single voice,
broadcast over the most powerful station in the Western hemisphere,
burst into those homes as though it had a God-given right to be there. It
was the voice of a small, bearded man speaking from a luxuriously
appointed private office in a mansion on the banks of the Rio Grande.
The voice was at once seductive and chiding, for he wished you to know
that he was a compassionate physician, a healer of thousands; at the
same time, he was an impatient builder of empires who would heal thousands more—no, *millions* more—if only they had the good sense to
come unto him. This was the voice of "Doctor" John Romulus Brinkley.

It was, alas, the voice of a quack, and a huckster and a scoundrel. But give the scoundrel his due, for Dr. Brinkley was also a genius in his way. In the midst of the Depression, he was hustling a million dollars a year from ordinary folk who had little money to spare. He'd sold them gallons of nostrums for gas, hemorrhoids, and just plain tiredness, as well as reams of rustic advice on female maladies. But his "specialty" was a male problem, a particular form of lethargy that sets in on men of a certain age, in a certain part of their bodies.

What is the use of pussyfooting around the subject? Why not drag it into the open? . . . No man wants to be a capon. Contrast the castrated animal—of any species—with the natural male or female. Note the difference, for instance, between the stallion and the gelding. The former stands erect, neck arched, mane flowing, chomping the bit, stamping the ground, seeking the female, while the gelding stands around half asleep, cowardly, and listless.

Doctor (he preferred to be called just "Doctor") had invented sundry "remedies" for male impotence. His most daring cure called for an operation in which Doctor grafted goat testicles onto the human items. For this, and like surgical services, he had charged some fifteen thousand men anywhere from $750 to $2,000 apiece. From an impoverished Smoky Mountain boyhood of corn bread and turnip greens, the fifty-three-year-old Brinkley had transformed himself into a multimillionaire. He owned mansions, limousines, an airplane, a yacht once used by presidents.

Even as a measure of desperation, it is hard to comprehend such success as Doctor Brinkley's unless one comprehends the power of radio. In the 1930s, radio was still a miracle. Electricity hadn't yet reached the country's remotest parts, but radio could wriggle its way into places not yet plugged in to the current of modern America. A single battery-powered radio set could pluck sounds out of the ether, just like magic; it provided unimaginable news from unimagined places, jokes of surpassing hilarity, and music that made listeners dance, cry, or just plain sigh. Americans didn't listen to a voice that came over a radio in the same way they listened to ordinary voices.

And if there was empathy in such a voice—if it seemed to understand "the pain, the grief, the wretchedness that is visited upon the innocent" in a time of national hardship—then that voice could have inestimable power over them. Doctor understood all of this, and he exploited radio like nobody's business.

He had begun his unlikely enterprise in a small, dusty farm town in the middle of Kansas. But by 1930 his radio-medico empire had made him one of the wealthiest men in the Sunflower State, and one of the most controversial. When the state board stripped him of his medical license, Brinkley staged a last-minute race for governor and was nearly elected as a write-in candidate. A few months later, feeling grossly underappreciated in his adopted state, Doctor moved to the Texas border town of Del Rio. A few miles south, in Villa Acuña, Mexico, he set to building a radio transmitter beyond the reach of the United States government and its bothersome regulations that limited stations to a puny fifty thousand watts. Two hundred thousand Depression dollars later, XERA, Brinkley's million-watt "Sunshine Station Between the Nations," thundered across North America. Locals claimed the XERA transmitter had turned on the headlights of cars parked in Del Rio and made children's bedsprings hum in San Antonio. All across Texas, they said, you could pick up the signal on a barbed-wire fence. In actual fact, there were nights when XERA nearly obliterated Atlanta's WSB and, 1,500 miles north, elbowed aside Chicago's WGN. As it crossed into Canada, the signal still had enough juice to muddy CKAC in Montreal. There had never been anything like XERA, nor would there ever be again. XERA reached farmers in the Mississippi Delta, steelworkers in Detroit, bridge builders in San Francisco, and coal miners in Alberta, Canada. The station got mail from every state in the nation, and fourteen other countries to boot.

By 1939, South Texas had blossomed with an outlandish industry built on XERA and other border stations that had sprung up around it. XERA's roster included the Reverend Eugene F. Smith, who hawked a book on how to prepare for the Second Coming ("A month from now might be too late!"), and soothsayer Rose Dawn the Star Girl,

Patroness of the Order of Maya, who promised to personally pray for any listener who sent her a dollar. Carter's Champion Chicks, a company that sold live poultry, also leased time from Brinkley; so did the makers of Kolorbak hair dye; Peruna, a tonic that prevented colds; and Sinose, a preparation guaranteed to clear up the sinuses in the unlikely event that Peruna failed to prevent infection. And just in case Sinose failed, too, the Sterling Company offered life insurance for only a penny a day.

Of course, even such superior products and services as these were insufficient to attract an audience. For that, entertainment was needed, and no entertainment was found to be more enticing to country people than country music. Consequently, Del Rio had become the "Hillbilly Hollywood." There was Cowboy Slim Rinehart ("Empty Saddles"), Patsy Montana ("I Want to Be a Cowboy's Sweetheart"), and the Pickards ("How Many Biscuits Can You Eat This Morning?"); there were the J. E. Mainer's Mountaineers, Doc and Carl, and countless others, all long forgotten. And there was also the Carter Family.

The Carter Family is not only not forgotten, but its influence still smolders in the popular music of the twenty-first century, both in the United States and Europe. The Carters aren't dusty old relics trapped on 78s. Seventy-five years after they first cut their voices into wax cylinders, their music is still finding an audience. Carter Family recordings have sold millions of copies, and continue to be remastered and remarketed to this day. For the past ten years, the Rounder label has been rereleasing original Carter Family recordings. Just last year, Bear Family Records of Hambergen, Germany, put out a boxed set of nearly three hundred of the Carter Family's original recordings. Carter Family songs like "Wildwood Flower," "Will the Circle Be Unbroken," "John Hardy Was a Desperate Little Man," and "Worried Man Blues" have been making new hits through eight decades, for stars such as Woody Guthrie, Earl Scruggs, Elvis Presley, Bob Dylan, Joan Baez, Johnny Cash, Emmylou Harris, Linda Ronstadt, the Nitty Gritty Dirt Band, and Lucinda Williams. To this day, the Carters' music is celebrated at festivals from Australia to the upper reaches of Canada, in Europe and in Asia, from Newport, Rhode Island, to Alaska. Above all, the Carters proved that simple songs about the lives of ordinary people can be as beautiful, as profound, and as lasting as music studied in conservatories. The nest of Doctor Brinkley and his fellow swindlers may seem an odd place to argue such a proposition, but that is where the Carters found themselves at the tail end of the Depression.

The border stations billed them as the *Original* Carter Family, because a dozen years' worth of enormously popular recordings had spawned scores of imitators. The Virginia-based trio had been willed into being by Alvin Pleasant Delaney Carter, a gangly, peripatetic man nearing his fiftieth birthday. A.P., as he was best known to his listening audience, provided an inexhaustible supply of songs, many of which he collected from Appalachia's remote mountain homesteads (as well as from its mills, factories, boardinghouses, and coal mines) and then "worked up" with his wife, Sara, and sister-in-law Maybelle. It was Sara's rich, expressive alto that had first attracted a producer from Victor records. At forty, she was still a riveting, dark-eyed beauty. Maybelle, the twenty-nine-year-old guitar player, was the virtuoso of the group, a fact which astonished many listeners of the 1930s, who would not believe that the agile licks and infectious rhythms were conjured by a woman.

Unlikely as it sounds, the Carter Family brought dignity even to border radio's raucous proceedings. They didn't play hillbillies or hayseeds or cowpokes. They were just regular folks making their own music. What set the Carters' music apart from the crowded field of country acts was the *intimacy* of their harmonies; the closeness of Sara and Maybelle, who sounded for all the world like a single person with four arms playing two instruments at once; and the unself-conscious ease with which A.P.'s high bass strolled in and out of each song, as if he were leaving the studio from time to time to chop some wood or hoe some corn, then returning to join the singing when the chores were done. There was nothing squared off or predictable about the way they made music, and their genius was giving a modern sustain to decades- and centuries-old songs. "They were the best loved in our valley," remembers one Arkansan whose entire family would walk three miles to the nearest neighbor with a radio. "They were singing our songs."

It is doubtful that A.P., Sara, and Maybelle could have been persuaded to spend six months a year playing in South Texas had times not been so hard. The trio had never spent much time on the touring circuit and didn't care to be away too long from their ancestral home in Poor Valley, Virginia, in the foothills of Clinch Mountain. Carters, they would say, never felt quite right unless they were enfolded by the mountains. But the border-radio appearances had reignited their popularity beyond even A.P.'s wildest imaginings. "Mercy, I never saw as much mail in my life," Maybelle once said. "When we left [Texas after the first year] and came home we had over five thousand letters that came in. We'd get mail every day, from every state in the Union."

Almost any music lover living in rural America at the time heard those broadcasts, including an entire generation of future country stars. Chet Atkins, as a fourteen-year-old living in Columbus, Georgia, listened in on a battery-powered radio he'd built from mail-order parts. In little more than ten years, Atkins would be a struggling musician hired out of obscurity by Maybelle Carter. The future architect of the "Nashville Sound" always credited Maybelle with saving his nearly stillborn career. In a farmhouse in Dyess, Arkansas, Johnny Cash listened also, never suspecting that he would one day marry Maybelle's daughter June, who was already appearing on the broadcasts, yodeling her eleven-year-old lungs out on "The Old Texas Trail." Twenty years later, Johnny Cash would make Maybelle Carter and her three daughters part of his road show; he would also credit her with saving his life. Maybelle would finish her career with Johnny, and he would preach at her funeral. "Having her in my show was a powerful confirmation and continuation of the music I loved best," he wrote in his autobiography. "It kept me carrying on the traditions I come from." In Littlefield, Texas, a small boy named Waylon Jennings would watch his daddy pull the family truck around the side of the house, pop the hood, and hook up the family radio to the pickup battery. Waylon would never forget the Carters' swirling harmonies, and after he and Willie Nelson had reoxygenated the stagnant country-music pond with their stripped-down "outlaw" style, both would pronounce Maybelle "the Queen Mother of Country Music."

But all the pronouncements and public approbation came later, when the country-music industry began to attach historical *significance* to the trio. Back in 1939, the Carters' impact was direct and immediate. "All the songs had deep-gutted meaning," says their niece Lois Hensley, who grew up on the music. "They were always about a feeling somebody had *had.*"

"A thing that especially pleased country folk," remembers Tom T. Hall, a future songwriter and recording star who grew up in Olive Hill, Kentucky, "was that the Carters were a *family.*"

Listeners came to regard the Carters as friends they knew, as people like themselves. There was A.P. wandering in and out of songs, Maybelle trying out new descending licks on her guitar, and Sara's voice deepening through time. There was little June flailing her way through a solo of "Engine 143." That little girl couldn't carry a tune to save her soul, but, by golly, she was a gamer. She and her sisters would even yodel. As with true country relations, the Carters' kinship with their listeners didn't depend finally on intimacy but on simply being there . . . every day. Where the *Grand Ole Opry* and *Barn Dances* and *Hayrides* were weekly affairs, special as church on Sunday, the Carter program was in the warp and weave of life. In fact, through the dark, shut-in winters of that fretful time, *The Good Neighbor Get-Together* on station XERA was there morning and night. Twice a day, in between Cowboy Slim Rinehart and the Mainer's Mountaineers, came the Carter Family, leading off every set with their theme song, "Keep on the Sunny Side."

For an hour a day, the Carters' radio show could close up the open spaces of lonesomeness that seemed to be widening all over the country. The railroads, then the Great War, then the gleaming economic engine of Henry Ford's America, then the Depression and the withering dust storms had enticed, begged, bullied, and shoved southerners and midwesterners (black and white alike) off the farms and toward the coal camps and mill towns of the South, up the line to industrial centers such as Chicago, Pittsburgh, and Detroit, and to the picking fields of California. Some folks made it to their destination; others were simply stuck somewhere along the road, having lost the memory of what precisely they'd set out for. Carter Family music was a song of what they'd left behind. The lonesomest, neediest, most cut-off listeners could lean forward toward their radio sets, hear those songs, and think, *That's just how it was. . . . They understand.*

Letters that poured into the station at Del Rio, or the post office at the foot of Clinch Mountain (where they were simply addressed "The Carter Family, Maces Springs, Virginia") testified to the Carters' way of making the forgotten feel a sense of belonging, and the sinner forgiveness: "Aunt Sara, this is from my heart," wrote one young man at the time. "Oh Dear God, hear my plea and answer the one prayer I feel in my heart. . . . I am poor and don't understand big words but you know my heart and thoughts, please keep Aunt Sara Carter singing your praises and songs like she has in the pass [*sic*]. Don't let nothing happen to her health and voice, and Good Lord if we both don't get to see each other in this world, help us to meet each other in heaven, and there I can hear her sing and play in person forever, in Jesus' name amen."

The odd thing was that their devoted family of fans knew little of the Carters themselves, or of their personal lives. Even among those selling the records there was a want of information about the family. Evalean Gowen, proprietress of the Gowen Grocery Company ("Dealers in Fancy Groceries and Notions, Distributors of Phonographs, Records and Accessories") in Grab, Kentucky, inquired directly: "Well Mrs. Carter," she wrote, "we have been ask [*sic*] by our customers about your family, is it man and wife and daughter; or is the girl your sister?" Sara never did answer the query. All three were preternaturally private, and as A.P. later said of their discoverer-manager, "Mr. Peer didn't want us to talk about that."

So when A.P. was suddenly—and without explanation—off the radio for a stretch in February of 1939, the Carters' vast and varied audience couldn't have guessed why. Nobody outside the family knew anything of the crisis that shook A.P., or of worried sponsors who pulled him off the show when they thought his agitation was actually coming through on the air. The Carters' following knew nothing of the fault line that ran right down the middle of "Country Music's First Family." So how could those same fans be prepared for what came next? How could they be prepared for the music to stop?

By the time the country had clawed its way out of the Depression and into war, the original Carter Family was no longer on the radio, no longer making records, no longer even *together*. Their parting was so sudden—and the silence that followed so eerie—that there was a rumor that the entire group had been wiped out in a car crash. Less-excitable theorists maintained that the Carters had simply outlived their popularity; tastes changed, and the audience was no longer interested. For more than half a century, the reason for the Carter Family's breakup has been a matter of uninformed reckoning. And no one in the family would talk about it. Not Maybelle, not Sara, and certainly not A.P.

The split was most wounding to A.P., who lost nearly everything that truly mattered to him. He would spend the next two decades pining for what was lost, and never gave up the hope of recapturing it. And while A.P. didn't go in much for irony, even he couldn't have missed this maddening fact: The true story of the breakup had all the makings of a mighty fine Carter Family song—new love in bloom and withering heartache, promise and betrayal, earthly sin and its painful consequences. But that's a story A.P. never would share with his public. That's a story he endured alone.

For six decades since the Carter Family broke apart, academics and music writers have been making hay with the proposition that the group embodied a distant voice from America's guileless, rural past. In the waning months of the last century, no less an authority than the *New York Times* was still writing that Carter Family music is set in "a mythic rural American Eden" and preserves "the idealized memory of the sim- ple life." If this makes the Carter Family more enjoyable to the Old Gray Lady, by all means, let her have it. The Carters' songs might have been simple. Their lives were not.

The Carters were possessed of a thorny ambition that grew even in the most unlikely American soil. From two remote and still valleys, they made themselves known to half a world. That was no mean feat in the 1930s, and it didn't just *happen*. To varying, sometimes conflicting, degrees, A.P., Sara, and Maybelle chased fame and fortune. They were, to quote a song lyric that may be the finest distillation of the American character ever written, "searching for the water from a deeper well." They didn't choose the easy path.

The Carters won fame—if not fortune—because they could recast the traditional music of rural America for a modern audience. And like their music, the Carters themselves had to negotiate the gap between the insular culture of preindustrial Appalachia and the newly modern America. Their lives were marked by the sheer want of rural existence, lack of a decent paved road or a decent school or cash money; by drought, flood, disease, meager harvest, and plain old loneliness. But their lives were also marked by the frantic demands of an American industry inventing itself. Work in the music business required regular travel for shows all through the remote backwaters of the South, and recording dates in Louisville; Atlanta; Chicago; Camden, New Jersey; and New York City. Moreover, it demanded of them *product*. A.P. had to go out into those Appalachian hills and scare up twenty or thirty new songs a year to feed the hungry maws of their record company and their fans. In the '20s and '30s there was nothing simple about bridging these two different worlds. The cost of trying was dear. And all of this is reflected in the Carters' songs, which are mostly about life's buffeting— about love and longing, hurt, loss, and suffering. In fact, it was precisely that clear-eyed and unwavering focus on the hard art of living that gave them such wide appeal.

Even on Brinkley's radio station, their music carved itself in relief to Doctor's insidious monument to quackery. The Carters weren't simply an act; they were the real deal. When they sang of the Virginia wild-wood, the cattle lowing in the lane, faith in the glory of the world to come, or the swiftest locomotive on the line, they were singing about their own story. And when they sang of orphaned children, worried men, tangled love, and bruised hearts, that was their story, too.

*Top row: Elisha "Lish" Carter and Mary Bays Carter (with their children),
Will Bays, Charlie Bays (holding Dewey) and Mary Bays, Mandy Groves,
Mollie Carter (obscured, holding Ettaleen); bottom row: Nancy Carter Bays
Hensley (Bob Carter's mother), Nathaniel "T'int" Bays and Levisy Bays
(Mollie Carter's parents), Bob Carter (holding Eck and Virgie), A.P. Carter,
Jim Carter (Stella Bayes)*

Opposite: Mollie Carter with grandchildren (Carter Family Museum)

Pleasant

Five separate mountain ridges cut on a southwest diagonal through Scott County, Virginia: Powell's and Stone westernmost, out by the Kentucky border; Clinch Mountain farthest south and east, not far from the Tennessee border; and in between, the Copper Creek and Moccasin ridges. Every big valley rolls and folds into itself, forming valleys within valleys, haunts and hollows that can't be seen from even the highest perch in the county, on top of Clinch Mountain, 3,200 feet up. So you'd have to have a pretty fair knowledge of the richly filigreed landscape, of the right roadless gap to take, to make your way into the deepest hollows. That inaccessibility, with its promise of well-hid treasures, has always been the heart of the romance of the Appalachian Mountains. "A mysterious realm," the writer Horace Kephart called the southern Appalachians, "*terra incognita.*" Kephart was a St. Louis librarian who had traveled widely in Europe and spent years cataloging a gargantuan collection of works by and about a fourteenth-century Italian poet. In 1904, with his penchant for the obscure surprisingly undiminished, Kephart moved to the America's southern mountains and began cataloging the culture of its natives.

Ten years later he brought out his book *Our Southern Highlanders* and introduced a people as exotic to his fellow academics as South Sea islanders or Eskimos. For a decade Kephart had plumbed the region's language, superstitions, work patterns, diet, and dentistry: "It was here I first heard of 'tooth-jumping,'" wrote Kephart. "Let one of my old neighbors tell it in his own words: 'You take a cut nail (not one o' those round wire nails) and place its squar p'int agin the ridge of the tooth, jest under the edge of the gum. Then jump the tooth out with a hammer. A man who knows how can jump a tooth without it hurtin' half as bad as pullin'. But old Uncle Neddy Cyarter went to jump one of his own teeth out, one time, and missed the nail and mashed his nose with the hammer. . . . Some men git to be as experienced at it as tooth-dentists are at pullin'. They cut around the gum, and then put the nail at jest sich an angle, slantin' downward for an upper tooth or upwards for a lower one, and hit one lick.'

" 'Will the tooth come at the first lick?'

" 'Ginerally. If it didn't you might as well stick your head in a swarm o' bees and ferget who you are.'"

It's no wonder Horace got caught up in the flat-out *oddness* of the remotest hollows (the "back of beyond," he called it), but his seminal work in the mountains had the effect of obscuring the regal and practical *breadth* of Appalachian culture. By 1913, it was way too late for *rural* to still be thought of as synonymous with *backward* or *isolated*. At the time Kephart was doing his fieldwork, a young native of Scott County, Leonidas Reuben Dingus, educated at the free schools near Wood, Virginia, was presenting his own postdoctoral papers, to wit: "Study of Literary Tendencies in the Novellen of Theodore Storm," "A Brief on Schiller's Esthetic Philosophy," and "*Beowulf* Translated into Alliterative Verse—Selections." It was with evident pride that Dingus was celebrated as "one of the ripest scholars the county has produced."

A full generation before Kephart arrived, Scott County had ninety-six public schools and two local newspapers, not counting the *Toledo Blade*, which arrived over the mountains by horseback in Copper Creek every two weeks. There was nobody who wasn't but a few hours' ride from a railroad station, and from there you could get to Kingsport, Nashville, Indianapolis, Washington. D.C., or New York. And the railroads could deliver *any* of the largest or most exotic items to be found in the Montgomery Ward or Sears, Roebuck catalogs. Usually that wasn't necessary, however, for most of what was needed could be got right in Scott County. There were forty corn and flour mills, fourteen sawmills, and two woolen mills, all powered by the creeks and rivers that ran through the valleys. Every wide place in the road, such as Fido, Osborn's Ford, and Nickelsville, had a general merchandise store that stocked everything from fine china to Cracker Jacks. Even the outlying areas were dotted with home manufacturers who could take a body from cradle to grave. You could buy a pram, a wagon, or a coffin, handmade locally.

In Hiltons, James P. Curtis was doing a fine trade in both guns and butter. He'd invented a churn that ran by the motion of a rocking chair, and a more efficient turn plow for the hundreds of dirt farmers scratching a living off of the land. But he is remembered best for his rifles. During the Civil War, Curtis had supplied nearly a thousand Kentucky rifles to the Confederate army. At the turn of the century, his long-shot rifles were still in wide use in the land disputes that had entered the American consciousness as "feuds."

More than anything else in Scott County, land counted. In the last decades of the nineteenth century, nearly four-fifths of Scott County's seventeen thousand residents farmed. Even at $2.26 an acre, no commodity was more precious than land. And it wasn't just the present value of the land that mattered, but the future value. In fact, the fastest growing trades in the county—as in most of Appalachia—were land agentry and lawyering. And most of the men practicing these professions were under the employ of the railroads and their subsidiaries, out on the prowl, quietly leasing mineral or timber rights from local farmers. "Inexhaustible beds of iron ore (red and brown hematite) are found in this county," boasted a local business directory in 1889, "and manganese, lead, coal, marble of various kinds, and limestone in abundance. . . . The extension of the Narrow-Gauge road through this county from Bristol in Tennessee, will open up its mineral treasures, which now lie buried awaiting convenient and cheap transportation facilities."

Already, in 1891, the railroads and their affiliates were clear-cutting tens of thousands of acres of forest for crossties and square-set mining timbers. Five separate mines were in full cry, blasting coal and iron out of the ground, filling up freight cars behind the gleaming new Norfolk & Western or Virginia & Southwestern engines, all headed for the more populated and higher-paying parts of America. The railroads were not a paternal force in the valleys, not by a long shot. Neither were the timber companies or the mine owners or the quarry operators. They meant to dig out of the land whatever value it held, and Scott Countians take the hindmost. By 1891, for better or worse, the future had rumbled into the valleys.

From her little one-room log cabin on the other side of Pine Ridge, Mollie Bays Carter couldn't hear the Virginia & Southwestern engines roll through Poor Valley. Not that she didn't have her ears open to them. It was the middle of the night and she was by the fire, still in her day clothes, sitting bolt upright on a cane-backed chair. On her lap she held a shotgun.

Mollie was just nineteen and she still held her beauty, which owed in no small part to the Cherokee in her. Her great-grandfather was a half-blood, and you could see it in Mollie's high cheekbones, her dark eyes, and her straight coal-black hair. She kept her hair long ("A woman's hair is her glory," they taught her at the Friendly Grove Methodist Church). When she let it down, it would fall well below her narrow waist. But Mollie rarely let her hair down. She plaited it every day and kept it tied in a fat bun on top of her tiny head. Above all, Mollie was a Christian woman and modest in her appearance.

In the cabin that night, she was alone except for her infant son, Alvin Pleasant Delaney Carter, who was born just weeks before, on December 15, 1891. That's why she was up in the middle of the night. Earlier that day, Mollie had spied a panther skulking around the farm. There was no glass in the windows of her cabin; she'd just hung sackcloth over them. That might keep out the wind, but it wasn't going to keep out a hungry panther. So Mollie sat alert and awake all night long, in frightened defense of her newborn son.

Where her husband, Bob, was she couldn't have said for sure. Robert Carter was part of a long line of roaming mountain men, from Daniel Boone (who had been so constitutionally unsettled that he had, at age eighty, still searched out new trails) to the novelist Thomas Wolfe (who would occasionally, and without purpose, walk the entire circumference of Manhattan Island). Bob Carter was a far-wanderer, a gangly, long-legged man, and, truth be told, a bit flaky. He never was much for work, and there were times when Mollie would look up and Bob was just plain gone. No telling where . . . or for how long.

One thing he liked to do was visit the sick. Bob could sit bedside for hours, praying over the afflicted. If somebody in the Valley was dying of cancer, neighbors might help plant the corn or bring in the harvest, but most made a point to stay well outside the plagued house, reckoning any sickness could be catching. Not Robert Carter. Later, during the big influenza epidemic of 1917, he was so stalwart and so fearless that he would earn the nickname "Flu-proof Bob." Another thing Bob liked to do was inquire about local happenings. He was an enthusiastic gatherer of news; some said gossip. One neighbor lady who was a bit peeved by some of Bob's more personal reporting took to calling him by the local newspaper name. ("Well, here comes the *Scott Banner*," she'd say, loud enough for him to hear as he approached. "He's got all the news.") But Bob never let the taunts slow him down. Comfort and news were Bob Carter's business, and that business kept him on the move. Later in the marriage, Mollie learned to read the signs. When Bob began chopping wood and stacking it high, she knew he was about to leave. The higher the stack, the longer he'd be gone.

"Bob, are you leaving your family again?" a neighbor once admonished.

"Well, if you can take any better care of them than I can," he shot back, "go on ahead."

"Uncle Bob would be walking by our homeplace and say, 'Well, where's your dad?' " his nephew Vernon Bays remembers. "He would ask a dozen questions: 'When did he leave?' 'When's he gonna be back?' 'What'd he go there for?' and he never stopped walking. Just walking and asking questions and bringing news."

Bob might be gone from home a day, or—say, he went to visit his cousin Amanda Groves—he might be gone a week. Mandy Groves was a striking woman, six feet tall and broad-shouldered, with flaming red hair she kept pulled back so it didn't fly into an unruly frizz. Mandy was nosy, too, and witchlike. She never forgot anything. She could give chapter and verse on what happened on a specific day forty years before. Neighbors who had no record of their birth date would go to see Mandy, and she'd know. *You were born July 6, thirty-eight years ago. That's the day they brought the wheat in over at Wolfe's. Looked like a storm all day, but never did rain.* Well, there was nothing Mandy didn't know, and Bob could put his feet under her table and get all the goings-on. Besides, over by Mandy there was always some land squabble. Her own husband, Abraham, once plugged Jerry McMurray with a bullet from the silver-plated rifle Old Man Curtis had made for him. So there was plenty of interest at Mandy's house.

In later years, when Bob was on the circuit, Mollie might be able to track him by telephone. There were only a few phones in Poor Valley, or over in Little Poor Valley, but somebody would have seen him, and they'd tell him to get on home, that Mollie said it was time to strip the tobacco. But way back in 1891, on that cold, dark night, Mollie Bays Carter had no way of knowing precisely where her new husband was. Maybe Bob had walked down the Little Valley to Hiltons, and then another half dozen miles along the Appalachian Trail to the county seat, where he could alert the sheriff of the "addition to the family" and record the birth of his new son, Alvin Pleasant Carter, in the Scott County registrar's books. Or maybe he was off to visit an uncle, see about work. It was hard to know.

From the beginning, Mollie Bays knew Bob Carter was going to be a project. She'd first seen him about 1888, not long after her family moved across Clinch Mountain and into Poor Valley so that they could be nearer the new railroad. She'd gone to a square dance, where she'd seen Bob playing the fiddle. And not only could he fiddle, but he could hit the back-step, too. He was more than six feet tall, fair-skinned, strong-jawed, and only a bit sunken in the chest. His hair was wavy and brown, shading to auburn. Whenever Mollie told the story of their meeting, she'd talk about watching him on the dance floor with his patent-leather lace-up boots with the blue bands around the tops and his "stri-ped britches." She always said he was the prettiest thing she'd ever seen and that she fell in love with him the minute she saw him.

But there were things about Robert Carter that could have given her pause. Bob had seen some of the world already, having just returned from a railroad job in Richmond, Indiana. And Mollie had pretty good reason to believe that Bob Carter had seen the business end of a whiskey bottle as well. ("Most Carters of that generation," says a family historian, "didn't hesitate to take a good sip of whiskey.") There was also the thorny question of his provenance. His Little Valley neighbors all said Bob was "base-born," a phrase, like many in the region, meant to muddy the actual meaning, a way of talking about things that kept outsiders in the dark. There were other such phrasings: If a man was "in his back," he was, in fact, drunk as a skunk; if in wartime he had gone "scoutin'," he was, in fact, hiding up on the mountain, dodging conscription. So the locals might have called him base-born, but to put it in the plain English of the day, Bob Carter was somebody's bastard son.

Bob's grandfather had been the first Carter to come over to the south side of Clinch Mountain. Dulaney Carter was the son of a well-off landowner from Rye Cove, twenty miles northwest of Poor Valley, and a descendant of one of the earliest and most esteemed settlers in Scott County. He had also married well. His bride, Rebecca Smith, was the daughter of John "Dutch" Smith, who'd got a land grant for exemplary service in the Revolutionary War. So when Dulaney arrived in Poor Valley in 1833, he was doubly staked, which was why when they spoke of him, his own children would say that Dulaney had managed to drink up *two* fortunes. "The bottle," says his great-grandson, "got the better of him. He had nothing when he died, and he left his children with nothing."

Dulaney's second child, Nancy Carter, had it particularly rough.

She was a big-boned woman, with a streak of independence as wide as the Delaware and a weakness for pipe smoking and men. At twenty, she'd married a teenager named William Anderson Bays. They had four children together before he went off to fight for the Confederacy in the War Between the States. Billy Bays didn't return from the war for nearly a full year after Lee's surrender, and when he did come back, his wife was pregnant again. Now, Billy was no scholar, but he could do the math. He'd been gone years. On March 20, 1866, Nancy had a son, Robert, to whom she gave her maiden name. She filed for and was granted a divorce from Billy Bays, who moved to the next county and started a new family. Several years later, Nancy Carter bore another son, named Elisha "Lish" Carter. There was much speculation about the paternity of these boys. For her own part, Nancy took a put-that-in-your-pipe-and-smoke-it stance. Somebody once asked her directly who was the father of one of her children, and she replied, directly, "Law, honey, when you run through a briar patch, you don't know which one scratched you."

Bob grew up mainly with Nancy's brother, William Carter, who had five strapping children of his own (including the witchlike Mandy). But in the years after the war, working bodies were always welcome. There was almost no hard cash in the Valley at that time—save Confederate currency, which had all the value of a two-legged mule. People lived off the land, raising table vegetables in a truck patch, hogs for meat, and corn and tobacco for bartering for other necessities. Over time, William Carter finagled his way into enough estate sales and land deals to build up a holding of nearly a thousand acres. On his death, each of his five surviving children got two hundred acres of land. Neither Bob nor Lish was written into his uncle's will.

In fact, when Robert Carter convinced Mollie Bays to marry him in 1889, he was a twenty-three-year-old farmer with next to no land, little ambition, no inclination toward hard work, no professed faith in God, and a passing acquaintance with the bottle. He was high-strung, and hardheaded to boot. It's a good thing he was fetching. And it's a good thing that Mollie Bays, at seventeen, had faith enough for the both of them. She was going to set him straight.

Mollie Bays was a God-fearing and abstemous young woman, but she was no stranger to odd men and scandalous women. Her grandfather William H. Bays was one of the most eccentric men on either side of Clinch Mountain. William H. Bays's father was heir to an early settler and well-off landowner in Scott County; his mother was said to be a full-blooded Cherokee. And this Bays never ran from either heritage. He had his father's blue eyes but his mother's jet-black hair, which he parted down the middle (he carried separate combs for each side) and wore in long plaits that fell over his shoulders. He carried his fiddle everywhere and was best known as "Fiddlin' Billy" or simply "the Entertainer." It wasn't just his music that made Fiddlin' Billy entertaining; he was born to perform, and he meant to amaze. He favored clothes that made a statement, such as long coats made of the finest and most colorful broadcloth, festooned with over-size brass buttons. Fiddlin' Billy's son said his father had a way of just appearing, almost out of thin air, then disappearing just as abruptly. And the Entertainer liked you to know that he might trust in God, but he didn't trust in banks or governments. He never had a nickel in a bank, but he never lacked for money. If there was something he wanted to buy, he'd disappear, and reappear hours later with a wad of greenbacks. It was said that Fiddlin' Billy had his money buried on some remote and thick-grown hillside, but he died without revealing to his own sons the whereabouts of his stash. If his family knew little of his finances, the local, state, and federal tax authorities knew even less. He was so stubborn about paying his taxes that one frustrated county collector finally reached across and ripped off a handful of Billy's brass buttons as payment in kind.

Fiddlin' Billy's wife was his equal. Eliza Morgan Bays would race her stud horse alongside Moccasin Creek, bareback . . and she didn't ride sidesaddle, and she didn't always ride sober. When a group of marauders came across the Tennessee border to prey on the women, children, and old men left behind during the Civil War, Eliza—it was believed—was one of the women who tracked the nine men to their camp one night and bludgeoned them to death with hickory sticks. Eliza was evidently a fiercely independent woman, perhaps too independent for Fiddlin' Billy. In 1870, after twenty-six years of marriage, there was, according to court records, "a devorsement of the parties." By that time the couple's eldest daughter had already given birth to four children, all base-born. So Bob Carter's personal and family history held no terror for Mollie Bays. In fact, there wasn't much at all that could scare Mollie.

They were—and are—ferocious doers, the women of Poor Valley, and if they grew up in the long years of want after the Civil War, as Mollie had, they put their faith in God, and in themselves. In those years even the grandest farm in Scott County—the Jett place—operated by the power of man and beast. The scythes were operated by hand, and the turn plows pulled by mule. But what the Valley lacked in machinery, it made up for in women. Women kept the Valley humming. For staying power, efficiency, and capacity, no combustible engine was their equal. The women in the Valley could work all day and all night. Most did so without complaint, save for an occasional sigh ("Law") or an aside meant for all to hear ("A man's work is sun to sun; a woman's work is never done").

To make a go of life in the Valley, a woman had to be able to make corn bread, worm tobacco, teach her children Christian prayers, plow a straight row, put up kraut and beans for winter, sew a proper school dress, tan hides, keep a house clean and a cornfield free of weeds. Above all, they had to know how to *stretch* what life gave them; they wasted nothing.

Take for instance the hog killing. There are women in the Valley yet who light up at the memory of that splendid tradition. Just put them in the living room and let them talk:

"It'd take several days to butcher a hog and get everything cut up and put away."

"It wasn't like it is today. I heard somebody say just the other day they threw away the liver! We never threw away a thing. We ate tongue. We'd boil them and peel them off. And the heart. I always liked the heart so good. Some fellow said he didn't like to put the head in sausage, so he threw it away. But you could salt that down, and my aunt Rosie could fry that stuff and roll it in buttermilk and flour. Granny made her mincemeat out of the head."

"What I like is the cracklin'. Render the lard and cook it down and make cracklin' bread."

"We always fed the ears to the dog."

"My grandmother pulled out the intestines and made soap with it."

"The bladder? They'd blow that up for a balloon for the kids."

"Honey, they used everything but the squeal."

Mollie Carter didn't have an electric icebox, or even a smokehouse, and meat had to keep. So she'd cure it with salt, black pepper, brown sugar, and molasses siphoned from wildwood pines. Even so, there was never enough ham or bacon or sausage to make it more than a side dish. At the heart of the table were the vegetables from the summer garden: kraut and beans Mollie put up to last through the longest winter. If all else ran out, there was always corn bread, and Mollie could always walk out her front door and wring a chicken's neck.

The Bob Carters never had enough land to reap cash. Mollie's dad had deeded them a farm in the Little Valley; it might have been forty acres, but so much of it was wildwood running up into the foothills that there wasn't room enough for a big corn or tobacco crop. They might have planted a pretty fair orchard on the side of those hills, where, according to the deed, the land "meanders to the top of the Poor Valley knob, thence west with the top of said knob." But with just Bob and the mules (and even later when his sons came of age), they never had the brute force required to clear the land. So they made do with small harvests, a milk cow, chickens, and a hog a year. Mollie could take milk and eggs through Jett Gap to Neal's (a general store that also served as the Maces Springs railroad depot and post office) to trade for what else they needed: coffee and sugar, soup beans and rice, fabric for clothes. In the leanest times, John Neal would even let Mollie and her neighbors buy on credit. With so many people in the Valley in the same harness, nobody had more riding on the annual harvest than John Neal. When the family was down to nothing but debt, Bob Carter would have to cut timber and drag it off the mountain by mule to sell to the railroad. The railroad was always in need of timber for ties, and Neal could act as an agent for the transaction and put it right on the train.

To her credit, nobody went hungry in Mollie's house, and nobody saw her struggle. Her method was making do, but her real genius was adding flavor to a meal. Every circuit-riding Methodist preacher in the area knew where to go for Sunday dinner; they'd even come scratching around Mollie Carter's door on weekdays, right around noon. When a preacher put his feet under Mollie Carter's table, he wasn't disappointed. She always set aside something special for the man of God. On Sundays, she made sure there was icing on her cakes.

Mollie wanted everything to be just so. If she turned out a corn bread that wasn't to her standards, she'd start over. Not that it went to waste! She'd open her door and fling it into the yard, "The chickens can have that." She never could get her biscuits to rise just right, so she stopped trying. But for blackberry jam, molasses cake, or apple butter, nobody could match her.

And it wasn't only the table that benefited from her care. She kept her yard *swept* and flowering, with the glorious aid of her chicken litter. All around her house were gladiolus, lilies, sunflowers, baby-rose bushes, elephant ears, and dahlias. She even talked Bob into building diamond-shaped beds to hold her most precious flowers and plants. Mollie's granddaughters, great-granddaughters, and great-great-granddaughters still have portions of a Christmas cactus she started more than a century ago, and to this day, that plant blooms in houses up and down Poor Valley.

Besides her gardening, Mollie loved music. Her grandfather, after all, had been Fiddlin' Billy Bays, and her brother Charlie Bays could saw a few tunes, too. "He played his fiddle around the house," remembers one family member. "He'd go hunting for a note to get it to sound just right. Sounded like a chicken plucking on that neck. He played 'Hog Molly,' a hoedown tune, and he played 'The Eighth of January,' which was the fiddle tune for the Battle of New Orleans. A lot of that music came out of Ireland. It was jig music." Mollie had seen jig music promote some un-Christian behavior at many a dance, so she was wary of the fiddle. But while she went about her daily chores, Mollie Carter would sing the hymns she loved best: "The Land of the Uncloudy Day," "Amazing Grace," or "The Gospel Ship." But she also sang traditional ballads, known as "English" songs, because the form—if not the songs themselves—had crossed the Atlantic with the English and Scotch-Irish who settled the southern mountains. These were story songs, hemmed and tucked and remade to fit each new generation, like the story of the Scotsman who met his beautiful Cherokee bride at the river and ended up with a slew of children. "White man wishing he'd never gone fishing . . . still, you are my pretty little Naponee." "The Wife of Ushers Well," Mollie would sing, or "Brown Girl," or one that was particularly close to home:

> *Single girl, single girl*
> *She goes to the store and buys*
> *Oh, she goes to the store and buys*

> *Married girl, married girl*
> *She rocks the cradle and cries*
> *Oh, rocks the cradle and cries.*

> *Single girl, single girl*
> *She's going where she please*
> *Oh, she's going where she please*

> *Married girl, married girl*
> *Baby on her knee*
> *Oh, baby on her knee.*

For nearly twenty years—and without respite—Mollie Carter had a baby to contend with. Alvin Pleasant Carter was born in 1891, then came Jim (1893), the twins, Ezra and Virgie (1898), Grant (1900), Ettaleen (1901), Ermine (1906), and Sylvia (1908).

After a while, there wasn't much room in the Carters' little one-room cabin for anything but four beds (they slept two and three to a bed) and the supper table. Another family with five strong boys might have been in the money. But taken as a whole, the growing Carter boys were a net loss. Maybe after a while, Grant held his own; he *learned* to work. But only Ermine inherited his mother's willingness. From the beginning he could put his head down and work like a mule. Once, before he was even a teenager, Ermine raised a potato patch that kept the family going an entire winter. As for the rest of the Carter brood, they kindly resembled Bob.

There were, however, two Carter boys who had ambition, if not focus. Those sons seemed to understand that the old mountain ways were about to be overrun, and some folks were going to get run over, and some were going to hop on the train. Those boys were Mollie's oldest, who was called Pleasant; and Ezra, called Eck. Eck was shy; he didn't speak a word until he was three, and not many more after. But from the jump, he had a gift for invention. "Oh, Lord," says his niece, Lois Hensley, "Ezra had a *busy* mind."

Eck was also a quiet, sneaky prankster, and his mischief might have gone entirely undetected if it weren't for his twin sister. Eck and Virgie had divided their father's personality right down the middle. Eck was restless, another wanderer. Virgie could sit still for hours, gathering news and gossip. In fact, Virgie took particular pleasure in keeping everybody up to date on Eck's high jinks. Sometimes, when Virgie would claim to be the older of the twins, Eck would counter, "Yeah, you got out first so you could tell everyone else I was coming."

Growing up, Eck seemed to be always looking for a way out of Poor Valley. Among the Carter children, only Eck finished high school—and that took some doing. The only school in the Valley was down through Jett Gap, on the way to Neal's Store. It was a two-story log building that doubled as the Friendly Grove Methodist Church, so during the big revival time, school would shut down for a week or more. And during the harvest season, attendance was sparse. Worse yet, the school went through only eighth grade. So when he graduated there, Eck was forced to walk up the Valley—four miles each way, every day—to attend high school in Hiltons.

His mother was the only person who really understood what Eck was aiming for. One day he was with Mollie at Neal's when the train went through. People were always milling around Neal's place, trading, getting the news, having a coffee, playing cards by the big potbellied stove, or just plain "meeting the train." Waiting for the train in the Valley was like waiting for the big paddle-wheel steamer to come rolling into port in young Sam Clemens's Hannibal. The buzz in the store always increased as the posted arrival time neared. Even if it was only a few people getting off, anybody at Neal's would be the first to know that the Hensleys had a cousin visiting from Roanoke, or that Mandy Groves just got something called a "player piano." There was no telling what treasures were inside those canvas pouches stamped U.S. MAIL. Disappointment was palpable when the train edged past Neal's Store, slowing but not stopping. If there were no passengers for Maces Springs, the railway mail clerk would make his pass on the move, tossing off a mail pouch and grabbing the outgoing mail from a swinging metal arm. The train would just keep on toward Bristol and Roanoke, then up to the state capital in Richmond and the nation's capital, Washington, D.C. Eck knew about those places; he'd read about them all. "Someday," Eck quietly told his mother as the train pulled through the station, "I'm going to put mail off that train."

The strangest case of the entire Carter brood was the firstborn, Alvin Pleasant Carter. Pleasant shook, all the time. From the day he was born until the day he died, he was possessed of a slight tremor, most noticeable in his hands. The family named it "palsy" and never saw cause to better Mollie's own theory. Like most mountain women, Mollie turned for answers to God and nature. Whenever anybody asked about this odd, shaky child, she would tell them about the day when she was pregnant with Pleasant and got caught outside in a thunderstorm while gathering apples fallen from a tree. A crack of lightning hit the tree she stood beneath and traveled like wildfire along the ground all around her and, as she reckoned, shot such a bolt of fright into her swollen belly that the baby inside would be afflicted with that very nervous energy for each and all of his days. Sometimes Mollie would say her eldest son had been marked. What that meant nobody was quite sure, but it must have given some comfort to a little boy with a difficult row to hoe.

Like the cause, the consequences of this affliction were not altogether worked out. There were some things about Pleasant that were laid squarely at the feet of this encounter with the lightning. He *was* odd. Even when he was a child, it seemed like Pleasant was always humming, or giggling quietly to himself in contemplation of some private joke. He wasn't much good in school, easily distracted, self-conscious about his shaky handwriting. In the classroom, the other kids did the giggling—constantly—at Pleasant's strange ways and shortcomings. By the time he was ten, Mollie had relieved her emotionally bruised son of the chore of going to school.

Another thing people put down to the lightning was how Pleasant appeared to be hooked up to some source of energy from which he couldn't unplug himself. The boy never could sit still. Even after he grew to his full height of six foot two, lanky and gaunt, all joints and Adam's apple, he could still unfold himself and raise up from a chair faster than a man half his size. He never stayed in one spot long; he'd jump off the porch, head out past Neal's, and down the trace, perambulating alongside the railroad tracks. In those days, most folks walked wherever they needed to go. And, like Eck, they might walk miles every day just to get where they had to be. But Pleasant Carter never appeared to be heading anywhere in particular. Neighbors would see him walking up and down those tracks, bent slightly forward as if walking into the wind, his hands folded behind his back, his long, thin legs taking the railroad ties two or three at a time and his jug-eared head bouncing atop his skinny neck.

It was matter of wide speculation whether his head bobbed from the act of walking or the act of thinking. Pleasant took so many notions that they tumbled over one another and fought for space at the front of his mind; he had a hard time ever keeping a single idea front and center and rarely saw one through to completion. He was forever leaving chores undone. As a grown man he would practice a variety of trades: farmer, sawyer, fruit-tree salesman, choir leader, carpenter, music-recording professional, and proprietor of a general store whose hours were neither regular nor predictable. He never did seem to care much about his income. When he found himself in some personal bonanza, he'd buy more land, or a sawmill. Forty years after his death, his family still doesn't have a definite inventory of the sawmills he owned. "A.P. was always a step out in left field," one of his nephews remembers. "Wifty" is how one niece describes him.

Finally, and most notably, the ever-present tremble gave A.P.'s voice a slight quaver, so that when he spoke, it was like a ripple on a pond, and when he sang, it was faster, like the shimmering rush of a mountain creek over mossy rocks below. All these things, everyone in the Valley agreed, were on account of the lightning.

Then, too, there were things about Pleasant that were not so clearly consequences of the thunderbolt but seemed, unlike the tremor, to come from the deepest part of him and simply *were* him and would have been there regardless. First there was his stubbornness, which could flare into real, and occasionally frightening, fits of temper. Then there was his need to see things of the world out beyond his ancestral valley, and to make himself *known* in that wider world. And, on the other side of that very ledger, there was his fear of leaving and not being able to double back home. Those conflicting impulses fused over time into a single inchoate longing that takes hold of boys and girls in the most isolated parts of this country, a longing for something they cannot put a name on, or that has yet to be named, or whose name simply hasn't reached their valleys. The longer Pleasant lived without knowing what to call that longing or how to act on it, the more enervated and absentminded he became. Even as he passed into adulthood, even when he had been up on the sill a good while and ought to have mellowed, Pleasant Carter, it was agreed, was strung a hair too tight.

The other thing Pleasant seemed to have deep within him was music—and it was music that brought him his first notice. Bob had quit playing dances at Mollie's request, but he'd still occasionally scrape out a tune around home. And when they were just boys, Pleasant and Jim got a fiddle to share between them. Jim practiced obsessively, but the only song he really mastered was "Johnny Get Your Hair Cut Short." So it wasn't long before everybody in the tiny cabin was sick of that tune. Pleasant showed a more supple feeling for the instrument and seemed to have a real ear for music. If he heard a new song, he could generally chord it out on the fiddle by the end of the day. But Pleasant's tremor continued to vex; he could barely keep his bow steady. It was his singing that got him recognized. When he became a teenager, his voice ripened into a deep, rich bass, and the tremor gave him what the locals call a "tear," embroidering his singing with an almost otherworldly tenderness. It was one mighty fine church voice—and that's where he had his first triumphs.

The church was the most important institution in Poor Valley. It served as a family of families and helped that larger family push back against the uglier potencies of nature: weather, disease, death, and the darkness in one's own heart. For Mollie Carter, it was the rock that held fast. Mollie had figured out early in the marriage that she wasn't going to inject any real drive into her husband, or take the edge off his stubbornness. But she did carry him to church and bring him into the larger community. First they attended the Friendly Grove Methodist Church with Mollie's own family: her sister Martha (who married Bob's half brother Lish Carter) and her brothers Charlie, Will, and Flanders Bays. In March of 1904, one of Mollie's uncles donated land for a new church building and a cemetery behind. Bob Carter and the other Sunday-school men felled trees and hewed out logs on Clinch Mountain. Pleasant and his uncle Charlie Bays ran teams of horses and mules, skidding the logs off the mountain and up a hillside to the building site. It took four horses to drag the colossal tree chosen for the church seal, and Mollie was in her glory: The chosen tree came from her farm.

In the spring of 1907, fifty-plus members climbed onto the hilltop overlooking the old Friendly Grove church and schoolhouse, and dedicated Mount Vernon Methodist Church and its cemetery. At Mount Vernon they continued a traditional worship, with the complicated, Old World King James Bible as text. Religion on the hilltop church was still practiced as a stalwart barrier against the forces of nature. One Sunday at Mount Vernon, in the middle of a crop-choking drought, an old farmer stood up and beseeched his maker: "Oh, Lord God, please send us a good clod-soaker. But oh, Lord God, don't send us no *damned* gully-washer!"

They talked to God, together, in that church. First they'd testify to faith in their personal savior, Jesus Christ, and to the glory of the Father. Then they'd plead for Him to walk with them in their daily struggles, to deliver them from the pain—and not just in the peace of the hereafter, but right now, on this earth, in this minute. They'd beg for His healing power. And from the start Bob Carter proved himself a prodigious voice in that church; his prayers were pleading and, in extremis, emotional to the point of weeping. Ruby Parker, who grew up in the church, still remembers: "Bob Carter just said a good old humble prayer—and he didn't leave nobody out," she says. "The saved, the sinner, sick, afflicted, everybody. Especially the sick. He always remembered them in prayer." One of his own granddaughters thought Bob's longer perorations timed out at about an hour, but Ruby would only offer that Bob "could pray on and on."

Prayer might have given Mount Vernon foundation, but music gave the church lift. The congregation rang in the service with song, and rang it out with song. So while Bob's solemn prayers were Mollie Carter's personal comfort, the songs were her joy. When the congregation sang her favorites, Mollie *belted* them out. Her granddaughter June Carter Cash once claimed that when Mount Vernon broke into "The Land of an Uncloudy Day" (and the wind was just right), you could hear Ma Carter at Neal's Store, nearly a half mile down the road.

So Mollie's face must have betrayed her motherly (if not altogether Christian) pride when her own son Pleasant showed himself to be the finest bass in the entire church and ready for the exalted church quartet. He'd been handpicked for that quartet by Mollie's brother Flanders Bays, who served the church as musical director. But nobody in the congregation thought to call it favoritism. Pleasant's talent was unquestionable.

Pleasant heeded his uncle's direction—and not just in the church. In fact, Flanders Bays proved to be the lodestar for Pleasant Carter. Fland was just nine years older than his nephew; he was of the Valley but somehow above it, too. Fland was a solid citizen in Maces Springs; he would also sit with the sick and dying, though he'd often put a dab of turpentine on the tip of his tongue to ward off germs. Like most people in the Valley, he worked a small farm, but he maintained a seigneur's dignity. He was nearing six feet, with dark hair and a patrician nose, and he wielded a wheat cradle (which was something like a scythe) with practiced precision. His sons claim that nobody in the Valley could work one faster, even while he sternly counseled them on method: "Keep your right elbow locked, or you'll really feel it in your arm." But it wasn't his uncle's handiwork with farm implements that fascinated Pleasant. It was the simple, stark fact that Flanders Bays was the first person he'd ever seen who could make a living away from the farm—and with *music*. Flanders had learned shape notes from a singing master at a normal school in Nottingham, Virginia. Based on a four-note scheme (diamond, square, triangle, heart), which made it easier for congregants to follow along, shape-note singing began in New England churches in the eighteenth century. By the turn of the twentieth century, shape-note singing had died out in New England, but in the South, it had evolved into a slightly more elaborate seven-note format taught at singing schools sponsored or encouraged by the South's efflorescent gospel publishing industry.

By the time Pleasant was twenty, Flanders Bays was teaching singing schools all over southwestern Virginia. Uncle Fland was much under the spell of James D. Vaughan, a publisher whose close-harmonizing gospel quartets were the new musical sensation of southern choirs. Four or five times a year, new gospel composition books would arrive at the Bays home from Vaughan's publishing house in Lawrenceburg, Tennessee. Then Fland would load up his horse with dozens of fresh new songbooks—*Crowning Praise* was a favorite—and head out through Hamilton Gap to the other side of Clinch Mountain, or farther out to Washington County or Russell.

"He had a burning desire for music, and to see people saved," says Fland's son Vernon. "He'd always open his schools with prayer and with a short Bible reading. And he closed it with prayer. It was a devotional, religious service."

Next to the annual revival, Fland Bays's dollar-a-day singing school was the biggest event of the year in hidden-away hamlets all over that pinched corner of Virginia. On the north side of Clinch Mountain, in Copper Creek, there might be thirty or more people who'd sign up for the school. They'd sometimes travel from neighboring towns and bed down with relatives for the chance to cram into the Saratoga schoolhouse every day for four or five hours, ten days straight, learning how to read shape notes, how to master their voices, and, as they advanced, how to *use* those voices in the close harmonies of southern gospel. "Everybody would go," says Daphne Kilgore Stapleton, who went with her girlfriend Maybelle Addington (later Carter). "All the young people would go to learn the notes and to sing up the scale and back down."

Fland Bays wasn't one to put on airs; he often presided over the school in his denim overalls. But he was never lax about the music. "He always taught us to be able to read three notes ahead," says Ruby Parker. "You would be singing notes to music, do-re-me-fa-so-la-ti-do, eight notes. And Flanders Bays would stand right over you and just listen, and when you missed a note he'd stop you, *that quick.* He could catch a sound as quick as anything. He knowed his stuff, buddy."

Sometimes, if Pleasant could get free of his farm chores, he'd go to his uncle's singing schools to help out. He'd willingly walk down the Valley toward Hiltons, then over Clinch Mountain, across Moccasin Valley, over Moccasin Creek, and across Moccasin Ridge to Copper Creek. That would be a difficult daylong trip, but once Pleasant was there, he could stay as long as he wanted. Mollie Carter had been born on that side of the mountain, and she had family there yet. Besides, travel suited him. He could walk all day in solitary contemplation, never minded being alone, and loved seeing what was around the next bend in the trail.

Despite A.P.'s talents, farming was still the surest way to make a living in the Valley, and that meant he needed a piece of land all his own. So in 1911 Pleasant followed his father's path to Richmond, Indiana, to take a temporary job as a carpenter on the railroad. More than twenty years earlier, a Bays in-law named John Smith had married an Indiana girl, moved up north, and found work on the railroad. Since that time, the Smiths had provided a pipeline from Clinch Mountain to Richmond. Young men from the Valley were always going to Richmond for high-paying work on the railroad. Like the rest, Pleasant figured that in a year or two he could raise enough money to buy a farm in the Valley, or maybe a sawmill. But Pleasant Carter didn't last long in Indiana. His first expedition outside Virginia was a bust. He returned home with a blazing case of typhoid fever and memories of gnawing homesickness.

According to his sister Virgie, Pleasant also returned with his first song in his pocket:

> *She clung to me and trembled*
> *When I told her we must part*
> *She said don't go, my darling*
> *It almost breaks my heart*
> *To think of you so far apart*
>
> *Carry me back to old Virginia*
> *Back to my Clinch Mountain home*
> *Carry me back to old Virginia*
> *Back to my old mountain home*
>
> *My mother's old and feeble,*
> *My father's getting gray*
> *I'm going back to old Virginia*
> *And I expect to stay*
> *At my old Clinch Mountain home*

Back home at Clinch Mountain, Pleasant's fever was so intense that they shaved his head to keep him cool. Mollie nursed her oldest boy back to health, and he not only recovered but grew back a head of hair his sister-in-law Theda claimed was more lush and wavy than ever.

Still, Pleasant had failed in his bid to stake himself. He tried to raise money doing farmwork for his uncle Lish Carter, but it must have been slow going on his uncle's wages. Lish was one of the workingest men in the Valley, and he expected hard work from his farmhands. He was also tight as bark on a tree. "Lish wouldn't give up a nickel for nothing," one niece says.

It was his musical uncle who rescued Pleasant. Flanders was acting as an agent for the Larkey nursery, selling fruit trees and house shrubs around Maces Springs. So pretty soon, he had his eldest nephew selling for the nursery, too—but Pleasant wasn't content with the trade in Poor Valley. One day in 1914, with his leather side-pouch, his subscription booklet, and a color catalog of handpainted pictures of fruit and flowering trees, Pleasant Carter walked over Clinch Mountain to try for some sales by Copper Creek. Somebody had suggested he try his mother's cousin Milburn Nickels, and Mil's mother, Aunt Susie Nickels.

The Nickels' homes were even farther than the Saratoga school, but Pleasant must have thought it would be worth the extra effort. It's a long, muscle-searing walk over Clinch Mountain, and the trip to Copper Creek probably took a few days, but as he crested the last little hill, where he could just see Aunt Susie's house, Pleasant Carter heard singing coming from inside it. The way he'd tell the story later, the music quickened his weary step. It was deep for a woman's voice, but a woman's voice for sure. "Aunt Susie had one of these tall, old-fashioned sewing machines, and I was standing beside it and my autoharp was on top of it, and I was just kind of playing around with it," the owner of that voice would recall many years later. "I remember I was singing 'Engine 143,' an old song I learned as a little girl, and this fellow knocked on the door."

Pleasant motioned for her to go on singing, and then stood very nearly still in Susie Nickels's front room, watching the young woman. Sara Dougherty was only sixteen and still wore her long brown hair down over her shoulders. While it was Sara's voice that first drew him, Pleasant always said it was the way her dark eyes held a constant play of sparking light that transfixed him. He listened to the entire song, a ballad about a train engineer burned to death in a bloody train wreck while trying to make up lost time. The engineer, it seems, hadn't listened to his mother's caution. And he ended up in a lonesome grave, pining for the engine he loved.

"I remember that he stood there while I sang," recalled Sara, "and then he said something like, 'Ma'am, that was mighty pretty playing and singing, and I sure would like you to play that over again for me,' and so I did."

Whether Susie or Mil Nickels bought a single tree or shrub from Pleasant Carter is lost in time. But the girl in the front room, Sara Dougherty, did manage to sell Pleasant a set of dishes out of her own subscription booklet. Pleasant and Sara's first child claimed the inventory included a set of glasses, a clear pitcher with a cranberry design, a berry set, six dessert dishes, a three-legged fruit bowl, and a vegetable boat.

Even Sara must have known that no bachelor traveling salesman needed six dessert dishes and a vegetable boat, but she made the sale just the same. For Pleasant, he liked to quote himself when he told the story. "I said to Sary, 'If I thought I had a chance with you, I'd take the whole book.' "

Sara Dougherty (Carter Family Museum)

Opposite: Thursa Mae, Sara (right), and their brothers, not long after their mother died (Carter Family Museum)

Sara

A.P. Carter was not without reputation on Sara's side of the mountain. He'd spent a fair amount of time around Copper Creek already, been seen *and* heard. "I thought he was a good citizen," the local schoolmaster, Ezra Addington, remembered seventy years later: "He was tall and slender, pleasant-looking, like his name." Stories of Pleasant's musical talents were also out on the vine. Besides helping out at Flanders Bays's singing school, Pleasant Carter had lent his trembling bass from time to time to Ezra Addington's choir, which met at the schoolhouse or at Ezra's home a few miles over in Nickelsville. Ezra had three altos and four sopranos in his regular group, along with a couple of tenors, but an extra bass was always welcome. Most of the time they'd sing Sunday evenings. After church services and Sunday dinner, the group would walk by lantern light over to Ezra's, gather around his eighteen-stroke organ and open their *Windows of Heaven* hymnals. "All we sang was hymns, church songs," Ezra says. "The men wore ties— not bows—but regular ties, and white shirts. Maybe there were a few short sleeves in the summertime. A.P. sung with us a whole lot. A.P. was a great singer back then."

Still, whatever pleasing qualities were attributed to Pleasant Carter, it's also true that the citizens of Copper Creek had a fairly rounded-out picture of him. Reports of Pleasant's "wiftiness" had also made their way across Clinch Mountain. As Ezra's own wife recalled, "He was a good boy, but he was a jumbled person, wasn't he?" Maybe that was the root of A.P.'s initial difficulties with young Sara. Or maybe one has to take Sara at her word. When Pleasant Carter first began to show interest in her, Sara told one relative she would never marry him, because she simply didn't like him.

Sara Dougherty was one to look at all sides of a prospect; she was not going to get swept away by romance. Her delicious brown eyes, wavy dark hair, and rich, textured voice might have launched scores of romantic flights of fancy among the local boys, but Sara had her feet planted firmly on the soil. She was a shy girl, a bit standoffish as she grew older, and later still, she could be downright remote. The earliest picture of her shows a four-year-old staring intently, almost broodingly, at the camera. The natural set of her already full lips pushes down toward a frown. That first picture captured precisely her own wide streak of stubbornness. Her girlhood nickname was Jake, in honor of her straight-backed bearing and her nearly masculine reserve. To this day, family, friends, and acquaintances are most likely to remember her as "regal."

Sara was one of five children, born to Sevier and Elizabeth Kilgore Dougherty on July 21, 1898, just north of Copper Creek in Wise County, where her father ran a shift at a sawmill in a growing coal-mining camp. But Elizabeth died of typhoid when Sara was just three, and that family was lost. Nobody remembers Sevier Dougherty doing much work of any kind after that; he just traveled around, staying with friends and relatives. Wherever he went, he carried a sack full of books. Sevier loved to read, to no real end but for the simple pleasure of it, for the escape. The three Dougherty sons—Bob, Nathan, and Stephen—spent their childhoods shuttling among friends and relatives, while Sara and her older sister, Thursa Mae, were sent to live with their mother's sister and her husband. Sevier was often at that house to see them, but he was never a steady presence in his daughters' lives.

Whatever hurt Sara suffered as a parentless child, she kept inside. Singing the ballads of death and dying, of family members cold in their graves, of orphaned children, lonely women, and jailed men seemed one of the few releases she allowed herself. Besides, what Jake liked best (though it was not always easy to see) was being in the middle of fun. Around Copper Creek, that was never very hard.

A.P. Carter's home came by its name honestly. The farmland in Poor Valley, especially as it recedes from the Holston River, is mineral-shy and arid, not the best growing ground. But Sara's childhood home, called Rich Valley, had dark and loamy land, with raw limestone out-croppings jutting through to announce the minerals within. And where the Poor Valley landscape was full of rocky escarpments that seemed to close in on its citizens, Rich Valley was wide open, with gentle, undu-lating hills. The farming was a little better, the fields a little greener, the pastures a little flatter. Life in Rich Valley was less severe. In Poor Val-ley, Mollie Carter sought calm in deep religious faith; in Rich Valley, her cousin Milburn Nickels found ease in the pure fun of living.

It was Milburn and his wife, Melinda, who took in Sara and her sis-ter. Uncle Mil and Aunt Nick (as Melinda was called) never could have children of their own, but over the years the couple raised or cared for more than a dozen orphaned children. Mil and Nick took all comers in their four-room, wood-planked country cottage . . . and they were poised for more. Aunt Nick kept her table set twenty-four hours a day, the food covered with a cloth, in case anybody—friend or stranger—happened by hungry. The Nickels never wanted for food. They cut ice from Copper Creek in winter and packed it in sawdust. It usually lasted deep into the summer, keeping the meats without curing. Even in the longest winter, the dug cellar was stocked to the end. Aunt Nick kept three waist-high staved barrels in the cellar: one for beans, one for kraut, and one for salted brine pickles. Uncle Mil did a little teaching, raised hogs, corn, and tobacco, laid out apple and peach orchards. When they got old enough, Sara and Mae (Thursa) helped out by picking berries for jam, pickling, canning, quilting, and keeping house. In the late spring and early summer, after they'd walked home from the Saratoga school, there was always time to go the extra quarter mile down the hill to the "bent" of Copper Creek.

Some afternoons Sara would walk over to Ethyl Bush's house to listen to Ethyl and her friend Eb Easterling play their five-bar autoharps. "They used to show me a lot about playing. I was just a little girl then, less than ten years old, I guess," Sara once said. "I was about ten or twelve when I got my first [autoharp]. I sold greeting cards to raise money and ordered it from the Sears, Roebuck catalog for about eight or ten dollars. It was an eight-bar."

Playing an instrument put Sara right in the swim of the Nickels house. Music was the fun in that house, as present as oxygen, and free to boot. Most days, Uncle Mil would rise before the sun, start the fire, pick up his fiddle, and play for an hour. He favored older tunes like "Pine Dreams," "Soap Suds," "Fatal Wedding," and "Johnny Put the Kettle On and We'll All Have Tea." Mil was the melody in the house, but he was always happy for his wife's makeshift accompaniment. Aunt Nick would grab her knitting needles and tap out the rhythm on the fiddle's wood frame, or follow along on a harmonica of her own making, a comb with a piece of paper pulled tight across it. Some Saturdays, Ap Harris—Rich Valley's blue-ribbon fiddler—would show up to play with Mil. When news got out that those two were making music together, people would head straight for Mil's house. The two fiddlers would do the fast tunes, and Aunt Nick and the neighbors would have to push back the furniture or put it out in the yard so that people had room to dance. It wasn't long before Sara was able enough on the banjo to join in, and then she was hooked for good.

Before Sara reached her teens, she had already formed a girl group with her cousin Madge Addington. Madge's home was a five-minute walk up the hill, and in that house, musical instruments didn't have to be improvised. The Addingtons had a banjo, a guitar, a five-bar autoharp, and an old-timey organ. Madge and Sara both played guitar, banjo, or autoharp, so they switched off, playing old ballads and gospel songs. In the first years of the twentieth century, older folks all over Rich Valley had songs to sing, and they were happy to share them with eager young girls such as Madge and Sara.

In Sara's childhood, before the phonograph, music was passed around Rich Valley in two ways. The first was a straight lineal transmission. Old fiddle airs and archaic Scotch-Irish ballads came across the ocean with forebears and were passed down through generations. Each generation added (or subtracted) verses to fit the times, but the songs retained a general integrity. When the local fiddlers played tunes at frolics, the songs were pretty close to the ones being played in North Carolina or Georgia or Texas, or even out in Montana where the Welsh and Irish were flocking to the mines—and also pretty close to the old airs still being played in Liverpool or County Cork. Ballads worked the same way. Around Copper Creek, old folks sang "The Storms Are on the Ocean" or "Sailor Boy Song" in the unaccompanied ancient modal way, with a high nasal delivery favored in the Old World.

But when Sara was a girl first learning the autoharp, a more modern mode of song transmission was taking root. New, professionally written songs were traveling, too. The old minstrel shows and the newer vaudeville and "physic" shows would come through Scott County, and even if the denizens of Copper Creek couldn't make it to the big town for a show, the music made its way around. After any show, sheet music was made available to the audience. The bigger touring vaudeville shows had rafts of sheet music, sold by the page or by the book. Even self-employed minstrels sold their songs on "ballets" they'd had printed up. So somebody might come back to Copper Creek from the Gate City theater carrying a new song to sing. The songs felt like their own, too, because newer songs written by Tin Pan Alley professionals owed much to the imagery and (often dewy) sentiment of traditional Anglo-Irish ballads. The new songs leaned heavily on mother and home (and the leaving of same), lonely wandering in the cruel, cruel world, and dying wishes. The songs also owed much to the first great American tragedy, the Civil War.

In the four decades since peace had been made, the war's horror and heartbreak had been furiously commercialized. Already in full swing was the very American way of selling a story back to the people who had been touched by it, and songwriters made great (and sometimes beautiful) songs from awful memories of that war. Loss of life, loss of love, and loss of home were copyrighted, printed up, and offered for pocket change. The beauty was, no matter where Americans lined up on the conflict itself, the experience of it was much the same.

Most everybody in Rich Valley had been affected by what was known there as the War Between the States. At the start of the Civil War, the Nickelsville Spartan Band was formed as one of four companies of the Forty-eighth Virginia Infantry Regiment, and over the next four years these farmers and farmhands fought their way through Romney, Chickahominy, Second Bull Run, Fredericksburg, Chancellorsville, Gettysburg, the Wilderness, and Appomattox. At Chancellorsville a third of their regiment was killed, wounded, or captured. At Gettysburg, where the Forty-eighth had pushed up Culp's Hill to within ten yards of the enemy firing line, another third of the regiment had been wasted. When Sara and Madge were young girls, veterans of those man-mauling battles still walked, ghostly and deep-socketed, among the living. Every family in Copper Creek and Nickelsville had a memory of the war, and memorabilia, too. The Hartsocks kept a yellowed clipping from the August 8, 1862, edition of the *Abingdon Virginian* describing the demise of William D., "gone all too soon for his sorrowing friends and bleeding country," at the Battle of Port Republic. "He fell to the ruthless hand of death by a shell; but he has gone from among us in the bloom of youth, with a heart warm with future anticipations to his last moments," says the *Virginian*. "We cannot tell in what mind he died, but of upright life, religiously inclined we may trustfully leave with a good God, who knew best when to call him hence." The Kilgore family held a letter written by the Spartan Band's company commander, Sylvester P. McConnell, who was in 1915 a mottled, white-whiskered retired clerk of the county court: "It is my painful duty to inform you of the death of your son, John D. Kilgore," he wrote in 1862. "I gave William P. Harris an order to the ward master for his money ($10) & his clothing & sent him to town to see him decently buried. We tried to take him home but the higher officer said it was against the order of the War Department . . . it is a sad occurrence indeed that he had to die so far away from his kinfolks, but remember he lost his life in a glorious cause." Official accounts and correspondence rarely offered much in the way of comfort, or explanation, but draped the awful, lonely, far-from-home deaths in the romantic cloak of martyrdom in "the glorious cause" of a "bleeding country."

Casualties were not confined to faraway field hospitals, war prisons, and battlegrounds. The McConnells still told the sad tale of Drusilla, whose betrothed was killed in action at Gettysburg. Drusilla went to an early grave, too, the victim of a broken heart. In 1915 a great-niece kept as a family treasure the last love letter William Patton Harris sent to Drusilla McConnell.

In the aftermath of the war, the binding sentiment, the one that traveled down through generations, was that nobody's loss—be it an affair of war or an affair of the heart—should be made small. That simple notion passed almost imperceptibly from generation to generation, through ballads such as "Poor Orphan Child," "Wandering Boy," and "I Have No One to Love Me." What McConnell could hear the lyric "Go dig my grave both wide and deep, / Place marble at my head and feet, / In the middle of the grave put a turtledove, / To show the world I died for love" and not shudder for poor dead Drusilla?

According to Sara, a neighbor named Myrtle Porter taught her a song about a girl whose once ardent young lover had forsaken her. Nobody knows the exact words Miss Porter left to Sara, but, according to scholar Charles Wolfe, they were most likely based on a song written a half century earlier by Maud Irving and J. P. Welch, called "I'll Twine 'Mid the Ringlets." As Irving and Welch wrote it, the opening verse went:

> *I'll twine 'mid the ringlets of my raven black hair*
> *The lilies so pale and the roses so fair*
> *The myrtle so bright with an emerald hue*
> *The pale aronatus with eyes of light blue.*

It's impossible to know if anybody in Rich Valley still had the published sheet music, but the song itself had been passed around from local singer to local singer. Over the years it was delivered again and again, with scores of musical midwives. It came out sounding different nearly every time. Albert Easterling of Nickelsville would claim for years that he'd written the song from scratch for his wife, Jane. He made that claim without fear of lawsuit and without shame. Songsters like Albert were constantly retuning and rewording. Given Appalachia's oral tradition, and the dense thicket of romantic poetry, the transmission of the song became a game of transgenerational telephone. What was whispered in at one end of the line came out the other end in sometimes nonsensical little couplets. By the time Sara popularized the song in 1928, the first line had become "I'll twine with my mingles," a line without literal meaning; the myrtle became bright with "emerald dew"; the pale aronatus was now "the pale and the leader," whatever that was. A later line, "the crowd I will sway," made its way onto the record as "in his crown I will sway." But what made it loud and clear through all the ancestral noise was the *point* of the song: that a woman ought to show a fierce and stoic pride in the face of rejection.

> *I'll think of him never, I'll be wildly gay*
> *I'll charm every heart, and the crowd I will sway.*
> *I'll live yet to see him regret the dark hour*
> *When he won, then neglected, the frail wildwood flower.*

Happily, the music Sara grew up with wasn't all about life's dark hours; it had a good bit to say about grabbing fun where you could, or just plain having fun with the song. "Chewing Gum" took potshots at the newly puffed-up middle class:

> *I wouldn't marry a lawyer, I'll tell you the reason why,*
> *Every time he opens his mouth, he tells a great big lie.*
> *I wouldn't marry a doctor, I'll tell you the reason why,*
> *He rides all over the country and makes the people die.*
> *I took my girl to church last night, what do you think*
>   *she done?*

*She walked right up to the preacher's face and chawed
her chewing gum.*

Sara and her pal Madge were exposed to all kinds of music: gospel, ballads, comic songs, and flat-out dancing music. The girls' grandfather Arnett Kilgore had been able to play any instrument he'd ever laid hands on, and Madge's mother, Margaret Kilgore Addington, played a five-string banjo and a Sears-bought autoharp. Madge's brothers played some of the best guitar on Copper Creek, and her baby sister, Maybelle, had pulled the autoharp down off a table and started playing by ear.

Those talents put the Addingtons at the center of the local social scene, and the highlight of Rich Valley's social season was October— corn-shucking time. The Easterlings or the Wamplers or the Blankenbecklers would invite all their friends and neighbors to come out and help complete the fall harvest, with promise of reward. The men went out in the fields where the corn lay cut, shocked, and tied to dry, and they shucked all day long, while the women stayed in the house and quilted or made molasses or cooked for the square dance that night. The younger kids milled around the yard playing Andy Over or London Bridge. As the sun dropped low, everybody left for home, but just long enough to spruce up. The men put on fresh overalls and clean white shirts, and the women stepped into their long skirts. The single girls, who were prospecting, generally took the longest time in preparation, and it wasn't until they were in tow that a party made its way to the square dance. Whether they went on horseback, in wagons, or on foot, there was always somebody sent out front to light the dirt paths so that whoever arrived first could see floating globe-shaped kerosene lanterns converging on that night's dance hall. The dance hall was really just somebody's house or, if it was a big party, the Addington Frame Church. In that case somebody had already pushed aside the pews to make the dance floor.

It wasn't long before the crowd was pretty well oiled. When the crop was good—and, tell the truth, even when it wasn't so good—there was always corn to spare for liquor. Madge's daddy, Hugh Jack Addington, who ran the Green Store, had a still. Uncle Mil Nickels made a pretty fair batch of moonshine, too. So there might be a half-dozen short pints warming the edges of the dance floor while the fiddlers sawed away at "Turkey in the Straw" or "Sallie Goodin." A banjo or a guitar gave the music body, but it was the fiddle that shivered the spine and made the feet go.

"They loved dancing in Rich Valley, and they could do it," says A.P. and Sara's son Joe Carter. "Breakdown, Virginia reel, buck dance, just flatfoot dance. Uncle Ermine used to go over courting them girls in Rich Valley. He said, 'You get out there and try to dance with one of them girls on a waltz and they'd walk all over you. Let them put on a hoedown and it sounded like a bunch of air hammers on the floor.'"

It wasn't just the dancing that drew the Poor Valley boys across the mountain. Sometimes the teenagers would sneak off for kissing games like Spin the Top, or Post Office. Post Office was a round-robin kissing tournament, where the lead girl would be sent alone into a room to call out the name of her favored boy and ask him to "deliver the mail." Once that mail was delivered, the postman got to stay in and call out his favored young lady. "They'd tell what they wanted," says Daphne Stapleton. "A letter with a one-cent stamp, you'd get one kiss; three-cent stamp, you'd get three kisses. If it was a package you'd get a hug. Sometimes you'd get people who were really a-datin', and they'd stay in there a long time."

Now, A.P. Carter shied from kissing games, wasn't keen on dance music, and wanted nothing to do with corn liquor, so he went about his courting in a more earnest and forthright fashion. He'd iron his stiffest store-bought collar, maybe wet it down and iron it a second time for shine, button it down over his tie, and go visit at Mil and Nick's.

Nobody really knows what melted Sara's initial resistance. Joe Carter figures his father flattered his mother, told her how pretty she was, and how smart. But over the years, Joe has developed a jaundiced view of romance, and that clouds his vision. Neither Sara nor A.P. confided the details of their courtship. What little evidence there is comes from something Sara told a fan who caught her off guard nearly fifty years after the wooing commenced. "A.P.'s main savior was his bass," Sara said. "I think he was the best. I've never heard anybody that could sing bass like him." For A.P.'s part, he was poleaxed in love. And he wasn't going to give up.

Even so, the courtship wasn't always easy. First there was the simple fact that A.P. had to walk a day or more—over one mountain, two more ridges, and a half-dozen creeks or lesser streams—just to get to the Nickels homestead. And like any sixteen-year-old beauty, Sara could be aggravating. Ezra Addington often saw Pleasant tied in knots. Sometimes when A.P. was visiting Copper Creek, he'd stay with Ezra. Ezra always remembered the time Sara took umbrage at something A.P. had done and refused his company altogether. "He sent his dog up," Ezra Addington recalled years later. "Put a letter of apology on the dog's collar to ask if he could come and see her. That's the way he got in."

Sara had to be impressed with A.P.'s resourcefulness and his staying power, but she must have also been aware that a man has his limits. She may even have been a bit chastened by her own sister's recently failed courtship. Four years earlier Mae had turned down a marriage proposal from William Joseph "Buff" Hartsock. Buff had been so upset that he hopped a train straightaway and hoboed out to Idaho for work in the zinc mines. So when A.P. proposed marriage in 1915, Sara accepted. Pleasant raced back home, took over some farmland in the Little Valley with the help of Uncle Fland, and went to work building a house. It was just a two-room cabin, but he meant to make it a fit home.

Alvin Pleasant Carter and Sara Dougherty were married on June 18, 1915, the month before the bride's seventeenth birthday. After the ceremony and the dance that followed, Pleasant loaded up his one-horse wagon and carried his new bride back to Poor Valley. They had to ford the winding Moccasin Creek five times just to get to the gap that let out onto the south side of Clinch Mountain. "I know that was a wonderful trip home," their daughter Gladys wrote years later. "Daddy always walked over the mountain as it was so much closer to go courting, but now he was bringing her home with her autoharp, all of her fancy crochet pieces, quilts, a few dishes; and, Aunt Nick had picked out twelve of her nicest pullets and a rooster and put them in a coop on back of the wagon. . . . They would be settling down with their horse, a milk cow called Old Brin, two good squirrel dogs Top and Brownie (which was a must in every family those days), a good 12-gauge shot gun, their chickens, a step stove, table, four cane bottom chairs, two iron beds, and a new dresser with a big mirror in it (very rare in those days) in a new little two room cabin which Daddy, his brothers, father and all the neighbors had pitched in to build as soon as he told them he was going to bring his bride home in so many days. He had to have his house on his own little tract of land."

For well over a half century, there were witnesses who spoke rhapsodically of the day A.P. brought his bride home to Poor Valley. "My mother always remembered the first time she saw Sara," says Barbara Powell, a daughter of A.P.'s cousin Elva. "She was the most beautiful thing she ever saw. Mom was so struck with her beauty and how she dressed. She had a huge, wide-brimmed hat with a red rose on it. She had that long, dark hair and big beautiful brown eyes. She was real young when A.P. brought her over the mountain . . . sixteen."

The day the newlyweds arrived, their cabin in the Little Valley wasn't altogether complete; unless Pleasant had *meant* to have a dirt floor. But it took him only a couple of days to carpenter a solid woodplank floor, and they were in business. Sara made a space for her autoharp on her cedar chest, and in time she framed and mounted the first picture of the A.P. Carters, their wedding photo. That picture was snapped right outside the Nickels' cottage, and Buff and Mae are in the photograph, too. (After five years Buff had come home, and Mae had accepted his next proposal. So the betrothed couple had stood up with A.P. and Sara that warm June day, as a dress rehearsal for their own wedding two months later.) In the photo, A.P. sits folded into a too-small chair, his legs crossed and his homburg still on his head. His shoulders are hunched toward his jug ears, and his mouth is curled at the corners in a sheepish grin. He looks a little like that old cat who ate the canary: pleased and proud in the moment, but aware the act he's just committed might have *consequences*. Sara stands at his side in a white ankle-length dress pulled fetchingly tight at the waist. She's looking dead at the camera, almost as if in a challenge. Her hand rests behind her new husband's shoulder, as if she's expecting him to lead her somewhere. In that captured moment, Sara Dougherty Carter can have no idea what she's in for.

The wedding photo (Carter Family Museum)

Opposite: Poor Valley (Lorrie Davis Bennett)

The Homeplace

They didn't live in the Little Valley long. By the time their first child was born in 1919, A.P. had bought a few acres just up the road from Neal's Store at Maces Springs, and built Sara a bigger cabin in the foothills of Clinch Mountain. A.P. had picked a spot up near the tree line, for comfort and ease of living. First off, he wanted to be close to the timber. About the only way to heat a house in Poor Valley was by fireplace or woodstove. For all the good burning coal in Appalachia, there was little in Maces Springs. By the end of the Great War, two or three freight trains a day would come down from St. Charles, Virginia, grinding through the Valley with dozens of cars, all full of coal dug out of the mines in neighboring Wise County. But those loads were bound for bigger markets; once they hit the railhead in Bristol, the coal would be switched to the Norfolk & Western's fast freights for points north and east. "A conveyer belt for coal masquerading as a railroad," one writer called the N&W. Once in a while the conveyer belt's flotsam would wash up in Poor Valley. The general store at Hiltons might buy a carload of coal to retail, and Fland Bays would drive over in his wagon (and later a Model T Ford truck) to buy a load. Even better was when the kids in the Valley could walk the tracks after the freight passed and pick up lumps of coal that had bounced out of overfilled cars. That was free fuel. And that coal would burn all night long, without a second's tending. But A.P. and Sara couldn't count on found coal. What they could depend on was going out the back door, sawing down a tree, and splitting it for firewood. After a long, cold night Sara might wake to find her bedspread sprinkled with frost, but she could always put a few more logs on the fire to get the house warmed again.

The other great advantage to A.P.'s chosen lot was its water. All over Poor Valley, streams ran down off Clinch Mountain, feeding the Holston River. So A.P. could have settled in the deepest part of the Valley and been a short walk from good, clean water. But the farther up the mountain one lived, the nearer the spring; the nearer the spring, the colder the water. And in 1920, when the only electricity in the Valley was up in the elements, and there wasn't enough still water to freeze over into deep blocks of winter ice that might last, Sara had to have cold water nearby to keep her dairy products. Like Mollie Carter, Sara kept her milk and butter under water, as near the mouth of the spring as she could, in a wooden (and later cement) box with bored holes to let the icy water run through. Only on the hottest days would she walk up to the creek and find the milk "blinked." But even on those airless summer days, A.P. and Sara were glad to be nestled so high and deep into the foothills that Clinch Mountain itself gave good evening shade.

And maybe best of all, the new Maces Springs home was an easy walk to Neal's; it was nothing to run over to the store to trade milk and eggs. Leonard Neal, who took over for old John, wouldn't just buy the eggs, he'd buy the chicken, too, or most anything else a body had to sell. Ermine Carter and his wife, Ora, used to pick huckleberries to trade for fabric, to make their children's school clothes. Leonard Neal stocked sturdy fabrics for making dresses and pants, flat bread (didn't have to have corn bread with *every* meal), and Cracker Jacks for the children. Into the twenties, that store remained the only place in Maces Springs to spend hard cash, and the single bustling spot in town. To get there,

Pleasant and Sara came down off the mountain and walked half a mile along the rutted dirt road that ran to the north and west through the Valley. They'd cut up onto the track bed and across the iron tracks themselves, then down onto the gravel holding area that fronted the store's uncovered wooden porch. On the way in, they'd nod greetings to whomever they knew, and if it was Pleasant, to those he didn't. People were always milling around that porch, especially when the flag was out and the train was going to stop.

Neal's was officially the railroad depot, the post office, and the general store; unofficially it was meeting place, town square, card room, and gossip corner all rolled into one. It was big enough to hold a crowd—thirty feet wide and a hundred feet deep, with a sturdy wood tongue-and-groove floor, and a big potbellied stove with a table and chairs next to it where people could sit for coffee and cards, or to listen to the radio. If there was a Jack Dempsey title fight, Leonard Neal would dial it in on his battery-powered radio, and the store would crowd up with men, while the women shook their heads, wondering what could be so desperately important about "a wrasslin' match."

That store was most notable for the people it brought together. At any given time it might hold the richest landowner in the Valley and the most low-down tenant farmer; a traveling salesman (a "drummer," they'd call him) in a city-sharp serge suit who got his car stuck on the muddy roads outside, and the local boys in their overalls who made half a living by waiting for chances to lift those kinds of cars out of the mud for a dime; a college man in Sunday clothes come to town to run the Maces Springs primary school, or a backwoods boy from way up in the hollows above Boozy Creek who rode over the mountain on horseback to catch the next morning's train to Gate City to fetch a doctor to look in on his daddy. He might be telling anybody who'd listen how he'd never bring his coon dog over to Neal's again. He'd rode over with the dog one time, and that was enough. When that hound heard the train a-whistlin' down the Valley, he hit that mountain and didn't come down for what seemed like a week.

More than anything, Neal's, like Poor Valley itself, was a way station—and a place so plunked down in the *middle* that it was the perfect vantage point to see old hat and newfangled, farm and city, past and future. Talk at Neal's wasn't confined to the Valley; there was plenty of talk about the world beyond. Local boys were starting to leave to find work elsewhere. Up in Wise County, the coal mines at Norton, Coeburn, and Appalachia were always hunting skilled carpenters and unskilled laborers. And they always needed men farther over in the big Pocahantas field in Tazewell County, and across the state line in Bluefield, West Virginia. A man didn't need anything but a strong back to get on a crew setting mining timbers, laying underground rails, or pulling coal cars by hand. The work could bust a man, and there were stories of coal leaders who drove their crew day and night and day again—thirty-six hours straight—letting up only for meals; and of foremen beating men with pick handles. But it paid better than a dollar a day; word was out on that. The idea was that a man could work in the mines a while, scrape together enough money to buy some land, and come back home. How could they know, sitting there in the sweet breeze of Poor Valley, that there were mine muckers who worked full-time and came out of the week in debt after they'd paid their rent and store bill to the company?

There were easier wage opportunities around now, too. Over in Bristol there was a pulp and paper factory, a leather goods factory, and a foundry for making mine cars. There were textile mills as near as Galax and Fries, and just a dozen miles away in Kingsport, Tennessee, jobs were going begging. Kingsport, especially, was coming up in the world. First known as the Boat Yard, Kingsport had long been a sleepy river town of a thousand souls where they built boats to haul staples such as bacon, salt, and nails up either fork of the Holston. But when the Clinchfield Railroad connected the city to Cincinnati and the Carolina coast in 1909, and started promoting the town, Kingsporters began to get the idea their city was on the way up, a Tennessee Zenith. The Kingsport Improvement Association hired a hotshot (aka European-trained) landscape architect and city planner, who laid out streets radiating from a town circle that was ringed with high-steepled *brick* churches. Then the Improvement Association bought up the big tracts in the flatlands near the fork of the Holston River, put in a power plant, and started selling the town to industrialists and investors. By 1919 they'd drummed up a cement plant, a tannery, a book manufacturer (they'd print the classics!), and a brick and tile factory.

Then they hooked the Big Fish. The self-appointed town fathers invited photography tycoon George Eastman to have a look-see at their new power plant and a nearby methanol factory. They took him pheasant hunting in the mountains overlooking the river bottoms, and made sure he came back with a couple of birds. But it wasn't just natural beauty and rich virgin timberland that attracted Eastman. The way he saw it, the town was blessedly free of the dark-skinned Mediterranean immigrants he blamed for the labor trouble in mills and factories in the Northeast. "Kingsport is . . . in a beautiful valley at 1800 ft. elevation," Eastman wrote later. "One of the nicest towns I have ever seen, with 10 000 inhabitants, only one of which is a foreigner." The locals, Eastman knew, would also work for a lot less than the urbanites of the North. Eastman shelled out a million dollars for the government-owned wood-alcohol factory, bought an extra three hundred acres, put in a narrow-gauge railroad to haul timber to his plant, and began mass-producing his own wood alcohol to be used in Eastman Kodak film base.

But even after Tennessee Eastman was up and running, the Improvement Association still had some good land left over in the bottoms, and some of that land ended up in the hands of Uncle Charlie Bays. Charlie was Mollie Carter's younger brother. He'd married a local girl named Mary Smith, and by 1918 they were living in her family homeplace, a big two-story clapboard house right up the road from Neal's. By the standards of the Valley, they were living high. The house was surrounded by fruit trees and a whitewashed picket fence; it had five fireplaces.

Charlie had a big farm in the Valley, but he had to feed three big sons—Dewey, Coy, and Stanley—and also his four daughters, Elva, Alma, Charmie, and Stella. Charlie had been around enough to know there were easier places than Poor Valley to claw a living from the ground. "Daddy was like a Viking," Stella remembers, "always looking for better land." In 1919 he bought a sixty-acre farm on a fertile four-mile stretch of bottomland in a long fork of the South Holston River. The cabin they built wasn't nearly as big as their house in the Valley, but it was so near the paper mill that they could hook in to its power plant. When Fland took five-year-old Vernon over to visit a few years later, the boy couldn't stop looking at the electric lights. He'd never seen anything so bright. And if Vernon would always remember the first sharp glare of those arc lights, his uncle Charlie's own children would be forever changed by living in the brilliance of that city light. Sometimes A.P. would stop by Kingsport for a visit; and he had to take but one look at his young cousins to know they were on their way up.

In the twenties there were more and more ways up and out of the Valley. And if you got far enough out, the roads were flat-graded and paved, made for fast travel. Nobody in Maces Springs knew that better than A.P.'s brother Ezra "Eck" Carter, who was by the early twenties a man on the go. When he was in town, people would see Eck at Neal's sometimes, and they'd watch him walk. He swayed a bit, holding his hands out from his hips as though he were trying to balance himself. This odd gait was, in fact, a sign of professional attainment. Just like he'd vowed, Eck had got that job as a U.S. Mail clerk on the rails. He'd ride the train from Bristol as far up the line as Washington, D.C., and he spent so much time walking the aisles of rocking passenger cars, he always looked uneasy on still ground. Eck's work made him known in Poor Valley, and respected as well. He had the best job in the Valley, that's what everybody said. For one thing, he was the best-paid man in Maces Springs, salaried, in fact, with all the guarantees and pensions Uncle Sam had to offer. But it wasn't just his walking-around money that distinguished Eck. He was the first of the Carter boys—and one of the few men in all Poor Valley—to make his living by his wits. And Eck let it be known, you had to be a sharp tool to do *his* job, had to memorize every post-office code in Virginia and the surrounding states, know the connecting lines to one-horse towns all over the South, and be able to speed-sort by hand, and on the move, sackfuls of incoming mail.

Above all, Eck was a proud man, and he wasn't above the subtle promotion of his reputation. He didn't have to do much, the way people were watching him. They'd see him return to the Valley from his trips north with the spoils of his success: a radio, a phonograph with a rack of hand-heavy but sleek black 78 records in their paper slipcovers, and books. Most folks in the Valley were lucky to have a Bible and a speller. Eck was always reading about practicalities that hadn't made it to the Valley: rotary engines, electric motors, dynamos, alternate and direct currents, and combustible engines. He was the first in the Valley to have a car. Eck's first—a Model A Ford—didn't make much time, but he liked to push it to the limit, with a seat full of friends, and people hanging off the running board. "They were just little ole cars, on dirt roads. If it rained, they'd just slide right off the road," says sister-in-law Theda Carter. "But back then, a small bunch of men could practically pick it up and put it back on the road."

It wasn't until the thirties that the state started grading and tending the dirt road that ran down Poor Valley, alongside the railroad tracks, but by then Eck had perfected his foul-weather driving methods. One of Flanders Bays's children would look up and see Eck pull off the road at a railroad crossing and hop onto the tracks. (Eck had the train schedules memorized, too.) The only problem was his wheelbase never matched the track gauge, so he wasn't so much riding the track as riding the ties. "He was always bumping up and down as he went by our house," Vernon Bays says. "He did that for about a quarter of a mile to the next crossing."

If Pleasant Carter was jealous of his dashing younger brother with his automobile and his pockets full of crisp dollar bills, he never expressed it. But what he saw happening all around him made it harder and harder for him to see himself as a lifelong dirt farmer. A.P.'s wandering gene was always getting the better of him. If his feet weren't wandering, his mind was. In the growing season, Pleasant (or "Doc," as he was often called by now) was especially restless. He'd get his crops planted every year, but then it would be months before he'd see the corn ripen or the tobacco leaf out. And those crops had to be worried over constantly, almost daily. The corn patches had to be weeded and reweeded; the tobacco plants had to be wormed and suckered. The constant press of tending, and the waiting, waiting, waiting, drove him nuts. And for what? Where was the money in that? So Pleasant started to avail himself of the other employment opportunities in the area. He worked at cutting timber, tanning bark, and framing tobacco barns. Just six miles up the rails, he got work for a company digging silicose sand out of the mountain for making glass. They actually made a town there, Silica, with a mail drop and a railroad depot for the freights hauling out the sand. "Daddy worked there beating rocks," says Joe Carter. "They'd go in there and shoot dynamite, blast it out. And then Daddy and them would take a hammer and break up the rocks until they could handle the pieces, put it in a cable car down off the mountain, where they'd put it in a big crusher and pulverize it into sand."

The jobs A.P. liked best were working sawmills and selling fruit trees. There were men who couldn't abide the whirring din of the rotary blade on hardwood, but Pleasant Carter could stand for hours listening for the changes in pitch and tune, the knothole melodies. That whir drowned out the rest of the world, so it was just him and his thoughts alone, as he smoothed raw wood into clean building lumber. He liked the tree selling because he liked the travel. In the winter months especially, he'd take off on foot, carrying his shoulder bag and his catalogs all over Scott County and beyond. In time, he was making ever-widening loops. He'd walk up through the Valley, following the Appalachian Trail all the way to Tazewell and even into Bland County, making acquaintances all the way, living by country hospitality. "Just hang around," people would say. "We'll wring a chicken's neck." He liked it best when he could stay with people who made a little music on their porch of an evening, after supper. A lot of times he carried his own fiddle with him, in a flour sack.

On the way home he'd circle back around through the hollows and coves, the little towns and mining camps of Buchanan County or Russell or Wise. And maybe he'd stop off in the big city of Kingsport, or Bristol, see what was new in the stores. He was especially interested in Cecil McLister's new place on State Street in Bristol, where you could buy the black vinyl disks that played music. Sometimes Cecil would wheel a phonograph over by the front door and pipe music right out onto State Street. People would gather on the sidewalks by the dozens to listen. Sometimes the local police had to send a man over to break up the crowd, or at least clear a path on the sidewalk. By the time A.P. got back home, he might have walked 150 miles of muddy wagon roads and mountain paths, might have even sold a few trees. But he always made new friends. And like Bob Carter, he had a little news of the outside world.

A.P. might be gone a week or ten days at a time, and he was a family man now. In 1919 Sara gave birth to Gladys Ettaleen Carter. A.P. was so nervous when Sara announced she was going into labor that he walked eight miles to Mendota, in the middle of the night, to get Doc Meade. Doc Meade probably would have suggested Poor Valley's best midwife. "Get Mollie Carter," he'd say. "She'll do as good as I would." Of course, by the time A.P. got back, Mollie Carter had delivered the baby without complication. His second daughter, Janette, was born in 1923, and he was away again, though nobody remembers exactly where.

Not that Pleasant was a great deal of help when he was home. As his daughter Janette wrote in her book, *Living with Memories*, "He would start jobs, go on to another, and not finish what he started. Mother spent her time telling him, 'Doc, change clothes.' 'Pick up your tools.' When Daddy finished a job, he never cleaned up; someone else did, while he just calmly walked off! He'd start something, then walk off till he took a notion to come back and finish what he'd started. It might be a month later."

More than anything, A.P. Carter's ways gave his home a restlessness; when he was around, the entire family lived in a state of constant readiness, as if they were on their way somewhere, frozen in that unsteady moment of excitement and fear that comes when the suitcases are packed but the conveyance hasn't yet arrived. It seemed as though A.P. was constantly looking for a way to confirm Mollie's prophecy of his being marked. "Someday, Sary," he once said, "my name's gonna *mean* something."

"Daddy would walk and walk and walk," Janette says. "He always seemed to be in deepest study. And he'd walk like that up and down the railroad tracks, always with his hands behind his back, in deep study. He was a-searchin'."

It was up to Sara to steady the household, and Sara Dougherty Carter was a woman meant for the task. She was prideful, and like Mollie

Carter, she measured herself by work. "I knowed her for taking a horse and dragging mining ties and everything else out of the mountain, run a grist mill, jack of all trades," says an old neighbor, Clyde Gardner. "I took corn out there for her to grind the day before [her third child] Joe was born. Somebody else started the engine, but she had it ground. And Joe was born that night." Sara's house had to be neat, her sheets white as snow, and her goose-feather pillows round and plump. "I know she believed in feeding her kids, but it was more'n that," Joe Carter says. "She had to have a vegetable salad with vinegar-and-oil dressing. And she would fix up vinegar and oil and add just this much sugar. She had a taste just like she had an ear for a song. She'd taste it, 'Needs a touch more vinegar.' And it was perfect every time. Every time the same. She could throw a meal together easiest of anybody there ever was. She'd grab this and that. Next thing you know she had a meal together. Not a lot of pains."

The idea was nobody should see her struggle. But anybody could see it in her hands. They were made strong from years of washing on a board, sometimes blistered from the frying grease popping out of the skillet where she cooked every meal, often dirty under the nails after a day of weeding a corn patch, or calloused from hours of keeping up her end of the crosscut saw. And Sara and A.P. had so little in the beginning, says one niece, Sara sometimes had only one dress that she'd turn over when it got too dirty. That had to be the hardest for Sara, because she was proud in one way Mollie Carter never was. She wanted to *look* good, all the time. Sara really did take the wild mountain flowers and twine them 'midst her ringlets and waves of dark hair; every day she used the little glass perfume dispenser on her dresser. It wasn't that she wanted to go out in the world and talk with people, or be talked about, but to look right confirmed her own sense of who she ought to be.

In fact, Sara might have kept pretty much to herself and her family, but in Poor Valley women still depended on one another. What would Sara have done without Dicey Thomas? In the summer of 1923, Sara was taking Gladys and six-week-old Janette back from Ma Carter's house when a train spooked the horse pulling their buggy. Janette was thrown clear into Dicey's rosebush, but Sara tried to hold the reins, and she was dragged down the rocky dirt road. Sara didn't get out of bed for nearly six weeks, but Dicey—who had seven children of her own—plucked Janette from the rosebush and nursed her the whole time. And that wasn't uncommon. Dicey, or Sara's sisters-in-law, Vangie Carter and Ora Carter, they'd all scoot over one of their own to nurse a niece, a nephew, or a neighbor baby.

Sara gathered a small group of girlfriends and became someone the others looked to. She wasn't one for confiding—nobody really knew her business—but Sara was full of sneaky fun, always had sharp little asides about the people of the Valley. "I loved Sara, ' Ruby Parker says. "She was funny as a monkey. We'd walk down to Neal's store together, and she always came up with something to make you laugh." And she could be counted on from the day she moved to Poor Valley. Out visiting one day, she found one of her friends, who was six months pregnant, in a hot fever of Spanish flu. And the woman was still on her feet, trying to feed her six children. Sara, then seventeen, put her to bed, with promises to fix corn bread and beans so the family could eat. And she kept coming back until the woman was strong enough to get out of bed.

Sara's friends loved her best for her solidity and her self-assurance; she might be quiet, but she was not to be crossed, and she did as she pleased. Like a lot of her girlfriends who worked so hard and so ably, she felt whatever freedom she wanted to take was her due. She might be bonded to work, but the bondage stopped there. Her granddaughters like to say that Sara was liberated before there was such a thing. She hunted and fished; she wore pants and smoked cigarettes. She danced if she wanted, even when her husband caviled. This "liberation" wasn't an idea Sara and her friends got from women's magazines. It came right out of life. They had earned the right to do as they pleased—and they did.

"The older women didn't cut their hair," says Sara's granddaughter Flo Wolfe. "It was biblical. A woman should never cut her hair. Sara had long hair when she moved to the Valley. Then Sara, Myrtle Hensley, Dicey Thomas, and Aunt Vangie, who all buddied around, they decided to cut their hair short, and didn't tell any of the men. The men probably didn't like that too much." Whatever the men thought, it wasn't of much consequence. The deeply religious Pleasant may have been chastened by his wife's newly bobbed hair, but all he could do was take the flowing (and now discarded) mane of hair and put it in a place for safekeeping.

The bottom line was, A.P. and Sara annoyed each other. But A.P. needed his wife like he needed air. He adored her (though he'd never figure out how to tell her), and not least for her musical talent. As soon as she moved over the mountain, Sara had joined in with Fland Bays's choir at Mount Vernon. When they went to singing conventions, Fland always wanted Pleasant and Sara along. In the twenties, singing conventions drew church choirs from all over Southwest Virginia. Hundreds of people would gather in front of a rigged-up stage, while a dozen choirs (or trios, quartets, and quintets) awaited their own call. At Gate City singing conventions, they even had a printed program, with a listing of all the groups and the songs they would sing. The stage would be set on the courthouse steps, and the main street had to be closed to traffic.

At the conventions, Sara would not only sing, she'd also accompany the choir on the autoharp. Ruby Parker remembers how Sara's lone contralto could move an entire gathering. "Everybody at the courthouse would be standing up, had their hands up in the air," Ruby says. "She could get down so low. She was a special talent."

"The first song my mother ever sang in public as a solo was in Bland County, Virginia," Gladys said. "She was there with Daddy and Uncle Fland Bays at a singing convention. They asked if anyone would volunteer for a song, so she took the harp and sang 'The Wandering Boy.' She said that the people came around and gave her money.

"I know Mommy said somewhere her and Daddy went and sang at a church and some man gave her ten dollars. That was a lot of money. She told the man he didn't have to give her anything, and he said you've got the prettiest voice I ever heard, and I want you to have it. It pleased her to death."

A.P. was starting to understand that music could mean money. And what with money being pressed into her palm, Sara wasn't oblivious to it, either. Still, it was only in extremis that she would pass the hat. In 1925 A.P. and Sara borrowed Eck's car to visit Buff and Mae, who had moved to Charlottesville. On the way home they'd barely made it out of Charlottesville when the car broke down. Dead broke and stranded more than two hundred miles from home, A.P. asked Sara for suggestions about raising cash. "All I know to do is sing," Sara said. So A.P. got the permission of the local preacher, booked a schoolhouse, and told the town storekeeper to put out the word: They were going to give an entertainment. By the time they'd finished, Pleasant and Sara had raised enough money to get the car fixed and had some left over when they got home.

Still, for Sara, music was mainly fun, for playing with friends and neighbors. Maybe the local postman, Price Owens, would join in, or Cleo Vermillion. They'd make music right in that little cabin at the foot of Clinch Mountain, and people would amble over to sit on the porch and listen, then Sara would invite them in for blackberry cobbler. The music got to be even more fun when her cousin visited from Rich Valley. The girl was just a teenager, but she had already made herself a queen of the guitar; she even had a way of plucking out the rhythm part under her own melody. Add Sara's lush voice and her autoharp and there was no better music in either valley. The two were so good that a local teacher invited them to play for her students at the Maces Springs School.

Seventy-five years later, one of those students can still conjure the picture of the two of them that day, sitting with their instruments at the head of the class. She can still see Sara, with her regal, stiff-necked bearing, and the young cousin's lively blue eyes, her curly dark hair. Sara's cousin was so tiny, she could have passed for a grade-school student herself that day. But she was like a miracle to those kids, working her Stella guitar so hard she busted a string—and went right on playing. "It was the grandest thing there ever was," the long-ago schoolgirl remembers. "Sara and Maybelle."

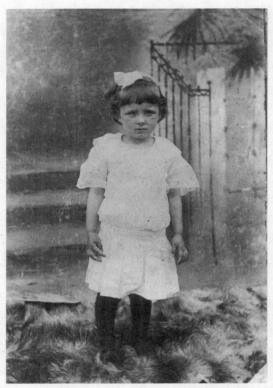

Maybelle Addington (Lorrie Davis Bennett)

Opposite: Maybelle's father, Hugh Jack Addington, sitting at right with high lace-up boots. Her mother, Margaret Kilgore Addington, standing with her hand on Hugh Jack's shoulder. Uncle Mil (sitting at far left) and Aunt Nick (standing at far left) raised Sara. (Carter Family Museum)

Maybelle

Not long after the schoolhouse performance, Maybelle was invited back to Maces Springs to perform with Sara and A.P. Half a century later, Maybelle remembered the date plainly, December 13, 1925: "I'd gone to Sara and A.P.'s to do a show at a schoolhouse," she told her good friend Dixie Deen Hall. "A.P.'s brother was in the play, and he was going with a schoolteacher there at the school. Well, he was supposed to take her home, but he didn't. He came with me back over to A.P.'s house, and that was the beginning of it. Everybody had been expecting him and this schoolteacher to get married, and I had a boyfriend, too, who was kindly disappointed "

That evening in December, Maybelle Addington fell for the most eligible young bachelor in Poor Valley: Ezra J. "Eck" Carter. That was Eck for you, charmed for life. Eck's friends and his brothers had been dragging themselves across Clinch Mountain in search of a Rich Valley girl, and one walks right in Eck's front door. And not just anyone, but maybe the finest flower in all Rich Valley. Here was a young woman—

a girl, really—who could sing, dance, play a guitar, ride a horse or a motorcycle or a running board, and bake a banana cream pie to curl your toes. She also provided instant ballast for Eck's orneriness. She could sit for hours making new friends while Eck would sneak off after "Hello." She never got rattled. Hard work didn't scare her a bit, and neither did hard play. Meanwhile, she also thought Eck Carter was the most beautiful man she'd ever seen, which was just fine with him.

Eck was so impatient (and Maybelle so undemanding) that they didn't wait for her seventeenth birthday, or even for Eck to build Maybelle a house of her own. "All of a sudden, the first thing I knew, we were married. I met him on the thirteenth of December and we were married on the thirteenth of March. We eloped . . . just slipped off and got married. I think I was only ever out with him three times alone—my father and mother were pretty strict on all of us, and one of my brothers always came along. We got married in the preacher's home in Bristol, and Virgie—Eck's twin—and her husband, Roy, were the only two with us. We didn't have a honeymoon. That night, the same play we had given in Maces Springs was supposed to be given at Hiltons, so we caught the train from Bristol and rode down to Hiltons. The snow was knee-deep, and you talk about cold! I had my guitar, because we were supposed to play, but the weather was so bad they canceled, and there we were in Hiltons . . . stranded. Well, we walked back up to Maces, to Uncle Lish Carter's, and my husband's first cousin Gordon Bays, who wasn't married, walked up the railroad track through the snow with us, carrying my guitar . . . not knowing I was married."

It should be noted that Eck let his cousin perform his chivalrous courting duty, without a word. "When we got to the house we told them, and Gordon just hollered, 'What! Well, I guess I'd better just go on home then.' "

On that snowy wedding night, March 13, 1926, Eck and Maybelle stayed with Uncle Lish. After that, they moved in with Bob and Mollie Carter, in the one-room cabin with the sleeping loft above. Even so, Eck was still living a charmed life. In the middle of one moonlit night not long after the wedding, a racket commenced in Pa Carter's front yard: first the tub-thumping, then the cowbells, and then the shouts and yodels. Poor Valley was there to shivaree Eck. A shivaree is a vaguely barbaric and unsettling old pagan ritual wherein a new husband (and sometimes a new fiancé) is stripped down, tied to a greasy pole, slathered with assorted and odoriferous substances, and carried around his house and outbuildings. Either it had been too long since Bob Carter himself was a newlywed, or he'd been fast asleep and wasn't thinking on a waked mind, so he went out onto the porch in his split-tail long johns and started jumping up and down, telling everyone to go home. This only got the party's blood up. So without further preliminaries, they tied Pa Carter to the greasy pole and paraded him around the house while Eck slept peacefully next to his new bride.

Actually, the living arrangement worked out just fine. Eck's railroad job took him away from home for three or four days at a time, and Maybelle didn't like being alone. So they stayed with Bob and Mollie nearly a year. Maybelle gladly helped her new mother-in-law with the cooking and the cleaning, watched the younger children, and added a warm and easy glow to the cabin. Even the cousins from the other side of the Knob started tramping over to see this new girl. "There was a sleeping loft in the cabin," remembers one of those cousins, Stella Bays. "We went upstairs, and Maybelle was sitting on the side of the bed with a guitar. She had bobbed hair, but long, down below her chin. Black hair. She had on dark-rimmed glasses, and she had freckles, brown freckles. Had a lot of freckles. She was sitting on the straw tick on the bed. Maybelle was a little shy at the beginning. At first, she never liked to play her guitar for just family. Whenever we'd say, 'Maybelle, play something for us,' she would hesitate. Then when she got started, she opened up."

Maybelle Addington was born May 10, 1909, across the mountain in Midway, Virginia, just a quarter mile from the Copper Creek home where Sara Dougherty was raised. Maybelle's mother and Sara's mothers had been sisters, both Kilgores. Maybelle's daddy was a sometime farmer, rolling-mill operator, storekeeper, and moonshiner named Hugh Jack Addington. Hugh Jack was a big square-jawed man with bright, piercing eyes, who proudly traced his family heritage back to a British prime minister, Henry Addington. The family freely admitted that Prime Minister Henry had been more or less run out of office on a rail, but not before he gave sage advice that led to General Wellington's shellacking of Napoleon.

The first of this Addington line in America was William, an educated young Londoner who emigrated for the sheer adventure of it. As a commissary officer in the Revolutionary War, William Addington had been charged with helping to feed and supply Washington's army. William nevertheless made it through the conflict without being shot by one of his own, and was at Yorktown to witness Cornwallis's surrender. After the war, William took his soldier's land grant and settled in Southwest Virginia with his wife and young son, Charles Cromwell Addington, who was born in 1777. In 1805 Charles moved to Copper Creek, where he lived until his death at the age of 104. When the town threw him a centennial party in 1877, the table was two hundred feet long, and its bounty fed more than a thousand people. By then Charles had been married three times, and accounted for 16 children, 107 grandchildren, and 443 great-grandchildren.

When Maybelle was growing up, Rich Valley was crawling with Addingtons, all close or distant kin. Her own schoolteacher was A.P.'s old singing buddy, Ezra Addington. Two of the three horseback mail carriers were Addingtons (and so was the first substitute). In and around Nickelsville, a town of 150 souls, there were *four* different Joe Addingtons. "There was Big Joe, Little Joe, Caverat Joe, and Pennywhinkle Joe," says Daphne McConnell, who grew up with Maybelle. "Pennywhinkle. Like the little shells they used to gather them on the side of the creek. Big Joe was my great-uncle. . . . No, Little Joe wasn't his son. Little Joe was Pennywhinkle's son. I know it's confusing. Like Opal Addington married Will Addington. Lot of Addingtons married Addingtons."

Hugh Jack married Margaret Elizabeth Kilgore, but he did his part in producing Addingtons: Their issue included Madge, Dewey, D.J. ("Deejer"), Willie B. ("Sawcat"), Norma, Maybelle, Linnie Myrl, Hugh Jack Jr. ("Doc"), Milburn B. ("Toobe"), and Warren M. ("Bug"). They moved all around the area—even got burned out of two homes—but always kept a big house. They lived in two-story English-style whitewashed cottages, with wood-rail fencing, cisterns for water, and walk-in cellars for winter storage. Hugh Jack liked to keep an ice house, too. In winter, he'd take a mill saw down to Copper Creek, cut out three-foot cubes of ice, and drag them up the hill with his team of oxen. During the flu epidemic of 1918, neighbors knew if they came to his house, Hugh Jack would gladly give over what ice he could to ease their fevered and dying kin. Even if the folks were hurried and fretting, Hugh Jack was glad for the company. Nothing made him happier than having a new ear to bend. "Hugh Jack was the big talker," says his niece Mary Bell Easterling. "I remember him sitting out on the porch telling tales. Hugh Jack was full of life."

He loved running the Green Store, which was his own general store that stood on top of the big hill running up from the "bent" of Copper Creek. Like they did at Neal's general store in Poor Valley, people congregated at the Green Store. Sometimes there were even fresh faces who didn't already know Hugh Jack's tall tales. And truth be told, his clientele always had a little more ready cash to spend—especially toward the end of the year, when wholesalers would come into the area and buy up geese and turkeys for Thanksgiving and Christmas dinners. Between that and a healthy trade in moonshine, a lot of folks had spare cash. So besides the staples like flour, beans, and coffee, Hugh Jack stocked his store for the up and coming. He had writing quills (a lot of unschooled farmers around Nickelsville were willing to pay to learn to read and write at the summer 'subscription schools"); new shoes (some people in Rich Valley had one pair of shoes for church alone; they'd walk to church in one pair, then change into a fresh unsullied pair before going in); a little jewelry (Hugh Jack liked bringing beads and crystals home to his wife); and sparkling sets of pressed-glass dishes. Margaret's pride was her store-bought pressed-glass punch bowl. When the Addingtons entertained, she'd fill that punch bowl to the brim and surround it with home-baked cakes.

But it wasn't just Elizabeth's food and Hugh Jack's drink that made the party. When Dewey was old enough, he started playing dance music with his uncle Steve Kilgore. Both could play banjo and guitar, and sometimes Ap Harris would join in with his fiddle. Passersby would see the furniture set neatly on the front lawn, with the rugs rolled up and set gently on top, hear that music, and know there was dancing going on inside.

When her older siblings first started making music, Maybelle was too young to join in, and anyway, she was her mother's daughter straight down the line: She wasn't one to step forward on her own. She had her mother's stature (when Maybelle first started going to school, she wasn't much bigger than the little doll she'd carry with her on the little rock footbridge that spanned Copper Creek and led to her school), and she had Margaret's temperament (nobody *ever* heard Maybelle raise her voice). As a young girl, she was so small and unassuming that she might have disappeared altogether in a crowd. But there was something magnetic about Maybelle. First off, her eyes were riveting. They were blue, but so pale they had a silvery, mirrorlike quality. And she had a way of making people see their own best selves in her eyes, because those eyes almost always looked pleased. Her hair was black and wavy, but when it was humid out, and especially when it rained, those waves would curl in unruly tendrils around her face.

Maybelle showed no particular genius at the Saratoga school, not in Ezra Addington's classroom and not even at Flanders Bays's singing school. But long before she hit her teens, she proved herself precocious in one way: After she pulled her mother's autoharp down onto the floor, she'd quickly learned to play it. Then she moved straightaway to "banjo pickin'" (which she learned from her mother) and claimed first prize at a Copper Creek banjo contest when she was just twelve. When she was thirteen, her brothers got a guitar. Around this time, Gibson and Martin were making guitars with stronger bracing for higher tension on the strings; the brightness of the new guitar sound captivated Maybelle.

Except for Uncle Fland's shape notes, Maybelle couldn't read music at all—and never would—but she studied her brothers and learned to play old songs by ear. She could take one of the old songs her mom played—"Weeping Willow Tree," "Sugar Hill," or "I Ain't Gonna Work Tomorrow"—and make her own tune of it. "The songs we learned were taught to us by my mother, who learned them from her mother before her, who had, in turn, learned them from her parents." What gave the old songs a modern flare was her guitar. "People hadn't been using the guitar in the country that much," says historian and musician Mike Seeger. "They had been singing unaccompanied, or they had banjo and fiddle for the most part. And the style of guitar that Maybelle played had a fluid, flowing, rhythmic sound, a way of playing the melody that was plain enough so that you could understand what it was, yet still brought you in because it had rhythm and life to it."

It wasn't long before her brothers were *asking* her to play with them at dances. Having Maybelle sit in was like having two musicians at once. Almost out of necessity, she was already developing a style of playing that would become known as the "Carter scratch." It wasn't necessarily difficult to master, but it was distinctive. And Maybelle got there first, on her own, transferring what she'd learned from her mother's five-string-banjo style. "I started trying different ways to pick it, and came up with my own style, because there weren't many guitar players around. I just played the way I wanted to," she said years later, when asked to explain her invention, "and that's it."

"She'd hook that right thumb under that big bass string," her daughter June Carter Cash once wrote, "and just like magic the other fingers moved fast like a threshing machine, always on the right strings, and out came the lead notes and the accompaniment at the same time. The left hand worked in perfect timing, and the frets seemed to pull those nimble fingers to the very place where they were supposed to be, and the guitar rang clear and sweet with a mellow touch that made you know it was Maybelle playing the guitar." Even when she was just thirteen, Maybelle had strong worker's hands—and staying power. She and her brothers would play until sunup. "You know" she once said, "I have square-danced all night and many a night in my life."

Another thing Maybelle did for entertainment was attend the Holiness revivals in the area. Maybelle didn't have so much interest in this hot new strain of American Methodism; the charismatics could be frightening, speaking in tongues, channeling the Holy Ghost itself. But for church-house music, there was no better. Maybelle would walk miles to a revival just to hear those driving hymns. "There was nothing else to do, so we'd go hear them sing," she once said, "just for the curiosity of it." It was wholly unchained from the old modal ballads and parlor songs so common in Rich Valley, and even from the more traditional shape-note gospel harmonies in Flanders Bays's songbooks. At bottom, the Holiness music had the rhythmic, free-form crackle of old slave spirituals, and Maybelle couldn't get enough.

For church itself, the Addingtons stayed closer to home. On Sundays they'd dress in their finest and ride in buggies over to the Addington Frame Church. Services at Addington Frame were less emotional and pleading than at the Holiness revivals, or even at Mount Vernon. By comparison, the Frame was subdued. But this Primitive Baptist church had a forgiving progressivism that Maybelle would carry with her all her life. By the time Maybelle came into the church, Addington Frame had a long history of social progressivism. During the Civil War, the area's Primitive Baptist central council threatened any congregation that aided the Union cause, and the Addington Frame elders fired back: "The advice given by the Association to the churches is contrary to the orthodox principles of the Baptists. It is unscriptural, uncharitable and full of bigotry." The Frame was also doctrinally charitable, to each and every individual. The Frame rejected predestination, which said that God had already chosen the few who would be saved and the rest were damned without appeal. At Addington Frame, Maybelle learned that *everybody* had an equal chance to earn his way into eternal life— from the wealthiest landowner to the poorest farmhand. It was between that person and God, and depended on both faith and works.

That's not to say the Frame didn't practice old-time religion. Once a year they had a foot washing, where members would humble themselves before God and community by washing another's feet. They also had furious, weeklong revivals, part spiritual and part social. "When we'd have revivals, all the young folks would go," says Daphne Stapleton. "And the deal was 'Can I walk you home?' Sometimes it would be midnight before you got home."

Those nights went so late because when a sinner was called to the altar, no schedule mattered. "Sometimes they'd start praying with somebody, and they didn't stop until they got them right, got them saved," says one woman who remains a force in a nearby church. "They might start in the afternoon and then come back at night after supper."

At every revival and every regular service there was music, though the singing at the Frame was more democratic than at Mount Vernon: They didn't go in for special quartets or solos. Everybody joined in. But despite their differences, Addington Frame and Mount Vernon were more alike than not. In a way you could say that Addington Frame religion *came* from across the mountain, and it came in the person of Big Tom Carter. Big Tom was a six-foot-six, three-hundred-pound servant of God and man. But he was no friend to his horses. For forty years he rode back and forth across Clinch Mountain from his home in Poor Valley to Rich Valley, where he pastored at the Frame.

Big Tom was cousin to Bob Carter (his father had helped raise Bob) and brother to Mandy Groves. He'd been a bit of a heller when he was young, even took a drink now and then. But when Big Tom got religion, he got it whole hog. After he was saved, he wouldn't touch a drop. When Big Tom wasn't preaching, he was serving his congregations in other ways: He delivered two hundred babies, performed more than five hundred weddings and twice as many baptisms. He also set broken bones and cured skin cancer. Anybody who thought they had a skin cancer would visit Big Tom, and he'd treat them . . . which is to say he'd burn off the growth. "You're gonna suffer," Big Tom would always tell people right up front. But he was not licensed to prescribe painkillers, so all he could do was suggest the best substitute for morphine he knew: whiskey.

That's another thing Maybelle took from her church: an understanding of provident al grace. Tom Carter always figured God had a highly evolved view of sin, that He took a good hard look at a person's circumstances before He judged them. In fact, when Big Tom was late in life and suffering from arthritis and other maladies, his doctor told him to take a sip of whiskey every night for health purposes. And he did. But according to his son Dale, he'd first lace it with goldenseal (an herb), so it tasted bitter as bile. "He figured if it didn't taste good and he didn't get any enjoyment out of it," says Dale, "it was okay."

Because Big Tom also led a congregation on the Poor Valley side of

Clinch Mountain, he made it to the Frame only once or twice a month. So when he was there, he'd preach Saturdays and Sundays, and that meant whoever was preparing the Sunday dinners could go to services Saturday morning. After services, Big Tom would do the dunking. "It was quite a ways from the church to the creek where they'd baptize," says Daphne Stapleton. "Baptism was on Copper Creek, down where Hugh M. Addington lived. There'd be all the people up on the hill watching, and buggies and horses. Wasn't hardly any cars back then.

"Maybelle and I were baptized at the same time, in 1924. There was a whole bunch of us baptized. There must have been about twelve or fifteen people. I was about thirteen, so Maybelle must have been about fifteen. Tom Carter baptized us."

What a holy day that must have been for Big Tom, more than a dozen souls washed clean in one fell swoop. Big Tom's call was strong, and he didn't act on it just within the walls of his churches. Back and forth across Clinch Mountain, Tom Carter was always prospecting for souls. He'd see some young farmhand on a plow and walk right up to him, voice booming: "Boy! Have you been *saved?!*" Probably that's why Eck Carter went the other way when he saw his preacher cousin coming. At the time he married Maybelle, Eck didn't care much for religion. He was busy chasing other things—like worldly goods. But Maybelle never pushed Eck, and she never judged him. The way she saw it, that was his choice. She loved him anyway.

How could Eck *not* love this girl? There was nothing he wouldn't do for her. Anything Maybelle asked for, he'd give her. But Maybelle didn't ask for much, so he'd give her things he thought she *might* like. When he got himself a motorcycle, he bought her one, too, a one-cylinder Indian. But even with the motorcycle, Maybelle couldn't keep up with Eck. Who could? And who wanted to? "Eck had him a big Harley-Davidson motorcycle, specially built," says his nephew Joe Carter. "And every time he'd go out, he'd come in clawed up. He'd run it through a fence or something. I believe he bored it out to eight [cylinders]. It'd outrun a scalded dog. And Eck thought he was a motorcycle man. He'd lay that thing down on a curve, and that little pedal down there where your foot rests, it'd leave a fire going all the way around the curve. If he'd a-hooked into something with that thing, he'd still be on the road. Ermine rode with him out of Bristol one time. Came near to scaring Ermine to death. Ermine said he fell in on one of them stiff curves and kept laying it down there and they was a-leaving a streak of fire behind them. He said, 'Eck, you better slow her down.' "

But Eck wouldn't slow down for anybody. He was on the move— on his way up. He'd had plenty enough lean years growing up, and his own house was going to be different. Eck measured his progress in the world by the bounty he brought home to his bride. Too much was never enough. Eck didn't return from the road empty-handed; he'd burst through the cabin door with bagfuls of bananas, grapes, and walnuts . . . and jewelry and perfumes from town. He bought Maybelle a radio so that they could listen to Riley "the Ball Mountain Caruso" Puckett and "Fiddlin' John" Carson—with his daughter, "Moonshine Kate"—on WSB out of Atlanta or the Grand Ole Opry (known then as the WSM Barndance) out of Nashville. Eck bought records for their battery-powered Victor Talking Machine Company phonograph. Cecil McLister didn't stock just Caruso and Broadway show tunes. Records were starting to sound like home: Vernon Dalhart's renditions of "The Wreck of Old 97," "The Ballad of Floyd Collins," and "Prisoner's Song"; Puckett's covers of "Little Old Log Cabin" and "You'll Never Miss Your Mother Till She's Gone"; and Henry Whitter's versions of "Lonesome Road Blues" and "The Old-Time Fox Chase." When they'd listen to them together, Eck would tell Maybelle there wasn't a musician on radio or record could hold a candle to *her.*

Around their first anniversary, Eck started to build Maybelle a house of her own. He bought some land way up in the foothills, just a few hundred yards from Mount Vernon Methodist Church, and built a big four-room cabin with a sleeping loft above. In fact, Eck might have built it a little too big. It was so nice that Bob and Mollie decided to move in, too. So Eck built a second, smaller cabin a bit farther up the mountain, where he and his bride finally set up housekeeping on their own. It was time, anyway: Not long after they celebrated their first wedding anniversary, Maybelle announced she was going to have a baby. But when Eck was away, Maybelle could still go down the mountain to stay with Bob and Mollie, or up the road less than a mile to stay with her cousin Sara.

Though Maybelle and Sara had grown up within a quarter mile of each other, they hadn't been close. Maybelle was only six years old when Sara married and went across the mountain. But once Maybelle got to the Carter side, the two women were like instant sisters. People could see it in the way they made music together: One would start in on a song, and the other could always follow along. And people could see it in the way the quiet would sit so easy between them for hours. They didn't have to talk. For Maybelle, who was just a teenager when she married, Sara's presence eased her way on the other side of the mountain. For Sara, Maybelle was like a lifeline she hadn't realized she needed. For the first time, Sara found almost absolute security in another person. In fact, she even felt confident enough in their sisterhood to risk it on a practical joke, the only practical joke anyone remembers Sara perpetrating. Just after Maybelle's first daughter was born, Sara made a stealth visit to Eck's house. While Maybelle was cleaning in the next room, Sara quietly removed the sleeping baby from her crib, hid her in the other bedroom, and left the house unseen. When Maybelle entered the nursery and found the crib empty, she fainted. They'd laugh about that one for the rest of their days. Nobody was more forgiving than Maybelle—and nobody was more fun. When she'd stay over at Sara's, Maybelle would help Sara cook for the children: Gladys, Janette, and baby Joe. Then they'd pull out their instruments and make music in the cabin. When A.P. was gone, they'd kick off their shoes and teach Gladys and Janette how to dance the buck and wing.

A.P. was gone about as much as Eck in those days, mostly on the circuit selling fruit trees. One time in 1926, he returned from a trip to Kingsport and somehow convinced Sara to ride back to town to sing for a man who was scouting "hillbilly" musicians for Brunswick, a "recording" company. But with Sara singing the lead, the scout didn't see a chance for the Carters. Women just didn't take the lead in combos, except maybe on race records. He thought A.P. should get out front. They could bill him as "Fiddlin' Doc." Partly for his mother (as he'd always claim later) and partly because he knew his own limitations, Pleasant demurred. But he left the audition with some cause for hope. The Brunswick man had said there was no need for them to be poor folks with voices like theirs.

How could A.P. forget that? Sometimes when he was home, he would pull out his fiddle and play along with Sara and Maybelle. And sometimes he'd just stop and listen. He knew how good the two were together. He'd heard all Eck's records, too, and the men were agreed: There was no duo or group better than their Sara and Maybelle. Not only that, the music they played—the songs themselves—were precious gems, A.P. believed. Pleasant Carter had a preacher's faith in the eminence of those songs. As Pleasant saw it, those old songs were more valuable than all the coal in Wise County—and a lot more lasting. That's what he was banking on in July of 1927, when he saw an ad in the Bristol paper for the local Victrola dealer, the Clark-Jones-Sheeley Company. DON'T DENY YOURSELF THE SHEER JOY OF ORTHO-PHONIC MUSIC was the headline, but in a box beneath it, the small type read, "The Victor Co. will have a recording machine in Bristol for 10 days beginning Monday to record records—Inquire at our Store."

A.P. went immediately to 621 State Street to see if Cecil McLister knew anything. And Cecil sure did. There was a Mr. Ralph Peer in just the other day, he told A.P., a representative of the Victor Talking Machine Company who had asked Cecil to put the word out and line up some music acts Peer could audition in Bristol. Cecil didn't see why the Carters couldn't have a tryout.

"[A.P.] came back home and he told us, said there's a man from Victor in Bristol looking for talent, you know, to make records," Maybelle told folklorist Ed Kahn twenty-five years later. "And of course we didn't think anything about it. I didn't."

A.P. couldn't think of anything else . . . and he couldn't stop talking about it. He told his wife that Mr. Ralph Peer was going to be paying fifty dollars for every song he liked well enough to record. Sara's reaction was characteristically blunt: "Aw, pshaw. Ain't nobody gonna pay that much money to hear us sing." Even when A.P. could point to the story that appeared in the Bristol paper a few days later, about a fellow named Stoneman, from Galax, who was making $3,600 a year in royalties alone, the reaction in Maces Springs generally followed Sara's. The toughest criticism came from Uncle Lish, who was himself a suspect character—he'd once set out to burn the lice out of his hen's roosts, forgot that it was attached to his barn, and burned the entire structure to a charred heap—but always ready to think the worst of his wifty nephew. "Well, Doc's going crazy," he'd say.

"Uncle Lish Carter was always on A.P.'s case," Janette Carter wrote in *Living with Memories*. "Doc had done some strange things, usually right backwards to other people. . . . So when Daddy calmly announced, 'I am going to make records if Ralph Peer in Bristol likes our act,' Uncle Lish said, 'Send him out to Marion [the Marion, Virginia, mental hospital]. He's completely gone this time. His family will starve, no doubt.' "

Eck was not altogether behind his brother's scheme, either. Maybelle was just eighteen years old, and eight months pregnant. Besides, A.P. didn't just want to borrow Eck's wife; he wanted to borrow his *car*. Eck did relent, but not before he made A.P. promise to weed his corn patch. Some good was going to come of this, Eck figured. On July 31, 1927, A.P., Sara, and Maybelle loaded up Eck's Essex for the trip. "I remember standing at the fence up there at Grandma Carter's, screaming and crying for them to take me, and they left me a-standing there," Janette says. "They took Joe. He was nursing."

Eight-year-old Gladys climbed aboard the Essex; she was going along to baby-sit Joe, in case their mother had to spend long hours auditioning. By the time A.P. got everybody loaded in, there wasn't much room for luggage. "When we got ready to leave, I said, 'Should I take my guitar?' " Maybelle told Kahn. "A.P. said, 'Why, sure.' Said, 'You can't make a record without your guitar.' " Had they rehearsed? Kahn asked. "We didn't do anything. Of course the songs we did then we already knew. We had been doing them together quite a bit around the house."

That deep-summer day was hot and humid; looked like a thunderstorm was coming, and Maybelle must have been miserable. She was eight months pregnant, and in the sticky heat her hair must have been curling like new leaves. Still, she probably never complained as A.P. drove them out of Poor Valley, through Jett Gap. If it did rain, the deeprutted roads would muddy and grab at Eck's tires. Then they'd be in trouble. But if they could make it out of he Valley, and ford the Holston River before it got up, they'd get be on a state highway. It wasn't paved, but it was graded, graveled, and oiled to keep the dust down. If they made it across the Holston, A.P. figured, it would be smooth riding from there.

 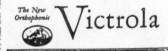
The Bristol News Bulletin *advertisement that lured A.P.* (Bristol News Bulletin)

Opposite: Mr. and Mrs. Ralph Peer (Carter Family Museum)

Mr. Peer

Ralph Sylvester Peer must have seemed an odd duck to the people who auditioned for him in his make-do "recording studios." Even when he was on his scouting expeditions, living out of suitcases, in the middle of wet-hot southern summers, Ralph Peer would be wearing his fine London-tailored suits with a silk handkerchief in his breast pocket. The hopeful musicians stood small in some cavernous and nearly empty warehouse loft, shuffling their feet, trying to introduce themselves to the New York record scout, and wondering what might be behind the thick blankets that hung from the ceiling, but Mr. Peer rarely took pains to put people at ease. Not that he was threatening. His rich baritone voice had command, but just enough midwestern twang to take the edge off. Even as he neared forty, there was something boyish about his smooth, moon-round face, and he was so naturally placid that people around him rarely got rattled. God knows, that helped in the recording business.

It took only one bad mistake to blow a take: could be an engineer or his assistant; could be a bandleader or an instrumentalist or a singer.

There were a lot of people who had to be able to do their jobs right. If just one fouled up, they'd have to shave the wax and start again. It helped having a head man who kept jangled nerves at a minimum. That's part of the reason Peer was in the driver's seat. He didn't waste time.

So when some new act was standing in front of him, shuffling nervously, Peer would dispense with preliminaries and tell them to get on with it, do the song they wanted to do, and do it their way. And when they'd start, Ralph Peer would lean forward in his seat, close his eyes, cup a hand behind each ear, and listen. He didn't care so much what anybody looked like. He cared to know only what they would sound like on record. Mr. Peer liked to cut to the chase.

That's not to say Ralph Peer himself was simple to know. He was an opera's worth of contrapuntal chords. By the end of his life, he had almost single-handedly built the world's largest music publishing company, but his own son would say he took just as much pride—and spent just as much time—cultivating his prizewinning flowers. He sat on the board of directors of the local camellia society, rarely missed the camellia club's Tuesday meeting at the California Institute of Technology, and kept up a correspondence with botanists around the world. He was a committed workaholic, but his idea of a well-spent Saturday was to sneak away from his desk and engraft camellias in the greenhouse out back. After a lifetime in the music business, Peer knew more music people than anybody, but he probably didn't spend three hours a year at industry parties.

In his later years, he could sit for days in perfect stillness at his home office in Los Angeles, reading a blizzard of memoranda into the latest-model Dictaphone (he was proud to keep *two* secretaries overworked), but he liked nothing more than to take his speedboat out onto Lake Tahoe and open it up while the deafening wind whipped through his hair. He was always, even toward the luxurious end of his life, sensitive about his education. When asked where he'd gone to college, Peer's answer was "University of Chicago . . . for two months." Naval officers' training course, he'd explain, First World War. It was a deft parry, and headed off further discussion of his deficiencies in formal schooling. But

Peer never lacked for confidence in his own capacities. "It's amazing how accurately I forecast what finally happened," he once mused out loud about a major turn in the music business. "I have a brain that likes to work."

Peer rarely talked of himself or his accomplishments. When he did, he could be surprisingly seductive: thoughtful, matter-of-fact, and modest. And then suddenly, wildly, egotistical. In 1953, during a two-day interview, he claimed credit for launching the careers of Jimmie Rodgers (true) and the Carter Family (true), coining the genre terms *race* and *hillbilly* for records (true), helping Gene Autry into the saddle (partially true), setting the foundation of the modern music-publishing business (glancingly true), and "inventing" Louis Armstrong (a whopper).

Peer was an unmistakable aesthete out claimed to care about little besides making a buck. His personal tastes in music ran to opera, chamber music, and big-band swing, but he staked his own business with forms of music he sometimes claimed to despise, what he called "the hillbilly and nigger stuff." Late in life, he still sounded ashamed that such "stuff" was the underpinning of his music-publishing empire. "I've tried so hard to forget them," he once said of the early race and hillbilly artists he discovered. He could speak of those same artists with a father's secret fondness for his wayward children, and then a blue blood's unconflicted coarseness. He also was prone to exaggerating the artists' shortcomings in a way that engorged his own genius. On bringing back harmonica player Henry Whitter for a 1923 re-recording session, he said, "Something was lacking. Then I discovered the dope could sing. He never told me."

"I wouldn't say Jimmie Rodgers was extremely clever," he said of the man who almost single-handedly made Peer his first fortune, "but that he had good intelligence from a hillbilly base. Above the average [for a hillbilly]." Actually, Jimmie was clever enough to put the shine on Peer from time to time. Right up to his last New York recording trip, in 1933, the tubercular Rodgers used his illness to procure from Peer the perquisites he would require. "We got him to the Taft Hotel and assigned a man to watch out for his 'incidental welfare.' If he needed more whiskey and whatnot," Peer said years later. "The tubercular person has three times the sexual activity of a normal man. There was nothing he could do about it, so he was just acting naturally."

When asked how Rodgers himself made out on the millions of records sold, Peer answered, "I looked after him. Of course, looking after him was giving him all the money he asked for. And warning him when he got in too deep. . . . I remember when he owed me a hundred thousand dollars at one time, so he must have made out okay. He wanted to build a great big mansion in some little town north of San Antonio. But I certainly never lost anything on Jimmie Rodgers."

Despite friendships with black professionals such as composer Perry Bradford, theater critic Tony Langston, and musician Louis Armstrong, Peer could be even uglier when he spoke of African Americans. Hillbilly records brought in an avalanche of correspondence from would-be artists, Peer said, but not race records. "Of course the niggers can't write," he explained, with a chuckle, "southern niggers." Louis Armstrong's second wife, Lillian, a woman of expansive intelligence who held a university degree, Peer called simply "an awfully nice ole nigger girl."

Still, nobody can gainsay Ralph Peer's place in history—or what he did for black and rural white musicians, and what he did for their long-ignored audience. He opened the field of recording to artists who had been left out, even while they held America's richest native musical traditions. And he opened it up at precisely the moment when those traditions were being reforged in the white-hot shuttle between old-timey country living and wage-slaving in the city. There were blues enough at both terminals, and most every mile in between. In the decade after World War I, huge numbers of blacks and mountain whites from the South were kicking the dust off their shoes and moving into mill towns, coal camps, and industrial cities all over the country. Even on meager wages, they had money to spend. Ralph Peer found out before anybody else in the recording business that there was a big world out there making music, with a lot of *different* audiences, and room enough for everybody; that the color that mattered most was green, and that sometimes a man had to just close his eyes and listen.

In the 1958 interview, sixty-six-year-old Ralph Peer tried to explain how he'd made his place in history: "I have a favorite saying: 'It's the art of being where the lightning is going to strike.' And how in God's name you can detect that, I wouldn't know. But I've always been able to do it. . . . Look at the accidents! Just why did those things happen?" If you were to fill up Ralph Peer with truth serum, he'd probably say there wasn't an ounce of school-bought genius to it. As a young man, he was flinty enough to cause a stir in the marbled halls of the "respectable" music business, and contrary enough to have enjoyed it. And there's little doubt he'd say he was addicted to the sheer adventure of it. More than brains, what he did took effort, energy, and endurance. Ralph Peer understood this: If a man chased the sound of thunder long enough, he was probably going to get hit by lightning. "The real secret," he said, "is continuous activity."

Ralph Peer and the recording industry grew up together. He was born in Independence, Missouri, in 1892, just as the first recordings were being sold to the public. The business was mostly a hard-science racket then, and the product a rich man's vanity toy. In 1892 Thomas Edison's Electric Motor Phonograph, fully loaded, sold for a whopping $190. Those machines read songs carved into heavy wax cylinders. Fidelity to the original music was iffy. And there was no way to copy the cylinders from a master. So even if Edison could get an artist to record one song over and over and over, production costs were high. Still, the phenomenon of recorded sound was enrapturing. Its future could be read in the wide-eyed, slack-jawed look of a virgin listener. When a New Orleans drugstore installed a "coin-in-the-slot" phonograph, it pulled in five hundred dollars a month. And once cash was on the line, the scientists and engineers got right down to business. A German immigrant named Emile Berliner started to carve songs into seven-inch wax disks, and to make as many copies as needed from a single master recording, while the two biggest companies in the business—Edison and Columbia—raced each other to improve fidelity and to drive prices down enough to make the phonograph a middle-class vanity toy. By the turn of the century, furniture stores all over the country were retailing the top-of-the-line Edison Home Phonograph for $40 and the Edison Gem model for just $7.50. Columbia's Home Graphaphone sold nationwide for $25, and its Eagle model (introduced for the Christmas rush of 1897) could be had for $10.

Phonograph sales were a boon to Abraham Peer, whose furniture store was the exclusive Columbia dealer in Independence. Business was so good that he didn't seem to mind that his ten-year-old son, Ralph, spent most of his Saturday workday listening to and cataloging the newest Columbia disks. Abraham even relented when his boy wanted to make the forty-minute train ride downtown to pick up the newest selections from Columbia's main retail office and warehouse in Kansas City. By the time he was eleven, Peer had won a summer job in the Columbia office, filling in for whichever stock boy or shipping clerk took vacation.

Peer was so sure of the business, and his own future in it, that he took a pass on his slot at Kansas University, married his high-school sweetheart, and settled into the permanent employ of the Columbia Phonograph Company's Kansas City office. For an eighteen-year-old with big dreams, the work itself lacked romance. Over the next five years he worked as a credit manager, a retail manager, a traveling salesman, and the assistant manager (without title, because he was too young) of the Kansas City operation. He was still 1,200 miles away from what he considered the real action, the recording studio. What went on in those New York studios was a tantalizing mystery to him.

He made a brief stop in Columbia's Chicago store, where he worked again as the assistant manager without title, and he followed that with an uneventful tour with the U.S. Navy during World War I. After Peer was mustered out, one of his old bosses, who had left Columbia, offered him a job at the General Phonograph Corporation. It was hardly the big time, but it was New York.

General Phonograph's bread and butter was the manufacture of phonograph motors, billed in their catalog as the "Motor of Quality." For the five years before Peer joined the company, General had spent most of its time trying to convince piano and furniture manufacturers to try their hand at phonograph production. The company's recording label, Okeh (the "Indian" word, they said, for "all right"), was barely that. The early repertoire—pressed at a button factory in Scranton,

Pennsylvania—didn't live up to the flashy Indian-head design on the label and sleeves; the first recording they issued was "The Star Spangled Banner," with the equally uninspired "American Patriotic Medley" on the flip side. Even after they switched over from the old vertical "hill-and-dale" recordings to lateral-cut disks and got down into the groove with "The Vamp" and "My Cairo Love," Okeh hardly made the established companies quake with fear. While Columbia, Edison, and Victor were riding a wave of record sales that pushed over $100 million in 1921, Okeh was lucky to claim 3 percent of the total market.

By the time Peer became director of recordings at Okeh, the postwar depression and radio were starting to pinch the record business. Within four years, sales would be little more than half the industry's 1921 benchmark, and Okeh had little margin for survival. Peer was trying new fixes, leaning hard on the ethnic markets, recording German oompah bands, Polish polka bands, Swedish chorale groups, Yiddish nightingales, and African-American blues singers. "We had all foreign groups: German records, Swedish records, Polish records," Peer said, "but we were afraid to advertise Negro records." He didn't have to. "Race records," as he named them in the Okeh catalog, sold big. Peer got reports of Pullman porters buying twenty-five records at a time, dollar a pop, and then carrying them off to southern cities such as Atlanta and New Orleans, where they could sell them for double the money.

Peer decided it was time to go out into the country and record local artists; there was almost no music he wouldn't try to keep Okeh afloat. In Chicago, he recorded selections in Italian, German, Bohemian, Lithuanian, and Greek. In Buffalo, he recorded Polish bands. In New Orleans, he recorded Dr. James Roach, a "Cajan" singer whose first cut was "Gue Gue Solingail," i.e., "Song of the Crocodile"; in Dallas, the Bel Canto Quartet and Jimmie Wilson's Catfish String Band. And in Atlanta, Georgia, in 1923, he recorded a local radio celebrity named Fiddlin' John Carson. Carson's record—"The Little Old Log Cabin" and "The Old Hen Cackled"—was the first southern mountain music Peer put out on Okeh. But he didn't have much hope for the release.

For decades the phonograph companies had been dabbling in recording the music of the southern mountains: mainly gospel hymns and old-timey fiddle music. The market had never been big. And when Peer got back to New York and listened to the Fiddlin' John selections, he was horrified. They were, in his phrase, "pluperfect awful." It wasn't that John Carson lacked talent, but the recordings themselves were terrible. In order to play in his angular style, Carson had stood so far back from the acoustic horn that the warehouse's roaring presence had been captured in the space between and laid permanently on the wax disk. Because the warehouse walls weren't properly muffled, Carson's voice and his fiddle played in maddening dueling echoes. Even so, the Okeh dealer in Atlanta insisted on having five hundred disks pressed and shipped right away. He said he wanted them for a fiddlers' convention, less than a month away. Peer was too embarrassed to even put a catalog number on the selections. But the local dealer was adamant, mainly because he understood the fiddle's place in southern mountain culture.

In the twenties, the fiddler was the knight errant of mountain music, traveling to well-attended tournaments all over the southern mountains, playing the same Scotch-Irish airs that had been handed down for generations. At the annual interstate old-time fiddle contest in Atlanta, for instance, John Carson competed with a fiddle that bore the date 1714. His great-grandfather had carried the instrument over from Ireland a century earlier, and when John was ten years old, his grandfather presented it to the boy. Besides the annual Atlanta event, there were dozens of regional fiddle contests. America's most publicity-minded magnates were even trying to cash in on the cult of the fiddle. Henry Ford and Thomas Edison halted their "vacation motor tour" to alert news outlets worldwide that they had discovered the greatest fiddler on earth, one Jasper E. Bisbee, of Paris, Michigan. Mr. Ford even sponsored his own round-robin of regional tournaments, which culminated in a national championship. Mr. Ford's first champ, a five-foot-tall construction worker named "Uncle Bunt" Stephens, won a thousand dollars and a new Lincoln automobile. Other contests had a more down-home feel to them, as did the contestants. There was Dexter Allison, an octogenarian from the Georgia mountains who started his fiddle-fight days by simply calling out any man of reputation. Stubbins Watts came out of western Missouri, claiming kinship to the original mountain man,

Daniel Boone, and offering his own recipe for success: "You can't fiddle if you don't pat your foot." From the Ozark Mountains there was "Hi" Taylor and his local adversary, Mrs. Lem Waterman, wife of a Baptist preacher. Mrs. Waterman was one of the few contestants who would do without a chaw of tobacco, but even without the benefit of nicotine jolt, her renderings of "Money Musk" and "Get Up and Go" always gave Hi a run for his money.

For the contestants, this was not play. The prize might only be bragging rights, but that was prize enough. The oldsters could still get testy when the judges had spoken on *tekneek* and *repertory*. When sixty-six-year-old William Stalcup edged out seventy-one-year-old "Uncle John" Llewellyn for the King of Missouri Old-Timers crown in 1923, Uncle John yelled that he'd been hamstrung. "Ef it had been wet times, I'd beaten the youngster out," he complained. "I learned to fiddle with my feet on a beer keg. I do my best fiddling with my knees half as high as my head." And there was more than a hint of sadness when ninety-year-old Wise Deacon of the Arkansas Ozarks said he could still play "The Arkansaw Traveler" and "Turkey in the Straw" just fine, but when it came to "Leather Breeches" and "Give the Poor Fiddler a Dram," he could no longer "put the tingle" in the dancing feet.

In the twenties, youngsters were streaming out of the hills with their grandfathers' hand-me-down-down fiddles . . . and their songs, too. Twenty-two-year-old Marcus Lowe Stokes blew down from the Blue Ridge foothills and captured Atlanta's annual fiddler's championship with a foot-stompin' version of "Hell's Broke Loose in Georgia." After that, the crowd wouldn't let Stokes off the stage at Cable Hall, and he was happy to oblige his audience: "We play till milking time in Cartersville," he said Stokes's rousing victory inspired Stephen Vincent Benet to write the poem "The Mountain Whippoorwill" ("My mother was a whippoorwill pert / My father, he was lazy / But I'm hell broke loose in a new store shirt / To fiddle all Georgia crazy").

In short, fiddlers always drew a crowd, and that's why Atlanta's Okeh dealer, Mr. Polk Brockman, wanted the John Carson records by the time the next fiddle contest convened. So on a hot July day in 1923, Brockman went to Atlanta's Railway Express Office to take delivery of the Carson disks. Then he raced to Cable Hall, where dozens of fiddle champs and an audience of six thousand people were gathering, climbed onto the stage, pointed the glory horn of an old German phonograph out toward the audience, and let fly with Fiddlin' John on record. In a few hours, Brockman's inventory was gone and he was calling New York.

"He got on the phone and said, 'This is a riot,'" Peer remembered. "'I've gotta get ten thousand records down here right now.'" When national sales hit half a million, Peer called Carson to New York: "I said, 'Get this fellow on a train right away. I've got to remake the record. We can't go ahead with that sort of thing. So we remade two selections and another eight or ten, you see, and we were off."

So Peer had another series to add to the Okeh catalog and a question about what to name it: Mountain? Mountain Country? Hill Country? It would be nearly two years before a five-piece string band from Galax, Virginia (Al Hopkins and the Hill Billies), gave Peer his inspiration. Next catalog out, the "hillbilly record" was born. Peer began trolling the mountains for more recording artists, and the mountaineers were waking up to it.

In the summer of 1924, a thirty-one-year-old carpenter in the coal town of Bluefield, West Virginia, was downtown killing time at the Warwick Furniture Company when the store manager put one of Peer's early mountain recordings, Henry Whitter's version of "The Wreck of Old 97," on the phonograph. Ernest V. "Pop" Stoneman was almost embarrassed for Henry; he'd worked with Whitter over at a cotton mill in Fries, and Pop knew the man was no singer. He sang "through his nose so bad," Pop told an interviewer in the sixties, "I said, 'Everybody's going to think we *all* sing through the nose. I can outsing Henry Whitter.' So I made me a harp rack and started working on a harmonica and autoharp combo. I said, 'They ain't got anything like that.'"

Stoneman was already moonlighting as a musician for hire, at three dollars for three hours most Saturday nights. But through that summer, he spent his free nights rehearsing with a local dance band. He wrote letters to both Columbia and Okeh. Columbia invited him to New York in September; Okeh said "come any time." But when Pop started saving up money and talking about his big trip, his friends mostly laughed at him. "You won't find your way out of Penn Station," somebody told him. "Others did," Pop said, "and I'll follow them."

Stoneman arrived in New York in September of 1924 with forty-seven dollars (less train fare) in his pocket, an autoharp, and a harmonica. The Columbia man offered him a hundred dollars to record eighteen sides right away. Pop didn't like the offer, so he just never went back. Over at Okeh, the audition went better. Ralph Peer had been charmed by the autoharp—he'd never seen one before—and he offered Pop twenty-five dollars *per song*. A few days later, Pop recorded "The Titanic" and "The Face That Never Returned," but when Peer sent the demos to Pop in Bluefield a few weeks later, he said Pop's songs were just too fast. Peer figured the key to hillbilly records was in the songs' stories. "You've got to make people understand it," Peer said. So Pop paid his own way back to New York and recut those songs, plus two others ("Freckle Faced Mary Jane" and "Me and My Wife"), and Peer signed him to a five-year contract.

What Peer loved about Stoneman was that he didn't do just the old traditional songs that everybody knew. He'd made something new of the *Titanic* poem—and could find newer songs with modern-sounding lyrics, such as "Sinful to Flirt" and "Don't Let Your Deal Go Down." And Pop could always pick up a new song in a hurry. That helped a lot in Okeh's hillbilly catalog. The best-selling songs were usually what Peer called "event" songs. "Any disaster that came along we'd have somebody write a song about it," Peer said. "This was the trick. This fellow Andrew ['Blind Andy'] Jenkins was just waiting there to get an idea. He had a wonderful retentive mind. He'd get people to read the paper to him. And he could write a song about any little incident."

The first big event song was Jenkins's "Floyd Collins Trapped in a Cave," about a Kentucky spelunker who got himself wedged into a dark, tight spot sixty feet underground. For three weeks in February of 1925, while a make-do crew from the local railroad raced to dig out poor Floyd, the nation had been riveted to the live-or-die drama. It was one of the country's first big media circuses, early reality programming. The story ran in newspapers across the country, and on radio broadcasts; newfangled newsreel cameras filmed as the heavy machinery tunneled toward Floyd, and a tiny *Louisville Courier-Journal* reporter managed to crawl far enough into the hole to interview Floyd. "Oh God, be merciful!" was how the special edition of the *Courier-Journal* quoted Floyd. "I keep praying: Lord, dear Lord, gracious Lord, Jesus, please get me out of this." Just as his rescuers got close, the roof of the tunnel fell around Floyd's head. Photographers snapped away at his doe-eyed fiancée, who looked on as the workers dug a second tunnel. When they finally got to Floyd, he was cold and lifeless. But what a story—and one the entire nation knew. Such a nice religious boy, and brave to the end . . . and the poor girl he left behind. It was an American tragedy.

Within six weeks, Fiddlin' John's version of the Jenkins song was on the market. And Jenkins recorded it, too, and so did George Ake and John Fergus and Vernon Dalhart. With the powerful Victor label behind him, Dalhart made "Floyd" a million-seller. And Polk Brockman *owned* the song. He'd asked Blind Andy Jenkins to write it, and bought the copyright. So Brockman was getting a royalty on every song sheet and every record. No matter who recorded it, or for what label.

After that, when there was a cotton-mill fire in South Carolina or a flood in Mississippi, Brockman and Peer would call Jenkins, or Kelly Harrell, and tell one of them to work up a song, fast. Peer could hand Stoneman the words to Harrell's new "Story of the Mighty Mississippi" on one day, and Pop could record it the next: "Ralph Peer put me in a room with a colored piano player who played me the tune," Stoneman said, "and I pinned [the words] up in my hotel room and learned them that night." That's why Peer had signed Stoneman to a personal contract, which made Peer his manager. And that's why Peer took Stoneman with him when he left Okeh for the Victor Talking Machine Company.

Since the turn of the century, Victor had been the label of Enrico Caruso and class. The Victor Red Seal series was the top of the line of the recording industry: operas, symphonies, silky urban dance tunes—only the best. But when company sales had dropped off a cliff—by 1925 revenues were just half the 1921 figure—Victor was suddenly anxious to get into the growing hillbilly music field. So they hired Ralph Peer to make it happen. Peer said he'd come on for no salary, as long as he could control the copyrights to all the songs he found. The way Peer saw it, this was duck soup: He'd get a royalty on every record sold, and Victor knew how to sell a record. No company sold more. When Peer first got to Victor in 1926, he recorded a new Stoneman record and it sold sixty thousand without an ounce of promotion.

That year, Victor began a new electric recording process and issued a new phonograph, the Victor Orthophonic, which was flying off the shelves. Victor still had money to burn, Peer found out, when he told the company's recording director what he was going to pay the hillbilly acts for each song. Nat Shilkret, a onetime clarinet prodigy who had played with the Russian Symphony, the New York Philharmonic, and the Metropolitan Opera orchestra, had paid out piles of cash to artists such as Nellie Melba and Caruso, and to the finest dance orchestras in New York. He almost fell over when Peer named the figure, the same one he'd paid at Okeh. "You cannot make any recordings for Victor at twenty-five dollars apiece," Shilkret said. "This is just entirely too cheap. It might get cut and we couldn't stand that kind of publicity."

"So make it fifty dollars each," Peer said.

When he told Shilkret he wanted a portable recorder to take on a southern expedition for Victor, Peer, as he later said, had to "put over the thought that the hillbilly recordings didn't have to have the same quality as Caruso. And, uh, they appropriated sixty thousand dollars for the trip . . . and they thought that was peanuts. I could have done it for half. But at that early age, I had the sense to conform to whatever the company wanted."

With the money in place—and a new and better recording system—Peer wrote Stoneman. He was coming to visit Pop at his new home in Galax, Virginia, and Pop should go up in the mountains and find some acts worth recording. After the auditions, Peer said, he'd have Pop and the other approved acts meet him in Bristol, Virginia, for Victor's first field-recording session. Recording in Bristol had two advantages: There was a strong Victor distributorship there, run by Cecil McLister, and it was a railhead. With two major roads and a half-dozen short lines running into Bristol, acts from all over Appalachia could get there fairly easily. If all else failed, Peer figured, at least he'd get some Stoneman recordings on wax. By the time Peer got to Bristol, that's about all he could count on. Pop hadn't turned up much talent besides his own family and one friend.

By the time Peer and Stoneman started recording on July 26, 1927, the whole expedition looked like a bust. So Peer got the idea of inviting the local newspaper editor to visit the rented makeshift studio on the Tennessee side of Bristol (downtown's State Street runs along the Virginia-Tennessee state line). The editor came over the next day. "Intensely interesting is a visit to the Victor Talking Machine recording station located on the second floor of the building formerly occupied by the Taylor-Christian Hat company in Bristol," said that afternoon's *News Bulletin.* "This morning Earnest [*sic*] Stoneman and company were the performers and they played and sang into the microphone a favorite in Grayson County, Va., namely 'I Love My Lulu Bell.' . . . Eck Dunford was the principal singer, while a matron 26 years of age [Pop's wife, Hattie Stoneman] and the mother of five children joined in for a couple of stanzas. . . . The synchronizing is perfect: Earnest Stoneman playing the guitar, the young matron the violin and a young mountaineer a banjo and the mouth harp. Bodies swaying, feet beating a perfect rhythm, it is calculated to go over big when offered to the public."

All this made nice publicity for Victor and Peer, but the real coup was when the New York executive took the *Bulletin* editor aside and told him about the money the group was making: two hundred dollars a day for recording, plus royalties. Stoneman had made $3,600 in royalties last year alone. (Peer neglected to mention that he himself had made $250,000 in royalties from the sheaf of copyrights he now controlled— in a quarter of a year.) Well, naturally the editor tucked Stoneman's financial windfall right into the story. "This worked like dynamite," Peer said, "and the very next day I was deluged with long-distance calls from the surrounding mountain region. Groups of singers who had not visited Bristol during their entire lifetime arrived by bus, horse and buggy, train, or on foot."

Most of the acts racing toward Bristol would go back home to obscurity, with nothing. Many of the mountain acts Peer saw repeated the same songs: hymns, centuries-old ballads, or popular standards that had been recorded already. Peer needed material he could copyright and cash in on, so he needed musicians who could write their own songs, or at least restitch the traditional songs enough that he could "put them over as new." Down in Bristol in those last few days of July 1927, Peer was holding musicians to a tougher standard than he had while at Okeh. As always, he'd let the groups do the song of their choice first—and it was usually a well-known song. Then he'd ask if they had any songs of their own. "If they did another popular song," Peer remembered, "I never bothered with them."

Few who climbed the two stories to his State Street studio could spin out something new, or new-sounding, but Peer was not discouraged. The dapper thirty-five-year-old had a certainty about himself and his ability to make a find. He never doubted his fundamental method: constant activity. On the first day of August, he spent the entire day in the overheated studio on State Street, recording two different bands. Both had decent fiddlers, but neither had much to offer in the way of new songs. He broke for supper but planned to come back that evening for another session—to meet with a Mr. and Mrs. Carter, from Maces Springs, Virginia.

78 (Eugene W. Earle)

Opposite: Gladys, Janette, and Joe, near the old porch (Carter Family Museum)

New Orthophonic Victor
Southern Series

A. P. might have been overly optimistic about the ride to Bristol. By the time they arrived at his sister Virgie's house in town, it was near dark—and everybody must have been in a foul humor. It had taken the entire day to drive the twenty-six miles from Maces Springs to Bristol, traveling the dirt road that ran up and down but rarely flat, curving around the foothills so that the horizon was often lost. Around some turns, the road mercifully opened onto a view of gently rolling farmland; around others, the high hills closed in from both sides, dwarfing the little Essex automobile and blocking the slanting sunlight until the path was all but darkened. Maybe the road hadn't been graded in a while, because it seemed to eight-year-old Gladys that they were bouncing off the seats all the way. Infant Joe squalled the entire time, and Sara had to keep him at her breast. And how often did Maybelle, just a month from giving birth, have to stop to answer to her poor weighted bladder?

There was certainly no shortage of stops. The rain held off, but a tire popped. A.P. managed to get a rubber patch over the inner tube, but the heat kept melting it away, so he had to stop along the road twice more to repatch and pump air back into the inner tube.

At Virgie's at least there were beds, but Gladys heard somebody walking the floor most of the night. Was her mother up in the night comforting the baby? Could her daddy have slept at all? He was anxious *every* day. What must he have been like that night, with his big audition at hand? It was a good thing they had all the next day to tune their instruments and run through the songs they'd chosen. As evening neared, they put on their best Sunday clothes. A.P. wore a dark blue suit. Sara and Maybelle wore their nicest dresses, cut just below the knee, with sheer silk hose fastened tight by garters. Gladys put on her best dress and her Sunday-school slippers. Then they all headed for State Street.

What confidence the trio had mustered took a shot when they got to the old hat warehouse downtown. On the sidewalk outside the building, and all through the lobby, there were people milling around, and it seemed like half of them were carrying instruments. The way they were dressed, they might have been from Richmond or New York or London. Years later, A.P. confessed to a friend that he'd been so shaken when they arrived that they decided to go around to the alley and climb the fire escape. They didn't want to walk though that crowd and let everybody get a look at their country clothes.

When they arrived upstairs in the warehouse loft, the walls were hung with blankets. The "recording machine" was partitioned off by a second set of blankets, and all they could see of it was one horn jutting through a small aperture. Mr. Ralph Peer was there, with his new wife (and former secretary), Anita Glander Peer, and with two engineers who ran the recording machine. The businesslike Mrs. Peer ushered Gladys and baby Joe over into the corner, while Mr. Peer calmly explained to the three nervous musicians that they would have to mount the jerry-built platform, get right up next to the horn, and direct their voices into it. So they climbed up on the wooden stage, drew in close to one another. Then Maybelle led in, bare-fingered, on Eck's little Stella guitar, and Sara's voice chased right after it:

My heart is sad and I'm in sorrow,
For the only one I love.

And suddenly, out of nowhere, A.P.'s quavering bass was registering right alongside Sara's contralto.

When shall I see him?
Oh, no never 'til I meet him in heaven above.

Bury me under the weeping willow,
Yes, under the weeping willow tree
So he may know where I am sleeping
And perhaps he will weep for me.

They told me that he did not love me.
I could not believe it was true
Until a man softly whispered,
"He had been untrue to you."

Peer wanted more. So he had his wife usher Gladys and Joe straight out of the studio. Anita Peer was an able businesswoman and problem solver. Before she'd married Ralph Peer she'd been a girl Friday around movie studios. She'd dealt with Hollywood producers, puffed-up actors, and stoned session musicians. But a crying baby was beyond her expertise. "Mrs. Peer fed Joe ice cream until he was about to burst, as it would have to do until his Mama finished singing," Gladys later wrote. The Carters recorded four songs that evening, and Sara's was the lead voice in all. Peer had been taken with her voice, but it was still a tad unsettling. In all the groups Peer had seen in Bristol—and all the mountain groups he'd auditioned over the years—none had a woman carry the lead vocals. And he didn't know if A.P. Carter had the force to hold the group together musically. Peer couldn't help but notice the way the tall, gangly fellow kept wandering away from the microphone *in the middle of a song*. After that first session, Peer pulled A.P. aside. "You didn't do very much," he told him.

"No," said A.P. "I just bass in every once't in a while."

When Peer invited the Carters back the next morning, A.P. didn't even show up. Sara and Maybelle recorded two more numbers, with Sara singing "Wandering Boy" and "Single Girl, Married Girl" as solos. They were done before noon. That same afternoon, A.P. loaded the family in the Essex for the trip home. He had no idea what was going to come of this venture. But he did know they were leaving Bristol with three hundred dollars more than they arrived with (minus the money he spent that morning buying Eck a new tire). On the way back home, Maybelle couldn't wait to tell Eck about the session. He would have loved the machines: the heavy spinning turntable covered with an inch and a half of wax, powered by a system of pulleys and weights housed in a tall wooden tower. The microphone ran off electricity. Maybelle couldn't have told her husband how the thing actually worked. And she didn't have words to describe the static jolt it gave her when they initially played back the sound; it was like she'd found her own image in the mirror for the first time. "When we made the record and played it back, I thought it couldn't be," Maybelle once said. "I just couldn't believe it, this being so unreal, you standing there and singing and they'd turn around and play it back to you."

When historians and writers came knocking at Peer's Los Angeles mansion in later years, the story he liked to tell about the Carter Family's Bristol session was the kind of hackneyed set piece that you could sell only in Hollywood: "They wander in. He's dressed in overalls [and sometimes in Peer's account they were splotched with mud] and the women are country women from way back there—calico clothes on— the children were poorly dressed. They were backwoods people and they were not accustomed to being in town, you see. They didn't know what to do. . . . But as soon as I heard Sara's voice, that was it. You see, I had done this so many times that I was trained to watch for the one point. . . . As soon as I heard her voice, why, I began to build around it and all the first recordings were on that basis." *New York talent scout discovers diamond among the rubes. History is made.*

But in private, Ralph Peer would quietly express a true sense of wonder about the family he met on that close August evening, dressed, in fact, in their Sunday-go-to-meeting clothes. "My father always said that what amazed him," says Ralph Peer II, "was that they were good, but they didn't seem to know *how good* they were."

In 1927 the Carters' public appeal was a hard thing for a city boy like Peer to appreciate—and he didn't. The family's music sprang mainly from the narrow traditions of white southern gospel and the balladry that had floated for generations in the thin mountain air of Appalachia. Over the years, the trio would seek out new forms, including coal-camp blues and black gospel, but they never added Dixieland, jazz, or pop instruments to fill out their pared-down autoharp-and-guitar arrangements. Adding frets or substituting a second guitar for Sara's autoharp was as radical as they got. They also showed little talent for the hit-chasing event song. A.P.'s one attempt, "The Cyclone of Rye Cove," sounded like it belonged to somebody else. The Carters were never much good at channeling public tragedy.

A.P., Sara, and Maybelle were at their best when they were plying the sharper edges of private and personal pain. From the first, that's what they cut down into the grooves of their most affecting records. Even from the wheeziest Victrola, their voices ricocheted off the bone, because they leaned so hard on their own notions of tragedy. How many times in their own valley had they seen righteous, innocent people simply wiped away—and without cause? Right around the time the Carters went to Bristol, their friend Price Owens had accidentally driven his new Ford off the dirt road and fifty feet down an embankment into the Holston River. He was long drowned by the time farmhands pulled him out. Uncle Lish Carter had a boy drowned in that same river. One of Uncle Fland Bays's sons fell into a well and couldn't be pulled out in time to save him. Neither boy made his tenth birthday. In 1927 Uncle Charlie Bays had just got news that *three* of his children had contracted tuberculosis; it was only a matter of time before they'd be in their graves.

Sara herself had been orphaned at three. Maybelle's sister Madge would die at twenty-eight, orphaning her three children. And A.P. had lost a thirteen-year-old sister; by 1927 A.P.'s sister had been gone as long as she had lived. Ettaleen Carter had been a perfectly happy schoolgirl picking berries one afternoon, fevered in bed that night, and dead by morning. Maybe her appendix had burst, the doctor said. Nobody knew for sure what killed her. When they showed her daughter one last time at the grave site, Mollie Carter must have wailed. But there was little time to mourn. Mollie still had five children at home to raise. She had to go back to the planting, weeding, cooking, canning, and sewing. After Etta was buried, Mollie took on even more. She wouldn't let her youngest girl, Sylvia, lift a finger. She doted on her, and saw that her hands were kept soft and filled with amusements.

But what could Mollie do for her dead daughter, whose short life was hard work from one end of the day to the next? For the next thirty years, she regularly climbed up to Mount Vernon's hilltop cemetery to plant flowers on Ettaleen's grave. "She would go up there and dig around and make it nice," Mollie's daughter–in–law Theda Carter says. "Just spend time up there." Mollie Carter *remembered*, for thirty years, when it would have been easier to forget. Mollie's shame would have been in forgetting, in giving in to the desolate, empty feeling that her daughter's short life, and the lives of all those who'd died in her valley, didn't finally matter.

In 1927 Thomas Wolfe—the first great modern writer to come down off a southern mountain—described the bone tragedy of his twelve-year-old brother's death in his autobiographical novel *Look Homeward Angel*. In the event, two undertakers take the boy's remains off the cooling board to be prepared for burial, leaving the grieving parents to themselves: "For some time Elizabeth and Gant continued to sit alone in the room," Wolfe wrote. "Gant leaned his face in his powerful hands. 'The best boy I ever had,' Gant said. 'By God, he was the best of the lot.'

"And in the ticking silence they recalled him, and in the heart of each was fear and remorse, because he had been a quiet boy, and there were many, and he had gone unnoticed."

The Carters had a way of giving voice to that unspoken dread. What they cut down into those early recordings (in songs such as "Will You Miss Me When I'm Gone?") was the sound of a single person facing down the desolate emptiness of uncaring time, a distant, ghostly cry from the darkest hollows: *Don't forget me. I mattered.*

But how could Ralph Peer and the boys in New York have the ear to recognize the amplitude of that keening pitch? In October of 1927, Victor released recordings by eleven different groups Peer had found on his southern expedition. The Carters' recordings were not among them.

Of course A.P. couldn't let it go. Didn't matter to him that nobody from Victor had contacted the Carters since Bristol. For A.P. it was still an article of faith; something was bound to happen. "A.P. had the strongest convictions of anyone I ever saw," his niece Lois Hensley says. "You couldn't change his mind! He was that stubborn." All through that fall, Pleasant was wound tighter than ever, and his temper could flare like a rocket. Anybody around could literally see the anger *rise* in him, as his tremor gained speed. So Sara just kept her head down and kept the house running. People never even saw her strain under the weight of it. She didn't lose her calm. She never raised her voice. And even when A.P. was away on a trip or just out walking the tracks in fitful contemplation, she never faltered. She arose every morning before dawn, added wood and chips to the fire—and a pine knot if it really needed a kick. The hogs had to be fed, and she'd feed them. The cow had to be milked, and she'd milk her. Gladys was old enough to get herself off to school, but Janette and baby Joe were underfoot all day—and they had to be tended. "My mother ran her home like clockwork," Janette wrote in *Living with Memories*. "I knew as sure as my feet hit the floor, I would be washed all over and scrubbed clean from my hair to my toes with old lye soap. Everything smelled of lye—my hair, clothes, skin."

Actually, Janette was little trouble. Nearing five, she could already be counted on for small chores: gathering kindling, bunching tobacco, or walking the railroad tracks to pick up spilled coal. Joe was a different story. The minute he could walk, he was a terror, always on the go. Even that young, he was on the circuit. "I think Joe nursed all the mothers in Poor Valley," Janette says. Sara could spend the day chasing Joe, but the corn still had to be weeded, the tobacco wormed, the corn milled, and the wood chopped. A few times a week she'd pull out the washboard and get a heavy, sloshing tubful of well water, add her lye, and scrub clean what few clothes they had. And every day, no matter what, meals had to be cooked. Sara always made sure to have corn bread put up. After the hardest days she could warm over beans, but most nights she'd try to make a real meal: tomato gravy, chicken and dumplings, green beans. If there were berries, she'd make a pie.

When the work was done, most everybody liked to take a swim in the Holston River, get the chiggers off after a long day in the field. But Sara never liked the water. Maybe she'd help the girls catch lightning bugs so that they could put them in a jar and watch them spark in the night. Sara could always make music, but there was so little time—and she had so little strength left at the end of the day. Besides, Maybelle had her hands full with her new baby, Helen, who was born that September. Most nights Sara's autoharp sat untouched on her cedar chest. Bristol was a fading memory.

Then one day in early November, Eck and Maybelle came back from the city with news. They'd stopped by Cecil McLister's store, and he had the phonograph piping music out onto State Street. The crowd was huge, and they were listening to the Carter Family's first record. Inside, the record was on display under the NEW ORTHOPHONIC VICTOR SOUTHERN SERIES sign. It was a double-sided 78 with "Poor Orphan Child" on one side and "Wandering Boy" on the other. Eck and Maybelle had come home and played it for A.P. and Sara on Eck's phonograph. And of course that wasn't the only copy in the Valley. Uncle Flanders Bays bought the record—and he didn't even own a phonograph. But that gave him a chance to take it to the Collinses' for a listen, and then on to the Denisons', where everybody waited in anticipation while Daddy Denison hand-cranked their boxy little Starr phonograph. "Flanders was so proud of that record that night," one of the Denison daughters remembers.

Sara suddenly had celebrity. Funny thing was, the sun didn't rise any later. The cow didn't milk herself, the weeds didn't stop growing, the tub of wash water didn't get any lighter, and corn bread didn't miraculously appear on plates every night. Day to day, Sara's life didn't change one whit. At least not right away.

Then, in early 1928, Peer released "The Storms Are on the Ocean" and its flip side, "Single Girl, Married Girl." That record took off. "Single Girl," a married woman's lament for the loss of her carefree girlhood, moved the disks. There must have been a lot of women out there who felt kin to something they heard in Sara's lone voice. ("Sara sang that one by herself," Maybelle remembered. "It's no harmony song.") It sold, and kept selling, all over the South. One day that spring, Cecil McLister himself drove over to Maces Springs and presented the Carters with a royalty check. It wasn't a lot, but suddenly the Carters were making money—for doing nothing. McLister had some other news. Mr. Peer had called. He wanted the Carters in Camden, New Jersey, right away, at the Victor Recording Studio. And that's when Sara's life changed. That's when it started to get hard.

LOOK!

Victor Artist

A. P. CARTER

and the

Carter Family

Will give a

MUSICAL PROGRAM

AT *Roseland Theater*

ON *Thursday August 1*

The Program is Morally Good

Admission 15 and 25 Cents

A. P. CARTER, Mace Spring, Va.

"Entertainment" poster (Gladys Greiner)

Opposite: Original Carter Family, circa 1930 (Carter Family Museum)

Home Manufacture

Pleasant Carter was in a frenzy that spring. Mr. Peer wanted the threesome in New Jersey in early May, and that was just weeks away. They had to have songs to sing, the more the better. Peer was still offering fifty dollars for every song they recorded, plus royalties for each and every one they could copyright. Sara and Maybelle knew plenty of old songs from Rich Valley. And according to Maybelle, A.P. even wrote a song he called "Little Darlin' Pal of Mine," about a jilted lover. The writing foretold A.P.'s best to come: sighing wind, a casket, a shroud and a grave, betrayed and lifeless lips still hoping for a last kiss, and the charming, to-the-point couplet "Thought I had your heart forever, / but I find it's only lent."

To round out the selections, A.P. leaned on family and neighbors. And who didn't want to help? Uncle Fland knew plenty of church songs and had stacks of the old shape-note hymnbooks from the publishers in Tennessee. Even A.P.'s flimsiest critic had a song for them:

"Now, 'Keep on the Sunny Side,' " says Joe Carter, "Daddy learned from Lish Carter."

A.P., Sara, and Maybelle would gather nightly, after the day's work was done, and work to squeeze every song down to three minutes or less, all a 78 could hold. Religious songs such as "Anchored in Love" were the easiest. They could take them right out of one of Fland's hymnals, and they rarely ran over. But the ballads were tougher. "You had to tell your story in three minutes," says Janette. That time, she says, generally allowed a simple pattern: verse-chorus-instrumental-verse-chorus-instrumental-verse. If a song ran over, they couldn't cut the words and short-circuit the story, so Sara and Maybelle would cut down the instrumental bridges. Then, most important, they'd work out the harmony. "They sang on one mike to record then," says Joe Carter. "Ain't like today. They couldn't adjust the levels after the fact. That's where better singing, closer harmonies, has to be on. The rehearsals were about getting the harmony real tight."

By the time A.P., Sara, and Maybelle boarded a train for Camden on May 7, 1928, they had rehearsed and re-rehearsed twelve different songs, squeezed each into the three-minute format, and tightened the harmonies down to a whipstitch. On May 9, after a night at the Camden Hotel (where they were treated to the marvels of indoor plumbing, hot and cold running water, and room service), they were driven to the Victor recording studio in downtown Camden. That first day the Carters laid down four songs, including "Meet Me by the Moonlight, Alone" and "Little Darlin' Pal of Mine." Maybelle must have been making her own separate study leading up to that session, because on both those numbers she played guitar in the fretted Hawaiian style, just like Frank Ferera's backing on Vernon Dalhart's big-selling record "The Wreck of the Old 97." She was likely inspired by listening to the Dalhart record Eck had bought for her.

The next day, the Carters raced almost flawlessly through eight separate numbers. That session was part old-time ballad ("Forsaken Love"), part hymn ("Anchored in Love"), and part pop song ("I Ain't Goin' to Work Tomorrow"); part Maces Springs fatalism ("Will You Miss Me When I'm Gone?") and part Rich Valley spirit ("Wildwood

Flower"), with dollops of slave spirituals ("River of Jordan"), country humor ("Chewing Gum"), and mining-camp lawlessness and regret ("John Hardy Was a Desperate Little Man").

If the Carters had never again returned to a recording studio, their work in that two-day session would have been enough to mark them for good. Those twelve songs sold from the start, and they had legs, too. The tracks they set down that May have been retraced and remade for nearly three-quarters of a century. "John Hardy" alone has been covered by Flatt & Scruggs, Doc Watson, Johnny Cash, Bob Dylan, Joan Baez, and Manfred Mann. "Wildwood Flower," named by National Public Radio as one of the one hundred most important songs of the century, is the closest thing country music has to a true anthem. Those first Camden recordings proved for good that a lone mountain woman's voice *could* speak to a vast audience (men and women, rural and not), flat-grading the road for singers such as Kitty Wells, Patsy Cline, Loretta Lynn, Emmylou Harris, and Lucinda Williams. In Camden, Sara's contralto alone carried the song of a jilted maiden ("Wildwood Flower") and the ballad of the murdering John Hardy. The Carters' small-group church harmonizing—which they also used on traditional ballads and love songs—set the standard for early country music, putting the voice ahead of instrumentation. "Guitar and autoharp was all they had," said one musician friend of the Carters'. "Their singing is how they got to where they wanted to be."

A.P. still only "bassed in every once't in a while," but he showed remarkable range, and a genius for finding his moment and his way in. On "Will You Miss Me When I'm Gone?" his distant harmonizing creeps in and out at unforeseen intervals, giving the song a haunting echo. A.P.'s voice sounds as if it's floating in the dusk-darkened treetops, the mournful wail of a man who no longer casts a shadow in this world.

By the end of the twenties, Maybelle's Carter scratch—graceful and thumpingly rhythmic at once—was the most widely imitated guitar style in music. Nobody did as much to popularize the guitar, because from the beginning her playing was as distinctive as any voice. "She could make that guitar talk to you," says Ruby Parker, who was schooled on the instrument by Maybelle. Maybelle's innovations crossed through musical genres. On the gospel songs they cut in Camden, Maybelle's scratch provided a rhythmic drive like the Holiness songs she'd heard at revivals, and even in the first recording sessions, she was already playing Hawaiian, and a sort of slide guitar favored by the black blues musicians around the South. Her style had a way of bridging geographic, ethnic, and social divides. Maybelle's version of "When the Roses Bloom in Dixieland" was the first song that guitar virtuoso Doc Watson learned to play; her "Wildwood Flower" was the first song the Italian-American city kid named Perry Como learned to play.

Of course, none of these future events was contemplated by A.P., Sara, or Maybelle as they left Camden that May. What mattered to the Carters was that they were carrying back to Maces Springs a cash bonanza equal to a good year's take from the farm: six hundred dollars. Mr. Peer had proven good as his word. He paid out fifty dollars per side and covered travel expenses on top. Better than that, Mr. Peer had signed the Carters to an artist-manager contract. They would continue to get fifty dollars per song. When it was one they could copyright, A.P. would own the copyright and assign it to Peer. That meant that the three would continue to get royalties. Mechanical royalties (record sales) amounted to a half cent for every record Victor sold. Publishing royalties (sheet-music sales) would bring them two cents per sheet. So Peer and the Carters were yoked now. If A.P. could continue to come up with new songs (or songs that could be "put over" as new), Peer would make sure Victor sold them. The more songs the Carters could come up with, the better for them all.

The minute they got back to Maces Springs that May, Pleasant started looking for a new house. With the Camden take split three ways, A.P. and Sara had four hundred dollars in the bank, and A.P. had faith the royalty money would keep rolling in. Less than a month after they returned, he put down $233.33 and moved Sara and his three children off the mountain and into a four-room house on a flat one-and-a-half-acre lot. When they moved in that spring, A.P. must have been in his glory. By the standards of Poor Valley, it was a splendid house. Out front there was a big cedar tree with a congregation of robins, bluebirds, and wrens. From the back, the family could hear the susurrous rush of the Blue Springs branch. If the wind was right, according to Janette, the smell of purple lilacs and red-flowered Japanese bushes wafted down from behind Neal's Store and right into the Carters' new homeplace. One day not long after A.P. had moved the family into the new house, Mr. Peer sent a photographer over to take pictures for the new Victor catalog, which would feature a nearly a dozen Carter Family songs. They spent the day posing like a mountain family hard at work. Maybelle and Sara thought it was ridiculous that they had to put on their nicest dresses and then go out and draw water from the well, and that they were posed in front of the most dilapidated and weathered outbuildings they could find. Sara and Maybelle hated the lies of those pictures, but they went along.

For A.P., the next few years were all possibility and payoff. He bought himself his first car—a brand-new red Chevrolet—which he immediately put to practical use. One day not long after A.P. and Sara moved, Bud Derting was out working on a road crew in front of the new Carter house when he and his partner saw A.P. circling around his new Chevy with a big sow.

"What in the hell is that man fixin' to do?" Derting's partner asked.

"He's gonna put that hog in there," Derting said. "Must be in heat."

"Ah, naw. He wouldn't do that. Not in that new car."

"Just you watch him."

And the two men did watch, as Pleasant took out the backseat, muscled the sow in, and drove her off for her date with a stud hog.

As handy as that car proved in the gnarly logistics of breeding hogs, it was even better for doing business as a professional "musicianer." A.P. could make much wider circuits for song hunting and promotion. And he wasn't one to return home empty-handed; his long, lean years of denial and poverty were over. On one trip to find songs in North Carolina, he found a deal he couldn't pass up. "About dark one night, we heard the most unusual noise coming up the road, and it looked like a Texas dust storm blowing in," wrote Gladys Carter Millard. "Mama said, 'It can't be. Surely Doc wouldn't pull that thing with our new car.' But it was Daddy all smiles with his new purchase. The Chevrolet was a little hot. Guess it is the only car in history to pull a saw mill boiler 200 miles up mountains and over dirt roads."

When he was in Maces Springs, A.P. began improvements on his new homeplace. The house, he decided, needed a new fence all around it. Of course, deep down, Pleasant was still Pleasant, so after he put up the swinging gate, he lost interest, and in the Carters' front yard stood a lonely hinged gate, and no fence. It was still like that the day word arrived that Mr. and Mrs. Peer were going to make a visit to Maces Springs—in two days—to talk business. The Peers were going to drive to Poor Valley, have supper, and spend the night. "My wonderful Daddy had to get a garage up quick," wrote Gladys. "It would never do to let a big Cadillac set out overnight." With a little help from his friend Worley Vicars, Pleasant built a four-square wooden garage, with sturdy side braces and a tin roof. With his sawmill, Pleasant planed out a door. Then he bought a big Yale lock for security and put a gallon of blue paint on the outside. (There were only two painted *houses* in town, and A.P.'s wasn't one of them.)

Maybelle and Sara began sprucing up for the visit, too, plumping the feather beds and throwing extra lime at the outhouse, frying chickens, making red-eye gravy and hams, baking desserts (including Maybelle's trademark divinity). They planned supper at Eck and Maybelle's, where there was a separate dining room that didn't take all the heat from the stove, and Maybelle pulled out her best dishes (untouched by a child's hand) and her brand-new china tea set (a recent present from Eck). The Peers' visit was a boon to Leonard Neal's grocery. Gladys watched the procession of neighbors who had saved up their eggs and chickens to have an excuse to pass by the house and get a glimpse of these New Yorkers and their Cadillac. Actually, the locals got a lot better look at the Peers' car than A.P. would have liked. The doorway to A.P.'s new garage was too narrow to allow the Cadillac entry into its beautiful new berth, and the garage itself was two feet shorter than the car.

Other than that, the trip was a grand success. The Peers drove off with a country ham and jars of dewberry jelly. They left behind the newest stand-up Victrola for A.P. and Sara, with a complete set of their records and a promise of another recording date. And why not?

Peer was making a pile off the Carters and other artists he'd signed to contracts. His other great find at Bristol, the yodeling brakeman Jimmie Rodgers, was making Peer rich all by himself Rodgers's record sales were five times that of the Carters. Every time Victor released a Rodgers 78, it sold nearly a quarter million copies And a few would go on to sell twice that. Rodgers was making a half cent on each record sold. As the holder of the copyright, Peer was making a lot more. The royalty arrangement had worked like a dream for Peer, making him a hero to many of the rural acts he signed. "Most of them expected to record for nothing," Peer once said. "When on top of this fifty dollars I gave them royalties on their selections, they thought it was manna from heaven."

But the truth was, Peer could have done a lot worse by the Carters. In the twenties, it was common for publishers to simply buy copyrights outright, for one hundred dollars or less, and take all the royalties. "I was too young to have the really vicious approach," Peer said of his early days in the business. Ralph Peer was also too canny. As long as he kept his artists happy, he figured, they'd keep coming back with more songs. And with a financial stake in sales, his recording artists were more likely to go out and hustle their records and sheet music. (Though the copyists in New York were having a devil of a time translating Sara and Maybelle's melodies into sheet-music notes.)

Peer's formula had been a happy elixir for A.P. Carter, and he was a spirited promoter for his own records, even if it took some doing. When record-store owners and fans started writing to ask if the Carters would make music in their towns, A.P. pushed and prodded until Sara and Maybelle agreed to go out and give "entertainments." First he broke off the end of an ironing board so that Sara could have a stand for her balkier new twelve-bar autoharp. Then he built her a real stand. He even had flyers printed up for the shows, and two weeks before a scheduled date, he'd show up in town and start posting them in schools, in country stores, even down the dusty, rarely passed side roads. A.P. especially liked a town with a lot of telephones. There were more poles to work with:

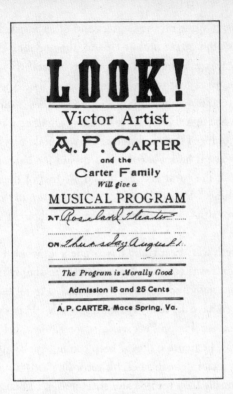

LOOK!

Victor Artist

A. P. CARTER

and the

Carter Family

Will give a

MUSICAL PROGRAM

AT *Roseland Theater*

ON *Thursday August 1*

The Program is Morally Good

Admission 15 and 25 Cents

A. P. CARTER, Mace Spring, Va.

A.P. was never strict about admission. He'd often let youngsters in for a nickel or a dime. The halt, the lame, and the blind he let in free of charge. The Carters performed at any place in town big enough to hold a crowd, which was generally the school or the church. "When we first started going out to schools and places like that, we didn't have microphones," said Maybelle. "We put on many a show without a mike in these schools. In fact, in a lot of schools we didn't have electricity, just had kerosene lamps."

The first onstage was always A.P., whose new success had given him an air of command and a surprising magnetism. He made it a point to introduce every song. If it was a ballad, he'd tell what he knew of the real story; when he told the story of "Wandering Boy," he'd often get himself worked up into tears. For other songs, he'd simply give credit due. "Hattie O'Neill over in West Norton learned this to me," he'd say. Sara and Maybelle rarely spoke from the stage, but for an hour or more they bent themselves earnestly to the task at hand. A.P., meanwhile, might join in, or he might simply wander offstage. Occasionally he'd play his fiddle, unless he forgot it, and then he was apt to cry out, mid-song, "Sara! Where's my fiddle?"

Sometimes when he came in late on a part, or missed it altogether, Sara would chide, "A.P., why don't you sing when you're supposed to?"

"Well, I'll get in there," he'd say. "Don't worry about me. I'll be there."

"If he felt like singing, he would sing," Maybelle once said. "If he didn't, he'd look out the window. So we never depended on him. We just let him sing when he got ready." There was one show in later years when A.P. never even made it to the stage but simply left the women to do the show by themselves. (They found him later that evening sound asleep at their host s home.) The emceeing was left to a local school-teacher who was not altogether familiar with the trio's repertoire, so Sara had to write out the set for her. But the light of the kerosene lamps must have been dim that night. "For their next number," the school-teacher said at one point, "the Carter Family will do 'Sad and Lone-some Dog.' "

Sara and Maybelle wouldn't even laugh at that. Even when things went awry, or Pleasant meandered, Sara and Maybelle stayed the course, reproducing as closely as possible the recordings their audience already knew so well. In the middle of a song, Maybelle might occasion-ally break into a sideways smile, but above all, the two women meant to project dignity. "Mama didn't believe in getting broke up onstage," says June Carter Cash.

"All of us felt about those performances just like you would feel about visiting some friends," said Maybelle. "They could buy our records else-where. They came to see us in person, and we came to please them." The best of those entertainments were pleasing in the extreme and occasion-ally had the spontaneity of a good Methodist revival. When things were really going good and the audience was right down with anything they did, A.P. might break out his fiddle and try his shaky hand at a dance song. Then Sara and Maybelle would call out the little girls to do a buck and wing. A.P. even bought five-year-old Janette an Indian costume for her stage time. It had a fringe of bells up the pants leg, and a headdress. "I loved to dance," says Lois Carter Hensley, who would have been six years old in 1929. "I'd dance my shoe soles off. Janette was sort of shy. And her daddy wouldn't let her dance at home. But Aunt Sara sort of picked on me and made me get out and dance at the shows. They wanted the whole family to kindly contribute a little bit."

But sometimes the entertainments were too far away to take children, and so it was just the three of them—or four if Eck was in town. Sara and Maybelle could always depend on Dicey Thomas and Myrtle Hensley or Mollie Carter or their sisters-in-law Vangie and Ora to take care of their brood, but they still insisted on making the trip as fast as humanly possible. They'd ride over, do a nighttime show, pack up their instruments, and head straight home. At least now they could count on the Chevy. Before that, Maybelle once said, "We'd go out in a little Model A Ford, with no lights, and have to tie a lantern on front to get home with. I recall one night all four of us, my husband, too, were all piled into a one-seated little coupe, and it was a-storming and lightning like mad as we were coming into Gate City. We were meeting all these cars, and I said, 'A.P., can you see?' He said, 'I can't see a thing.' About that time, bang! we hit a car on the left-hand side of the road, mind you, and my head hit the windshield. I was picking glass out of my head for months.

"Another time we were going around a mountain when a pickup truck with a barrel on it comes around the bend, and A.P. was so busy watching it he ran off the road himself, and there we were astraddle this big log."

Fortunately, though, most of the trips were uneventful. On those quiet nights after the show, Maybelle and Sara slept in the backseat, while A.P.—his driver's license taped to the steering wheel—piloted his new Chevy through the still, dark hours of morning, over the winding highways and rutted dirt roads that led back to Maces Springs. He was never happier.

Mr. Peer had set a second Camden recording date for February of 1929, just eight months after the first. Victor had sold nearly one hundred thousand copies of "Wildwood Flower" and "Keep on the Sunny Side," and the rest were selling steadily. The Carter audience was proving loyal, and Peer only had to check the sales of Victrola phonographs around the South to know that the record-buying audience was growing. In the late twenties, the way rural mountain people got their music was taking a radical—and modern—turn. Take for instance the Adamses of Buchanan County, Virginia. Minnie Adams was just eleven years old when the Carter Family records first came out, and her dad worked for a state crew digging out a road between the Premier Coal Company and the town of Grundy, Virginia. Up to then, the Adamses had never had a radio or a phonograph, so their music had been familial, and catch-as-catch-can. "My mother's people were wonderful singers," says Minnie. "My granddaddy played songs, had a beautiful voice. My mom had heard songs from Grandpa Blankenbeckler. He sang a lot of English songs and Irish songs. The songs all had stories. That's what I liked about them. 'Barbara Allen' was one of my favorites.

"There was an old fella used to come by our house, must have been going someplace to perform, maybe. He would pass our house, and he always wore a blue serge suit and carried his banjo. And he'd always stop at our spring and get him a drink of water, and we'd ask him to sing 'Barbara Allen.' Oh, that voice rang all over the hills. And he'd pick it on his banjo.

"Sometimes we went to performances at schoolhouses or courthouses, but there were not a lot of dances. There wasn't room for dancing. Anyway, Buchanan County was a mining spot, but it was beautiful up on these mountains. And we'd walk so far then, about five miles, to hear the Carter Family records because they were tops. We didn't have a Victrola, so we'd walk over to friends' through a flat place. They told ghost stories and ate apples around the fire, popped popcorn, and played Carter records. People come from miles around. The Carters were the main attraction.

"And then my daddy finally got a Victrola, and we thought it was the grandest thing on earth. Everybody was getting one by then. It wasn't a very expensive one. Just a little music cabinet."

Anybody who was lucky enough to be living near Maces Springs could still be treated to a little live music most any night around harvest-time in 1928. Once the day's farmwork was done, Maybelle would haul her guitar over to A.P. and Sara's new homeplace to rehearse for their February recording date. "I used to go out there on the railroad and sit there and listen to their practices," says Fland Bays's son F.M. "They'd rehearse on the front porch. I'd hear them rehearse, so I'd walk over there and sit right by the tracks and listen. You could pitch a horseshoe from their front porch where the railroad tracks ran. It was maybe fifty or seventy-five feet away."

"We walked everywhere we went," says Chester Hensley, who was a teenager working on a road crew in 1928. "I worked on these bridges up here at the county line, me and two more boys that lived here about my same age. We walked up there—eight miles—do a day's work, and walked home. And sometimes we'd come home and eat supper and go about three miles over here to the New Hurland Church to a revival meeting." But if there was no revival meeting for entertainment, or if it was Baptists—they weren't like the Methodists; they'd come into the audience and grab you right out of your seat to get you saved—Chester and his buddies would cross the Knob and go to the Carter homeplace. "I'd walk up this road here, and the river is just on the other side of the hill. Nanny Hawkins would take us across in his boat. When we'd get to A.P.'s house, we'd just lay down there on the grass, there on the yard, and listen. They allowed anybody who wanted to come in. They didn't care who come in."

"Neighbors would come in," says Janette, "and they'd let them listen to these songs they was gonna put on the records. 'Now, you listen to this and see what you think.' And if the neighbors didn't like 'em or the family didn't like 'em, most of the time it was because they weren't right. They were very serious songs, but they all had to have that Carter style. It all told something. It had meanin' to it. The songs that they sang, people wouldn't forget 'em. They'd linger in their minds, if you know what I mean."

For that February date, A.P. still relied heavily on neighbors. Aunt Myrtle Bays suggested her favorite songbook number, "Little Moses." Big Tom Carter, Bob Carter's preacher cousin, gave A.P. the sheet music for "The Grave on the Green Hillside," a hymn that was a favorite of his parishioners. Bud Derting, who has lived near the Holston River for ninety-four years, saw A.P. and Sara rambling around on song-fetching trips in those days. If they were passing Bud's place, there was no mystery about where they were heading. Everybody around knew there was a mother lode of songs on one particular porch on the other side of the Holston. "A.P. and Sara had to come across the north fork in boats," says Derting. "Everybody that lived on the river had a boat then. Maybe four or five times a day somebody on the other side might holler, 'Bring over the boat!' and here they came. They'd do it, pole across. Then you had to walk four or five miles, instrument on your back, to get to Mancy Groves's."

In 1928 Amanda Groves was sixty-five years old, still more than six feet tall and still in possession of flaming red hair and an astonishing mental capacity. Her old visiting cousin, A.P.'s father, Bob, liked to tell A.P.'s sister, "Virgie, you've got a good memory, but not as good as mine. And the best there is, is Amanda Groves."

"Amanda Groves was an old lady when I was a kid," says Derting. "She was a great big old tall healthy woman like all the Carters, square-set face, dressed in black with a big black hat on. She just remembered so good. People came to her to find out stuff. . . . Amanda Groves knew a lot of songs. They bought her an old-time piano way back years ago, a huge piano. It took a good man to pick up one corner of it. They probably hauled it in there in a wagon, maybe in parts. Anyway, they'd have singings in that house."

"When I was a little boy, she'd set out on the porch of their little log house and she'd sing to me," says Dale Carter, a nephew of Mandy Groves. "She had the prettiest clear voice, and she'd set there and rock and sing all these old songs. One of them I particularly remember because Burl Ives came out in the fifties or sixties and said he had discovered a long-lost song, completely lost: 'The Wayfaring Stranger.' Well, Lord, Aunt Mandy sung that to me when I was a little kid. She'd sing that, 'Barbara Allen,' 'Sourwood Mountain.' She had all of these. She loved to sing. So A.P., that's where he got some of his early songs, from Aunt Mandy Groves."

It's hard to know just what songs A.P. did get from Mandy. Derting thinks she gave him "Clinch Mountain Home," though Virgie and Sara always said A.P. wrote that song himself, years before, on his trip to Indiana. In fact, though A.P. is the sole writer and composer of almost three hundred songs—according to the filings at the U.S. Copyright Office—it's nearly impossible to know the paternity of many of those compositions. There are historians who have spent years tracing Carter songs and lyrics back to hymnbooks, previously copyrighted parlor songs, and traditional ballads. Charles Wolfe traced "Sweet Fern," a song the Carters prepared for the February 1929 session, to a parlor song called "Sweet Bird," written in 1876 by Thomas Westendorf and George Persley. Maybelle thought A.P. got it from somebody while out hunting songs in East Tennessee.

Meanwhile Gladys always insisted her father authored the song. "I can tell you where Daddy wrote a song one time," she said in 1990. "Right over behind the house here. The blackberries was ripe. And Mommy said, 'Doc, go a-back out in the holler and pick me some black-berries, and I'll make a pie.' And there's a little old bird up in the tree a-singin' and Daddy was a-throwin' berries, and hitting the bucket, and he come back—'Sweet Fern.' He got the tune to it from that bird a-singin' to him and [the berries] a-hittin' the bucket. And it went ding, ding, ding. And he come back and said, 'Sary, I thought up a song,' and he wrote it and they made that record. And I was just a little kid just eight years old when that happened, 'cause I was eight years old when we moved up to the house, and Joe was just a baby and Janette was a lit-tle girl. But I can remember that as if it'd been yesterday."

The historian and the daughter are probably both right, in a way. Like as not, A.P. did get some lyrics or sheet music for "Sweet Bird" from somebody up in the Tennessee hills just beyond the Groveses' house. And like as not, he did get the idea for the call-and-response arrangement of "Sweet Fern" from his blackberry expedition. And like as not, Sara and Maybelle took A.P.'s notion and remade the melody and instrumentals into something barely suggested by the old sheet music. The Carters' method of "lining out" a song was collecting, home manufacture, and invention all rolled into one, like Old Man Curtis's

rocking chair–powered butter churn. Its separate parts might be familiar, but in combination, they constituted something entirely new.

The process started with A.P., who was happy to leave behind his
farm chores to go off hunting songs. "He loved meeting people, loved
visiting, and he never forgot people he met," says Janette. "My daddy's
hands always shook. I always remember that from when he took my
hand, or when he touched my head. And they were so warm. And he
had big hands. And when he took my hand I would have followed him
to the end of the world and jumped off. When I was little, I would
scream and cry until he'd take me with him when he was hunting songs.

"He was known in the Valley and in the area, and people would tell
him if they heard somebody had a song, and he'd go see them. Or sometimes he'd just be driving by and stop and go up to a little house up in
the hills to see if they had a song. It's a wonder he didn't get dog-bit.
He'd just tell 'em who he was and that he was looking for songs. Sometimes he'd stay all night at their house."

"A.P. would put his feet under anybody's table and stay," says his
niece Fern Carter Salyers. "He'd stay with black people. Once Janette
and A.P. got stuck and stayed over at a black family's home, and Janette
couldn't get over how the woman had turned out the corn bread right on
the stove." In fact, the Carters recorded the African-American spiritual
"River of Jordan" in 1928.

Anybody who could pick up an instrument and play a tune for him
A.P. called a "musicianer." But if the person could only sing out the
lyrics, that was a "songster." And there were a lot of songsters around,
and most of them carried lyrics in their head.

Oftentimes A.P. got back home with scraps of paper bulging from
his pockets, each with lyrics, or pieces of lyrics, scribbled in his shaky
hand. Then he'd get out and walk those tracks, hands behind his back,
cogitating on ways to fill up the holes in the lyrics. When a notion for a
lyric hit him, no matter when it hit him, he had to act on it. "He'd go to
bed and have a tune or something up in his mind, and holler for me to
get up and hold the lamp," said Gladys, "'til he could write down what
he thought of, a chorus or something."

Melody was not A.P.'s strength. There was no way he could write down all those notes. The best he could do was carry back what he remembered from his collecting trips. "He had the tunes in his head," said a friend of A.P.'s who sometimes traveled with him. "He would hum it until Maybelle and Sara would catch the tune of it." A.P. told Maybelle that every song should have a distinctive instrumental intro, so the audience could recognize it from the first chords, but other than that, he left the melodies to the women.

Even when A.P. brought home sheet music for old parlor songs or long-forgotten pop tunes, it didn't do Sara and Maybelle much good; neither one could read music. When A.P. brought home lyrics with no tune at all to work with, Sara and Maybelle would fashion the melody by ear, drawing heavily on the old fiddle songs they'd heard Uncle Mil Nickels or Ap Harris play over in Rich Valley—or even tinkering with a melody they'd already heard on a record. "Meet Me by the Moonlight, Alone," Maybelle once said, was more or less the same tune as "Prisoner's Song," which had been a hit for carpetbagger Vernon Dalhart in 1924.

Not only did they take a melody from "Prisoner's Song," but A.P. also lifted pieces of its lyrics for a song he called "I'm Thinking Tonight of My Blue Eyes," which they cut in that February 1929 Camden session. But what set apart that song was the tune. "I'd known that one for a long time," Maybelle once said of the melody, so it must have been from something she'd heard as a girl from Mil Nickels or Ap Harris or her own mother. Whatever the provenance, that melody became of one of the best known and most copied in country music. It was as if the melody was so deeply encoded in country music's double helix of performer and audience that every time a singer sneaked it in under his or her own lyrics, the songs hit with the reflexive thump of recognition. Roy Acuff used it for "Great Speckled Bird," and it became a signature song. Kitty Wells used it on "It Wasn't God Who Made Honky-Tonk Angels" and charted a hit.

That February in Camden, the Carters also recorded "My Clinch

Mountain Home" and "Sweet Fern," some ballads of unhappy love, a number of gospel songs (including Big Tom's "Grave on the Green Hillside" and Aunt Myrtle's "Little Moses"), and even an old "scaffold song" called "Don't Forget This Song." "Don't Forget" was the sort of ballad that had, for centuries, celebrated Irish rebels who liked to make subtly mutinous speeches from the gallows before their (surely unjust) hanging at the hand of the British crown. That sort of song, if not the song itself, had traveled back and forth across the Atlantic for more than two hundred years. A.P. found his scaffold song on a farmstead in Russell County, Virginia, no more than thirty miles from his own front porch.

A.P. also convinced Sara to do "Engine 143," the song that had drawn him to her. Peer copyrighted every song they recorded in A.P.'s name. In all, they cut a dozen more songs—and walked away with another six hundred dollars. Royalty checks from the last session were coming in every three months now, for hundreds more dollars.

For once, A.P.'s fortunes seemed to be running with the tide. At the beginning of 1929 America—and Americans—had never been so rich. Even the impoverished rural South was making its way into the modern industrial world. Southern farmers and laborers might have less time on their hands, but they had more cash. A.P. could see it all around him. The Jetts were no longer the only family around Maces who could afford a motorized tractor. Eck and A.P. weren't the only ones around with cars. Doc Meade had given up his horse, whip, and buggy, and he was making emergency calls in a new automobile. Uncle Fland had got a Ford pickup truck and was hauling coal back from Hiltons nearly every week. Over on the outskirts of Kingsport, builders had made an entire development of whitewashed two-story clapboard houses, with big basements to hold coal-burning furnaces, indoor plumbing, electricity, polished wooden floors, and flowered wallpaper. White City, they called it, and regular working people were buying those homes for thousands of dollars. But the thing A.P. saw that he liked most was this: When Cecil McLister put new Carter records on sale at his music store in Bristol, they'd be gone in a day's time. And that was just around home. With the Victor machine pushing Carter Family records all over the country, A.P. knew the Carters were going to keep making money. So did Eck. And Maybelle. And Sara.

For the first time in their lives, they had spending money. Sara bought new dresses and slacks, fancy hats, and a fur stole. She'd buy bottles of her favorite perfume, Blue Waltz, and bright red nail polish. Maybelle got clothes, too, and more china. Eck bought a seventy-acre homestead on Clinch Mountain and spent $275 on a new Gibson guitar Maybelle saw at the music store in Kingsport. But A.P. had the biggest eyes. Three weeks after they returned from the Camden recording date, A.P. bought seventy-five acres of the best farmland in Little Valley from Uncle Will and Aunt Myrtle Bays. He gave the then stunning sum of $3,500 for the land, taking over payments on Uncle Will's $1,124.15 mortgage from the Federal Land Bank in Baltimore, Maryland. Uncle Will agreed to hold notes for the remaining $2,375.85 for two years, payable at 6 percent interest.

Suddenly, A.P. had one of the biggest farms in the Valley. But he remained one of the least interested, and most intriguing, agriculturalists in the entire state of Virginia. One day he decided he was going to use his new sawmill boiler to power his plow. "Pleasant wanted to plow with a steam engine," says Bud Derting. "He got it on wheels and rigged it up to the plow, plowed one row, and he was done. Guess he done what he wanted to do, and he was happy. He'd get something in his head about a steam engine, and he was gonna do it."

"He wanted me to plow some up there in the Little Valley where he owned his land," says Clyde Gardner. "I went up there one morning and said, 'Where do you want me to plow, Pleasant?' He said, 'Ah, just anywhere you want to.' I told Janette that and she laughed. Said, 'That's just like him.'

"I heared one fellow talking about going up to the Little Valley where Pleasant had his farm, and Pleasant had a horse and a mule there, and he was going to rake hay. He hooked his horse, put it in the reins, and he couldn't catch the mule for a while. And this fellow said,

'Pleasant got up on that rake and set there a while and never did catch the mule. He just got the horns off of that horse and went on home.' "

"Sometimes he'd walk through the Gap to his farm in the Little Valley," says his niece Lois Hensley. "There was no road, so he'd take Kit [his mule] up to the Valley to work. Maybe he'd plow one row, and then he'd quit. He just didn't have any staying power."

There were only two things Pleasant Carter wouldn't quit: his music and his home. In 1929 he could have moved his family to one of those beautiful new houses in Kingsport or to Bristol or up north to be near the recording studio in Camden; he could have gone to Nashville or Atlanta or Chicago, where radio stations were blasting out their barn dances week after week. But the more A.P. traveled, the more he knew there was only one place he could live. He had to be surrounded by his mountains, and he had to be surrounded by his home people, who knew him best and were willing to make allowances. Folks around Maces Springs knew how to forgive and forget. Mount Vernon, for instance, didn't turn its back on anybody.

One Sunday, a three-hundred-pound congregant worked himself into a frenzy powered by an alternating religious current of guilt and righteousness. First, he called out his secret mistress and demanded she wash his feet. Then he started jumping up and down in a craze until he went right through the floorboards, terrifying the other Methodists. "Mr. Paris got so upset, he jumped out the window," remembers one woman who was there that day.

It was decided that the wayward sheep would have to be restrained by the flock, so the best wrestler in attendance was sent in first. "I can throw him," said Daddy Denison, "but I can't hold him." It took every man in church that day to get Haven Larkey tied down to the floor, and in the confusion, poor Ernest Wolfe got knotted up with Mr. Larkey, too. "You gotta let me go!" Ernest kept yelling. "You gotta let me go!"

Once the storm had passed—and the floor was fixed—Mr. Larkey was welcomed back. But people did like to tell the story on him. A.P. Carter knew people told a few stories on him, too, but there was no harm, and he never minded. Not now that he'd achieved fame outside the flock. "When did you say you were born, Pleasant? . . . Well, I never did see nobody born in December that amounted to anything." But Alvin Pleasant Carter had amounted to something. In a two-year period ending in 1930, the Carter Family sold seven hundred thousand records across the nation.

Carter Family Songbook (Flo Wolfe)

Opposite: Jimmie Rodgers with the Carters in Louisville (Flo Wolfe)

Fire on the Mountain

O f course, Mr. Peer wanted more, and A.P. began piloting his new Chevrolet in wider and wider circles, searching for material. Remote hollows, tenant farms, mining camps, big-city factories—A.P. would go anywhere in search of a song. In Kingsport there was a group of black musicians who had come down from the mountains of Tennessee, Virginia, and North Carolina to work at the local mills and factories. There was Steve Tarter, a blues guitar player who had reputation enough for recording artist Blind Lemon Jefferson to seek him out when he came through town. There was a guitar player named Ed Martin, a fiddler named John Evans, and his guitar-playing brother-in-law George "Duff" McGhee, who played at farm workings and city dances both. There was McGhee's son Brownie, whose polio had bound him to a wheelchair but gave him plenty of time to practice his guitar, and his other son, Sticks, so named for the way he'd wheel his brother around downtown Kingsport. The teenage Brownie, who would go on to fame as a world-traveling blues musician, remembered the excitement when

A.P. Carter pulled into town in his big new red Chevrolet bought with record royalties. In the black section of Kingsport, A.P. found a group whose music had plenty in common with his own—their home sound also came off the porch and out of the church. That neighborhood's left-handed five-string banjo player plucked out a version of "John Henry" that was much the same as the one Maybelle's mother used to play on her own five-string banjo, on the porch overlooking Copper Creek. But the music these black Kingsporters made was starting to get the bluesy feel they'd picked up on old Scott Joplin–like ragtime records and the recordings of Blind Lemon Jefferson, Blind Blake, and Barbecue Bob.

One Sunday morning, somebody in Kingsport sent A.P. to see John Henry Lyons, who had a blues song called "Motherless Children Sees a Hard Time." Visiting the Lyonses' house that day was a young black guitar player who had learned to play watching Ed Martin and Steve Tarter. His given name was Lesley Riddle, though he always asked friends and family to call him "Esley." "I happened to come by the porch there, and so John Henry gave me his guitar and told me to play Mr. Carter a piece," Riddle told Mike Seeger more than thirty years later. "So I was playing pretty regular then and I played him a couple of pieces. He wanted me to go home with him right then and there. I went over to Maces Springs with him. Stayed over there about a week. From then on, he and I got to be good friends. I continued for about three or four years, going over to his house and going where he wanted to go. I went out with A.P. about fifteen times to collect songs.

"He'd just go in [to people's homes] and tell them, 'Hello, I was told by someone that you got a song, kind of an old song. Would you mind letting me hear it?' So they'd go and get it and sing it for him."

Over the next ten years, Riddle had some real down-home country-road adventures with A.P. One day, when Riddle was visiting his mother in his native home of Burnsville, North Carolina, he looked up and saw the big red Chevy coming down the road. Next thing he knew, Esley was on his way to Charlottesville, Virginia, where A.P. had heard about some songs he wanted to get. Logistics were difficult for a black man and a white man traveling together in the Jim Crow South, and

A.P. was always in a fix to find places that would have his young friend. On the trip to Charlottesville, A.P. stashed Riddle with a family of Cherokees, or melungeons, or some such. Riddle never did know, because his hosts never said much. "I stayed up there for five days," Riddle said, "and the whole five days I was up there, every meal, we had rabbit. Rabbit They didn't call it rabbit, they called it 'rob-it.' We had rob-it for dinner, we had rob-it for breakfast, we had rob-it for supper. After I was up there for five days, Mr. Carter came over one morning, and I told Mr. Carter, 'Mr. Carter, I can't stay here at these people's house.' He said, 'What's the matter, Les?' I said, 'They're feeding me nothing but rabbit, and I'm getting sick and tired of it.' They got fried rabbit, dried rabbit, stewed rabbit, boiled rabbit, and rabbit hash, and every way in the world you could fix a rabbit they had. So Mr. Carter told me I'll see if I can find you somewhere. So he taken me way down in the country to an old man named Ole Man Brown. They were real old people—he and his wife. We went down there. Mr. Carter taken the car and went into town, and he got a whole carload of groceries. I don't know what they was feeding him over there where he was staying, but anyway he went to staying with us, went to eating with us."

Sometimes they'd be driving down a country road, and A.P. would start yelling for Esley to pull over. Sure enough, there would be some torn-down sawmill, and A.P. would start scrambling around picking up hardware to bring home for parts. It was an operation Riddle never quite understood. He says he never witnessed A.P. saw a single piece of lumber off the sawmill in his backyard. But the older man's salvaging instinct was one Riddle had come to appreciate. "He was just gonna get old music, old songs, what had never been sung in sixty years," Riddle said. "He was gonna get it, put a tune to it, and record it."

The coal-mining town of Norton, Virginia, was always ripe for song gathering—and A.P. had family there, too. His brother Jim was living in Norton then, and his mother's cousin Henrietta Nickels O'Neill. Hattie O'Neill had married a New York Irishman who had moved south for work as a foreman in the coal mines, and then on the L&N Railroad. William O'Neill made a good wage, had a big house, and, like many striving middle-class Americans, owned a new parlor organ. There was an array of music in that house. Most of the O'Neill children preferred the old-timey music of southwestern Virginia, and daughter Kate was already playing guitar with her band, The Lonesome Pine Specials, at radio station WOPI in Bristol. Hattie O'Neill, meanwhile, was partial to hymns. But William O'Neill, the old Irishman, was fond of the lachrymose songs of his homeland and sentimental Tin Pan Alley parlor tunes. He bought lots of sheet music for his parlor organ, and some of it ended up in A.P.'s hands. "He'd come back from Hattie O'Neill's with a fistful of songs," says Jim Carter's daughter Lois. "He'd stop at the O'Neills' and eat and get some more songs." Sometimes A.P. would take Kate O'Neill around the area to hunt more songs. He'd write down the words; she'd catch the tune.

"He'd go ninety miles if he heard someone say that someone had an old song that hadn't ever been recorded or didn't have a copyright," said Riddle. "One time he and I went way to the other side of Gate City and some old lady about ninety years old, and she had some music her grandmother had left her. We got a whole stack of that music and come back. Couldn't nobody understand it. Couldn't nobody read [music]."

Much of the sheet music A.P. collected was crumbling yellow pages from the post–Civil War boom in commercial song-making. In the forty years between the Civil War and the advent of the phonograph, a song's success was judged by its sheet-music sales. A hit song might sell hundreds of thousands of copies of sheet music, which landed in parlors all over the nation. By the late twenties, the writers of those songs were more or less forgotten men: an Indiana reform-school teacher named Thomas P. Westendorf, a black railroad porter, Gussie Davis (who is credited for, among other songs, "Goodnight Irene"), and the Jewish New Yorker Charles K. Harris. In 1892 Harris had produced one of America's first megahits, "After the Ball," which sold 5 million song sheets and is still rendered nightly in the Broadway musical *Show Boat*. Davis and Harris were northerners working on Tin Pan Alley in New York, but these men understood, or came to understand, what appealed to a post–Civil War southern audience; they specialized in sentimental story songs about home, mother, wandering boys, and orphaned chil-

dren. But when Harris wrote "Mid the Green Fields of Virginia," what
the composer knew about the Old Dominion would not fill a page. As
Harris once explained to Booker T. Washington, "I had to inquire if
there was corn raised in Virginia and if there were hills in Carolina.
This information was given me by my office superintendent, Mr. Blaise,
a native Southerner, and my imagination did the rest."

But A.P. could take these turgid old parlor-piano songs and, with a
good cleaning (there was usually an underbrush of moldering Victorian
poetics to clear away) and a little melodic rendering by Maybelle and
Sara, work up a song that seemed kin to latter-day down-home mountain balladry. A.P. found the parlor songs of William Shakespeare
Hays especially useful. Will Hays was a Louisville Kentucky, newspa-
perman/poet and probably the most prolific southern songwriter of the
late nineteenth century. Hays was fond of pale moons, withered flowers,
aging mothers, and dying children. His songs could be egregiously
maudlin, but A.P. shaved off some of Hays's dewy theatrics and made
nice little songs of "Jimmy Brown, the Paper Boy" and "You've Been a
Friend to Me." Others, like "Little Log Hut in the Lane," required
drastic minstrelectomies. In the Hays version, the lyrics went as follows:
"I'll never hear dem singin' in the cane, / And I'se de only one dat's left
/ Wid dis ole dog ob mine, / In de little old log cabin in de lane." A.P.
remade it entirely: "I'm going from the cotton field / I'm going from the
cane, / I'm going from that little log hut, / That stands down in the
lane." Even when he sang from the perspective of a black slave, A.P.
meant to give voice to a certain human dignity.

Song-hunting trips got a lot easier with Riddle as his traveling companion. Much of the time A.P. could leave Esley to drive the big new
Chevy, so he could daydream in peace and not worry about running off
the road. Best of all, Riddle could remember lyrics and a tune, something A.P. could never do. "I was quick to catch on to anything," Riddle said. "If I hear you sing, I could sing it, too. I was his, what you call,
his Poll' Parrot. I was his tape recorder. He'd take me with him and
he'd get someone to sing him the whole song. Then I would get it, then
I'd learn it to Sara and Maybelle."

Besides his work as the human recorder, Esley Riddle also brought his own repertoire to the Carters. The mixing of races was an unusual thing in Poor Valley, but then, A.P. had never hied to convention. He and Sara would have Riddle at the homeplace for a week or more at a time. "They were just like home to me," said Riddle. "I was with them off and on for four or five years. They all lived in the neighborhood, almost in hollering distance. His father, mother, sisters and brothers, Maybelle.

"I'd be settin' over there sometimes, you know, and pick up the guitar and play something. Four or five months from then, I'd be coming down the street and I'd be hearing it. The Carter Family would be singing it.

"You know, as many times as I was over at the Carter Family, I never got them together to sing for me but twice the whole time I was over there. They never sang for me. I'd have to do all the picking and singing while I was over there."

The Carter Family would record their own version of a blues song Riddle learned from a Blind Lemon Jefferson recording, and a retooling of a song Riddle's uncle had been playing for decades, "The Cannonball." It's a familiar down-home tune, put to many a song. Charlie Poole and his white North Carolina string band took the melody for their McKinley assassination song, "White House Blues." But black musicians pushed the melody into the space between ragtime and blues, as in Furry Lewis's version of "Stackolee" and Mississippi John Hurt's "Frankie." Woody Guthrie would take the same melody and write a Depression-era song called "Dirty Overalls."

A.P. took the scant lyrics Riddle had sung with the tune, added his own, and came up with a song that included this delicious and vivid phrasing: "My baby left me, she even took my shoes . . . She's gone, she's solid gone." In the recording session that May, A.P. screwed up the courage to make "The Cannonball" his first turn as a solo vocalist.

Years later, Maybelle would tell Mike Seeger that Riddle had taught her how to play the blues licks in "The Cannonball," but Riddle always demurred. Maybelle was just like him, Riddle would say. She was *always* paying attention, *always* watching. "You don't have to give

Maybelle any lessons," Riddle remembered thirty years later. "You let her see you playing something, she'll get it. You better believe it."

The Carters even recorded one of the few songs Riddle claimed to have worked up himself. "I was sitting on my shoeshine stand—that's what I was working at—one morning, and it was raining and I hadn't made no money and I was lonesome," Riddle told Mike Seeger. "I had my old guitar over there. I got that guitar and picked up the words and went and got me a piece of paper, up on the shoeshine stand, and wrote them down." A.P. and Sara recorded the song, "Lonesome for You," as a duet, passing the lead vocals back and forth like a hot potato.

In fact, in the two recording sessions the Carters did in 1930, they reached well outside the narrow traditions of Clinch Mountain music. A.P. was showing real artistry. That year he wrote a beautiful and thoroughly modern song, "The Birds Were Singing of You," which captured a single suspended moment of grief. Under the stillness of a pale moon, a lonely man can't shake the whispering memory of his departed lover. Did the lover die? Run off? Marry another? We never know. In that void of knowledge, all that exists is his gnawing pain. In that moment, the birds were singing of her. Heaven was thinking of her. And all the world was sighing, sighing for her.

A.P. wrote two of the songs they recorded that year, and Sara herself wrote two. But of the nineteen songs the Carter Family cut, nine were either church-house blues or sacred songs from the black Baptist or Pentecostal churches. Both those musical movements were fed by absolute, existential loneliness, far beyond the comparatively feeble homesickness of Anglo-Irish and white southern traditional music. In the African-American song, there might not even be a home or mother to get back to.

The body-altering flights of Pentecostal music, especially, rose out of that emptiness. When there was nothing holding people to this cold world, why wouldn't they sail right out of it on the righteous note? Though the Holiness revivals Maybelle had attended were gatherings of southern whites, the movement got its musical release from the children of slaves. Pentecostalism was Wesleyan Methodism hot-wired by the notion that the Holy Ghost was at large in the land, and it was the first American religious movement to scramble the boundary line of race. In fact, the white-led Pentecostal movement would have flamed out in less than five years had it not been for one particular African-American man, a son of former slaves, William Joseph Seymour.

As a young Methodist working the cane fields in Louisiana, Seymour began to hear the call to preach, and the call drew him toward Houston, Texas. He walked there and found himself on the doorstep of a whites-only Bible college, where the minister Charles Fox Parham was converting laymen to his new Pentecostal church. When Seymour arrived at Parham's Bible college, he was refused admission. But day after day, Seymour came back to sit on the steps and listen to Parham describe the underpinning of his new mission: The minister told of the Pentecost, fifty days after Passover, when the apostles of the crucified Jesus gathered and, with flames over their heads, began "speaking in tongues," channeling His word in a way that broke down all barriers of manmade language. At his own church, Parham said, on the first day of the new century, one of his followers had risen out of her chair and, in ecstatic release, had begun speaking in tongues. This was a sure sign, Parham said, that the Holy Spirit was again present in the world, and that He might soon cleanse it in a flame of fire, leaving the holy and faithful to a better life on earth.

Seymour never did make it through the door of that Bible college, but he'd been led there by the Holy Spirit, so he took what he heard there on those steps as the gospel. He began making his way west toward California, preaching about a new Pentecost, which was there for the asking. By the time he arrived in Los Angeles in 1906, Seymour had worked up his own twist on Parham's teachings: If God meant to break down the barriers of language, didn't He also mean to break down the barriers of race?

The official Pentecostal story marks April 9, 1906, as the day "the power fell." At one of Seymour's services, in a private home on Bonnie Brae Street in L.A., a small group of black laborers began speaking in tongues, wildly, ecstatically, noisily. One neighbor lady walked over to see what was the commotion, began channeling the Holy Ghost, and fell on the piano, making music though she'd never played an instrument in her life. For five days, Seymour's quiet preaching drew a slowly growing audience, but it was mostly a local curiosity. The crowd watched as people among them twisted with the contortions of out-of-body conversions, and strained to hear Seymour's description of the imminent flame-licked apocalypse. On the fifth day, when an earthquake hit San Francisco and great stretches of the "Queen City of California" were consumed by fire, Bonnie Brae Street really started rocking. Seymour had to move his growing revival out of private homes and into a drafty abandoned stable on Azusa Street in downtown Los Angeles.

William Joseph Seymour was not by nature a charismatic; he was a smallish, soft-spoken man with a wispy beard and a glass eye. But his message had force, and it appealed first and foremost to the illiterate. Pentecostalism promised them "primal spirituality," an experience of the Holy Spirit that didn't depend on an ability to read or understand the Bible. Illiteracy was no disadvantage when the Holy Spirit could put the Word straight in you.

For nearly three years, the Azusa Street "Apostolic Faith Mission" revival pressed on, growing every day. As the movement grew, converts were no longer just African Americans from the Azusa Street neighborhood. Blacks, whites, Asians, Latinos—they all came to hear Seymour. People made pilgrimages from Europe and Africa. "One token of the Lord's coming is that He is melting all races and nations together," Seymour wrote, "and they are filled with the power and glory of God." A *Los Angeles Daily Times* headline screamed, WHITES AND BLACKS MIX IN A RELIGIOUS FRENZY. One white convert stated firmly, "The color line was washed away by blood." Services were carried on from morning until midnight, seven days a week. People came by the thousands. The neighbor lady's ringing piano was accompanied by the *tchokking* rhythms of everything from cow's ribs to thimbles. There was shouting, crying, screaming, wild flights of channeling, and near orgasmic release. "The power of the Lord was so great," said one in attendance, "it seemed to tingle your spine and your hair stood on end." Through it all, Seymour sat up front with his white preacher-partner, often with his head inside a shoe box or a wooden crate, trying to blot out the earthly noise so that he might hear the Spirit speak to him. Most of Seymour's talks were quiet teaching sermons, but sometimes he'd suddenly jump out of his chair, screaming, "Repent!" or he'd begin speaking in tongues.

Some local newsmen were terrified by what they saw: "Disgraceful intermingling of the races, they cry and make howling noises all day and into the night," wrote one. "They run, jump, shake all over, shout to the top of their voice, spin around in circles, fall out on the sawdust-blanketed floor jerking, kicking and rolling all over it. Some of them pass out and do not move for hours as though they were dead. These people appear to be mad, mentally deranged or under a spell."

The first furious revival was over by 1909, and also gone was the hopeful brotherhood of the races. White Holiness preachers had co-opted many of Seymour's white converts and split them off into their own "Assemblies of God" church. When Seymour converts carried the Pentecostal message back to the South and the Midwest, they usually split down racial lines. There was the Church of God in Christ (for African Americans) and the Fire Baptized Holiness Church (whites only). By 1930 the Ku Klux Klan had burned down a number of black Pentecostal churches in the South. Seymour's Azusa Street church had vanished.

But what lived on was Pentecost-fired music, with its wild abandon, its rhythmic, driving flight, and its stark, lyrical imagery. In those songs, people weren't just orphaned—they were orphaned, crippled, *and* blind—but they still had their train ticket punched for heaven. Jesus was likely to be nailed to a tree, and the world was always about to be consumed by fire.

At the time he met A.P., Esley Riddle was singing a lot of sacred songs he'd learned in church. When A.P. heard Riddle's friend Pauline Gary sing in Kingsport, he brought them both into the Valley to give entertainments for all his white friends. "She sang sacred songs," said Riddle. "He wanted her to come to Maces with us, so we taken her up there and she stayed up there about three days. We had a big old audience up there. Had a houseful. All the rooms full, three rooms, then they were standing all out in the yard and everything. Of course she was a really good singer We had two programs up there, two nights."

In 1930 the Carters had begun to put African-American sacred songs on record: "On a Hill Lone and Gray," "I'm Working on a Building" (which was a "Holy Ghost building"), the rousing "Let the Church Roll On," and "On My Way to Canaan's Land," in which A.P. would shout in Seymouresque exclamation, "Praise God!" In "Canaan's Land," it didn't matter if mother, father, sister, and brother weren't going on high, the singer was going it alone with Jesus. Maybe the best was "When the World's on Fire," which had been recorded as "Rock of Ages" by Blind Willie Davis, a black singer-guitarist from McComb, Mississippi. On the Carter record, Maybelle played in Davis's bottleneck-guitar style. Woody Guthrie would be so taken with that melody that he'd make it the basis for his American anthem to inclusion, "This Land Is Your Land."

A.P. also had an instant affinity for the secular country-blues music Riddle brought him. Riddle, who used to lock himself in his room and make music when he was feeling down never saw the blues as a racial statement. For him, it was just a way to channel a feeling toward sonic release. "Sometimes I'd get the blues and I'd be making chords that I can't even remember. Get the blues and take off," Riddle once said. "Blues ain't nothing but a man feeling sad." Woody Guthrie, another man who traveled back and forth between the worlds of white and black musicians, didn't see any great divide between the races where the blues was concerned. "I always just called it just plain old being lonesome," he told Alan Lomax in 1940. "You can get lonesome for a lot of things. People down around where I come from, they're lonesome for a job. Lonesome for some spending money. Lonesome for some drinking whiskey. Lonesome for good times, pretty gals, wine, women, and song like they see stuck up in their face by other people. Thinking maybe that you were down and out, disgusted, busted, and can't be trusted gives you a lonesome feeling. That somehow the world sorta turned against you or there's something about it you don't understand. . . . Blues are awful popular in jails."

The way Guthrie saw it, though, the most potent blues started with one of America's most isolated indigenous wanderers, the runaway slave. He noted that "Lonesome Road Blues," the song used in the 1940 film of Steinbeck's great Okie story, *The Grapes of Wrath*, came from just that man. "It was wrote by a colored slave that run off from his master and went up north," Guthrie told Lomax. "It's pretty cold up there. He worked up there a little bit, stayed in jail, got treated like a dog. So he wrote this song, or got it started." The runaway slave was America's ultimate existential man, cut off from a heritage of his own, beyond family, without home. And in this song, even after he makes it north to freedom, he finds no peace. The terrifying discovery at the end of the road is that he's got *no place* to be, no place except maybe the road itself. The best he can hope for is to get "where the climate suits my clothes."

A.P. knew what it was to be lonesome for something. He'd grown up set apart by odd and undefined longings, and had always been on the road to a destiny he couldn't describe. With his ear to that tune, and with Maybelle's ability to pick up the guitar licks Riddle showed her, the Carters began making some pretty convincing church-house blues. Their audience responded to it immediately, making "Worried Man Blues" their biggest seller of the year.

In "Worried Man Blues," a man goes across the river to sleep, wakes up a prisoner in chains, and has no idea what he's done wrong. That song spoke a simple unjustifiable truth: Some men were born to the poor and lonesome class in America, and despite the national promise, that class was hard to escape. Even if somebody did, the hellhounds stayed on his trail. Having come up in Poor Valley, A.P. had to know deep down his own good fortune could vaporize, and without reason. If life in Poor Valley taught him anything, it taught him that truth. But when the nation started to slide deeper into economic depression in the early thirties, the Carters were still doing a lot better than their neighbors. They were doing better than most of their professional brethren, too. By 1931 Pop and Hattie Stoneman's royalties had dried up, and they hadn't saved a dime. The Stonemans and their many children were living in a lean-to shack with an old army-issue canvas tent for a roof. Other musicians were failing to make recording dates. The Norton, Virginia, banjo player and singer Dock Boggs missed a date because he simply couldn't raise the train fare. Record sales were down to a tenth of what they'd been in the high times of the late twenties. Okeh was bankrupt and gone.

The big record companies were starting to cut their losses, putting money into already established acts such as the Carter Family. By 1931 no mountain group sold better, and even while sales dropped precipitously, Carter records had found a floor. After the two recording sessions with the Carters in 1930, Peer called for two more in 1931, and two in 1932. Ralph Peer was always looking for ways to spark sales, and he dreamed up a record that would introduce the Carters to the vast audience of his biggest-selling artist. Peer asked the Carters to come to Louisville in June of 1931 to make a record with Jimmie Rodgers.

Of the hundreds of acts Ralph Peer had recorded, none had sold like Rodgers. Neither Peer nor anybody else at Victor saw it coming, nor did they make it happen. "Hits were accidents," Peer's old expedition mate Polk Brockman liked to say. "Nothing was planned." In fact, Rodgers had to be pretty pushy to make it happen. According to his biographer, Nolan Porterfield, just a few weeks after Jimmie recorded at Bristol in August of 1927 (and before a single record had been released), Rodgers had already printed up new business cards and a letterhead: "National Radio Artist—Victor Recording Artist." When his first record was finally released in October of 1927, Rodgers badgered the Victor office for sales figures. And when he wasn't summoned by Peer, he hied himself to New York, checked in to a Manhattan hotel befitting a "Victor Recording Artist," and gave Peer a call. Just happened to be passing through town, Rodgers said. Did Mr. Peer want him to stop over and cut a few more sides?

Peer didn't hesitate. By the time he'd made a second set of Rodgers recordings, the Victor man understood that this was a singer made for commerce. Rodgers wasn't the "Blue Yodeler" for nothing. He had a way of being what listeners wanted him to be. He had enough Mississippi fried catfish in his voice to read "cracker" to any listener, but he was also bluesy enough to get with "the race" and randy enough to put a blush on the twenties' most cynical café-society crowd. He was also young enough to find his way into the "lost generation." (The first song he ever recorded for Peer in Bristol, "The Soldier's Sweetheart," was about a young girl who lost her lover to the "no-man's-land" of the Great War.) Rodgers could also do something Peer had rarely heard. The other song he recorded at Bristol, "Sleep, Baby, Sleep," was an old vaudeville song without much pop; Jimmie's own wife called it "a thousand-year-old lullaby." But Jimmie worked his way from chorus to chorus in a warble of throaty, high-pitched bawling so encompassing that it sounded like a railroad gandy-dancer shout, a roundup cattle call, and Polish polka yips all at once. At the second session, Rodgers re-created it on "Blue Yodel" (aka "T for Texas"). "I thought his yodel alone might spell success," Peer said. "Blue Yodel" would go on to sell a million copies.

Over the next few years, Peer never stopped trying to put Rodgers over as a popular star, backing him with Dixie string bands, juke-joint pianos, blues combos, and jazz orchestras. It paid off. Nearly every song Rodgers recorded sold a quarter of a million copies, and some would eventually top a million. Even at a fraction of what they had been, Rodgers's 1931 sales were still well in front of the field. Jimmie Rodgers was arguably the first modern pop star. He was also, like so many pop stars who would follow, hard-drinking, hard-living, and hard-loving, and his music never obscured those hard facts. Rodgers's "What's It?" is a bouquet of unrestrained lust about a two-hundred-pound cornfed mama who likes to get out in the dark and pet.

> She takes her little what's-it where she goes,
> Her what's-it never grows.
> When she walks down the street,
> Her what's-it can't be beat.
> She's my gal, my dog-faced gal
> From Nashville, Tennessee.

What made Rodgers's randiest songs modern was that they were leering but never menacing. When mountain men got their blood up in song ("I been in the bin with the rough and rowdy men"), their women friends tended to end up in shallow graves. Jimmie wasn't out to *possess*, and he had a way of letting a gal know he wanted to be pleased, but he wanted to be pleasing, too. Jimmie Rodgers didn't know how to stop. Though Maybelle never would talk about it, her daughters all got the idea the Blue Yodeler made certain unwelcome advances at the session in Louisville. In June of 1931, however, Jimmie might have been all bark and no bite. He was so weak with tuberculosis that Maybelle had to play his guitar parts at the recording session. He could barely get through the cornpone skits he and Peer wrote:

"Hey, hey, howdy folks, *yodel-ay-ee-hee*, so this is Virginia, huh? . . . Gee, I've been waiting to see you folks for a long time. . . . Say, what ole mountain is that laying over there? Ain't that a pretty ole mountain? What is that mountain laying over there?"

"That's Clinch Mountain, Jimmie."

"Izzat that ole mountain you all been singing about so much? 'My Clinch Mountain Home'? Izzat it? Izzat that ole Clinch Mountain? 'My Clinch Mountain Home'?"

"Say, Jimmie, things is getting good up here now. I went out last night, and my ole coon dogs treed two possums up one tree."

"Huh?"

"Two possums up one tree."

"Two possums up one tree?"

"Yessir."

"*Yodel-ay-ee-hee!* Boy, that's too many possums up one tree. . . . Doggone, I ain't never heard of that before. What kind of tree was it?"

"That's a black gum tree."

"Uh-oh."

None of the four showed much capacity for delivering this kind of tricked-up showbiz palaver, but throughout the session they all seemed game. Jimmie did two vocal duets with Sara, including "The Wonderful City," which was the only gospel song he ever recorded. All four joined in on the decidedly un-Carteresque "Hot Time in the Old Town

Tonight." Porterfield has noted that not one of them seemed to know the words, but he also called it "the wildest, most audacious thing on the record—a scant twenty seconds of country scat, Sara in the lead, Maybelle solidly behind her, A.P. boldly bassing in, Rodgers filling in the gaps with the shimmering little yodels punctuated at the end by a big one. 'Hey, hey,' says Jimmie, heading off for another snort. 'Boy, tell 'em 'bout us.' "

Porterfield has also noted that by the time of the Louisville recording session, Ralph Peer had hit upon a central tenet of the modern music industry: To boost sales, record companies needed more than performers—they needed stars. The audience wanted more than music; it wanted personalities. And though the Carters were never hungry for celebrity, they were willing to do almost anything to keep their new livelihood on track, to keep away the Depression-era woe they saw all around them. More than anything, they were eager to please their audience, no matter the size.

It was around this time that Minnie Adams's father moved the family over to Hiltons, where he had been hired to fix up another state road. Living not more than five miles down that road, Minnie found out, was the Carter Family. "We were overjoyed," remembers Minnie. "My aunt and me walked from Hiltons on the railroad all the way to the homeplace to see them. We didn't know them at all, but we were so anxious to see them because we had heard them all this time."

When Minnie and her aunt got to Maces Springs, they asked around until they found A.P. and Sara's home. But when they knocked at the front door, A.P. and Sara weren't there. Gladys was there alone, taking care of Joe, while their parents were out of town giving an entertainment. It was getting toward dark, so Gladys brought the two girls in, fed them supper, and let them spend the night. When A.P. and Sara came home the next day, Gladys told them how the Adams girls had walked all the way from Hiltons to meet them. So the Carter family sat the girls down and gave them a private entertainment. "Sara took off her shoes to get comfortable, and they made music right in the front room for us."

"Oh, their [celebrity] didn't make them no different," says Clyde Gardner. "They acted just about like they always did."

"I never did think I was very famous," Maybelle told a young musician thirty years later. "Honey, I just didn't look at it in that way. I was happy because our records were selling and people liked them."

Mary Bays at her son Dewey's grave (Stella Bayes)

Opposite: Sara (center) with Stella, Stanley, Alma, and Coy (clockwise from left) (Stella Bayes)

Sara's Problem

Sara Carter happily would have chosen comfort over fame. To put it
plainly, as Sara always did, she couldn't stand "all the folderol."
Though earnings from the music had given A.P. and Sara some margin
of comfort in desperate Depression times, the demands of the business
put extra weight on their marriage. For one thing, Sara was growing to
hate the entertainments. She never could get comfortable onstage,
behind the rigged-up lights, with an audience full of strangers *staring* at
her. "Let's just cut some more records," she'd say. She soon began to
balk at performing for live audiences, even when her husband pleaded.
So A.P. would grudgingly fill out the act with his sister Sylvia and leave
Sara behind with the children.

It was one more thing to argue about in an already tense household.
Running the house now fell to Sara alone. A.P. was constantly away on
song-hunting trips, and the truth was, the way he spent money on big-
ticket items, there wasn't always a day-to-day cash margin. "You'll hear
Joe say [his father] would go out song-collecting and leave Sara with

three kids—in February—up on that mountain, with no firewood, not a nickel to buy flour or sugar, and be gone for weeks at a time," says one of A.P.'s old friends.

Sometimes when Pleasant was gone, Sara would have to drag timber down off the mountain to sell to Eastman Kodak for a few dollars to keep the family fed. Bud Derting once saw Sara across the road at A.P.'s sawmill, chopping wood to fire the steam boiler. He says she was sweating hard in her work dress that day, barefoot, muddied up past her ankles, with little Joe at her knee playing in the ashes. "She'd be cutting down wood, pulling mining timbers out of the mountains—and Daddy out somewhere trying to learn a song," says Joe. "He never stopped to think what effect it might have on his family."

Even when he was home, A.P. was not inclined toward the mundane, day-to-day tasks of scratching a living from the Valley. Some days, A.P. would grab Lesley Riddle and his guitar and they'd go sit under a tree, A.P. telling stories about the recording trips or the entertainments, and Riddle straining to teach A.P. to play a guitar. "I tried my best to learn him how to play, how to chord," Riddle said. "I got so he could make G, C, and D, but he never could keep them in line. Instead of playing G, C, and D, he'd play D, G, and C. He turned around and played it backwards all the time. He tried to learn to play 'Wabash Cannonball.' He could sing it, but he tried to learn how to chord it, too. I don't think he ever did learn. I had him so he knew two or three pretty good chords, the match-up chords. C, G, and D and things like that.

"He liked to sing. He liked music. And he'd sit out there half a day if I'd sit with him. Lot of times I'd get disgusted and just get on up and go somewhere."

As frustrating as he could be as a pupil, Pleasant Carter was becoming even more difficult as a husband and father. A near solipsistic self-involvement had always been A.P.'s most maddening tic, and now that he was consumed by the recording business and the Carter Family's place in it, it seemed Pleasant never stopped to think about anything or anybody else. When he was at home, he was more distant than ever, more jealous of his own thoughts, more apt to flare in anger when something impinged on his valuable songwriting time. "Mother never spanked me. Her voice was kind and calm. Daddy had a violent temper," Janette once wrote. "I felt, if she said, 'Punish Janette,' he would. He always used a razor strop, if not a wild cherry switch." The tenderness he put on record, the way his own quavering voice graciously supported his wife's star-vocal turns, was often missing at home. Sara bore her husband's lack of regard in her stoic unsentimental fashion. If A.P. had dropped to his knees and professed his undying love for her, Sara probably would have rolled her eyes and said, "Aw, pshaw." That was the sort of thing, she'd always told herself, that she could do without.

But there were times when life simply wore Sara down, when exhaustion made her tender in ways she never suspected. Returning home with the children one day, Sara found the big cedar by the house chopped away, cleared out to make room for a new maple A.P. was going to plant. Janette watched in wonder as her mother sat on the front porch and wept. She had never seen her mother cry over anything, and never would again. "I've often thought about that," Janette says almost seventy years later. Even then, not yet ten years old, Janette knew this was about more than just a tree.

Sara continued to wipe her children's tears, cool their fevers, patch their cuts, bruises, and burns, and keep them in relative security. It was Sara who took the three children by train to Bristol to outfit them for school each year. She'd buy them each gloves, galoshes, cotton socks, new shoes, and Sunday dress-up clothes. Gladys and Joe got new winter coats, but Janette could always wear Gladys's hand-me-down. Sara would also buy material so that she could sew the girls' everyday dresses, which she did every year with the help of her friend Myrtle Hensley. After the shopping was done, Sara would hop on the train and haul the kids and the loot back to the Valley.

As they got older Gladys and Janette took on some of the workload, but Joe . . . well, Joe just made *more* work especially after he got his legs under him. "I had a race with a train and throwed my clothes off," he remembers seventy years after that race, from a living room looking down on the very same spot where the track once ran. "I was streaking. I laid down streaking in this country. That old engineer had ahold of that whistle"—here he stops and lets out the low, wet cry of the whistle—"I put the hammer down. I was getting it, and he just kept jerking on that whistle. I run it way up there about where you turned up to the crossing. Somebody come out of there and hollered at Mommy. Said, 'Get over here. This young'un is running up and down this road bare nekkid.' And Mommy she come through that bottom, and I seen her get a switch. I went under the house, and got up in there. She said, 'You come outta there.' I said, 'No, I ain't coming out.' She said, 'You'll come out sooner or later. And when you do, you're gonna get it.' She sent Janette in there. Well, I just laid back there where them old chickens had worked that dirt into powder. And I waited until Janette got up there, and I started throwing dirt. I made thunderhead. She went a-hocking and spitting. It was in her nose and eyes and everywhere, crying. Then she sent Gladys in there, and I gave her a noseful of the same thing. And that just made Mommy even madder. So I stayed under there and it was getting dark. And there was rocks along there where they poured that porch. And I got the idea this was an ideal-looking place for a copperhead. And I eased out of there, went around the house, and went in that front room, got up in that bed and pulled the covers over me and got down just like a lizard. You wouldn't hardly know I was in there. First thing I know, Mommy jerked those covers back and she had a switch. Hit me. I was nekkid. Had nothing to break that lick. I deserved that."

A.P. wasn't entirely unmindful of the hardship his absences visited upon his wife. For a while he put his friend Brown Thomas on retainer to do some of the chores around the house. Brown was the brother-in-law to Sara's great friend Dicey, and he was as odd as a seven-dollar bill. He lived just up the hill from the Carters, in a drafty cabin heated by fires he built in discarded tin drums. Brown did his farm chores in suit clothes, until they nearly fell off of him. He also told the wildest tales in the Valley and expected everybody to believe them. Sometimes he'd say of Sara, whom he insisted on calling Cary, "Cary give you a mattock and ask you to move Clinch Mountain." Truth was, Brown didn't do a lot for Sara. He could split wood and carry knotty pine down off the mountain to get a fire going. But he wasn't good for much else. She didn't want to leave him to baby-sit, for instance, and Brown could not be trusted to drive; modern mechanics overawed him. The first time Brown saw an airplane fly through the Valley, he exclaimed, "Thar's something up thar in the elements."

But as luck would have it, A.P. found Sara somebody else who could help out: his cousin Coy Bays, just returned to the Valley from Kingsport. Coy was a mechanical whiz; he always kept a car running, even if it was just a tied-together heap of metal. A.P. asked his cousin if he would be willing to help out by driving Sara around when he was gone on his song-hunting expeditions. And Coy was happy to help, happy to have something to keep his mind off his own troubles. So it seemed like a blessing all the way around.

It was the hard luck that brought Coy Bays back to Poor Valley in the spring of 1931. He'd left the Valley fifteen years before, at age eleven, when his peripatetic father, A.P.'s uncle Charlie Bays, had moved his entire brood to Kingsport to make his fortune. Uncle Charlie started off with a little barbershop downtown, just two chairs, one for him and one for his oldest son, Dewey. But Charlie hated the trade, so he sold out and bought a sixty-acre farm from the Kingsport Improvement Association. Dewey stayed in town and kept at barbering, but the other children—Coy, Alma, Elva, Stanley, Charmie, and Stella—moved with their parents to the farm, and soon enough into a big story-and-a-half farmhouse with a sleeping loft. The house drove Coy's mother crazy. Mary Bays swept and swept and swept and couldn't keep the sand out. The farm was full of sand and gravel, but Charlie found a way to make even that pay. He had Coy and Stanley scoop load after load of sand into the back of the family pickup and haul it just across the river to sell to the Kingsport Glass Factory.

Charlie made a great success of the farm, raising corn, hay, and hogs for market, and building a stock of fourteen prize dairy cattle. He even picked up a little extra cash letting his Rich Valley moonshiner friend land bootlegging planes at a makeshift airstrip on the farm. In 1925 he went in with Dewey—who now ran his own seven-seater barbershop downtown—on a big whitewashed Tudor-style colonial in

Kingsport's White City. The house had a seven-thousand-dollar price tag, but with Dewey's income from the barbershop and Charlie's from the farm, the payments were a cinch. The house had three stories (counting the attic room), four big bedrooms, papered walls, and hardwood floors throughout. In the basement was a coal furnace, and in the kitchen, an electric icebox. There was room enough for Mary's new mahogany dining-room set and her player piano. The only downside was chemical fumes from the Eastman Kodak plant nearby, but Dewey figured it wasn't any worse than the inside of his own shop, now that it was full of chemicals for the girls who wanted their waves and marcels just so.

By 1927 Dewey's shop had added all the services of a beauty parlor, and he was training his sister Charmie to handle the new clientele. He was making more money than ever, working harder than ever, and playing harder than ever, too. At just twenty-seven, Dewey Bays was something of a swain around downtown Kingsport. He was tall and lean, almost fragile, but he was suave. Dewey could talk a streak, quote near-epic poems from memory, and loved to tell women he was "part Injun," that his great-grandfather Fiddlin' Billy Bays was full of Cherokee blood. Dewey ran with the sort of crowd who honored the scent of halfbreed danger—a fast crowd. When the workday was done, he'd close up shop and race out with his hat tilted rakishly to one side, a flask at his hip. His ragtop roadster was always filled with young adventuresses in short skirts and long pearls, with marceled hair perfectly sculpted down over one cynical eye and a lit cigarette in hand. Dewey and his crowd spent their nights at speakeasies or nightclubs or, when it was warm enough, at the river, where nobody would bother them. A lot of nights Charlie and Mary would sit up at the kitchen table fretting over Dewey and his friends. A siren would start wailing somewhere, and they would be gripped by the vision of the ambulance drivers scraping their boy off the Kingsport pavement. They talked to each other about why Dewey wouldn't settle down, make a home with a nice girl, but there wasn't much they could do. Times had changed, and Charlie and Mary had raised city kids. Besides, they adored Dewey. He was so full of life, so much fun, so generous. How could they deny him his pleasures? He'd bought Mary the player piano, helped pay for Alma's wedding, given Charmie her job at the shop, and now he wanted to pay for music lessons for his youngest sister, Stella.

Still, they knew Dewey was not so dexrous that he kept himself out of trouble altogether. There were plenty of young men around who didn't like Dewey getting too close to their girlfriends or their fiancées or their wives. And if Dewey ever did get in a fight, somebody might snap him in half. That's why Coy set himself up as Dewey's protector. Coy was big and rawboned. Barely twenty, he was six foot three, with outsize features he hadn't fully grown into. He was never menacing, but the size of Coy Bays's hands alone gave one pause, and the bulge beneath his coat suggested to any would-be assailant that Coy's holster was not empty. Dewey always knew he could count on his younger brother; Coy worshiped Dewey. That's why when Dewey started to get scared in 1927, he turned to Coy.

First Dewey got sick, and he couldn't shake it. This wasn't just a day-after malaise but weeks and weeks of heaviness in his chest. When his legs swelled and he could barely walk, he knew he had to see a doctor. But Dewey didn't want to frighten his parents, so he asked Coy to drive him over to a doctor he knew in Virginia. The doctor saw it right away. Dewey had tuberculosis, and it was already advanced.

Once Dewey was diagnosed, Mary started to worry for the entire family. When the county health clinic offered free TB tests, everybody got chest X rays. Then they waited. "We were peeling apples in the kitchen," says Stella Bays. "And I remember the phone rang and my mom answered the phone. They told her that the results were back and that Charmie had TB, and Stanley, too. It was like writing out a death certificate. There was nothing they could do. They did give us hope about going to a sanitarium."

Stanley refused treatment, but Uncle Charlie made arrangements for Dewey and Charmie, who was just sixteen, to go to the Catawba Sanitarium in Salem, Virginia. Even with the state paying half the cost, payments were too high for Charlie to keep up. With Dewey out of work, Charlie knew he couldn't make the medical payments and the house payments, too. So Charlie sold the big Tudor house in White City and moved the family back to the farm, where Coy watched his father turn into a bent, white-haired old man. Charlie sold off his prizewinning dairy cows one by one. And every day he worried over his firstborn son and his daughter Charmie—the most carefree of his children—who sounded so blue in her letters from the sanitarium.

"Dear Dewey," Charlie wrote in a letter just before Christmas of 1930. "You should be very careful and not overdo yourself. You shouldn't be the least bit neglectful for it means a whole lot to get on good ground. I have not sent yours and Charmie's board bill in yet. Times are so hard that I can't ever hardly sell anything for the cash, although corn and hay and hogs is all scarce and will bring me in some money when I can find buyers. So I have got about five hundred dollars worth of corn, hay and hogs that will go a right smart way in taking care of you and Charmie at Catawba. . . . I am thinking of hauling my corn to Bristol. The mills is paying a hundred dollars per bushel. But they won't be but a few bushels at a time. I will close. Will write again soon. From Daddy."

By the spring of 1931, Charlie Bays was out of cash, out of livestock, and out of plans—until Eck Carter stepped in. He told Charlie he'd buy all the materials for a house in Poor Valley, up in the clean mountain air. They could build it on the land Eck owned back behind his own house, way up on Clinch Mountain. They'd make a screened sleeping porch for Dewey and Charmie, where they could see the hillside Eck had planted with apple trees. It would be like their own private sanitarium, with family all around to wait on them. They could come home.

So in June of 1931, Charlie and Mary Bays gave up their Kingsport dream for good and moved back where family and friends were already pitching in to build the house. The patients—Dewey, Stanley, and Charmie—all moved in. Alma was already married, so she stayed behind in Kingsport, and so did Elva, who had a good job at the Kress Department Store. But the youngest daughter, sixteen-year-old Stella, moved to the Valley to help nurse her ailing siblings. And Coy came back, too. He was twenty-six years old in 1931 and could have stayed and made his own life in Kingsport, where he'd grown up, but

Coy was the only healthy young man left in the family. The way he saw it, it was his duty to move back to Clinch Mountain.

People from all over the Valley came to look in on Dewey and Charmie that summer. Bob and Mollie Carter came the most often. Dewey had never been religious, but he wanted Mollie there, praying for him. Bob and Mollie had always been close to Charlie and Mary, and tell the truth, they were happy to see them back. The four could always laugh together. One day sitting at the Bayses' kitchen table, Bob said to Mollie, "If you could make apple butter like Mary's, I'd eat it."

And Mollie said, "Bob, I *brought* the apple butter you're eating."

For the kids, the best was when Eck came to the house. "When Ezra came to visit, it was just like sunshine. It was just like sunshine," says Stella Bays. "He had this little wit about him. He was a joker, a teaser like Coy. And he loved a good time." Every time Eck walked into that house, he brought something for somebody, but he didn't like to be on the sick porch much, with Dewey. Eck had walked to school every day for years with Dewey, but he wasn't comfortable watching his cousin die. So that summer he'd coax out Coy, Stanley, Stella, and even Charmie, and drive them to the river for a picnic and a swim, or he and Coy might spend a little time up on the mountain, at their still. They'd both been around, seen some of the world, and they understood each other. "Eck, if he didn't like you, he didn't like you. And my brother Coy was the same way," says Stella. "If he didn't like you, you knew. He could show it."

Toward the end of June—after returning from Louisville, where the Carters had recorded with Jimmie Rodgers, who was himself visibly wasted by tuberculosis—Sara started making regular visits up the mountain to look in on Dewey and Charmie, and Mary. "Sara would come from down in the Valley," says Stella. "She'd take a near cut right up in front of her house there, and she'd climb the mountain. It was pretty steep. It would take a half hour to climb the mountain, but she always walked up there." Sara never had much to say when she was visiting; Mary liked her quiet, strong presence. She could sit and listen to Mary talk for hours. Sara knew how to let her be sad, never expected false cheeriness, and never affected it. When Charlie and Mary asked, Sara loaned them $320.

That was a hard summer for Mary, who was used to getting her way. But there was nothing she or anybody else could do for her Dewey. Sometimes they'd wheel him into the house through the big French doors so that he could have a bath near the fireplace, away from the breezes, but mostly he was on the porch with Charmie. Charmie was better, and even talked about her hope for a cure, "a lung operation." At the sanitarium she'd got the idea that they could cut out her bad lung, and the disease with it. But out on the porch that summer, Charmie saw a preview of what the doctors said awaited her. By July, Dewey was nothing but skin and bones, barely able to walk out of the house. By August, he was too weak to walk at all and spent all his time in the bed on the porch. When Charmie was at the house, she'd stay in the room with the fireplace, unwilling to watch what was happening on the other side of the French doors. Charlie was too weary to deny the hard truth any longer. "I don't believe we're going to have Dewey with us very long," he blurted out to Stella on a hot August morning. But even as he said it, Charlie bent to his task of milking a cow, unable to look at his daughter. One Sunday that month, for Charlie and Mary, Mount Vernon had its services on the porch, at Dewey's bedside. "I remember Dad sang and asked Dewey if he was a Christian," says Fland Bays's son Vernon. "He asked Dewey if he had accepted Christ in his life. And Dewey said, 'Yes.'"

A few days later, early on the morning of August 20, Elva went out on the porch to look in on her brother and came back into the house, whispering, "Mama, I believe Dewey is dying." When Mary went to the porch, Dewey asked for his aunt Mollie. When Mollie got there and began to pray for him, Dewey said to her what he could not bear to say to his own mother. "Aunt Mollie, I'm ready to go." A few minutes later he was dead.

While Mollie sat and prayed over Dewey's body, Mary reeled out of her house and let out a wail that echoed through the Valley. Two days later, Mollie was at Mary's side as they buried Dewey high on the hill, not far from Mollie s own dead child, at Mount Vernon Cemetery.

In the last days of Dewey's dying, and the first long months of mourning, there was a separate crisis secretly unfolding, one that would rip the Carter/Bays family right down the middle and tear at the bond Mollie and Mary had long sealed. But in the fall of 1931, the family had a powerful need to return to the quiet rhythms of daily life. So even if somebody did see another crisis coming, it was left unspoken—as if silence would render it harmless.

Despite the sadness of Dewey's passing, the event itself had cleared the way for a more normal life. The death siege had taken its toll on Charlie Bays and his family, and they had neither the wherewithal nor the energy to restart life in Kingsport. So they just settled in among family. Coy and Stella, and even sick Stanley and Charmie, lent a buzz of electricity to the Valley. They'd put on their jodhpurs, lace up their riding boots, and go flying down the Valley Road on Harley-Davidson and Indian motorcycles. Or they'd pack a picnic, pile into Coy's old canvas-top Hupmobile, and drive to the river for an all-day swim. When they did that, Eck and Maybelle would join them. "Maybelle was a big sport," says Stella Bays. "She would do anything with the rest of us. She was young, a young mother. And Ezra, he was just as big a kid as the rest of us."

For a while, Eck and Maybelle's house was the gathering place. Eck was gone on his mail train most of the time, and Maybelle still hated to be alone. Besides, she always needed help with the girls. Helen was four, and the new baby, June, was up and walking already. But it wasn't just work. "That was the fun place," remembers Stella, who was sixteen at the time. "Saturday, the young people from the Valley would meet there. Mr. Neal, of Neal's Store, he had sisters; one was Vivian. And he had a nephew by the name of Beverly Neal, a young fellow about my age, and he was there a lot, the Larkey girls, my brothers Coy and Stanley." There'd be music from the Victrola, and dancing, or games in the front yard. Maybelle would even let them play the old kissing game from her childhood across the mountain. "Some of those girls were very popular," says Stella. "The Larkey girls were very popular with the Post Office game.

"One night—Ezra had planted a new piece of lawn out by the side of the house—we decided we were going to play Drop the Handkerchief. It was nighttime and there was no electricity, but I think the moon could shine the brightest I've ever seen there on Clinch Mountain. Well, the next morning Maybelle got up and looked out the window. She said, 'Stella, look out there. Look out there. Eck's gonna kill me.' We had torn up that fresh patch of grass. It was in a circle, and it was like horses had been tramping around it. She'd say, 'Eck's gonna kill me.' And then she'd laugh." She knew Eck would never be bothered by a little damage caused by fun. Whatever it was, it could be fixed.

That was Eck. He never shied at the cost of living high. He'd still burst into the house from his work trips with armfuls of bounty. "Ezra would come back for Christmastime, and he'd always come back with a lot of food," Stella says. "He'd come back with walnuts and grapes and bananas and oranges. Ezra loved to have plenty of food. He loved to have plenty of food in the house all the time."

Sometimes Stella would visit Sara at home; the younger girl wanted to learn to play the autoharp. Just being in Sara's presence made Stella feel stronger, steadier, more of a woman. But Pleasant and Sara's house wasn't like Eck's. It was a bit somber, and a lot less plentiful without the sure and steady income of a federal job such as Eck had. A.P. was making a little change from the three families renting on his farm in Little Valley but still wasn't taking much out of the land for himself. By the end of 1931, the Depression was closing in on them. Record sales were slower than ever: The recording with Jimmie Rodgers had sold only seven thousand copies, a tenth of what they might have sold three years earlier. Royalty checks were next to nothing. People didn't have the spare fifteen cents for Carter Family entertainments, even when Sara did agree to go on the road. The good news was that Ralph Peer wanted them in Atlanta in February of 1932 for another recording session. And he wanted to renew their contract.

The contract Ralph Peer presented A.P. that February was a bit different from the one that was expiring. The new contract was with Ralph Peer, and not Victor, which was now merged with RCA. Peer had bought his way out of Victor and hoped to stake his Southern Music Publishing Company to a chance to make hits where the real money was—in pop music. Besides the money he made on the copyrights for music in Hal Roach motion pictures, Peer's only real income was from the artists he had signed up for Okeh and Victor—his race and hillbilly music. In return for the book value of the Southern Music Publishing, RCA Victor agreed to let him take all the copyrights and all the artists he'd signed up to that point, and not to try to re-sign Peer's artists for five years. So Peer made A.P. Carter this proposition: If the Carter Family would sign an exclusive five-year artist-manager contract, he would up their pay to seventy-five dollars per cut, with a guarantee of four sides a year. But in return, Southern Music would get *all* the publishing royalties from the songs A.P. copyrighted in that time. With RCA Victor precluded from making an offer, the Carter Family was not going to get a better deal. So Pleasant signed the deal, and the trio was back in the recording studio, where they cut eight sides over the next two days.

The eight cuts that came out of that session were right in time with the national mood. Taken together, the theme of the sides was hopeless and irretrievable loss: lost homes, lost parents, lost loves. In fact, young Stella could testify that the session was a lot less a reflection of Eck and Maybelle's swirling home than of A.P. and Sara's tense, somber dwelling. Not one side had the driving rhythm of Maybelle's best guitar playing. Taken as a whole, A.P. sounds more distracted than ever, and Sara flatter. But that doleful, resigned tone and feeling put the Carter Family solidly in sympathy with their Depression-weary audience. The signature song of the session (if not the best) was "Tell Me That You Loved Me," a grave plea from someone leaving a lover.

It is impossible to know when exactly Pleasant Carter understood that loss was bearing down on him. He may have felt the uneasiness come over a room when he entered, and he may have heard the whispers. But Sara

Carter was the kind of beauty around whom swirls all sorts of unsavory and unfounded talk. It's impossible to know exactly when Pleasant realized that the talk was no longer completely unfounded. It's impossible to know exactly when Pleasant understood he had a problem—and that the problem was his own cousin, Coy Bays. "I would say Coy was a show-off," says a niece of Pleasant's. "He and A.P. were totally different. Coy was more of a fancy guy, and he may have turned [Sara's] head. It may have been years ago when she and Uncle Doc weren't getting along."

Coy was almost fifteen years younger than Pleasant, slightly taller, and a bit more stout. He had about the same amount of schooling as Pleasant had had, but the way he told it, the end to his schooldays was a swashbuckler. One day in fourth grade, he simply started from his seat, crawled out a window, and never came back. He had other plans. Coy loved anything that traveled: motorcycles, automobiles, and most of all, airplanes. "Coy was mechanical-minded," says his cousin F.M. Bays. "He was a wizard."

When they were living in Kingsport, Coy and his brother Stanley were always building model airplanes from scratch, with rubber bands and hollowed-out sticks for the skeleton. The things actually flew, though the steering was problematic, and on a few occasions they took out some of Mary's chickens. Later, when Charlie's bootlegger friend's pilot crash-landed on the jury-rigged airstrip at the Bays's Kingsport farm, Coy helped him rebuild the plane, pulling the lightweight strips of canvas over the frame and applying steely-smelling lacquer for stability. In return for his help, the pilot taught Coy to fly the plane.

Flying was perfect for Coy. He loved the quiet above the earth, where nobody could bother him about his drinking or what needed to be done: what needed carrying or loading or rewiring. "Coy could do anything with his hands," says Vernon Bays. "He was not overzealous, perhaps, to do a lot of hard physical labor, but he could do anything with his hands."

Most of what Coy wanted to do involved having fun, or making it—and he kept at that all day long. He was a jokester, a teaser, and a tickler. Unlike most of the men around the Valley, and unlike A.P. Carter, he was naturally an affectionate man. To this day, some in the family speculate it was Coy's gift for showing affection that attracted Sara. Nobody knows exactly what it was that turned her head, but it clearly wasn't something she thought out. The way she said it, it was a feeling she simply couldn't control: "I loved him better than anything I ever set my eyes on," she'd say later. Or, "I fell in love with him the first time I laid eyes on him."

Either Coy and Sara didn't do a very good job of hiding it, or they didn't try. Pleasant was often away hunting songs—Mr. Peer wanted them back in October—so it wasn't hard for Coy and Sara to get time alone together. Sometimes they'd leave and be gone for two and three days at a time. One of the Poor Valley transplants in Richmond, Indiana, tells a story of seeing Coy come riding up to his farm on his Indian motorcycle with Sara on the back. After a while, Pleasant knew, and he was furious. "Actually, it was kind of scary," says Stella Bays. "There were guns carried on both sides. They didn't have any love for one another. It wasn't a family love right there."

There were plenty of stories around the Valley about shooting scrapes. Chester Hensley used to collect them at the local country stores. Mandy Groves's husband, Abraham, had had a famous shootout with the McMurrays. "He said, 'Yeah, old Jerry'—that's the McMurray was shooting at him with a shotgun—'old Jerry was eating us up with that shotgun,'" Hensley says. "They were down at the bottom where they didn't have nothing to get behind and Old Man Abe had a cap-ball rifle up there with him. He said, 'Jerry stuck his old belly out from behind them white walnut trees and I put a rifle bullet through his belly. That brought him out of there.' He did. He shot him right through the stomach with a cap-ball rifle. Jerry got over it, but that hurts, you know. That's bound to hurt. That was over a line fence.

"One woman was a-building a hog lot, and Squire Bill McMurray started pulling up her posts. She split his head open with an ax. That happened back in the early twenties. She died in prison. I remember it quite well. I was small, but I remember it quite well. Her name was Martha McMurray. She'd married Chubb McMurray; that was Bill's brother. She killed her brother-in-law. Over a piece of land that I wouldn't give my pocketknife for."

The ax fell over land, and it fell over love, too. When one Valley woman found out her sister was fooling around with her husband, she hit her sister in the head with an ax. "It didn't kill her," remembers one local, "but it left her in pretty bad shape for the rest of her life."

Bob and Mollie Carter and Charlie and Mary Bays were not going to let anything like that happen in their family. They all decided it was time for Coy to leave town. Charlie dressed it up pretty good. He said he was moving the entire family west where the dry air would be better for Stanley's and Charmie's diseased lungs. He said he had a line on a ranch he could buy in Portales, New Mexico. He said he needed a fresh start away from the Valley. And everybody agreed it was best. Stella was thrilled for the adventure. She picked out Zane Grey novels and started reading about the Old West.

Charlie and Mary auctioned off their big furnishings, including the player piano Dewey had bought for his mother, and her mahogany dining-room set. Maybelle wanted them both, but she was out of town during the time of the auction, so she sent Mollie to bid for her. Mollie had to fight off one of the Bays cousins, but Maybelle got the piano *and* the dining-room set. After the auction—and after Charlie bought a Cadillac limousine from the undertaker in Kingsport—Charlie and Mary had three hundred dollars cash to start a new life in the West.

By the first week in February of 1933, the caravan was ready to go. The Valley road was rutted and iced over, but the Bayses weren't waiting for the sun to come out. Their two cars were full to busting, and so were both of the trailers. The whole family was going, even Alma. (That morning, Alma had shown up—eight months pregnant, with her three-year-old daughter in tow—and announced she was going to California, too. She was leaving her husband in Kingsport and didn't care if she ever saw him again.) Stanley was at the wheel of the Cadillac, and Charmie reclined in the backseat, which was filled with pillows and throws for her comfort. Coy—in his driving cap and goggles—was at the wheel of the Chrysler.

"The Cadillac was a seven-passenger car," Stella says. "Two little seats that let down behind the front seats. It was a family funeral car— lot of room. Coy and Stanley built trailers that were tarped over. And over the wheels of one trailer Coy built a box that Mama carried her pots and pans in. We put our mattresses, quilts, bedding, pillows in one trailer. In the other trailer, Mama had a barrel of flour, she had meal, we had smoked ham with us, bacon. In between the Cadillac and the second trailer we had a cage built, and we took Charmie's goat with us. Charmie drank goat's milk.

"That was a sad day when we took off from Virginia. A very sad day. The day we left there was quite a few people there. My aunt Mollie came over. Maybelle was there with the girls. Oh, they was hugs and they was tears and they was prayers. June was only about three, and even she could remember." In her own book, June described the scene: "Daddy tied the last crate of chickens on the rear bumper of the Cadillac, just before the trailer that hauled the tent, the pots and pans, pillows and blankets. . . . Mommie and Aunt Sylvia cried."

Then the Bayses were gone, disappearing down the Valley road, with the icy Poor Valley mud cracking under their wheels for the final time.

Sara in Rich Valley (Gladys Greiner)

*Opposite: Joe, Janette, and Gladys in front of the homeplace
(Carter Family Museum)*

From a Business Standpoint

Within weeks of Coy's departure, Sara Carter removed herself from Poor Valley and went to live across the mountain, at the only other home she'd ever known. It might have been shame that made her run. It might have been anger at the cabal that enforced her separation from Coy. It surely had something to do with her husband's temper. A.P. was hurt by his wife's affair, and embarrassed. Sara would later swear under oath that he would sometimes tell her to get out of his house and never come back, that he threatened her with physical violence, and that he had, on occasion, acted on those threats.

When Janette looks back at it, she does not dwell on the worst times. The way she sees it, her parents' separation seems nearly preordained. The wonder was that A.P. and Sara lived under the same roof for seventeen years. Both her parents were proud, and stubborn, and A.P. wasn't the only one who had real cause to be jealous. For most of her marriage, Sara fought a mistress that couldn't be faced down and couldn't be satisfied. "The thing that really mattered to Daddy was his music," says Janette. What Janette can't understand is how her mother could have left *her* and Joe and Gladys. Gladys was thirteen years old that winter, Janette was nine, and Joe barely six. In all the years after, their mother never offered the three an apology, or an explanation that sufficed. Sometimes Sara would repeat the plain truth: "I loved [Coy] better than anything I ever laid eyes on." But that was cold comfort to her children. She left them to reckon her decision as best they could. It's a legacy the two survivors struggle with almost seventy years later. "It never was right in a way after they broke up," Janette says, "but they did. They just separated. And it's no fair to put blame on somebody. I couldn't have left my children, but she didn't have no job. She didn't have nowhere to go. She had people back there [in Copper Creek]. She went back over to Uncle Mil and Aunt Nick's."

Sara's return to the Nickelses' farm must have felt like a double homecoming, for it conferred on her once again her orphan status. She'd first come to live with Mil and Nick after her mother died, dropped there with her sister Mae because her father could not raise them. In the winter of 1933, Sara returned to Copper Creek as an exile from the family of her own making, cut off, in no small part, by physical distance. It was less than a dozen miles as the crow flies from Maces Springs to Uncle Mil's cottage, but it was a hard journey. On foot, it began with a steep two-hour walk up Clinch Mountain's loose-rock trails, and when the weather was mildest and the climbing easiest, the trails teemed with copperheads. The down side of Clinch Mountain was more slippery. And even after the traveler had found the flatland, he still had to cross Moccasin Creek and Moccasin Ridge. It could take all the light in a long summer day just to get to Copper Creek. By car, the trip was still long and treacherous, over winding roads that were impassable when Moccasin Creek ran high and fast. Even when it was down, the winding creek had to be forded five separate times. By train, the passenger was dropped at the flag station in Dungannon, which left a good six-mile hike to the Nickelses' farm.

Even so, Pleasant would not withhold the children from Sara. "We'd go back across the mountain," says Joe. "Daddy would take us over sometimes, me and Janette both, for a week." After he dropped them off, Pleasant could head over to a town called Ben Hur, in Pennington Gap, where his friend Mutt Skeens would have new songs, or to Herbert Springs to visit his distant cousin Bobby Bays. Bobby always had new coal-mining songs he'd play for A.P. on his harmonica. In later years, A.P. would take Joe to Ben Hur, and Mutt would teach Joe to play the guitar. But for now, Joe was more than happy to stay with his mom on Copper Creek.

Uncle Mil and Nick always had plenty, and they still kept a jar of candy under the bed—all the kids knew that. Joe would listen to his uncle Mil play the fiddle, or watch him cook down a panful of tree sugar for molasses. Sometimes Joe and his cousin Paul Hartsock walked to the bent in the creek, where they could throw rocks at the biggest bullfrogs he'd ever seen, or watch Uncle Mil gig carp. For a six-year-old boy, Uncle Mil was a fascination. "Mil Nickels was a little old squatty man," says Joe. "Not very tall at all. He'd go up to harness the horses about four o'clock in the morning when he woke up. He'd feed his horses and put the harness on. And if he was feeling good, he could step up and get ahold of them joists in the barn. He'd get the joist from the underneath side, and he'd pull hisself up, and he'd go to hand-walking with his grip. And hand-walk across that barn. He was built in the shoulders but skinny below, so he could handle his weight.

"He had two thumbs on one hand. One that turned up like a sprout on a tree. He could pinch a piece out of you with those two thumbs. Get ahold of you and clamp down with that thing. You think a piece is gonna come out of you. He had a grip like a vise."

Janette's memories of those visits were less about the staying than the leaving. In her own book, *Living with Memories,* she writes of a time when Pleasant dropped her and Joe across the mountain to spend Christmas with Sara. "I can still see Daddy walking away through the fields—alone. My heart broke. I started running, and crying, 'I want to go with you!' So he took my hand, and we spent that Christmas together in Poor Valley."

From the start, Sara's removal threatened more than the emotional well-being of the family; it threatened her husband's dream of continued renown in the music business. Just weeks after Sara left, A.P. informed his wife that Mr. Peer was ready to set dates for a recording session in Camden, New Jersey. Sara said she'd pass on that. Besides, she pointed out, Mr. Ralph Peer still owed them money for songs they recorded the previous year. So she left it to A.P. to tell their personal manager that the recording session was off. On April 15, 1933, A.P. wrote to Peer, explaining the situation as best he could and suggesting that they might have better luck with his estranged wife if Peer agreed to record them near home. "Nobody will go to the expense of sending out a recording expedition," Peer wrote to A.P. on April 25. "Please let me know when you are ready and I will get everything lined up. I expect to get more money for you on this trip, although I think you will come out all right on the last recordings as soon as you are paid for the extra numbers."

But Sara stubbornly refused, and Peer, who counted on income from Carter Family records, asked his wife to get into the fray, woman to woman. In the first week of May 1933, Anita Peer's letter arrived in Copper Creek, betraying a certain amount of desperation. "My dear Sara, . . . Of course, it is really none of my business. . . . I realize it would be distinctly awkward for both you and A.P. to work together again, but on the other hand, the 'Carter Family' has become well known and there is a chance to make some more money, even in these days of depression. Let me know if there is anything I can do. I have been divorced once myself . . . so I can sympathize with you perfectly, and I will be glad of a chance to talk to you and perhaps give you the benefit of my experience. . . . Isn't there some way you can get together and fix up some songs for recording? . . . I'll do anything you suggest to get things organized again. Even if you never live together again you could get together for professional purposes like movie stars do. Practically all of them are divorced or should be."

Anita Peer's letter did get to the heart of the matter: There was still a chance to make money. Sara had no other way. If she could give little else to Gladys, Janette, and Joe, she could give them the benefits of money. So as the June recording date neared, Sara began spending time again in Maces Springs, and the Carter Family fell into their old rhythms. They'd work the fields by day, and gather at Eck and Maybelle's in the evenings to rehearse new songs. But now when the music was done, Pleasant would head back to his house alone. Eck and Maybelle had made room for Sara, and she stayed with them whenever she was in Maces.

The uneasy reuniting did breed hope. Ralph Peer had already sweetened the trip by booking the Carter Family on a live radio show, to be broadcast from RCA's fabulously plush new Radio City Music Hall—in the heart of New York City. Sara and Maybelle went out and bought new blue outfits and fox-fur pieces though the furs caused a panic in young Joe, who was greatly discomfited by the fox eyes. Joe yanked the piece from Sara's neck with such a force that she had to spend the better part of an afternoon mending a rip. The purchase of those new outfits was just a warm-up for the big day of shopping the women had planned. They were going to go to the finest department store in New York City, from whence each would walk out with the most stylish dress and hat on the rack. The two women wanted to take Gladys along, too. They'd celebrate her fourteenth birthday on the trip, and Maybelle would buy Gladys a city dress of her own, in thanks for six years of baby-sitting.

For Gladys, this bounty was due. From the first session in Bristol in 1927, when the little girl had been charged with watching Joe, Gladys had faithfully executed her baby-sitting cuties for both her siblings, as well as Maybelle's daughters, Helen, June, and the new baby, Anita. And when her mother left, Gladys had become—at thirteen—the de facto cook, seamstress, and hand of discipline in her father's house. "I never had a chance to play music," Gladys once said. "I had to feed hogs, milk cows, and wait on young'uns."

So that June, A.P., Sara, Maybelle, and Gladys loaded up the Chevrolet and headed for Camden, New Jersey, where they would make their recordings. The night before the session Sara wrote out on a piece of stationery provided in their room at the Plaza Club Hotel ("Camden's Newest and Largest") a list of the songs they would do. And like the songs themselves, that lineup, written in Sara's flowing hand, is a record of what might have been lost had she not seen the need to keep making music. In a single day, they recorded sixteen songs, including "I

Never Will Marry," "I Loved You Better Than You Knew," and a three-part harmony of the hymn "On the Sea of Galilee." If Sara had any reluctance about continuing the music, it was not discernible on record. She was spectacular that day, ranging up to get the higher notes on "Sea of Galilee" and then performing spirited yodels—which she always hated—on "Home by the Sea" and "When the Roses Come Again." She also performed a song that would so touch Emmylou Harris forty years later that she would record it herself. " 'Gold Watch and Chain,' " says Harris, "God, the first time I heard that song, I mean, I thought about my grandparents and I cried. There are these emotional memories that maybe aren't even yours; they belong to your grandparents and your great-grandparents, and somehow it strikes a familiar chord in you and you just, you know, you respond to it. And I found [the Carters'] music very haunting."

Whether A.P. and Sara's uneasy separation added a feeling to the song that particularly touched Harris is hard to know. But both rancor and tenderness were left unspoken between them in 1933; their emotions joined only in music. On every chorus of the song, A.P. "basses in" in solid support of his estranged wife.

> Oh I'll pawn you my gold watch and chain, love
> And I'll pawn you my gold diamond ring
> I will pawn you this heart in my bosom
> Only say that you'll love me again

That day, they also recorded their first version of what would become a classic, "Will the Circle Be Unbroken."

Once the marathon session was done, they set off for their date at Radio City Music Hall, a cash payment due from Mr. Peer, and a trip to the fanciest department store they could find. But hard luck and a stubborn pride got the better of them. "The car tore up in New Jersey before they were to get paid the next day," Gladys wrote in *I Remember Daddy*. "When it was paid for, it left 35 cents in the whole crowd. It took the dress money and my savings of $5.20 that I'd saved for almost a year. My dear parents and Maybelle would have starved before they'd ask for their money [a day early] and let the Peers know they were flat broke."

A.P. did, however, call Peer about needing new transportation to the city. Mr. Peer sent his chauffeur, installed them in a New York hotel, and messengered over tickets to a Broadway show. But there was still a problem. "They didn't send a bit of food along," Gladys wrote. "The next morning Daddy, Mama and Maybelle walked to a little café on the corner. Coffee was then 5 cents a cup and doughnuts 5 cents each and no tax. That left 5 cents for me to get a doughnut. They knew Mrs. Peer would feed me, as she was going to show me the town while they broadcasted, and the coffee and doughnut would do them until dinner, even though they had no supper the day before. Only these people, whom we were hoping would treat us to a dinner at noon like we eat, had their dinner from nine o'clock to midnight."

Before Anita Peer swept off with Gladys to show her the town, she insisted on taking Sara and Maybelle to the store to help them pick out hats. The Carter women demurred, but Mrs. Peer insisted. After all, there was an hour and a half to kill before the broadcast. "Of course, they went along and tried on the most beautiful hats in the world and had to find faults with them all, as there wasn't a red cent in anybody's pocket," wrote Gladys. "That was a miserable hour for them to pass, and I guess Mrs. Peer thought she would never take them hillbillies on another shopping spree. They left for the radio station, and I was on my own with Mrs. Peer, starved to death, in my first pair of high heels and my feet killing me."

In her chauffeured limousine, Mrs. Peer took Gladys up one side of New York and down another: to the zoo, the *Queen Mary*, Coney Island. "I had all the souvenirs I could carry for myself and the children. I'd have gladly exchanged them all for a bag of popcorn." At around five, the Peer limousine returned to Radio City Music Hall and whisked the entire entourage away for "a drink." Anita Peer had champagne, the Carters lemonade . . . and not a bite of food among them. "They got paid, the goodbyes said, and the chauffeur was to drive us through the big Hudson tunnel and get us on the right road home before dark," Gladys wrote. "Daddy told him to stop at the first hamburger joint across the river. I don't know what he thought of us, the way we ate, but we never told him either."

When asked if the Carters' return to the recording studio gave her and Joe hope that their parents might reconcile, Janette is firm: "I never did think so." And then Joe adds, "No, but if I knew then what I know now, I'da had a heart-to-heart talk with Daddy. I blame him more for not getting back. Mommy waited around a couple of years hoping that they could work things out. Daddy put the Old Testament as a barrier between him and her. And he just wouldn't forgive her. That's the way I see it. I'da told him, 'You're wrong, man! You're leaving the woman that loves you. You're deserting them kids out hunting songs.' Mommy was taking care of us kids, chopping wood, and all that. I'da said it right to his face."

"Your opinion and Daddy's opinion is different, Joe," says Janette. "You looked at it your way, and he looked at it his way, and that's the way it was."

What is so maddening for Joe, to this day, is that he believes his parents' feeling for each other wasn't extinguished. "They still had love for each other, but they were just so contrary, they wouldn't back down," Joe says. "Daddy put the Christianity strong. . . . He'd go back on the old Bible. If he would have just said, 'Well, you've done wrong; I'll forgive that if you forgive me.' . . . but they didn't come after it like that. The longer they was separated, the further apart they got."

The widening gulf most affected the middle child, who was so like her father, sensitive and easy to bruise. When Janette Carter talks of her childhood, she paints vivid, near photographic moments: of waiting for the train in hopes her mother might be on it, or of sicknesses that always fetched her mother. "Her hands were soft," Janette says. "She had a kind of a square hand, short, stubbylike hand. And I know one time, when she'd come to the Valley after they separated, I was sick and my head was a-hurting. She was up at Maybelle's and I was crying, so somebody went up there and told her. And here she comes. She said, 'Sit down there by the bed. Now what do you want?' And I said, 'Mother, would you sing to me?' So she sung—'My Native Home' and 'In the Shadow of Clinch Mountain.' I always loved that song ['Clinch

Mountain']. And I know I kept a-crying and she was wiping the tears away."

Of her father, Janette best remembers those moments when he was simply *there*. "When someone died, somebody would go ring the church bell. You could pretty well hear it up and down the Valley. I guess you could hear it in Little Valley, too. You'd more or less know who it was because this person probably had been sick for a while. They'd have the funeral and the service and carry them out to the graveyard and put the coffin down in the ground. And then they'd start shoveling the dirt before they took the family away. They'd start right there. That just about killed me to hear them clods, and young'uns—when it was their mother and daddy—running around a-screamin' and a-hollerin'. I'd clutch my daddy's hand, because I was glad he was there."

She also remembers the few times her father raised his hand to her, like the time she announced she was tired of dishes and she wasn't washing any more. "Daddy never did whip me but three times, once when Joe and I was fighting—"

And then Joe cuts in: "I got three in *one day*, I can remember. . . . Daddy was always mad when he whipped. You couldn't reason with him. [When Mom left] that made it worse. Aside from that he was easygoing, but he had a lot of pressure. Mother was constantly on his mind."

By 1934 Pleasant Carter was wound tighter than ever. His house was being more or less run by his oldest daughter. "I was just thirteen years old and I didn't know beans about cooking or nothing, and Esley [Riddle] was over at our house part of the time, and he showed me how to make corn bread," Gladys once said. "Grandma and Mommy showed me a little bit, but not much. But Esley, he would help cook some at our house." Not that A.P. could do much for his friend Riddle. Money was becoming scarce. Payouts for the songs the Carters recorded the previous June netted them around three hundred dollars apiece after they'd split it three ways. And copyright royalties on phonograph records, music rolls, and sheet music were no longer a solid hedge against the fierce winds of the Depression. Even with 76,027 records sold in the first quarter of 1934, the Carters' take was only $69.94 apiece. Worse yet, RCA Victor was releasing fewer of the songs they recorded. In the previous session they'd recorded sixteen songs, and barely more than half were released. RCA Victor never even released the original version of "Will the Circle Be Unbroken."

A.P. was still trying to kick up a few extra bucks from entertainments. Sometimes he'd get Mutt Skeens to go along and join in with his dobro or flattop guitar, or he'd get his cousin Kate O'Neill from Norton, but for a lot of dates he'd take his sister Sylvia to fill in for Sara. Aunt Syb was an able stand-in musically, but she proved a less than seasoned road warrior. On one trip, A.P. was barreling down a country road when he heard a yelp from Sylvia and turned to see her hanging off the door, which had swung open over the road when she leaned on it to throw out an ice-cream cone. He slowed the car as fast as he could, but Sylvia let go and all A.P. could see through the haze of dust was his youngest sister rolling like a ball down the gravel road. She walked away from it unhurt, brocaded with road gravel and angry at having lost her wristwatch in a ditch.

With the music money drying up, the family depended even more on what they could raise from the farm. But things hadn't changed much on that account, either. The way Pleasant worked his land, his family was headed right back to poverty. Sometimes he'd take Joe and Janette over to the farm in Little Valley, set them atop boards he'd laid on the harrow, and lead his mules, Kit and Maude, up and down his field. Even his children knew enough to make suggestions—Joe telling him it was too wet to plow; it'd leave nothing but dried clods after the sun came out. But if A.P. did take his son's advice and wait, he was sure to wait too long. "Sure enough it'd get so hard you couldn't stick a pick in it," says Joe. "He always waited. Never had a tobacco bed. He'd get a plat when other people did and he'd always get it out late and then you'd have to cut it green and it wouldn't ever cure out right. He was no farmer at all."

By the time he neared ten, a lot of the work fell to Joe, who was strong for his age but not a natural-born worker. Some days he'd get into epic bouts with Kit that wasted away an entire morning. "Kit would run my legs off [when I was] trying to catch her," Joe says. "A hundred and some acres. She'd run three hours and then she'd finally give up.

I'd finally get on her back, mad as anything. I'd say, 'You've run me all over this pasture; now I'm gonna get you.' I'd have a nail and poke it in her backbone, and she'd reach back and snap at me, trying to bite me, run me up against a fence trying to rub me off.

"In Little Valley one time, Daddy had one mule and he was wanting to do something that day that needed two mules, so he told me to go to Uncle Ermine's and get that mule of his, ole Roadie. I went out there and Ermine was gone, so I turned around and went back home. I told him, 'Ermine's gone and Aunt Ora said he'd be gone awhile. I can't catch Roadie.' Daddy got mad. He said, 'Why can't you catch her?' I said, 'Nobody catches her but Ermine. You touch her ears and she'll kick you.' He said, 'Give me that bridle. I'll catch that feather-headed mule.' "

"A.P. came out and said, 'I want Roadie,' " remembers Ermine's daughter Fern. "Daddy wasn't home. And Mama said, 'Now, Doc, you can't catch Roadie. Nobody can catch him but Buck. She called Daddy 'Buck.' He would not listen. He went up to the pasture field, and Joe was helping him corral it in a corner."

"Roadie had her head across the fence and Sue was there, too, standing in a V, and one was as bad as the other for kicking," says Joe. "And he walked up behind her—'Whoa, Roadie, whooooa'—up her back, talking to her, patting her on the back, up the mane on the neck. Her head raised up, ears went straight up, and eyes walling. And me telling him, 'Daddy, you better back out of there.' Before you could snap your fingers, Roadie wheeled and kicked him with both feet. Right in there on his belt. And he went down. Had the breath knocked out of him. I was there chewing my tongue. I knew he'd kill me if he'd a-heard me. Biting my tongue 'til blood was coming out of it to keep from laughing, and him laying there a-grunting."

"He laid there and moaned," says Fern. "Joe would say, 'Are you hurt, Daddy?' Giggle. 'Are you hurt, Daddy?' Giggle. Uncle A.P. went to the house and went to bed and stayed there for the rest of the day."

Looked at in a certain Poor Valley–Methodist way, the entirety of A.P. Carter's travails could be seen as the Lord's will, a humbling from on high. God didn't favor those who strove too keenly for worldly success and fame. (A.P. had to look no further than Jimmie Rodgers, who had risen higher and faster than any of Peer's recording artists. The Blue Yodeler was dead and gone, struck down by TB while recording in New York in May of 1933.) Even A.P.'s children suffered. A Carter sister-in-law remembers a time when one of Pleasant's children went to Neal's Store to buy food on credit, and Mr. Neal refused them because they were too much in his debt. Around that time, A.P. and Sara were even forced to put up their house and their farm as security on a five-hundred-dollar loan.

Still, Pleasant Carter jealously tended the field of his dreams. Peer had set another recording date for May of 1934, and A.P. was working up new songs. Without Sara around, it was harder than ever. "Daddy would write music in the house," says Joe. "He'd get the beat and start writing. He never used the guitar much to write, but it had to be quiet. He'd do it right in the living room. And he'd get upset when Janette and I were fighting. He was always telling us to be quiet." There were the times, though, when A.P. found his own nagging problems an inspiration. Once, he woke Gladys in the middle of the night so that she could hold a lamp over him while he wrote out the words to a song he called "It'll Aggravate Your Soul." It was one of the songs that A.P. wrote entirely from scratch, and at the recording session in Camden on May 8, 1934, he performed it as a tremulous solo. He did have the powerful good sense to change some of the salient autobiographical details, but it was a long-awaited answer to Sara's lament for the "Married Girl."

> *She wants a new coat and a hobbled skirt*
> *And you can't get in for the young'uns and dirt*
> *And when she gets out, oh, how she'll flirt*
> *It'll aggravate your soul*

> *Now, young men, take a warning from me*
> *Don't take no girl to Tennessee*
> *For if you get married and don't agree*
> *It'll aggravate your soul*

It's another bracing set, that spring 1934 session. Pleasant was still hunting hard, but songs were coming in over the transom all the time now. People from all over the country sent the Carters sheet music, poems that could be turned to music, or little snatches of lyrics. A.P.'s house was filling up with them, and Sara's trunk in Copper Creek also. The June 1934 session—as much as any—bespeaks the variegated musical fruit dropping from the trees: hymns from both black and white churches, cowboy songs, country blues, English story songs, remade parlor songs.

Even with sales so slow, Peer wasn't about to give up on the Carters. He had them back in the studio a second time that year, and this time they cut a remarkable twenty songs in a single day. One was a song Pleasant had written with the help of Riddle, the surprisingly hopeful "March Winds Goin' to Blow My Blues All Away." But it would be six years before the Carters recorded for RCA Victor again.

For nearly five years, Ralph Peer had been in a death struggle with a RCA Victor executive named Eli Oberstein, and the Carters found themselves caught in the middle. In the eight years Peer had directed the de facto division of hillbilly and race records for RCA Victor, he had essentially eaten up the competition. Even after he bought back Southern Music Publishing from RCA Victor in 1932, he continued to work for the company as he always had, scouting the talent, coordinating the recording sessions, making final selects for pressing, and promoting them as best he could. As RCA Victor went, so went Southern Music. Peer had hired Oberstein away from Okeh and set him up as a salesman in the field who could get southern distributors excited about RCA Victor's new catalogs. But right from the start, Peer was sure Oberstein coveted his job, and he was sure it was Oberstein who started rumors that Peer was padding his expense reports and pocketing huge sums of money. All of that Peer could have lived with, if Oberstein hadn't approached A.P. Carter with the idea of dumping his exclusive contract with Ralph Peer and signing a separate recording contract with RCA Victor.

Had he played it with subtlety, or cunning, A.P. surely could have gotten a nice new set of contracts with both RCA Victor and Peer—one that didn't give Peer *all* the publishing royalties from new copyrights. And one that was more in line with the sums RCA Victor paid its pop artists. It wasn't that Pleasant Carter was entirely without guile, but he had a strong sense of loyalty. Ralph Peer had given them their start; without him, their success would have been impossible. Besides, A.P. had signed Peer's contract; he wasn't going to weasel out of the deal. So no matter how many times Oberstein pointed to the inequities in Peer's business scheme, or to the money the Carters could be making, A.P. would not betray Peer. And when he told Peer about Oberstein's approach, that more or less tore it with Ralph and Eli.

Ralph Peer walked away from RCA Victor, giving over the hillbilly and race operation to Oberstein, but not before he signed the Carters to a recording contract with a new conglomerate called American Recording Company (ARC). He set the first ARC sessions for May of 1935, and Oberstein fired off a desperate letter that March to try to persuade A.P. to stay with RCA Victor. "[Peer] is naturally trying to keep things for himself and get all he can. . . . I offered to get together with Mr. Peer but as usual he wants everything and would like to give you people little or nothing. . . . The point he is angry about is that we want to give you copyright royalties and he wants those for himself with a very small portion to you. . . ." Of course it was more or less true. Peer *needed* the money. He was struggling mightily to set up Southern Music as a player in the pop music–publishing industry. And in spite of a hit with the Hoagy Carmichael/Johnny Mercer song "Lazy Bones," Peer was swimming upstream. His library of hillbilly and race songs was all that kept him afloat. "It was the worst year we'd ever had in the music business," Peer said. "I remember talking to [established publisher] Sol Bourne. We had lunch together. He said, 'Ralph, I'm going to get out of this business. We just can't do a thing with it.' He was ready to give up completely. And he had Irving Berlin!"

As tight as money was at the Pleasant Carter homeplace, he was not going to forsake Ralph Peer. Sara and Maybelle were less sanguine about their personal manager. Sara had already begun questioning the royalty statements. Even then, she and Maybelle knew the score. "Mr. Peer made us famous," they both used to say, "and we made him rich."

In fact, the move to ARC immediately put more cash in their pockets. The Carters recorded forty sides for their new record company over four days in May of 1935. At Peer's rate of seventy-five dollars per side, A.P., Sara, and Maybelle walked away with a thousand dollars apiece for that session. And the session itself was like cherry picking. Besides new sides, ARC wanted the Carters to re-record their tried-and-true hits. The Carters did new versions of "Keep on the Sunny Side," "River of Jordan," "Single Girl, Married Girl," "Wildwood Flower," "My Clinch Mountain Home," "Little Darlin' Pal of Mine," and "I'm Thinking Tonight of My Blue Eyes," among others.

The middle years of the 1930s were A.P.'s most prolific as a song-writer. Without Sara in the house, he had to keep vigilant watch on both the children and the farming. Consequently, his song-hunting trips were less frequent, and A.P. was thrown back on himself. Woody Guthrie used to say he could write only about what he saw; Pleasant Carter was writing about what he felt. One of his most fascinating songs of that period was a retooling of the Blind Lemon Jefferson song "See That My Grave Is Kept Clean." In the Blind Lemon song, the singer's heart stops, his hands get cold, a coffin lid slams shut, a church bell rings, and two white horses cart the dead singer to the graveyard. There is a haunt-ing plea from inside the coffin, for one kind favor: that his grave be kept clean. But the request evaporates, like the peal of the church bell, into thin air. There is no family in attendance, no friend. The departed is absolutely alone.

Despite his marital woes, and maybe because of them, A.P. Carter's version of the song "Sad and Lonesome Day" leans on the bond of fam-ily. In A.P.'s rendition, the song becomes the story of a mother's funeral, with mourners in attendance. "They carried my mother to the burying ground, / And watched the pallbearers let her down."

In 1935 the Carters also re-recorded the unreleased "Will the Circle Be Unbroken," another mother's funeral song A.P. had rewritten. For a melody, the Carters used a tune similar to the one they'd used on the gospel number "Sunshine in the Shadows." It was a melody familiar to a lot of folks outside the Carters' main audience. The tune was summoned, for instance, by the hallelujah shouters of The Elders McIntorsh and Ed-wards Sanctified Singers—of the Church of God in Christ, Chicago's hotbed of black Pentecostalism—for their 1928 recording "Since I Laid

My Burden Down." The Carters' version of "Circle," when finally released, was their big seller of 1935, and it would go on to be one of their best-known and best-loved songs of all time.

Throughout the mid-thirties, Sara's absence remained a daily hardship and an artistic spur. Much of what A.P. wrote in those years was about love and abandonment, and the records themselves sometimes sound like the uncomfortable release of feelings he had always found too hard to talk about with Sara. There was the romantic hopefulness of "My Virginia Rose Is Blooming," the sweet sadness of "Lover's Lane," the bitterness of "Dark-Haired True Lover," and the menacing jealousy of "Gathering Flowers on the Hillside."

Sara was writing material for those same recording sessions, such as the sad lament "Farewell, Nellie."

Fly across the ocean, birdie
Fly across the deep blue sea
Take this message to my darling
She'll be glad to hear from me

When the whippoorwills are singing
Across the dark and lonely sea
When you're thinking of ten thousand
Will you sometimes think of me?

By 1936 Sara Carter was just a few years shy of forty and more alone than ever. When she was at Copper Creek, she had nothing but time on her hands. She'd work around the house, maybe work up a song or two, but sometimes she just had to get out and go. "She was still living with Uncle Mil and Aunt Nick; she stayed down there a long time," says Daphne Stapleton. "She'd sing and play for you, you know. She came to our house one time and played for us. We lived in a little house down in the hollow, and she was real friendly to everybody. She was by herself. Back then, people walked for miles by theirselves. You didn't have to invite people. They'd just come to the house. She was just passing by and just stopped."

For more than three years, Sara had been cut off from the day-to-day lives of her children. Gladys was getting serious with a boy named Milan Millard. Janette was winning scholarship ribbons. Joe was learning to play the guitar. When Sara did go to Poor Valley, she'd spend time with them at the homeplace, but she stayed overnight with Eck and Maybelle, who were now akin to royalty in that valley. Eck and Maybelle had a house filed with stuff, including Mary Bays's mahogany dining-room set and piano. Their three little girls—Helen, June, and Anita—were like princesses, always with new outfits, and a full set of schoolbooks, bought *new*. They were, people said, the prettiest girls in the Valley. In fact, people said it all the time, until one day, Sara couldn't stand it anymore. "Your children might be pretty," she said to Maybelle, "but mine are a lot healthier-looking."

Whenever Sara came back to Poor Valley, she made it a point to bring presents for Gladys and Janette and Joe, and also for the cousins who didn't have as much as Maybelle's girls. Once when Sara came across the mountain, she brought her niece Lois a dark blue silk dress with a sleeveless leopard jacket. It took Lois's breath away; it was the finest thing she'd ever owned. Sara Carter's gifts, like her person, were growing more exquisite.

In the years Sara spent away from her family, her bearing had become more regal than ever. She made it a point to look perfect always, as if she didn't want her children to remember her any other way. To some of her nieces she might well have been the Queen of Sheba. Fern Carter was fixated on Sara's hands. They were not like the hands of her mother or the country women Fern knew. In the late thirties, Sara's hands were soft-looking. She wore rings and bright red nail polish. One day when Sara was visiting Fern's parents, the little girl sat and stared at Sara's hands, desperate to touch them. 'I wanted to see if they felt as pretty as they looked," she says.

That was how Sara seemed to so many people now: untouchable, remote. She wore her self-containment as a shield; she wasn't going to let anybody get close enough to see her hurt. She was beginning to think the business with Coy Bays had been a colossal mistake. When Coy had first gone west he sent her letters, and Sara could track his movements through New Mexico and Arizona and up into California. Sara wrote him faithfully, until she realized that his letters had stopped. First it was a week, then a month, then months, and no word from Coy. News came that his sister Charmie had died at a TB sanitarium in northern California. And then his brother Stanley passed. And what of Coy? Was he stricken with consumption now, too? Or had he found somebody else to love? Sara had no way of knowing.

Meanwhile, attempts to reconcile with her ex-husband went nowhere. There were times when A.P. was cold, and times when his anger still flared. In the first week of June 1936, one of Sara's sister's daughters overheard him talking to Sara: "He said that just as soon as he got back from making records that he was going to get his divorce and that he was going to bring him in a woman. He said that he already had her picked out."

Sara finally gave up on any chance of putting the marriage back together. On September 3, 1936, she went to Gate City to see a lawyer named L. H. Bond and told him she wanted a divorce. Bond wrote to A.P. and told him Sara's wishes and that A.P. could probably sue for divorce. He certainly had grounds. But A.P. wrote back that he would never ask for a divorce, and that he would fight any suit Sara might bring. Two weeks later, the Scott County Sheriff's Office served the papers. A.P. Carter was to appear at the circuit court the following Monday "to answer a bill in Chancery in our said court against him by Sara E. Carter." This was not what A.P. wanted, and he sat down and wrote Ralph Peer to ask his help. Peer passed on that. As long as the Carters kept recording, the exclusive artist-manager relationship did not extend into domestic quicksand. Peer wasn't wading in there for double the royalties. "[A.P.] apparently wanted me to exert some pressure upon you," Peer wrote to Sara, "but I told him that this was a matter which people had to settle for themselves and something in which I did not want to interfere." He did, however, wish to add his two cents on one count: "From a business standpoint," he wrote, "it is important that the Carter Family should not be too badly broken up."

When Sara's divorce complaint did reach the judge, A.P. did not fight it, but neither did he acknowledge it. As the October 15, 1936, divorce decree stated, "the defendant has failed to demur to, plead to, or answer said bill," and Judge E. T. Carter ruled that "said marriage be, and the same hereby is, dissolved and annulled. The court doth further adjudge, order, and decree that the custody of the children . . . be awarded to A.P. Carter, with whom they shall remain but the said Sarah [*sic*] E. Carter shall be permitted to see and visit the said children at seasonable times and intervals."

"When A.P. and Sara divorced, I can remember Ma Carter going up and down that valley to check on them kids," said Maybelle's daughter Helen. "You know, she'd walk a mile, back and forth. I'm sure it broke her heart."

In a separate filing at the Gate City courthouse that same week, A.P. Carter agreed to pay Sara $1,200 for a farm she had bought in the Little Valley. The document laid out a plan of payment: Half of A.P.'s portion of the royalty payments were to go directly to Sara, until the $1,200 (plus interest) was paid in full. All transactions regarding the marital split, in fact, were rendered in coolly precise, matter-of-fact language. No document betrayed a hint of emotion or loss or pain. In an odd way, the land agreement temporarily bound A.P. and Sara closer than ever, professionally. The more recording they did, the greater the royalty payments. The greater the royalty payments, the faster A.P. could pay off his debt to Sara.

By the time of the divorce, the Carters had a new recording company. Peer had set them up with Decca, whose management wanted lots of material, and wanted to license it to the Montgomery Ward catalog. In separate recording sessions in 1936 and 1937, the Carters cut a total of nearly sixty songs for their new label. Even after the divorce was official, the Carters could still knock them out. In the June 1937 session there was a flat-out upbeat song called "Funny When You Feel That Way," and the classic "Hello Stranger," sung as split solos by Sara and Maybelle. In fact, some said it was the best-sounding work they'd ever done.

The 1937 session was a great relief to Ralph Peer; his greatest hope for the family had been delivered. The Carter Family was not too badly broken up . . . from a business standpoint.

Ezra "Eck" Carter, also known as Pop (Carter Family Museum)

Opposite: Maybelle with Helen, Anita, and June (Lorrie Davis Bennett)

Stuff

I t was a point of pride among the Carters that they rarely had to do more than one take of any song, even under the most difficult conditions, like, for instance, recording twenty songs in a single day. This distinction owed in part to the Carters' diligence in preparation, but by the mid-thirties, Maybelle understood the other factor at play: Mr. Peer and his engineers simply weren't that particular. They took every song the Carter Family offered, even when Maybelle would try to point out the flaws. "This song don't make no sense," she'd say. "The words aren't working right." But Mr. Peer always said it would make no difference to their fans; people would get the gist of the story. That was bad enough, but what really galled her was when she'd make a mistake on her guitar and they would tell her not to worry. It was fine.

Maybelle knew what was fine, better than they did. She was never too loud about it, but she would gently prod Peer to let them do another take. Maybelle could make it difficult to say no. She wasn't a pleader, but she had a way of looking at people with her striking pale blue eyes—the "tragic look," her daughters called it—that made a person turn back on himself. That look registered such disappointment—*in you.* So sometimes Mr. Peer would relent to another take, but more often he would try to joke his way through, tell her it was okay to make a mistake because it made the record sound "authentic." Or he'd tell her people would listen closer, maybe listen over and over to see if they made the same mistake again. Maybelle might smile and move on, but her performance was no joke to her. Even thirty years later she was still grousing, though she always softened her most pointed jibes with a little chuckle. "Maybe I'd persuade them to do it over," she told Ed Kahn in 1963. "Then they'd put out the one with the mistake on it. They were certain to do that."

A.P. got the women out of the house, into the recording studio, and onto the stage, but from the beginning Maybelle was the most musically adventurous. Maybelle was a natural musician; she heard a tune and she could just do it, even if it meant playing in an entirely different way. Most of her earliest melodies were tunes she'd heard her grandmother or her mother play on an old five-string banjo or what her uncle played on banjo or what the local fiddlers played. Many melodies were generations old. Often as not, Maybelle didn't even have a name for them. "Sometimes I didn't know what I was playing," she said. "Just songs I'd always heard."

But from the day the Carters began recording in earnest, Maybelle sought out new tunes and new ways of playing them. When A.P. brought Lesley Riddle around to the rehearsals, Maybelle sat and listened to him play for hours, picking out blues licks she could use. If she was going to play the lead (and rhythm) on one of his blues songs, she would do it right. When the songs got too fast for her bare fingers, she would use a flat pick. She learned that from watching her brother Duke. More than her band mates, Maybelle had a feel for the compact between audience and performer. She understood they owed their fans *variety.* "She took the guitar and she used it in a way that nobody had thought of before, and not just the thumb lead, but listen to this," says John McEuen of the Nitty Gritty Dirt Band, picking up a guitar and playing one of her descending licks. "Like on a guitar lick. Nobody had done that before. And, you know, like ['You Are My Flower']. That lick. Hear how that string rings [on 'I'm Thinking Tonight of My Blue Eyes']. People don't usually think of playing an F chord with that A note ringing. Just like she'd play a C chord with a low E note. She was trying to get every note she could outta that thing! So it's pretty cool how that happened—playing up high sometimes."

Maybelle was always watching for something new, and her ears were always open. Sometimes, after Carter Family entertainments, Maybelle would hang around the schoolhouse stage. A.P. and Sara were quick to leave, but if she could, Maybelle might stay for hours, jamming with the local musicians, picking up a new trick here and there. And by the time she started branching out, phonograph records and radio had made it possible for Maybelle to hear about any kind of music she wanted. She took what she could. "Anything to get a little something different," she once said.

As early as 1928 she was playing steel and slide guitar on "Little Darlin' Pal of Mine" and "When the World's on Fire." Maybelle had picked up the Hawaiian style listening to Vernon Dalhart's version of "The Wreck of Old 97," a hit record in 1924 featuring the backing of guitarist Palakiko Ferreira (aka Frank Ferera), a Honolulu native whose early recordings had popularized the style on the mainland. "She played in three or four different styles, and she listened to the contemporary music of the day and incorporated some of the ideas into her music," says the musician and musicologist Mike Seeger, who knew Maybelle and played with her in the sixties. "She heard people playing Hawaiian music in the late twenties, and she said she really liked that, and then she started playing some of those slidey recordings. What she did is she put a little thing under the nut of the guitar, that's the fretted end, to raise up the strings, and then she played it with a Hawaiian bar."

At one early recording session, Maybelle forgot her slide, so she borrowed a bottle of Sara's Blue Waltz perfume, which proved a less than ideal improvisation. In the middle of the song there was a crash of glass, and a shriek from Maybelle: "Law, Sary, I broke your perfume." But they laughed about it, wondering how many days it would take to clear the studio of the overpowering fragrance of Blue Waltz.

In the studio, or stage, at home, Maybelle seemed always imperturbable, but Sara and A.P.'s jangly relationship had put her in a difficult spot. She had long been witness to the sharpest edges of her in-laws' existence together. In the worst times, Sara would retreat to Maybelle's house. So Maybelle was one of the first to know of Sara's affair with Coy—a secret she kept, and would always keep. In rehearsals, in recording sessions, on the road, it was Maybelle who had to steady the uneasy balance between A.P. and Sara. Maybelle kept the peace because she didn't take sides. Nor did she turn the "tragic look" on either of them by way of judgment. When the two separated, she and Eck also opened their home as the best option for rehearsals. Their house had a big coal furnace that kept it warm on winter nights, and it provided neutral ground for A.P. and Sara.

Despite the growing size of their family—by 1933, they had three daughters—Eck and Maybelle's house could be made quiet, partly because A.P. struck such fear in the girls. He'd walk in and say, "Well, it's okay for you girls to go out and play now," and the girls knew it was time to skedaddle. Serious business was about to take place.

But when A.P. and Sara were no longer working in tandem at keeping a home and career, A.P. had trouble producing the number of songs Mr. Peer required. In 1935 he wrote a song called "The Fate of Dewey Lee," about the man who killed Dewey and was shipped off to the pen in Richmond. It was based on a true story and ended with his own timeless verse: "Money won't hire a lawyer, / When you stand before your God." But after they recorded it and shipped it out into the world, A.P. came to regret the pain it might have caused the Lees. "Somebody gave him a poem about it, and he wrote it," says Janette. "But he used to say, 'He's still got people living. I shouldn't have done that.'" Once A.P.'s production started to slow, Maybelle began to pick up the slack. She suggested "Little Black Train" and "Sweet Heaven in My View," which were old hymns she'd heard sung at Holiness revivals years before. She even began to work up songs on her own. Her method was like musical quilting, a patch here and a patch there, stitched by a practiced hand. She'd find a poem she liked, rework it, and put a tune to it. "There's No One Like Mother to Me," which the Carters recorded for Decca in June of 1936, was almost word for word from a poem Maybelle cut out of a magazine. So was "You Are My Flower," recorded two years later. But "You Are My Flower" was another subtle but surprising turn; she gave the song the styling of a Mexican cantina tune.

She got the idea for the melody from the radio. Among the stations Maybelle was dialing in were the big blasters that originated just across the border from Texas. By planting their transmission towers in Mexico, the American-owned stations circumvented the U.S. law that limited a station's power to local range. By the mid-thirties, XERA, XELO, and XEG could be heard from the tip of Texas up into Canada, from one coast to the other, and every evening in Maces Springs, Virginia. "I used to love to hear Mexican music," said Maybelle, "and I started messing around with it and came up with that tune [for 'You Are My Flower']."

One thing Maybelle had going for her was the steadfast support of her husband, Eck. In fact, Eck was a lot more excited about the music business than his wife. Maybelle didn't lack for confidence where music was concerned. "Mama always knew she could play anything she wanted to," her daughter Anita once said. "It never crossed her mind that there was a stringed instrument she couldn't play." But it was Eck who first understood how far those talents could take them both. Eck may have caviled at A.P.'s notion of taking his wife off to Bristol to audition in 1927, but when he started seeing those Carter Family records being sold in towns up and down the railroad line, Eck became his wife's biggest promoter. It was Eck who replaced Maybelle's little Stella guitar with a new Gibson L-5 archtop from a music store in Kingsport. The Gibson cost $275, a fortune in 1929, but Eck saw it for what it was: an investment in their future. "Daddy had the vision," his oldest daughter, Helen, said. "He's the one who got Mother out of [the Valley], and us. We'd never have done anything had it not been for Daddy."

Like his older brother Pleasant, Eck Carter could never be still. And like Pleasant, Eck was not naturally communicative but seemed to be always engaged in his own private dialogue. In a way, Eck had it worse. Where A.P.'s constant milc tremor was a kind of release for his nervous energy, Eck's energy was like an electrical storm trapped inside him. Where Pleasant was deliberate, almost plodding, Eck sought release in speed.

Where Pleasant was content to walk the railroad tracks in quiet contemplation, Eck Carter lived for the locomotion of throttled fire. Trains, automobiles, motorcycles—anything with a combustion engine, Eck rode. Eck's idea of a great time was to fill his Packard full of children—his own and others—drive over to Highway 58 where the road was paved, and race at full speed around the curves and hills until the car literally flew up off the pavement. He kept one eye on the road and one eye on the rearview mirror so that he could watch the little bodies bouncing around the backseat like cans of peas. Occasionally he would put his daughter June on the back of his motorcycle and race all the way to Bristol or Kingsport. In Kingsport, he and June might even take a joyride in some barnstormer's airplane. Then Eck would talk the pilot into flying low along the Valley Road so he and June could shout and wave to Maybelle as they flew by. Eck got a kick out of scaring his wife, and he knew she didn't scare easy.

Eck was different from A.P. in another way. He was ferociously competitive, with a streak of meanness. When Eck insulted somebody, he could cut deep. What he competed for above all else was notoriety. When he was growing up, Poor Valley was full of cocky young men who measured themselves against one another. Life in the Valley was a physical endeavor, and the first measure of a man was physical strength. Tests were likely to include drinking and fighting. One local boy gained fame by successfully wrestling a circus orangutan. "Give him the fifty dollars before he kills my monkey!" was the way everybody quoted the animal's distraught handler when they told the story. From that day until his death, the young Poor Valley champion was known as "Monk," in honor of his great triumph.

Still, with so many young men, and so little chance to shine, talk sometimes got ahead of ability. "Willie Gardner, for instance, was a smart-ass," says Chester Hensley. "He could do more than anybody else. He could drink more whiskey. He could fight better than anybody else. Anything that come up, he was the best. Once some fellows went over [to the Jetts', who had a legal still] to get them some whiskey. Willie told Mr. Jett, said, 'I'll drink a pint of the strongest stuff you've got here if you'll give it to me.' Mr. Jett kindly grinned and got a tin cup out—

now, they held a full pint. Filled that full of whiskey. Willie drunk it straight down, stood right up there about thirty minutes, and fell just like a beef that'd been shot. He was laying there the next morning, yet.

"Then there was the time Lindsay Bright raised a racket. He thought he was smart; thought he was tough. He was up there in Bristol about half drunk and raised a fight with a fellow right on the street there. And that fellow hit him and knocked him plumb through one of them glass windows [into a store]. And I asked Lindsay once, 'What'd you do then?' So Lindsay said, 'He come in there and we tried to fight again.' I said, 'How come you didn't?' He said, 'They held us . . . but I wasn't hard to hold.' "

While Eck was more than happy to take a drink, he never made a contest out of it. And he sure didn't go in for fighting. Eck preferred a battle with less fleeting rewards; he measured himself by his stuff. From flatware to phonographs, automobiles to produce, appliances to clothes, Eck wanted to have the first, the most, the best. He wanted to be known throughout the Valley as the man with the finest. With his job as a railway mail clerk—steady pay, government-issue firearm—he was. And he jealously defended his position. The truth is, A.P.'s first success kind of galled Eck. "Ezra was a little bit jealous," says his niece. "He didn't like other people in the family to have money."

But when A.P.'s family life began to fall apart, and the Depression cut into his music money, Ezra was ascendant again. He was still making good money on the railroad; the U.S. Treasury check came every month, and it cleared, too. Everybody in the Valley knew where Eck stood; they didn't have to look any farther than his home. He'd bought a little cottage from Beecher Hartsock, and he immediately began making improvements. He had plenty of help. When Maybelle's father's old hollow-sounding lungs gave up to pneumonia, she'd invited her younger brothers, Bug and Toobe, to come and stay with her and Eck. A year later Maybelle's sister died, and her boys, Ford and Jack, were invited in, too. Eck found plenty for them to do. The house was surrounded by blue spruce and pine trees, but he added a big early-blooming magnolia tree out back, and ringed the front with boxwood bushes. Behind the bushes, Eck and the boys built a wraparound, three-sided porch, and they added a top floor. Then he dammed the little creek that ran beside the house, rigged up a waterwheel, and ran a generator off it so that his was the first and only house in the Valley with electric lights. When he was done, there were nine glorious, good-size, well-lighted rooms. They were filled, of course, with stuff, and with people, and Eck kept the entire household hopping, literally. When he decided he had to have a basement to hold a coal furnace, he ran into a giant piece of ledge right underneath the house. He read up on it and figured the fastest, most efficient way to crater out a basement was . . . dynamite. "Every once in a while he'd yell, 'Everybody out of the house!' " said his daughter Anita. "Boom! You had to move pretty fast."

The entire enterprise of "Life with Eck" should have driven Maybelle right around the bend, but she had perfected a kind of down-home Zen. The crazier Eck got, the more placid Maybelle became. The more Eck teased her, the less attention she paid to him. Before their third daughter was born in March of 1933, Eck kept telling Maybelle he was going to name her Ina, after the schoolteacher he'd almost married. For a while, the birth seemed no laughing matter. The baby was so big, and Maybelle's labor so difficult, that they had to call on Doc Meade, who came racing down the Valley Road from Mendota to help Mollie Carter oversee the delivery. Eck and Maybelle's little girls, Helen and June, were sent away from the hushed house to stay with the neighbors. Nobody was sure Maybelle was going to survive the birth. After it was over, and Eck was allowed in, he found his wife nearly bloodless, her normally rosy complexion paled to the color of white chalk, her lips shading to blue. Eck dutifully sat by her side until she regained herself, but once it was clear she was okay, he picked up his rotund baby girl, put her in a U.S. Mail pouch, and carried her to Neal's Store. "How much will you give me for this?" Eck yelled as he put her on the scales, where she weighed in at an astonishing ten and a half pounds.

Then, sure enough, Eck named her Ina Anita Carter. But his wife got the last word; one look from Maybelle was all it took—nobody *ever* called that girl anything but Anita. That included Eck. It was poetic justice—or flat-out payback—that Anita Carter proved a thorn in her daddy's side from the beginning. She was rambunctious, athletic, and

contrary. "Daddy was just really nervous," said Anita. "And I was not
very quiet when I was young. Daddy's mind was clicking so much that
sometimes he just couldn't stand the noise. When he would come home,
we'd have to be very quiet. He'd work three days, I think, and then he
was off four. And I made the most noise. Mom said I never went
through the house walking. I went through doing cartwheels and hand-
stands and all of that. That's how I traveled. Wherever I was going,
that's how I went. I imagine that was hard on someone who was nervous. He just couldn't stand the noise. And I was the noise."

Sometimes, when he was driven most crazy, he'd fix a look on Anita.
"You can't be mine," he'd tell her. "You've got to belong to Brown
Thomas." But Eck knew when he was beat. After a while he didn't even
try to stay in the house. He made himself a lair in the top of the smokehouse
across the creek, and when he'd come off the rails, he spent most of his time
there. "Eck was shy," says his sister-in-law Theda Carter. "He just didn't
talk much. Whenever there was company [which was pretty much always],
Eck would make an appearance, say hello, then he'd be gone."

Eck's smokehouse space had all sorts of advantages. It was quiet, it
was off limits to the girls, it was his. Down below, he made a little wood-
working shop where he stored his collection of exotic wood until his
friend Garn Larkey could carve it into new furniture. Up above, he
made a replica of the slot-box in his railway mail car, so he could practice sorting, keep himself sharp for the proficiency tests the government
was always throwing at him. Or he could read his science books and
magazines without disruption. Maybe best of all, the smokehouse was a
place where he could have a quiet drink of whiskey from his mountain
still without being bothered about it. But given Eck's prodigious ener-
gies, his whiskey nights were not always safe, like when he'd get a load
on and fire up his grist mill. "Once he couldn't get it shut down, and it
was hotter than a two-dollar pistol," says a niece who was a teenager at
the time. "He lifted me up there high enough to turn it off. It was a wonder I didn't get burned."

Eck tried to keep his drinking confined to when Maybelle was on
the road, but as his girls got older, Eck found himself sandwiched, gen-
erationally speaking. The women in his family were too numerous and

too observant. "I found it—right behind the toilet—as big as life—a dirty old bottle of liquor hidden in the bushes," June wrote in *Among My Klediments*. " 'Daddy, Daddy, somebody left a terrible bottle of whiskey behind our toilet. Daddy, I have it here with me.' He ran to me. I'm sure he was trying to figure a way to save his precious bottle and its contents. But just as he reached me, I sailed that thing out over the waterwheel and it broke into a thousand pieces. He never said a word to me, just hung his head and walked slowly toward the shop, with me trailing along, hollering, 'Who do you think that terrible person could have been, Daddy? Who could have been so bad to bring that horrible old liquor and hide it behind the toilet? You'd whip him, wouldn't you, Daddy? I know you would. You'd give it to him hard.' "

The women around Eck meant to save him from his wicked ways, and they were sure they had the Lord on their side. "Ma Carter would take me to church with her, and this was before Daddy was converted and we weren't going to church as such, you know," said Helen, "but Grandma dragged me out to church and I sat up there with her, and I can remember her praying for Daddy and his brothers, you know, that were considered being sinners at that time."

"It was really Grandma Carter who put an end to his drinking," wrote June. "Daddy would sometimes go into the mountains and stay all afternoon. I remember him out late one night with Uncle Grant—both in their panama hats—and Daddy's red eyes gave him away. It was then I realized that the terrible bottle I'd heaved away with great gusto had been his. Soon after that, Grandma Carter fixed Daddy good. She went into the mountains one day and came out pulling a big copper kettle hooked over the end of a stick, dragging it downhill all the way, calling, 'Ezra, Ezra, come here, Ezra. I've found the dandiest copper kettle for making apple butter.' She neglected to mention all the copper tubing that went with the rest of that still. But Daddy's still days were over, and we had dandy apple butter that winter."

Maybelle's ways, of course, were subtler. In the push-pull tug-of-war for Eck's soul, Maybelle was the gentle pull. She wasn't one to chide or lecture. But she had a way of making Eck understand what was expected, without actually saying it. He'd watch her take the girls to Mount Vernon

Methodist Church, or dress them up and hand them off to Ma and Pa Carter and Aunt Sylvia for the trip up the hill to the church.

He had to hear Maybelle's cries of joy when one of her daughters was saved and announced her intent to be baptized. "My heart is so happy!" she'd shout through the house. But until deep into the 1930s, Ezra avoided Mount Vernon like the plague. He refused to cross its threshold because, among other things, it was a noisy place for a nervous man. "We had preachers who were called to preach, from the community," June remembers. "Neither one of those had ever learned to read, but when they were saved, they could read the Bible. They would preach hellfire and damnation. There would be shouting in the church; there were women in the church who shouted 'Praise the Lord!' and 'I'll see You, Jesus!' They would praise God and their hat would sometimes fall off the back of their head, and the only thing that would hold it on would be a little hat pin. And that little hat would flump up and down. People would come to the mourners' bench and get on their knees and grieve and ask God to forgive them until this conviction they had on their hearts was lifted. And when God lifted that, it was as though the top came off that church, and the whole church would be shouting and singing!"

It must have sounded like an army of Anitas to poor nervous Eck. Even so, he began moving toward the church, literally. On Sundays, he'd follow the congregation up the hill to Mount Vernon but stand outside underneath a window, listening to services. "Once Eck went to church revival when there was snow on the ground," remembers Ruby Parker. "And he crawled under the church and laid there listening to the sermon, but he would not come in." All of a sudden, one Sunday, Ezra Carter entered the church, accepted Christ, and was baptized. And he had made Maybelle's heart truly happy.

Of course, Eck being Eck, he went about religion in his way. To begin with, he started reading up on it. Along with his books about science and electricity and aviation, Eck began adding to his library religious tracts from the publishing house in Dayton, Tennessee. But despite his born-again status, he was still the same old Eck: nervous, busy, prideful, and competitive. (In fact, he quickly collected the *most* religious books in the Valley.) He was also, as always, generous in his way. As the Depression settled deeper and deeper in the Valley, Eck's father, Bob Carter, intensified his prayers. "I can remember Grandpa Carter putting his walking stick in the air and standing up and praying," said Helen. "During the Depression he'd pray for all the poor people, pray for better times." Eck was still not comfortable in that raucous church, and even when he was there, he was too shy to start making speeches before God or any man. But he was like a one-man New Deal in the Valley; what money he had was on the circuit. He ran his grist mill on Saturdays, grinding corn for anybody who needed it, and for the neediest, he forgave them the 10 percent toll he usually took. And he was always inventing new work, and new ways to pay wages to the hard-luck Valley men who had little more than a small tobacco crop and an occasional government handout that many refused to take.

Eck had plenty of ideas about work to be done, and he had money to pay workers. He'd hire some local men to haul river rock up through the gap to wall off his new basement and undergird the house, or rent extra land and send a platoon of young men out to work the fields. He even tried to conduct a little agriculture on his land way on top of the mountain. Of course, there was almost no way to get there. So he bought himself a bulldozer, and his crew scraped out a new road—which turned out to be such a triumph that Eck could drive his new Packard all the way to the top. The farm itself was less successful. In fact, at first it was less a farm than a forest. Eck's crew had to start by clearing a field. The way his nephew Ford McConnell remembered it, they were literally pitching timbers off the side of the mountain until they finally got a workable plot and planted acres of beans. "We didn't take a single bean," Ford said of the adventure. "I guess it was too dry up there. . . . But we didn't know beans about beans."

Ezra didn't have extra beans that year, but he did have a bulldozer, which he put to use clearing his front yard of rock and ledge. And when he was done with his yard, well, he still had a bulldozer. "Then he went around and moved the neighbors' yards around, getting the rocks up out of their yards," said Anita Carter. "He just couldn't stand rocks." All the while, Eck was keeping the Valley in coin, and he was an equal-opportunity employer. "There were men who were known in the Valley as chicken thieves," says Vernon Bays. "And he took them because nobody else would hire them. Eck was the most generous-hearted man I've ever known."

But for Eck's grandest plan, he needed all the manpower he could get. He was always fretting over his feeble creek-driven power plant. "Just about every big rain that came, that dam would go out," Maybelle once told her friend Dixie Hall, "and I remember one day we were in Bristol and my husband says, 'Oh, we've got to get home; my dam's fixin' to go out, and we're up here in Bristol.' Well, we took off like mad, trying to beat that storm home. I think he just hit the high places [on the road], and I was scared to death down those crooked roads. When we got there, sure enough, it had washed out, clean to the bottom of the hill, and we had no lights."

"Every time it rained, the lights would get real dim," says June, "and he'd cuss that thing and he'd say, 'I've got to have a bigger power plant.' Well, he dammed up the blamed Holston River." Now, the nearest spot on the Holston was across the Knob, and well over a mile from Eck's front door. But he was undeterred.

"My father owned a sixty-acre farm we referred to as the 'River Farm,'" says Fland Bays's son Vernon, "and Eck went down there and put in a turbine wheel under the water."

"He paid Dad twenty-five dollars for the rights to put that turbine wheel in there," says F.M. Bays Jr.

Once the wheel was secured to the bottom of the Holston, Eck's crew had to sink big twenty-foot-high electrical poles along the entire route from the turbine engine back to his house, then string the electrical cable. But with help, he got it done. "Ezra was going to furnish electricity to himself and us," says Vernon. "He put in a transformer and ran lines to his house. He was coming to our home with a line when the Appalachian Power Company, of Bristol, bought him out."

Eck drove a hard bargain with the power company, a bargain as singular as Eck, and just as odd. "When the power company came through, Dad told them he wanted all the appliances from the World's Fair in Chicago—what was that, 1933?" said Anita Carter. "He said, 'I want all the electrical appliances that were displayed at the World's Fair. And they said, 'Oh, we can get you some of those.' He said, 'You don't understand. I don't want [replicas]. I want the ones that were *at* the World's Fair.' And he got them. I don't remember not having a dishwasher."

"Eck come over here one day and he told my dad, 'I've got some extra poles,'" says Clyde Gardner. "'I'm going to sell it out to the TVA. Haul those poles up there, and we'll put the line in and it won't cost you nothing.' We hauled them up with horses. That's how we got electricity."

It wasn't so hard for Eck to be generous. It was as if bad times never even scratched Ezra Carter. The Depression didn't set him or his family back a bit; in fact, it had the effect of separating them further from their neighbors. They just weren't like everybody else. Some Sundays after church, Eck put Bach or Beethoven or Mozart on his phonograph and piped it out into the Valley over the big ballyhoo speakers he'd attached to the front porch. Even without indoor plumbing, Eck Carter's home was the finest spread in all Maces Springs. His daughters were the best-dressed, best-scrubbed, best-fed girls in all the Valley. Once a week the light-bread truck came to Neal's, and Maybelle would press two nickels into June's hand—one for bread and one for salad dressing—and ship her off to the store. To Janette, every meal at Eck's house looked like Sunday dinner. Maybelle always had young women in her house to help with the cooking and cleaning and baby-sitting. Ruby Parker was around quite a bit, and Ruth Hensley practically lived there, doing household chores for a dollar a day.

For her part, Maybelle could concentrate on the sweeter things in life, such as music, or learning to ride a motorcycle, or dessert. She'd make homemade candy—chocolate fudge and Seafoam, a confection of boiled syrup and egg whites that practically floated above the table. In the kitchen, as in the recording studio, Maybelle was particular. "She was always telling her help what to do," says Ruby Parker, "showing us how to do things properly." So even when Maybelle had to be away recording or performing, things were done just so, and meals didn't suffer . . . unless maybe Ezra decided he'd cook, which he effected by making a heaping broth of every vegetable, meat, and marrow substance he could find in the kitchen. "Sons-a-bitchin' Stew," he called it, though rarely in front of Maybelle. *"Now, Daddy!"*

By 1938 Eck's daughters were like royalty in the Valley. Helen, June, and Anita knew no lack in their own lives, except what they saw around them. When they got new school clothes every year, their cousins might get their hand-me-downs. But none of the cousins seemed to be bothered. In fact, when June's cousin and best buddy, Fern Carter, got a secondhand coat from her one winter (Fern's dad gave June a nickel for it), Fern was thrilled. "I was living in the Little Valley and walking a mile and a half to Maces Springs School every day. So that coat came in handy." Some of the cousins might also have to stay back a year in school so that they could start with a younger sibling and share a set of textbooks. Who could afford two new sets? Well, Ezra Carter could. And in the fall of 1938, things were only getting better for his family.

The radio job came out of nowhere, but Eck was all for it. An adman in Chicago named Harry O'Neill made the offer. His client, the Consolidated Royal Chemical Corporation, would buy time on the biggest border radio station of them all, near Del Rio, Texas, and the Carter Family would do two shows a day, for six months. They'd be paid seventy-five dollars a week, *each*, with six months of paid vacation. For appearing on XERA, O'Neill was guaranteeing almost four thousand dollars a year, per person. Eck was still riding the mail rails, and Helen and June were in school, but the opportunity was too good to pass up. So they started making arrangements. Maybelle's mother and Eck's sister Sylvia agreed to move into the house to take care of the older girls, while Anita, who was just five, could go to Texas with A.P., Sara, and Maybelle. By October of 1938, the Carter Family and little Anita had arrived in Del Rio, Texas, and were met at the city limits by a welcome sign that reflected the spirit of Val Verde County's first great law-giver, the renowned Judge Roy Bean: YOU'RE IN GOD'S COUNTRY, SO DON'T DRIVE LIKE HELL THROUGH IT.

Soon after, the Carters were invited to the home of XERA's founding owner, Doctor John Romulus Brinkley. For worldly goods and hired hands, this man put Eck in the shade. The renovation of the Brinkley estate was so grand that its completion had transformed plain old Hudson Street into Del Rio's own "boulevard," for what else could the dustiest Texan call a thoroughfare lined with palm trees, an ornamental iron fence, and a row of five-globe lights that burned through the night? The day of their visit, the Carters drove onto the sixteen-acre grounds through a big arched gate that held the sign DOCTOR BRINKLEY. From the circular drive, the Carters could see Doctor's flourishing greenhouse ("Just a Little Bit of Heaven," he called it); his two fountains shooting thirty-foot-high sprays of water (at night the sprays were illumined with colored lights, all controlled by a single General Electric switchboard in the front hallway of the house); and his prize statuary: a marble copy of *Three Graces* and a bronze reproduction of *Romulus and Remus*. Doctor had forked over more than two thousand dollars for the bronze alone. And he delighted in telling visitors how he'd commissioned it while on his European tour of 1937. The statues were the work of Italian masters, he said, Chirazzi and Frilli (late of Florence and Naples). Even in Doctor's uninflected and mangled pronunciation, the *sound* of the sculptors' names alone was jaw-dropping impressive. Behind the main house were a tennis court and a swimming pool. The pool had state-of-the-art underwater lighting, a ten-foot-high diving tower, and was surrounded by palm trees, evergreen shrubbery, and a dozen Italian cypress trees. Doctor had successfully transplanted the palms in the Texas desert by burying four-hundred-pound blocks of ice at the roots. Inside the greenery, the pool was ringed by a ten-foot-wide tiled walkway. Doctor had kept a team of a dozen tilers busy on the property for months. The year before the Carters arrived in Texas, Doctor had nearly two dozen people on the payroll at the mansion alone—cooks, gardeners, tilers, masons, laborers. A chauffeur looked after a fleet of cars, the jewel of which was his sixteen-cylinder fire-red Cadillac limousine, with a "Brinkley" hood ornament and *JRB* scrolled into each polished stainless-steel hubcap. Then there was the staff at the radio stations and hospitals, his yacht crew, complete with a chef and a wireless operator, and the pilot for the Lockheed Orion monoplane, which rested comfortably inside the Brinkley Hangar at his airfield outside town.

Inside the house, the Carters could see Doctor's collection of Italian mirrors, Swiss grandfather clocks. There were chairs from the Holy Land, Persian rugs, a six-hundred-year-old Chinese tapestry, a Reuter electric pipe organ. In his vivid and seminal biography of Brinkley, Gerald Carson described the living room thus: "From a single vantage point a visitor could see six photographs of Doctor Brinkley, including the top eye-catcher of them all, illuminated with the soft glow of its own indirect lighting. It was five feet tall, hand-colored, showing Doctor full figure in his naval uniform, with gorgeous epaulets, the tunic laced with gold braid, bicorne hat and ceremonial sword " There was also a photograph of Doctor in a more modest uniform of the sea, in front of a gaggle of admirers, keeping a proprietary grip on the back fin of a 788-pound fish that hung limp beside his yacht. He claimed that this catch was a North American record, eclipsing the mark of western writer and adventurer Zane Grey. Two Octobers previous, he had paid Kricklers Studio fifty-eight dollars for enlarging and hand-coloring the photograph, which he referred to as *Tuna Fish and Self.*

Had Eck been there, he might have done cartwheels amid such splendor. Here were rooms paneled floor to ceiling in bird's-eye maple, and others in oak; cedar closets big as a bedroom; a dining-room set carved out of Panama cedar. There was a Holy Bible, bound in wood, with the inscription "Bought by me in Bethlehem." But it was the systems of the house that would have awed Eck. There was a furnace the size of his entire basement, a gas-fired Sunbeam made by the Fox Furnace Company. The unit didn't just heat the house in winter; it also blew cold air through the very same set of ducts, providing a cooling system equal to the hottest day of a Texas summer.

Five-year-old Anita would never forget that day, for nothing she'd seen—not even the huge Galápagos sea turtles out by the Brinkley fountains—had prepared her for Doctor's actual person. Nothing had prepared her for the small, goateed, bespectacled man, led ever so slightly by his round paunch, dressed in a tailored three-piece suit, with his numerous diamonds asparkle even in the soft glow of his indirect lighting, as he descended his grand marble winding staircase. "He came down the stairs and he had a monkey on his shoulder," she remembered, "with its tail around his neck. I certainly had never seen anything like that."

"I met Doctor Brinkley once when I was down in Del Rio," Joe Carter says. "You could tell he was upper crust."

Tuna Fish and Self—*Doctor Brinkley with a prize catch* (*Whitehead Memorial Museum*)

Opposite: Coy and Sara in Texas (Carter Family Museum)

XERA

Like his person, Brinkley's radio station was a dramatic presence. XERA was a five-hundred-thousand-watt powerhouse unlike any radio station that came before it, and unlike any that has come since. For the Carter family, that station would be a metaphysical being like unto God, part natural phenomenon, part celestial; power, providence, and fate all rolled into one. XERA was a giant pinwheel whistling in the Texas desert; by sheer centripetal force, the station would suck in the entire family, but as that force diminished, the Carters were released into a set of separate hurtling trajectories that—for good and ill—none would escape for the rest of their days. That transformation owes much to John Romulus Brinkley, for station XERA would never have existed without his singular capacities.

Doctor Brinkley was an American success story suited to his times. When the Carters met him, Brinkley was not only fabulously rich but as famous as a movie star. He had overcome humble beginnings—a lack of breeding, of inheritance, of formal medical education—to become one of the nation's most successful businessmen and best-known surgeons. "For a poor boy, up from barefeet in Jackson County, North Carolina," Brinkley liked to say, "this, dog me, is something." Even at the pinnacle of his career, while insisting on being called Doctor, Brinkley never forgot where he came from. And he didn't want anybody else to forget, either. Brinkley was a champion of the common people, he said, and it was only in *their* service that he flourished. Dr. Brinkley was a man of the people in the same generously accommodating mold of the other "Great Commoner" of the day, Louisiana's Huey Long. Long was once taken to task by the Louisiana legislature over his extravagant spending at New York City's finest restaurants, nightclubs, and brothels. At a hearing, he calmly explained to Louisiana legislators that he wasn't spending the taxpayers' money for himself. He'd visited New York once before, he told them, as a poor country hick, and was happy enough staying at the YMCA and eating in cheap diners. But on this trip, said the governor, he had been representing the people of the great state of Louisiana. "And the people of Louisiana," he said, "deserved the finest."

Now, Doctor could get right in behind that line of reasoning. Here was a man, like Brinkley, who had had to overcome great obstacles and face down countless small-minded persecutors. And when Long was shot dead in 1936 in the marbled lobby of the grand Louisiana statehouse he built, Doctor must have been ever more confirmed in the wisdom of having commissioned a bulletproof vest, and in his decision to keep Pinkerton guards on the payroll at upward of two thousand dollars a month—for protection and other, more creative services. No, men whose rise engendered so much jealous rage among the ruling class—a class of people Brinkley likened to the Philistines—could not be too careful.

The rise of John Romulus Brinkley from dirt-poor farm boy to the lofty heights of professional attainment was almost too fantastic to be believed and would likely have been impossible, except that Doctor's path to fame and fortune was mercifully free from the bothersome snags of human conscience. In 1918 Brinkley was a country doctor living in

Milford, Kansas, and it was beginning to look like the $150 and the six weeks of grueling study under the watchful but untrained eyes of the faculty of Kansas City's Eclectic School of Medicine was not such a great investment after all. Even with the medical degree from that storied institution, a passable understanding of human anatomy, and an impressive facility for tossing Latin terms into casual conversation, the thirty-two-year-old Dr. Brinkley was foundering. *Until,* as he always told the story, a local farmer came in to see him about having lost "the pep" in his marriage. Together, the two men cooked up the idea of grafting goat glands onto the farmer's own testicles. A year later, the farmer's wife delivered a healthy baby boy, whom the couple christened "Billy."

At first, the medical success was a local phenomenon, with nearby farmers quietly looking for the "kick" the Brinkley operation promised. But Doctor had big eyes even then. He trotted out young Billy in a publicity campaign and caught the eye of *Los Angeles Times* publisher Harry Chandler, himself in need of a little tune-up. In 1923 Chandler invited Brinkley to California and was so thrilled with his post-op revivification that he began suggesting the surgery to his prominent friends. When Doctor left California (with the state medical board fast on his heels), he took with him forty thousand dollars in fees and an idea that would prove even more profitable. While Brinkley was in Los Angeles, Chandler had shown him around his new radio station, and the Kansan decided that this radio business was another ripe idea.

Back home in Milford, Doctor erected a sturdy brick studio on the grounds of his hospital, and next to that studio a one-hundred-foot-high steel antenna. In September of 1923, after receiving a broadcast license from the Federal Radio Commission, Dr. Brinkley's KFKB ("Kansas First, Kansas Best") went on the air. With a ready mike just a few short steps from his office, Doctor could tout his newly christened Kansas General Research Hospital, with its splendid operating theater; its seven-thousand-dollar, electrically operated, high pressure–steam sterilizing machine; and its highly advanced Victor X-ray equipment, whose cleverly designed "Bucky Diaphragm," eliminated shadows from the photographs. But much of the programming was Doctor's frank talks about the ravaging physical and psychological consequences of male impotence: "Observe the rooster and the capon. The rooster will fight and work for his flock. He stands guard over them, protects them, but the capon eats the food the hens scratch up. He will even set on their eggs."

The radio-doctor business was a cinch, and Brinkley was soon fetching patients from all over Kansas—Lenexa, Cherryvale, Wakeeny, Parsons. Grant Eden, of Osawatamie, took a week off from his caretaker duties at the John Brown State Park to get fixed up. Pretty soon it wasn't just Kansans. Men were coming from as far away as Cherokee, Oklahoma; Columbus, Nebraska; Corsicana, Texas; Denver, Colorado. They'd arrive on the Union Pacific spur line from Junction City, met by the Brinkley hospital bus—"the machine"—which sped them to the front door of the hospital. There they were met by Doctor's wife, Minnie, who would say in a reassuring voice, "Here come my men." Besides acting as official greeter, Minnie was also a handy assistant in the operating room, where she worked as anesthetist, side by side with recent Eclectic graduates Brinkley had hired to keep up with the stream of patients his radio program produced.

Behind the hospital was a pen full of four- to six-week-old goats, for each week Doctor received a new shipment of Toggenburgs from a goat and bee man down in Gilbert, Arkansas. Doctor preferred Toggenburg glands because his early experiments with those of Angoras had left a couple of men with an odor that gave pause to even the most ardent and intrepid lady friends. If a Brinkley patient so desired, he could go out back and pick his match from the herd. Occasionally a patient alighted from the train in Junction City, cradling his own goat in his arms. No matter, the cost was the same: $750 per operation. Payable in advance. Doctor did not suffer deadbeats. He was a man of the people, after all, and he wasn't going to let his other patients incur the costs of those who skipped out on a bill.

As performed by Brinkley and his staff, the operation was breathtakingly simple. It could be done under local anesthesia, in just fifteen minutes. "I took and cut a hole in the man's testicle," Doctor once explained, "and took a chunk out and filled the hole up in the testicle with the goat gland." Despite specific promises in the hospital's literature, Doctor and his doctors didn't waste t me connecting arteries and nerves. But how hearts must have leapt when patients were wheeled into the operating forum and saw the agents of their rejuvenation, the tiny dried pellets resting on beds of soft cotton on a gleaming stainless steel tray. For seventy-seven-year-old Nebraskan A. B. Pierce, the surgery was something of a mystery, but he claimed results nonetheless. "I suppose a goat gland is a good deal like a potato," Pierce once said. "You can cut a potato all in pieces and plant it and every eye will grow. I suppose it's the same with goat glands. Just so you get a little piece in you, it will give you a kick, all right."

Doctor was constantly wowed by the results; he was sure he was making real scientific breakthroughs in that knotty thicket of medicine, urology, and most especially in the treatment of the male prostate, that "troublesome *cuckle*-burr . . . that robber gland," he called it. "I began to take out half to an inch of the vas deferens " he wrote. "It seems to me the more of the vas I removed, the better results I obtained so later I resected the vas to the globus minor to the epididymis and ligated there with linen. Also injected the vas with 5 to 10 cc of a 2-percent mercurochrome solution, lavaging the vesicle." After the "compound operation," proper hormone balance was restored, Brinkley said, and the patient was the immediate recipient of any number of unexpected side benefits. Reports of unforeseen benefits always increased at prize time, as when Doctor offered a free Oldsmobile for the post-op patient who wrote the most stirring essay completing this thought: "I consider Dr. Brinkley the world's foremost prostate specialist because. . . ." Brinkley patients claimed the fifteen-minute surgery had cured them of back pain, chest pain, hydrocele, diabetes, Bright's disease, and varicose veins. Doctor also claimed he had successfully treated dementia praecox. "My second case of insanity was a young bank clerk brought to me from a State Institution," he wrote in one paper. "Following gland transplantation, his mind cleared completely and he is now head of a large banking institution."

With KFKB (the "Sunshine Station in the Heart of the Nation") running full steam fifteen and a half hours a day, news of these myriad successes didn't have to be hidden away from the people, limited to the stuffy journals of medicine. With a microphone right at the hospital, Doctor Brinkley could sandwich his talks in between Bob Larkan and His Music Makers, agricultural commodities price reports, French-language instruction, the *Shut-In Program for Invalids*, and Roy Faulkner "the Lonesome Cowboy." He'd spend an entire half hour reading letters from his reinvigorated patients. Not only could Brinkley trumpet the great—and always greater—benefits of his gland operation, he could also give fair warning to the consequences of delaying treatment: "Many untimely graves have been filled with people who put off until tomorrow what they should have done today."

Doctor plied the airwaves with the honey-voiced concern of a healer and the canny nerve of an entrepreneur. In 1928 he instituted the fabulously popular half-hour segment *Medical Question Box*. Listeners would write Doctor, detailing their various and vague ailments, and Doctor would answer with stunningly specific instructions, to wit: "Here's one from Tillie. . . . My advice to you is to use Women's Tonic Number Fifty, Sixty-seven, and Sixty-one. This combination will do for you what you desire if any combination will, after three months' persistent use." And it wasn't only Tillie but other women listening in who, by gosh, were suffering the same symptoms. They'd need the same tonics, which could be purchased at the nearest druggist's carrying Brinkley medicine, which was shipped to the pharmacy directly from Milford. For drugstore owners in reach of the Sunshine Station, a quandary ensued: Doctor's pricey medicines were little more than castor oil or diluted syrup of pepsin, bottled, corked, colored, and numbered. But Brinkley traffic meant as much as a hundred dollars a day in new drug business, and few businessmen were willing to forgo the markup on that much product.

So by 1930 Brinkley was more successful than ever, his hospital bigger, his Milford Goats baseball team more stylishly uniformed, his bank accounts bulging. He'd bought his first airplane, his first limousine, his first yacht. He'd even managed to trump his Eclectic degree with a writ of diploma from Italy's Royal University of Pavia; he received the sheepskin after a lavish banquet in honor of the faculty. Doctor paid for the entire affair—the consommé frappé à l'Imperatrice, the Vol au Vent à la Toulousaine, Flaus de egumes à la Financière, the Glacé à la Napolitaine, the bottles of silky Italian Bardolinos and Barolos, the Piper Heidsiek champagne. He also paid a handsome fee to a local chamber orchestra, which augmented these gustatory delights with the soft strains of Mendelssohn, Puccini, and Irving Berlin. And all this was as pennies compared to the generous donation Doctor visited upon the Royal University's College of Medicine.

But 1930 is also when Brinkley started to draw real fire, on multiple fronts. The Federal Radio Commission began an investigation into just how exactly KFKB served the "public interest," angling hard to rescind the station's broadcast privileges The *Kansas City Star* ran an investigative series on Doctor Brinkley's background, education, moral fitness, and surgical methods. The *Star* reporter found him wanting on all counts. The American Medical Association's *Journal of American Medicine* began a campaign against Doctor's "blatant quackery," and in April of 1930, the Kansas Medical Society made an impassioned plea to the State Board of Medical Registration and Examination to revoke Brinkley's license to practice.

At the medical board hearing that July, Dr. Brinkley produced a parade of satisfied customers so long that the presiding judge called a halt to oral testimony, finally agreeing to receive into the record written statements from five hundred other healthy affiants. Unfortunately, by then, Doctor Brinkley's character and reputation had been badly wounded. Leading urologists in the field testified that the operation Brinkley performed was, at best, worthless. "Where Brinkley said he borrowed a nerve and hitched into the new gland to give it kick, [Kansas University School of Medicine professor] Dr. [T. G.] Orr said that was absolutely impossible because the nerve he described was not there at all," reported the *Star*, "and even if it was it could not be diverted to that use." Brinkley's defense was not much helped by his own expert witness, a former Eclectic instructor who had no formal medical training, signed his own diploma, and touted a cancer remedy that turned out to be a concoction of alcohol, sugar, glycerine, licorice, burdock root, senna, and water. A slew of anti-Brinkley witnesses told grisly tales of being sent home with nasty open scrotal or abdominal incisions, which led to painful, oozing local infections, and sometimes to blood poisoning. One decidedly unsatisfied customer testified that a Brinkley doctor instructed him to affix a rubber boot heel to the festering incision to act as a drain. This was all damaging enough, but the evidentiary capper was a stack of death certificates numbering forty-two. Each of the departed men had expired as a direct result of their short stay at Brinkley's hospital, though Doctor pointed out in his own defense that it wasn't the surgery that killed these men but infection. That September, the medical board revoked Brinkley's license to practice in the state of Kansas, finding Doctor guilty of "gross immorality and unprofessional conduct."

A man of less sturdy constitution might have folded up his tents and left the state altogether. Brinkley decided to run for governor. Just seven weeks before the 1930 election, he threw his hat in the ring. Candidate J. R. Brinkley took to the airwaves daily, promising free textbooks, free medical clinics, a lake in every county, a tax cut, and, for the poor Kansas dirt farmers, increased rainfall. Flying his private airplane from campaign stop to campaign stop, Doctor offered political succor to the forgotten rural masses. Through the beginning of October, political pros in both major parties ignored Brinkley's "sideshow." The political neophyte had entered after the ballots were already printed, so he'd be a write-in candidate, they pointed out. Maybe he'd poll thirty thousand, not bad for a man without an organization.

But Brinkley didn't need organization; he had radio. He was on it six or seven hours a day, playing to the sympathy of all those forgotten people who didn't think much of big-city newspapers such as the *Kansas City Star* and "that Topeka crowd." Among his supporters, Brinkley's best-loved campaign slogan was "Let's pasture the goats on the statehouse lawn." As November neared, party pros began to take notice of the profusion of Brinkley bumper stickers, of the thousands of pencils inscribed with "J. R. Brinkley," of the question most heard on Main Street: "Votin' for Brinkley?" The election pros revised their predictions for the Brinkley vote up to seventy-five thousand but said it was still no threat.

Just days before the election, Brinkley's plane appeared in the sky over a Wichita wheat field, circling the biggest crowd ever assembled for a Kansas political rally. Once on the ground, Brinkley told the gathering he wasn't there for politicking at all. It was Sunday, and he told the Easter story instead, reminding them of this: "The men in power wanted to do away with Jesus before the common people woke up," Brinkley said. "Are you awake?" On election day, Democratic candidate Harry Woodring polled 217,171 to squeak by Republican Frank Haucke by 257 votes. Best estimates are that John Romulus Brinkley got about 230,000 votes, but with so many write-ins disqualified for improper spellings, his officially recorded total was 183,278. By the power of write-ins, Brinkley had also carried three counties in Oklahoma, proving what Doctor knew better than anybody: Radio knows no borders.

Just three months later, KFKB signed off the air for good, stripped of its license by the Federal Radio Commission, citing the station's lack of "public interest." But that's where the radio commissioners had it all wrong, Brinkley knew. The public was nothing if not interested. *Radio Digest*'s audience poll of 1930 overwhelmingly voted KFKB the most popular station in the country. The Brinkley's station outpolled the *Kansas City Star*'s own WDAF 357,000 to 10,000 votes. Alas, popularity could not save Brinkley's license. And when he shut down KFKB, Doctor climbed immediately onto the cross. "Persecution!" he liked to say. "Even as Jesus of Nazareth."

Doctor never wanted for zeal of mission, and he wasn't about to quit his service to the common man. Playing on the Mexican government's anger at the United States government's refusal to share any of its 550–1,500 kilocycle radio broadcast band, Brinkley won the right to set up a new station in Mexico. As folklorist Ed Kahn succinctly put it in *American Music*, "Here was someone who would invest in the necessary broadcasting equipment and at the same time really irritate the U.S. Government." Basically, Mexican officials gave Brinkley license to do anything he wanted, and there was a moribund little Texas border town of wool and mohair producers then lamenting the Depression-era price drops in greasy shorn domestic wools on the Boston market, and in dire need of a little bump in the local economy. "My dear Doctor Brinkley," wrote Del Rio chamber of commerce secretary, A. B. Easterling. "We certainly hope that you will at least pay us a visit. . . . The Mayor of Villa Acuña [across the Rio Grande from Del Rio] has already assured the Mexican consul that their city will furnish, free, adequate land for the purpose of erecting your station thereon. However, they will welcome a visit from you and will be pleased to go over any proposition you might have to offer. Del Rio has a splendid flying field, located about one mile northwest of the city. The six-story Roswell Hotel has the name Del Rio painted on its roof and an arrow pointing to the field."

When Doctor arrived in town to stay, the *Del Rio Evening News* gushed, "When a man comes along who can hold his dream of helping mankind in front of him consistently and constantly until he makes it come true, he is a man who stands out and dominates his generation. Such a man is John R. Brinkley, M.D."

"When we came to Del Rio it was pitiful," Minnie Brinkley told a local reporter decades later. "One of the banks had closed, but we deposited money in two of the banks and kept them open." The Brinkleys circulated money all over Val Verde County. Even in the Depression, the local economy boomed. Brinkley's generous patronage of the Del Rio Steam Laundry funded a complete modernization of a business that was failing badly before his arrival. Local printers, rooming houses, department stores, and eateries flourished. Unemployment dropped precipitously. By 1935 Doctor had spent half a million dollars erecting a five-hundred-thousand-watt transmission tower in Villa Acuña. With its directional dish, station XERA ("The Sunshine Station Between the Nations") was twenty times more powerful than any station on U.S. soil. There was no place in North America so cut off that its citizens couldn't dial in to XERA at 735 kilocycles, smack in the middle of the U.S. government's broadcast band. This was the high-water mark for Doctor. In Texas, he was licensed to practice medicine, which he did with renewed gusto. The Brinkley Hospital, operating out of Del Rio's Roswell Hotel, was in full swing, with increased services to men *and* women. "Don't forget the estrogens we are now able to give you for loss of sexual strength," Doctor would tell his radio audience. "They are a God-send and God-blessings to men and women who had despaired of ever having any sexual strength anymore. They even produce wonderful results for women who have lost their ovaries, to men who have lost their glands. For men and women who still have their glands, if they'll come to us and let us clear the infection out of their bodies before the estrogens are administered, wonderful sexual strength may be returned. . . . It's a blessing to those of you who are prepared to receive it. Many are called, but few are chosen. And I hope you'll keep that thought in mind. . . . This is all so clear and so obvious that it needs no explanation. I'm looking for you in the Brinkley Hospital immediately. And this is Dr. Brinkley inviting you to come at once."

Doctor also founded a second hospital in San Juan, Texas. Now, the two facilities were not to be confused, but Brinkley's instructions were straightforward and very nearly unforgettable. "Remember," he would tell his audience, "Del Rio for the prostate, San Juan for the rectum." In his nightly radio talks, Doctor Brinkley could troll for patients at either of his facilities in the same sluicing stream of thought. "If you know anybody that's suffering from a rupture, tell them that we correct ruptures without cutting and without putting a patient to bed," Doctor said. "If they have piles, tell them that we don't cut or their piles, or cut them out. We don't even put them to bed for their piles. And the job is guaranteed for as long as they live. We feel like that a guarantee to you for as long as you live is long enough. I wouldn't see any use of guaranteeing it after you have died. I think during your lifetime is sufficient length for a guarantee to be made. . . . If your prostate's involved, infected, enlarged, and some doctor tells you to have it cut out, don't listen to him. Removing your prostate gland is removing one of your important sex glands. You're no longer a man after that gland is out. You're an old has-been. Yes, you are the equivalent of a capon. Do you want to be a capon? Most red-blooded American men do not. . . . I invite you to get on that road to good health, as so many thousands have done. This is Dr. Brinkley personally urging you to begin that journey right now, to our hospital."

Doctor's silky drawl summoned as many as 226 new patients a month to the warm climes of Del Rio, and nearly half that many to San Juan. In 1936 the Del Rio hospital grossed $676,587. In 1937, $838,163, and Doctor controlled cash flow as he would a spigot. When he was strapped, Brinkley overwhelmed Del Rio's postal workers with pamphlets, flyers, and fire-sale offers ("Guaranteed Prostate Treatment for June, July and August, for only $250") and took extra time making the hard sell during his radio talks: "Sensible men [who] came to me have their prostates. They're all man. They're whole man. They're not a half-man or a has-been. . . . You hear me read letters from men who have come to me years ago and continue to be well and healthy and happy. Other men who have not come to me have had their prostate glands removed and many of them are dead. It's results that count, ladies and gentlemen." Doctor's hype got results. In February of 1937, for instance, the hospital took in a meager $66,861, but after a promotional push, his March receipts jumped to $190,218.

By the time the Carters arrived in Del Rio for the winter of 1938–1939, John R. Brinkley's remarkable successes and lavish lifestyle were again drawing fire, and not just from his old foe the AMA ("American Meatcutters' Association," he called the organization). The IRS was killing Doctor for back taxes. In 1939 he parted with almost seventy thousand dollars every three months, settling tax debts going back to 1933. He was also paying a battery of attorneys and accountants to keep him ahead of the law. His monthly payments to the Pinkertons regularly exceeded two thousand dollars, because besides providing protection for the Brinkleys and their son, Johnny Boy, detectives also had to seek out the growing number of dissatisfied former patients and convince them to cease and desist from their disparaging remarks about Doctor, if they knew what was good for them. Still, Brinkley could show compassion. There were a few times when the Brinkley Hospital even refunded payments to the widows of patients who had died of post-op peritonitis.

Most disheartening to Doctor was that his adopted hometown of

Del Rio had allowed a mountebank to move in on Doctor's prostate-surgery business. J. R. Middlebrook, M.D., set up shop right down the street from Brinkley, undercut his prices, and sent an army of drummers to snatch patients bound for the Roswell Hotel. West Garfield Street in Del Rio started to look like the Texas of Judge Roy Bean's day. One passionate Brinkley supporter stepped in when he saw a Middlebrook agent at work outside the Roswell. "He was trying to rob Dr. Brinkley of his patients," said Henry "Coonie" Crawford, "and I just floored him. He slid halfway up under the car."

The besieged Doctor Brinkley tried valiantly to keep his good humor. He still illuminated his fountains every night for the delight of the passing townsfolk. At Christmas, he still trucked in loads of bananas, apples, oranges, candies, walnuts, filberts, and Brazil nuts, which were sorted, bagged, and passed out to the children of Del Rio. But by 1939 a pall had descended on the Brinkley mansion. Sitting in peaceful luxury in his private barber chair, with "Eggs" Coffield giving him his daily trim and shave, fifty-two-year-old Doctor felt like a hunted man. The siege weighed even on his ten-year-old son, Johnny Boy. "The doctor worshiped Johnny and denied him nothing," remembered a boyhood playmate. "But Johnny was the unhappiest person I've ever known."

Within three years, Doctor would be crushed under the weight of IRS demands, legal bills, and a flood of medical-malpractice judgments against him. He died a broken man in May 1942, a year after the Mexican government forced the closure of XERA in accordance with the recently ratified Havana Treaty, which allotted to Mexico specific radio frequencies throughout the United States in exchange for its shutting down the most egregious megawatt border stations. But Doctor John Romulus Brinkley had unleashed a powerful force in the world, and he had shined a light on the miracle and possibility of *broad*casting. Even after XERA shut down, smaller copycat stations remained: XELO Ciudad Juárez; XEG, Monterrey; XERB, Rosarito Beach; XEPN, Piedras Negras. And from 1938 to 1943, the Carter Family was on them all, riding the airwaves as far out as Edson, Alberta, Canada, 250 miles north of Spokane.

In a tiny cabin in a coal camp in Alberta, Ed and Elsie Romaniuk, ages nine and thirteen respectively, sat hunched over their new radio every night, ready to copy out every song the Carters did. The next day they would pull out their notebooks and try to perform the songs themselves. That music made bearable the dull aching days of life as coal miner's children; hearing the Carters on border radio changed the Romaniuks' lives. But in that damp cabin in the gray sloping foothills, those children never could have dreamed what effect border radio would have on the Carter Family.

It was the promise of a steady income that lured Sara to Texas. She hated to leave her home, but the radio job was the first bit of solid certainty she'd had in her life in a long while. All she had to do was go into the station twice a day, make music, and collect her seventy-five-dollar-a-week check. No Mr. Peer to deal with, and none of his complicated royalty statements to double-check for accuracy, no more entertainments, no more live audience for her to please. But the deal was not without cost. Janette and Joe were still in school, so they were left behind to live with Ma Carter. Gladys was now married to her sweetheart, Milan Millard. On August 30, 1938, just ten days before the Carters left for Texas, Gladys had made A.P. and Sara grandparents. But they had to say good-bye to their first grandbaby, little Flo. By the time they returned in the spring, Sara would have already missed the first seven months of her granddaughter's life.

For Sara, it was another leave-taking in a long, sad series of them, and she was not a happy woman. Sixty years later, tucked away in Flo's upright filing cabinet at her house in Maces Springs, is a set of unrecorded lyrics Sara had written around this time:

> When shadows fall I'm lonely
> For dear you are far away
> Though miles between us are endless
> I love you is all I can say.

> (Chorus)
> I'm alone in this world and so lonely
> I miss you wherever I roam

It seems, my dear, you've forgotten
I'm alone in this world, I'm alone.

You've broken your vows and your promise
I've waited so long and in tears
Please say you mean to return, dear
The days now have turned into years.

As always, though, Sara bore separation with a stoic composure.
She had not shed a single tear as they drove up the Valley Road on
their way to Texas. There would have been enough hysteria for them
all at Maybelle's house anyway, where June and Helen were distraught at their mother's departure. A half a year was like forever, and
how it broke those little girls' hearts when Christmastime came and
went and there was no package from their mother. It arrived late, probably held up at the Del Rio post office by the deluge of Brinkley mail.
"I felt very lonely at times about them being away," says June. "The
contact we had with them was mostly trying to listen to them on the radio." Maybelle's daughters did have the unique privilege of being able
to dial in to XERA and hear their own mother's voice, every morning
and every night. One night, they even heard their baby sister squeak-
ing through. "When Anita was out there the first time, I never will forget it, she sung harmony with Mother on 'Little Buckaroo,'" Helen
remembered. "Oh, we were so thrilled. 'Close your sleepy eyes, you
little buckaroo.'"

Anita's first half year in Texas was quite a ride. She lived happily
enough in a Del Rio boardinghouse with her mother and Aunt Sara,
and on balmy winter evenings, Maybelle would take her across the border for promenades around Villa Acuña's town square. Anita would
stare wide-eyed at the color-splashed ponchos and giant sombreros. She
even talked Maybelle into buying a sombrero to bring back to Grandma
Addington. But so much of the time was spent at work, or going to
work, that it could wear out a little girl.

The Carters were now a part of America's lively "and-now-a-word-
from-our-sponsor" industry. XERA's audience was decidedly rural, so

hillbilly acts had elbowed every other musical form off the station's daily program. When the Carters arrived in Texas in 1938, they were joined by Cowboy Slim Rinehart, the Pickard Family out of the mountains of Tennessee, Lou Childre, and Essie and Kay—the Prairie Sweethearts. Together, these performers heralded the *Good Neighbor Get-Together*, airing live every night from six to ten (and again the next morning), sponsored by Consolidated Royal Chemical Corporation. Morning and evening, the Carters drove over the Rio Grande on the new steel-trussed International Bridge, headed for the little mission-style studio building. In the studio, if Anita was truly tired, she'd crawl into her mother's guitar case for a nap while A.P., Sara, and Maybelle were being introduced by announcer Harry Steele. They'd lead off with "Keep on the Sunny Side," do a few more numbers introduced by A.P., then give way again to Steele for a word from Consolidated Royal Chemical Corporation: "Now, friends, if you're one of those folks who's always bothered with bad colds during the winter months, . . . why don't you do as thousands of others in the same boat have done? . . . Take the new Peruna to help build up your cold-fighting, cold-chasing ability. . . . If you want to try Peruna right away, all drugstores have it, and you get it under the maker's guarantee—you must be satisfied, or your money back for the asking. Is that fair enough?"

Peruna was a healing tonic that soothed whatever ailed a body. It was effective, too, but only in the short term, owing to the fact that it was 25 percent alcohol. Long-term effects were nil, but at least Peruna was harmless. The other product Consolidated Royal advertised was less benign: "Don't let gray hair cheat you out of your job and cause you a lot of worry. No, sirree, that isn't necessary anymore. And here is all you have to do. Get a bottle of Kolorbak from your nearest drug or department store. . . . under the maker's positive guarantee, it must remove every trace of grayness and make you look five to ten years younger and far more attractive, or your money back." The dye in Kolorbak did produce results, but used too enthusiastically, it also caused lead poisoning.

The beauty of the whole Texas arrangement was that the Carters didn't have to do the hard sell. They just made their music and let the announcers make the pitch. But they were still the draw. In fact, they were the biggest draw. Harry O'Neill, Consolidated's adman, had devised a way to track the selling effect of their *Good Neighbor Get-Together*. On the air, Steele would make this offer: Any customer who sent in a Peruna or Kolorbak box top to the station, care of the Carter Family, got a Bible in return. O'Neill figured each letter was worth about fifty cents to the company. The Carters were soon pulling in as many as twenty-five thousand letters in a single week, and Consolidated began to tuck photographs of the family into the Bibles before they sent them out.

It wasn't long before listeners began to understand the miraculous powers of XERA, the way it could shrink a vast continent down to the size of a small village. And that gave hope to desperate people in desperate circumstances. In 1939 a woman from Sherwood, Oregon, sent this note, addressed "The Radio Station, Del Rio, Texas": "Sirs, will you please send out a report on the air for my son . . . who is missing. He does not know where I am. Tell him if he will contact his Granddad, [in] Abilene, Texas, he will let him know where his mother is. He will have a home with me out here. He has been in a juvenile home in Bexar Co. but he has run away from there. He was put into this place without my knowing this. I have remarried again and would like to get my son."

None of this was lost on Sara, who was herself feeling some measure of desperation. One night in February of 1939, she decided to send a message out to someone long since lost to her. One night, in an act beyond her normal character, she bravely stepped to the mike in that cramped studio in dusty little Villa Acuña, Mexico, and announced she was dedicating the next song to Coy Bays, in California. Whether A.P. joined in, nobody remembered, but Sara let loose.

> 'Twould been better for us both had we'd never
> In this wide wicked world had never met.
> For the pleasures we both seen together
> I am sure, love, I'll never forget.

Oh, I'm thinking tonight of my blue eyes
who is sailing far over the seas.
Oh, I'm thinking tonight of him only
and I wonder if he ever thinks of me.

Oh, you told me once, dear, that you love me
and you said that we never would part.
But a link in the chain has been broken
leaving me with a sad aching heart.

Oh, I'm thinking tonight of my blue eyes
who is sailing far over the seas.
Oh, I'm thinking tonight of him only
and I wonder if he ever thinks of me.

When the cold, cold grave shall enclose me
won't you come here and shed just one tear?
And say to the strangers around you
a poor heart you have broken lies here.

When the show was done, all Sara could do was wait and, like the distressed mother out in Sherwood, Oregon, hope that the message had found its mark.

In the six years since Coy Bays and his family headed west out of Poor Valley, Virginia, a lot had changed. Even in the chill February of 1933, the Bays family had begun as a huge and hopeful traveling party: Charlie and Mary, their healthy children (Coy, Alma, Elva, and Stella), their tubercular children (Stanley and Charmie), and Alma's two-year-old daughter, Anita. The day they arrived in New Mexico, Alma had given birth to a son, Johnny, which the family took as a sign of rising fortune. Then there were Charmie's goats, the family bulldog, Caesar, and Stella's kitty. But along the way, the party had dwindled, and the hope, as well. The Bays family had worked its way across New Mexico, Arizona, and then up into California's Sacramento Valley, picking cherries and peaches, packing lettuce, cooking and cleaning at ranches. They lived under tents in camping parks or in abandoned houses given them for little or no rent, making their way with hard work and tiny kindnesses from produce foremen who kept the family employed even when there wasn't much work. (The Bays girls were lookers, and the bosses liked to keep them near.) Even so, Charlie had to swallow his pride and apply for state aid to keep little Johnny and Anita fed. That was how the Bays suffered their first loss, their name. " 'Bays' became 'Bayes'—with an e—by accident in California," says Elva's daughter Barbara Powell. "They were filling out some Social Security or state-aid papers, and some clerk wrote it wrong. It would have cost money to go back in and change it, so they just left it be."

That was the least of the losses. Stella was left behind in Linden, California, after the growing season of '34 to marry one of the scions of the profitable DeVincenzi ranch. She was just eighteen when she got engaged, and as the wedding neared, Stella realized she wasn't ready to be a wife. But the rings were bought, the wedding was planned, and she didn't want to break her fiancé's heart. Besides, if she married, it would mean one less person for her parents to worry about. So Stella said "I do" to give her parents a small break.

After Stella's big ranch wedding in November of 1934, Charlie and Mary left the Sacramento Valley for the mountains of northeastern California. The party was lighter than ever Elva and Alma had good-paying jobs in Stockton and decided to stay behind, leaving Alma's children to be raised by Charlie and Mary. So Coy and Stanley piloted the Chrysler roadster and the big Cadillac north into the Feather River Valley, ascending more than three thousand feet from the little town of Oroville into Greenville. Greenville was next to nowhere, 180 miles from Sacramento, 250 from San Francisco, and ringed by seven-thousand-foot-high mountain peaks. But Charlie watched with a pang of recognition as the flatlands began to roll and climb and the scrubby chaparral and manzanita bushes gave way to a fragrant mix of pine, fir, and spruce. It reminded him of home. "Dad ran into this Seventh-Day Adventist family [in Greenville]," says Stella Bayes, "and they said to my dad, 'If you would like, I do have a little ranch house down here. I won't charge anything for rent if you think you can live in it. Go look at it.' It was heaven to them."

If Greenville was next to nowhere, the Bandy ranch *was* nowhere. The ranch house was not much more than a cabin, and well out of town. It had no electricity, no running water, and the well was a long haul. But it was in the mountains and there was a daytime chill in the air, which Charlie reckoned would be good for Charmie and Stanley. Unsupported by any doctor, Charmie clung to the notion that she still had one good lung, and if the doctors could take out the bad one, she'd survive. But the constant movement—and the tuberculosis itself—had dimmed Charmie's hopeful gaze. In the first weeks in Greenville, she was weaker than ever, and Mary was worn thin with worry. She and Charlie even started going to the Adventist church, whose members took the Bayes family on faith, without rebaptism.

Christmas Day, 1934, was Mary's fifty-sixth birthday and her thirty-fifth wedding anniversary, but it was hard to celebrate. Charmie was so weak that one of the Adventist members, Dr. Morrell, suggested the sanitarium at Weimar. After the New Year, Coy offered to take his sister on the hard two-day drive south toward Sacramento. But before Charmie left Greenville, the entire family gathered at the little woodframe Adventist church on Main Street, where elders heated the water so Charmie could be baptized.

She had her twenty-first birthday at the sanitarium. It was her last. "Charmie only lived three weeks after she got [to Weimar]," says Stella. "Stanley and Coy were both with her when she died. She knew she was going to die. She felt it. She said, 'You all meet me in heaven.' And my brother said it was sort of a stormy day and there was a little almond tree in full bloom right out her window. And he said the sun came out just as she was passing.

"We could not afford a casket, only a little redwood box. I think they put a lining in it. She was taken to the closest mortuary, about two or three miles away in just this little village of a place. They put a little shroud on her. And we viewed her little body and they put her in a

hearse and took her back over to the sanitarium. There was a big cemetery on a hillside. In fact, it covered two hills of a little valley; when you
walk out there, you would think you was in a military cemetery. There
were hundreds of white crosses there. They were all TB cases. But we
didn't have the money, and it was too stormy to take her to any other
cemetery to bury her, so she was laid to rest there under a little pine tree.

"Stanley said, 'I want to go home to die.' So Stanley went home [to
Greenville]. He lived all through that year, and then he passed away the
beginning of 1936. Stanley had it in the bone and he had big sores that
would come up, boils. He got the boils n the last stages."

When the eight-year-long siege of sickness and death was finally
over, Charlie decided to make a clean start. He bought a lot in
Greenville, where he and Coy built a new cabin for the family and a
big garage with a loft above for guests. Coy was nearing thirty-five,
but he was still living with his parents. It was his duty, he figured,
because he was now the only son on whom his aging parents could
depend. For a while, he and his father worked up in the mountains,
cutting firewood to sell, but then he took a regular job at a sawmill
and continued his pinched existence in that far-flung California valley. "We tried to get him interested in other girls," Stella says.
"There was a beautiful girl up in Greenville. Her father owned a little store up there. And she would come out to the ranch quite a bit,
and she liked my brother real well. So we tried to get him to go with
her, but he wouldn't. Didn't have any interest. Didn't seem to care
about getting romantically connected."

At the time, Stella didn't know exactly what Coy was waiting for.
By the time Stanley died, Coy had stopped talking about Sara, because
somewhere along the way, her letters had stopped coming. This was
because somewhere along the way, Coy's mother intercepted them.
"Once in a while he'd get a letter from Sara, but among the family it
didn't get to him," says Stella. "Mama and Papa were opposed to it.
They loved Sara, but . . . this was a very sad thing in our life. It was a
very embarrassing thing, because it was their nephew [A.P.], and their
son. And both loved the same woman."

In 1939 Coy hadn't seen Sara in six years, and they hadn't corresponded in nearly that many. As far as Coy knew, Sara had simply lost interest. So he was just like any of the thousands of people who tuned in every night to hear her on XERA's *Good Neighbor Get-Together*. At least, that's how he felt until that cold February night, when he heard her call out to him from across twelve hundred miles and six years. "Coy wasn't sure that Sara still cared for him," says one of Coy's nephews, "until he heard her dedicate the song on the radio."

"Sara dedicated a song on the radio," says Stella. "She said, 'I'm gonna dedicate this to Coy Bays in California. 'I'm Thinking Tonight of My Blue Eyes.' I think he said, 'Mom, I'm gonna go get Sara.' And Mama says, 'Well, Coy, I guess you better go get her.' "

Coy sent news back to California right away. He and Sara were married February 20, 1939, in Brackettsville, a little town just outside Del Rio, and he kept the family informed with buoyant little postcards to Greenville, like the one dated March 8, 1939: "Sat. Nite. Hello Folks. Here in Mexico having a good time. Harry [Steele], Mae Bell, Sara and I are eating at the cafe on the other side. Love. Coy and Sara." It was cherry-blossom time before Coy finally carried his new bride back to Greenville. They arrived in the fire-engine red '39 Dodge that Coy bought new in Texas. That regally streamlined new coupe was a car fit for his new wife, the national radio star. Coy also had a new 8 mm camera, and his own movies of Brinkley's place in Del Rio, of the zoo in San Antonio, of him and Sara just clowning around. After so many years, so much distance, so much loss, the Bayeses were thrilled to see Sara again, especially Mary. "They didn't come as soon as I thought they was going to," says Stella. "But when they did arrive, it was welcoming. All of us loved Sara. It was nothing but joy."

"Coy would tease her," says their niece Barbara Powell. "He would sometimes kind of kiss on her, and she'd say, 'Oh, go on now.' Or he'd pinch her a little bit. And she'd say, 'Oh, go on. Go on.' And she'd just laugh a bit. He was affectionate with her."

"This was not a fling thing," says Stella. "It was not just an affair. It was deep love. If she sat on the couch, he sat down with her. And they would talk. My brother liked to tease her, talk baby talk to her. Sometimes she'd get a little embarrassed or something. They loved one another. It just showed."

Helen, June, and Anita in San Antonio (Lorrie Davis Bennett)

Opposite: XERA, circa 1938 (Whitehead Memorial Museum)

A New Act

A. P. could never say how he felt about Sara, or demonstrate it in a way that showed. In fact, it was hard to tell exactly what A.P. felt. When people who worked with them on radio saw him passing notes to Sara in the studio, some saw it as evidence of animosity between the two. But their children always said they got along better after the separation and maintained a constant watch on each other's well-being. And maybe the studio missives were meant as a nod to their courting, to the time when A.P. tied a handwritten note of apology to a dog's collar and sent it scurrying down to Uncle Mil's porch. It was hard to know what exactly was in Pleasant Carter's mind, until Coy showed up in Texas. "When Sara left him, it broke his heart in two," says his granddaughter Rita Forrester. "In Texas, whenever he'd see Coy coming down the street, he'd cross to the other side."

"He had no zeal, it seemed like, after that," says Joe. "He was lost."

Sara and Coy had married so fast it made A.P.'s head spin. "He became nervous and ill at ease after Sara's marriage to her second husband," the announcer Harry Steele told Ed Kahn, "and the agency for which we worked decided that he was transmitting his mood unwittingly over the air." Harry O'Neill's agency actually sent A.P. home a month early, leaving Sara and Maybelle to finish out the last month of the contract. Eck was in Del Rio visiting Maybelle at the time, so the two men drove back to Virginia, together with Anita. "Oh, my Lord, that was a trip," Anita remembered. "To put a little kid in with those two! My dad just jerked my pants on me and put them on backwards. Well, I had a zipper up the back and couldn't hardly sit down, and it was hurting and I kept hollering and Daddy was nervous and A.P. was nervous. Daddy'd say, 'I don't wanna hear it, Wimp.' (I loved hamburgers and he'd call me Wimpy.) Oh, Lord. It was not a time to travel."

Eck and Anita's homecoming was a bright day in Maces Springs. Eck presented Helen with a two-dollar guitar he'd bought for her in Mexico, and Anita handed June and Helen crisp dollar bills from the stash Harry Steele had given her for her "Little Buckeroo" performances on XERA. Of course, Anita held back eighteen dollars for herself. The most exotic gift of them all was the big Mexican sombrero Anita had bought in Villa Acuña for Grandma Addington. "She thought it was a rug," remembered Anita, "put it down on the floor, and tried to stomp it down in the middle." To Helen and June, that sombrero might well have been a *flying* carpet, exotic merchandise brought back from that great secret world Anita had seen for herself.

After Maybelle got home there was news. Big news. Consolidated Royal wanted the Carters back in Texas. All of them. Harry O'Neill was willing to let Helen, June, and Anita perform on the show, for pay. Eck could see what was coming. Sara's marriage to Coy and her removal to California might mean an end to the Original Carter Family, but this meant opportunity for him and his girls. As Helen said years later, "When we started out as little girls, our daddy said, 'Don't let the name die. There's something there. Don't let it die.'"

Eck had long been nudging his daughters to think outside the bounds of the Valley, sending them to piano lessons with a local preacher's sister, or making them practice the Hallelujah Chorus on Sundays after church. More than fifty years later, those girls would still get together and marvel, without regret, at what their father demanded. "Daddy was a classical-music lover," said Helen. "We had to listen to Beethoven and Bach and Tchaikovsky, so we all learned to play Minuet in G and all that stuff. Daddy put us on the train and sent us down to Hiltons to play the piano."

"I was just six when we had to learn the Hallelujah Chorus," Anita said. And June chimed in. "It hurt my throat somethin' terrible. [Here were] these little peepy voices singin' the Hallelujah Chorus."

"Daddy's one ambition for me was to learn to play 'Moonlight Sonata,' " said Helen. "He *loved* 'Moonlight Sonata.' "

"Sometimes the girls would be out trying to play, and Eck would make them come in and practice," remembers their cousin Lois Carter Hensley. "Maybelle was more easygoing. Eck always enforced it."

By 1939 Helen, June, and Anita were already learning to negotiate Eck's expectations, but in their own ways. Nearing twelve, Helen was a lot like her father, shy and nervous at once, and desperate to please her mother. She was anxious to master any musical instrument that came her way, from piano to guitar to accordion. He en was a homebody. She'd happily cook for a dozen-man threshing crew but wouldn't go within twenty feet of a milk cow. She was also a bosom companion of Ma Carter, who still carried her to church Sundays—and even took her to clean the graves out behind Mount Vernon. Ma Carter was still diligent about cleaning and decorating Ettaleen's grave, and she took care of Dewey's, too, with his mother all the way off in California. To Helen, Mollie Carter must have seemed part pal and part living history, a real mountain woman, with her long plaited hair still wound tight in its bun, her straight ankle-length dress covering a pair of mismatched socks. She was so modest that Helen figured Ma Carter never once undressed in front of her own husband. She was scandalized when Gladys had allowed Milan to touch her dress when she got it caught on a barbed-wire fence, and to kiss her on the night *before* their wedding. "Grandma Carter was like an explosion," Helen said of her. "She would have whipped you before you knew what happened to you if you didn't mind her, you know. But I loved that old lady; I think it was because I lived in the house with them when I was little. She always said that you had to be a lady, you had to conduct yourself as a lady in all things. Your reputation's all you have. Once your reputation's gone, you've lost it all."

With an early interest in boys, Helen began to understand that she wasn't going to be protecting her reputation all by herself. For Eck, it was inconceivable that his daughters would live the whole of their lives in the Valley, the way his own mother had. "All the young men in the Valley were scared of my daddy," said Helen. "Daddy always said that he wanted us out of that valley. He just didn't want us to get involved with any of the men in the Valley. He just didn't want us to get married and stay there. He always used to say that there was a world out there, and we should see it before we died. . . . He always told us, 'There's so much out there you haven't seen.' "

Anita was still the noisiest, and the most contrary, and in the midst of her own racket, she was willfully oblivious to her father's insistent demands. Anita was the most gifted singer of the entire Carter family, Sara included, but she shared Sara's trademark unconcern. "You could never get Anita awake or singing," says Fern Carter Salyers. "Anita just didn't have the *want-to*. It was hard to tell whether she really liked music that much." Says Lois Carter Hensley, "She'd rather be playing with her friends, always doing cartwheels, walking on her hands through the house. I believe we saw her butt more than we did her face."

June was the boy Eck always wanted. She rode airplanes and motorcycles, walked a plow, drove a truck. "Either June would stay with me, or I was at her house or at Grandma's house a lot," says Fern. "Before we started to like boys, we would go up the mountain and go climb trees. We tried to get up to a crow's nest once, almost fell out. We'd do that kind of thing. We'd go to Grandma's across the creek, and we used to climb on the rocks in the creek at a place called Breakneck Place. June was the first one up to milk the cows. We'd go to the river and go fishing, go swimming. We were tomboys." June also had Eck's eye for the main chance. She seemed to be channeling every ounce of his ambition, and her own besides. "Someday," she confided to Fern, "I'm going to dine with queens."

Now, that was Eck's ethic boiled down to its essence, and as much as he loved his standing in the Valley, June understood how her father chafed under its limitations. The radio show gave them a way out, but it had its complications. As much as June wanted to please her father, and as anxious as she was to get out into the wider world, she wasn't sure exactly what she could *do* on the radio program. That summer, June took inventory of her talents. She could shoot a rifle, climb a tree, harness a mule. She could drive a tractor. She could make her stomach muscles move in eye-popping contortions fit for a carnival sideshow. But XERA was no sideshow. This was a real radio program, heard throughout the *entire* country. Anita had already sung on radio. Helen had been singing with Janette for a couple of years, and she could play a passable guitar, even if she was a bundle of nerves. And June? "Mama looked at me like, *What in the world are you gonna do?*" June remembers. "And she said, 'Can you sing?' I said 'I don't know.'"

At the end of September, Ezra and the family loaded up their new Packard and headed west for Texas. Along the way, the girls sat in the backseat running through the dozen or so songs they'd prepared for radio. June would sing lead, because she couldn't be counted on to carry a harmony part. So Anita did the tenor part, and Helen the more complicated alto. June didn't have much of an ear, but she always knew when she got off-key. Helen would give her the tragic look (it was just like Maybelle's), and Anita could pinch like old Uncle Mil. Sometimes even Eck would turn around from the steering wheel and screw up his face. By the time they hit the Texas state line, June was getting scared. She didn't know what she was going to do, and it was beginning to look like they were entering an alien land. "It was a time when there was cotton rows as far as your eye could see," says June. "And then it just got so flat we couldn't believe it, and it was dry. We just died for green grass." The roads turned into long straight ribbons of pavement, the hills flattened out altogether, and the horizon came up unbroken; it was like looking at forever. Like the land itself, June's new fears seemed to stretch on without an end. Of course, it didn't help when Anita would get up in June's ear and blare out a song in perfectly rendered mimicry of her sister's off-key vocal stylings. "If you're going to be on the world's largest radio station with us," Maybelle said to her middle daughter, "we'll need some kind of miracle."

For her miracle, Maybelle turned to the Sears, Roebuck catalog. She'd ordered a new autoharp for June, and right on the instrument she wrote out the notes, the words, and the chord changes for a song. "Mama said, 'You will learn to play the autoharp this week.' And I did learn to play. I mean, to flail the daylights out of it. I learned eleven songs in that week."

For the 1939–1940 season, Consolidated had a new scheme, involving Presto transcription disks. The Carters would live in San Antonio and go to a studio once or twice a week to record their shows onto acetate-and-aluminum platters. A.P., Sara, and Maybelle had recorded some shows on disk at the end of their stay in Del Rio the season before, but that was to save them a trip across the Rio Grande in the predawn darkness for the morning show. The XERA announcer could just replay the *Good Neighbor Get-Together* from the night before. But Harry O'Neill had got the idea to run off as many copies of the acetate transcription disks as they needed and ship them to whatever station wanted them. Four other border radio stations wanted them right away: Rosarito Beach, Piedras Negras, Ciudad Juárez, and Monterrey. Consolidated would cut in the commercials after the fact, along with intros, outros, and station breaks suited to each. In fact, the new announcer, Brother Bill Guild, could do them all, right in the studio in San Antonio: "This is station XET, Monterrey, down Mexico way. Now here's that well-known and better-loved family of radio, The Carter Family: A.P., Sara, Maybelle, Janette, Helen, June, and Anita. And it looks like we're on the 'Sunny Side.' "

The Carters were often able to knock off an entire week's worth of half-hour shows in a single afternoon in the studio above the garage at the home of Consolidated's San Antonio agents, Don and Dode Baxter. Suddenly, the Carters' audience was bigger than ever. The group even got raises. Helen, June, and Anita were getting fifteen dollars a week each. They'd take themselves to the movies, buy ice-cream cones or new roller skates. Janette was making twenty a week, but with what she spent on Joe's footlong hot dogs and trips to the zoo, she had a hard time saving money to pay her way back to Poor Valley for Christmas.

Janette was the most miserable of them all; she'd been forced down to Texas against her wishes after Ma Carter warned A.P. that Janette was getting too serious with a certain young man. So in the autumn of 1939, A.P. had pulled Janette and Joe both out of the school in Hiltons and taken them to San Antonio. The trip itself was a trial. "I was looking forward to going to Texas," says Joe. "My dad had an old '35 Chevrolet, and we was driving along and came into a dust storm. It was raining, and muddy water was hitting the windshield. That was the big dust years."

"I never seen so many flat tires," says Janette. "I think we had three in one day. We hit them hot highways and them blacktops, and I remember one time we had a flat tire and Daddy went off under a bush or a cactus and said, 'Now you and Joe fix it.' And some man stopped and I think I was in tears. I'd had about all the flats I wanted. I was a-burnin' up and was homesick. So that man fixed the tire."

"Between Texarkana and San Antone all through there we had flats," says Joe. "Those tires was so hot, you could hardly handle them. And when you stepped off the pavement, you's in sand burrs and something was sticking to you."

"I thought my life had come to an end," says Janette. "I never did like Texas."

Janette and Joe both went to Alamo Heights School, where Joe was forever in trouble. "I had a French teacher, and she had a whistle in her accent," he says. "Every day she went to talking and I'd go to sleep. I couldn't stay awake." The school was so big that sometimes Janette found it impossible to find her way from one class to another, but she never felt comfortable asking her fellow students for help. "They'd come up to me and talk to me, but they weren't trying to be friendly," Janette says. "They just liked my accent. They wanted to hear me talk and then make fun of my accent."

"They did me the same way," Helen said. "I was in junior high and they'd take me behind the building and make me talk and just break up. And I thought, 'Well, you idiots, I'm talking fine.'"

All the Carter kids were alien beings in Texas. They'd ask for a "dope," which was a Poor Valley colloquialism for Coca-Cola, and the other kids would look at them like they were crazy. "I was always asking for a 'poke' to put my candy in, and they'd look at me like I was a snake," says June. "They had no idea what a 'poke' was, and I'd say, 'Don't you know anything? A poke! I need a poke to put my candy in!' Finally I had to go behind the counter and show them I wanted a paper bag." Where Janette and Helen could be hurt by the teasing, June began to see there was something to being *odd*. And she started to work on her own kind of hillbilly minstrelsy, the country equivalent of "blacking up." On the radio shows, she even started playing the poor country girl, reading ads for Kolorbak hair tonic with an extra-thick helping of gravy on her Poor Valley drawl.

Actually, with the girls added, the Carters' radio show was even better than the year before. It probably helped that Coy wasn't in Texas at the beginning of that season. A.P. had regained himself; in fact, he was at his best. More and more he braved solos, accompanying himself with guitar. And while his playing wasn't top-notch, his singing came from the deepest center of him. His best work was heartbreaking to hear, even if the radio audience never knew what had transpired between him and Sara. His voice had a way of ranging from proud defiance to hopelessness, all in one breath. The tenderness he brought to the Gussie Davis song "One Little Word" was almost unbearable.

> One little word would have changed my future life
> One little word would have made her my wife
> Too late. Too late. Now my fondest hopes are dead
> One little word, that word was never said.

On gospel tunes like "Lonesome Valley" ("Everybody's got to walk this Lonesome Valley, / We've got to walk it by ourselves") his bassing in was more forceful than ever. A.P. seemed to thrive in the Texas warmth that winter. He looked healthy again, and even put on some weight eating the local Mexican cuisine, though he did stop short at fried rattlesnake. "On the weekends we went over to the zoo, Breckenridge Park," says Joe. "There were hippos, snakes in there, every species of ducks, flamingos. Daddy liked that. He'd go down and watch that with me." Part of Pleasant's ease owed to Sara's presence. Even if they were no longer married, even if they would never be married again, A.P. felt better that his former wife was near, that they could still make music together.

Meanwhile, Sara and Maybelle could sound buoyant. When they'd knock off "Dixie Darling" or "Funny When You Feel That Way," the old Rich Valley joy bubbled up through the surface. The women tried new cowboy songs they'd picked up in Texas, or straight instrumentals such as "Chinese Breakdown." "You get tired of singing the same old things over and over," Sara told Kahn.

"We had to just learn songs or think up new songs," said Maybelle.

Maybelle made only one real mistake that winter. She loaned her Gibson guitar to the "least good" of their *Good Neighbor Get-Together* compatriots, Cowboy Slim Rinehart. Cowboy Slim went on a bender and lost the guitar to a local army airman in a poker game. "[Maybelle] had to get the base commander to intercede," says her grandson, who owns the guitar now, "but she got it back." That incident was a little bump in an otherwise smooth road.

Even the new announcer added real country flavor. He was a minister, with a charismatic's energy. It wasn't money that enticed Brother Bill Guild onto the radio show, but Don Baxter's promise that he could fit his radio schedule around his church work, and that he could mention God on the program whenever he felt like it. "Brother Bill would almost shout every time we'd sing an old hymn," remembered Sara.

The girls, meanwhile, were holding their own . . . even June. She started by singing so low she could barely be heard, but eventually braved a solo on her autoharp: "Engine 143." It wasn't a thing of beauty, but the audience was apparently willing to forgive the artistic shortcomings of a ten-year-old. Like their mother, Helen, June, and Anita were getting sackfuls of fan mail, and so was Janette, in spite of herself. Janette had agreed to perform on radio, but not without trepidation. "I remember the first song I ever sang on the radio was 'Dark-Haired True Lover,'" she says. "That was the first time I ever stood in front of a mike, and I remember wondering, 'Where on earth is my voice a-goin'?' It seemed like my whole breath was goin', you know? I was trembling. But Mama and Daddy and Maybelle was standing over nearby." Meanwhile, Joe took a pass. He was scratching around on the guitar at the time, but he refused to perform in public. "I kinda had stage fright," Joe admits. "I dreaded to get up there."

Still, Joe did like to be around. When the family drove down to Del Rio to do the occasional live show, Joe always went with them. But he wouldn't go into the studio. There was too much fun to be had outside. "The old building itself had this half-tiled roof that held water, and bats lived under that tile," says Joe. "Hundreds of them. After nightfall, I'd get me a bamboo pole and stand out there and whack at them. Every now and then, I'd hit one. They'd squeal and carry on up there.

"There was this little concession stand outside the station. Little old shanty built out of reeds. I could buy a soft drink for a penny each, because the exchange was five to one. I think I just about bust open drinking Coca-Colas. Handful of pennies and as much pop as I wanted.

"And that radio station was so powerful, you'd touch a barbed-wire fence right next to the station and it would burn you. It wasn't even connected, just the molecules through the air, I guess. This ole boy who ran the concession stand, what he had for a radio was a wire from the roof of his shanty that went to a tin can sitting on a solid piece of metal. You could hear entirely what was going on in the studio." Somebody down at the station even showed June that if she angled the iron gate at the XERA driveway just right, it would pick up the signal.

But the power of the X-station signal did not explain the power of radio. Gutzon Borglum, the sculptor who in 1939 was carving Mount Rushmore on a granite outcropping in far-off South Dakota, called radio a gift to cut-off rural America: "Radio suggests whispering messages from the heart of the world across the heavens to every listening soul; it stirs the imagination; it reaches into unlimited space—joy, tears, song, the very dream of life, vibrating its way toward the stars." Beyond Borglum's pronouncements of radio's stirring grace, there was also this: Radio could cut against the loneliness of the country's age of dislocation, could find the homeless wanderers who had escaped the rural South for dreams of better lives, and then lost their own sense of where they belonged.

That winter of 1939 and 1940, border radio allowed the Carters to soothe a dust- and Depression-ravaged rural population, and a dislocated nation. The *Good Neighbor Get-Together* was different from the other big cross-country radio shows such as Nashville's *Grand Ole Opry* and *The National Barn Dance* out of Chicago. And the *Get-Together* was perfectly suited to the Carter appeal. The other radio shows were performed before a l ve audience—a *big* live audience—which added a call-and-response feel, pushing musicians to dig deep, like preachers competing for souls at a big revival. But he live audience also reminded those listening that because they weren't there, they were missing much of the event. The listeners couldn't see what that new star Roy Acuff was wearing, or how much the fiddle player cocked his elbow. Or what sideman was reaching for the fruit jar to get something cool—or not so cool—to drink. When Uncle Dave Macon set the Opry crowd to shouting and stomping with "Go Away, Mule," the radio listener had to wonder if "the Dixie Dewdrop" had his banjo up over his head or down between his knees.

Roars of approval washed through the gleaming metallic threads woven into the fabric of Sears's new Silvertone radio . . . for things that could never be *seen* by a listener in his living room. It was a reminder that the action was somewhere else. Moreover, that big crowd presence on those radio shows had a way of nudging and wheedling a listener, of telling them what they should be *feeling*. At *The Good Neighbor Get-Together*, no noise got between the Carter Family and their listeners. Without that live audience, the action seemed to be happening right there in the listener's own living room. Sara Carter might as well have been five feet away, with her autoharp in her lap and her shoes kicked off.

That winter, a young kid in Johnson County, Arkansas, named Bud Phillips could listen to Janette Carter sing "Cowboy's Wild Song to His Herd" and conjure his own private image of her beauty. For Bud, it was well worth the three-mile trek through the river valley—even in a snowstorm—to get to the only neighbor who owned a radio. And Bud wasn't walking that valley alone. His family, his friends, and his neighbors all gathered to listen to the Carters. "The Carters were the best-loved in the our valley," says Phi lips. "They were singing our songs." Johnny Cash listened in, and Chet Atkins and Tom T. Hall and Waylon Jennings.

The Carter Family gave rise to their own fevered dreams. Buck Owens, whose own family was chased out of Texas by the dust and stranded fourteen hard years in Mesa, Arizona, listened faithfully to the Carters on the border stations. And how many others like Buck? But so, too, Lesley Riddle's sister, now living far away from home in Detroit, could be soothed by the sacred songs of her Burnsville, North Carolina, youth. And how many others like her?

Meanwhile, all Janette could feel was her own frightening disloca- tion; she just wanted to go home. As Christmas neared, Janette announced to her father that she'd saved enough money to get herself back to Poor Valley. A.P. had other ideas. Janette was a good singer, and getting better. She kept a notebook full of collected songs, poems she could put to music, or pieces of lyrics she'd written herself. She could do songs her parents didn't even know, such as "The Orphan Child," an inversion of the Little Orphan Annie story, where a poor lit- tle locked-out orphan girl ends up frozen and lifeless on the rich man's porch. Janette already sounded like a pro, and A.P. wanted his daugh- ter to make a little investment in the future. "Daddy was trying to get her to buy that guitar out in San Antone," says Joe.

"He wanted me to buy that guitar, and I wanted to come back home for Christmas, and I wouldn't buy it," Janette remembers. "But he bought the guitar, and he says, 'If you give me your money, what you got, I'll take you home.' I think I had seventy-five dollars."

New Year's, 1940, Joe and Janette were back in the Valley, and happy for it. They planned to stay right there. But their cousins Helen, June, and Anita were still in Texas, spending their Thursday afternoons at the Baxters' in San Antonio, cutting the weekly transcriptions. Some- times they'd strap on their roller skates and hit the Baxters' driveway while somebody else was recording in the studio, until one day Don Baxter came out and pleaded, "Girls, you gotta quit skating. It's coming through. We're picking it up on the recordings." It was hard, but they stopped. Eck's girls had become pros now, too. They'd sing. They'd play. They'd yodel. "On 'Chime Bells' we yodeled so high!" remembered Helen. "We were three yodelin' little mice." At six, Anita was already writing songs, taking inspiration from the double features they'd go to every Saturday.

"You can tell," Anita said later, "I went to a lotta westerns." Her first song the girls performed on the radio included these lyrics:

> *Saddle ole Paint on a prairie*
> *Just heading for a great big ride*
> *Ropin' and a-ridin' on a prairie*
> *Out on the Great Divide*
> *Git along, little dogies*
> *We're headin' for a great big ride.*

National celebrity had made the Carter girls plainly different from their friends and family in Poor Valley; in fact, they were living a life almost completely insulated from the hard times that were ravaging most of their listeners. They got a look at that when they made a trip to Hugo, Oklahoma, to perform a live show. "When we got into Hugo, there was a big crowd outside the building where we were playing," says June. "But when we got inside, there couldn't have been more than fifty people in that building. We looked outside, and the place was just covered with people. But they had no money to come in. Well, Uncle A.P. went down and opened up the doors and let everybody in, and we sung. But we didn't play any more dates. We just stayed on the radio."

Sara Carter Bayes, meanwhile, was simply biding her time until the end of March, when the season would be done, and she could go back to California. She lived in a boardinghouse with Maybelle and the girls. It was a trial. Helen was terrified, for instance, of fire. And every time a fire engine went by in the middle of the night, she would wake in a terror, and Sara would go comfort her. "I can remember her taking me all over the house to show me it wasn't on fire," Helen said. Coy was once again an eager and able correspondent, and his typed-out postcards were always welcome: "Sara Bayes, 303 San Pedro Avenue, San Antonio, Texas. Just in from deer hunting. No buck yet but have eight more days to hunt, yet. You bet we will be hunting when I get down there. I fixed that up that morning at the breakfast table in Del Rio. Well, hon, hope you are feeling fine by now. I listen to your records XELO 630 Pacific Standard Time, evenings. So by [sic] til next time. Your Hubbey."

Toward the end of the 1940 stay, Coy came to San Antonio, and he and Sara set up a separate household for themselves. Sara had hoped maybe Coy would live in Virginia again after the radio season was over, but her husband made it clear he meant for them to keep California as a permanent home. So at the beginning of April, Sara and Coy got back in the big red Dodge and headed west for Greenville, California, while A.P. piloted his own Chevy back through the dust toward Poor Valley.

When A.P. got back to the Valley, he found out that Janette, who was just sixteen, had dropped out of school and was getting married. Ma Carter, Aunt Sylvia, and Maybelle all tried to talk her out of it, telling her she was too young, but Janette pointed out that she was just as old as her mother had been when she married, and just as old as Maybelle had been, too. The way Janette saw it, marriage would bring her something she'd not had: security. Finally, there would be somebody who thought of her *first*, who would look out for her above all others. But she was afraid to tell her father, partly because it would be the end of her music career, and partly because she was marrying Jimmy Jett.

The Jetts were prominent in the Valley, but for all the wrong reasons as far as A.P. was concerned. First of all, they were Democrats. Party affiliation generally went back to the War Between the States, and even seventy-five years after, there were still venomous feelings on both sides. The big landowners in the Valley, like the slaveholding Jett family, had been Democrats, strong for secession. The farmhands, tenant farmers, and "rabble" often went for Lincoln's Republican party. And they stayed. A.P.'s father was a stout Republican. Even in the trough of depression, Pa Carter would not stand for people sniping at President Hoover.

The deepest undercurrent of Republican resentment ran right down to the north fork of the Holston River to Livingston Creek, where the Jett family farmed the richest bottomland in Poor Valley. At the time of secession, the John Jett place was the biggest estate in Scott County. The main house was a two-story Georgian made of bloodred bricks from the family's private kiln. There were fourteen rooms in the main

house, all with twelve-foot-high ceilings the sleeping quarters; the big
parlors with looms, spinning wheels, and musical instruments; and a
chandelier-lit dining room that gave off onto the rear house. The back
house held the ovens and kitchen, and quarters for the kitchen help. A
covered walkway connecting the two buildings was called the "Whistling Breezeway," because slaves delivering food were obliged to whistle
all the way over to the dining room so that the Jetts could be sure their
charges weren't eating any table food on the way over. At the outbreak
of war, John Jett owned hundreds of acres and seventeen slaves; and he
sent two sons to fight with General Robert E. Lee.

The Jetts lost their slaves in that war, but it hardly brought them to
their knees. Both sons returned from battle (one with an arm shot off),
and when they did, the family still held the best of the land. Seventy-five
years later, they remained the richest family in the Valley—and the most
talked about. Around Neal's Store there would be stories of the raucous, unchristian goings-on at the Jett place. They always had booze on
the table, people whispered. A cousin in Bristol even had his own dis-
tillery, when it was legal and when it wasn't. There were tales of bac-
chanalian socializing at the Jett places, about dances made risky by hard
fiddling and hard drinking. More than a few of those Poor Valley cotil-
lions entered into local legend. One rainy night, while the dancing and
drinking were going strong, the river got up and nobody could get out.
So they just kept the party going, for three solid days and nights. There
were tales of men pulling out their pistols and firing at the spinning hoop
skirts of dancing women, just to see if they could hear the ping of the
bullet glancing off the wire undercarriage. There were rumors of one
drunken fracas where guns were pulled and a cousin was shot dead.
When the circuit judge rode over a few days later to make an inquiry, a
posse of well-armed Jetts met him at the edge of the property to explain
that there would be nobody prosecuted on Jett land. Well, that's how the
story was told, anyway.

The Jetts weren't all bad. Back when there wasn't a car in the Valley, and surely no hearse, Clarence Jett offered his wagon, no charge, to
carry the dead to the bereaved family's cemetery. If somebody died
away from home and had to be shipped back to Maces Springs by train,

it was Clarence who met the body at Neal's and carted it wherever the family asked.

By the 1930s, the Jett stills were all bonded: taxed and legal. But the Jetts were still doing devil's work as far as A.P. was concerned, and Janette was afraid her father wouldn't approve of her marriage to Jimmy. So Janette told Gladys her plan and asked her to tell their father.

A.P. was not pleased, but he knew something about feeling alone, and he didn't try to stop Janette. "Well, I do hope she'll have some happiness in her life," A.P. said to Gladys. "She's not had much happiness." Still, the day Janette got married, A.P. went up the mountain to pick huckleberries and refused to come down. Janette and Jimmy got one of the Jett cousins for a witness, and the three drove over to Gate City on May 25, 1940, to collect the license and the preacher. When Preacher R. T. Carter asked if they wanted to drive back over to Maces to get married, Janette said they didn't have to go to the trouble. "My family's not there anyway," she told him.

The preacher drove them just outside Gate City to a nice spot he knew, where he performed the ceremony beneath an apple tree in bloom. He nudged the car in under the tree, and the wedding party never even got out. Jimmy's cousin witnessed from the front seat, next to the preacher. Jimmy and Janette said their vows from the backseat. After that, she and Jimmy moved to Bristol, and Jimmy wanted her to give up the music so that they could concentrate on starting a family of their own.

It was odd. Pleasant Carter was more famous than ever, and completely at sea. Losing Janette was a blow. The homeplace he'd bought for his family was now empty. Joe was living with Gladys and Milan, going to school up the road in Mendota. A.P.'s old buddy Lesley Riddle had moved north for work. Pleasant kept himself busy scouting and buying land, which he sometimes kept and sometimes held for a few years and turned around for a profit. Sometimes he and Mutt Skeens would go out and give entertainments. They spent a lot of time doing shows down around the Sandhills in North Carolina, where the pair had girlfriends. But those women moved away to California to try to get into the movies.

A.P. still loved to get out and go, and there wasn't much keeping him home. One time Jerry Parker asked him to look at a sawmill north of Roanoke. So Jerry and A.P. and Vernon Bays hopped in Jerry's pickup truck and took off. All the way up, Jerry and Vernon kept up a friendly patter, but Pleasant just stared out the window, humming. "Every once in a while he'd break out into a song," remembers Vernon. "It was strange. He just wasn't in the conversation." Then, all of a sudden, he'd come out with some arcane factoid: "If you want to know how big a town is," A.P. would say, "just start looking at the telephone wires as you get near. The more wires, the more people."

Just west of Roanoke, A.P. told Jerry to pull off of Highway 11, where he wanted to show them something. He took them over to see the grave of an old farmer who wanted to be able to see his land after he died. They'd buried him up in the hills, standing in a glass coffin. "A.P. had been all over, so he knew about this kind of stuff," says Vernon.

Before A.P. left for Texas for the winter season of 1940–1941, he made a move to put a little life back in the homeplace. For one dollar, and "the further consideration of his natural love and affection for his daughter, the said Gladys Millard," he deeded it to her and Milan. They moved in there with Joe before A.P. took off for San Antonio.

Actually, the Carter Family headed to Texas by way of a Chicago recording studio. Even with Doctor Brinkley's world crumbling around him, the radio audience was bigger than ever, pushing Carter Family record sales up out of their Depression-era slump. RCA Victor was reissuing old cuts, and now they wanted new recording sessions in Chicago and new material. In separate sessions in October of 1940 and 1941, the Carters cut a total of thirty-three songs. The songs weren't much different from the Carters' best-known guitar and swirling-harmony stylings, but the recordings reflect the startling distances these three people had traveled. Maybelle and Sara contributed more than ever to these sessions, including the first songs Maybelle wrote from scratch: an up-tempo but sad cowboy song, "Buddies in the Saddle"; "Why Do You Cry, Little Darlings?"; and "Lonesome Homesick Blues." The last song was down-home blues, with that old Lesley Riddle lick. Maybelle wrote it while living in Texas, where she was missing

Eck. "I'm gonna ride that ol' lonesome train, / To the one I left back in Maces Springs," the song went.

"Keep on the Firing Line" and "Fifty Miles of Elbow Room" were hymns Sara said she heard in California, at Charlie and Mary Bayes's Adventist church on Main Street in Greenville. She even wrote a blues song of her own, "Bear Creek Blues." And they also recorded a song they got in San Antonio from Brother Bill, a Holiness hymn called "There'll Be No Distinction There" ("For the Lord am just, the Lord am right, / And we'll all be white in the heavenly light").

The radio show had made A.P.'s singing more confident than ever, and the last solos he performed on Carter Family recordings, "I Found You Among the Roses" and "There's Something Got Ahold of Me," were as good as any he'd done. For all his troubles, Pleasant Carter's own joy cuts through. And why not? His dream of recognition for himself, for his family, for their music was complete. In the fall of 1941, *Life* magazine sent a photographer to Poor Valley to shoot a spread on the entire family.

Nobody in the Carter family, *nobody*, was more excited than June. "He was from New York, and we couldn't understand a word he said," June later wrote. "He made motions and we all smiled. Anita did her sitting-on-her-head routine, and not to be outdone, I showed him I was still a pretty good stomach-mover." When the photographer left, June pulled all the spent flashbulbs out of the trash and saved them. At twelve, June knew she'd never have her sisters' musical talents, but she'd already figured out how to deflect attention from her shortcomings and to get the applause she craved. It was a lesson she'd learned back at the San Antonio middle school.

Just before the *Life* photographer showed up, the Carters were playing a show in Birmingham, and Maybelle brought June over to meet the Grand Ole Opry's resident comedienne, Minnie Pearl. "Maybelle told me that June wanted to be a country comic, like me," Minnie Pearl once said. "I told June then not to imitate me, but to create her own country character."

The next week June got a letter from Minnie Pearl, with a collection of some of her best-loved Grand Ole Opry routines. But June took

Minnie's advice. "I never used one of those routines," June once wrote. "I developed my own."

Fern Carter remembers her father coming home from Eck's house one night, bragging about June. She'd done a comedy act for a bunch of friends and neighbors. It was corny as could be; her country character made that old Clinch Mountain hermit Brown Thomas look like David Niven, but everybody had loved it. June performed her act live for the first time at a show at Midway High School in Rich Valley. Between songs, she crossed the stage dragging a big wooden plank.

"Hey, where ya goin'?" Maybelle asked.

"I'm looking for a room," she answered. "I've got my board."

A.P., back in Poor Valley (Carter Family Museum)

Opposite: Anita, June, and Helen in Richmond (Carter Family Museum)

On the Road . . .

The big spread never ran in *Life* magazine. The week after the photo shoot, bigger news squeezed out the Carters: Japanese fliers bombed Pearl Harbor, and the country was, officially, at war. But the *Life* photographer, a Jewish émigré–New Yorker who had photographed Rachmaninoff and Stravinsky, framed a shot of himself and A.P. Carter and kept it on display at home. A.P., he said later, was the most exotic subject he'd ever photographed. It's a picture that captured Pleasant Carter at the end of his long climb to recognition; even without an appearance in *Life*, his celebrity was never greater. But A.P. Carter must have found the attainment of this lofty height akin to gaining the balding peak of Clinch Mountain. Once on top, there was very little to sustain a man. The only way off was down.

By the end of the 1941–1942 season in Texas, the Carter Family transcriptions were still winging out of the San Antonio studio to the X-stations along the border, but the Mexican government had shuttered Brinkley's XERA. How long could the others last, now that the Mexicans had made their peace with the United States government? Harry O'Neill decided he was going to get out while the getting was good. For the next winter, he bought time for Consolidated Royal Chemical Corporation, newly christened Consolidated Drug Trade Products, on station WBT, a fifty-thousand-watt shouter in Charlotte, North Carolina. Then he asked the Carters to be part of the new program. A.P. was in without question, but Sara had a decision to make.

By 1942 Sara and Coy had made their home in California. Sara had made real money in Texas, and she and Coy went in with Charlie and Mary to buy a house and a ten-acre cherry orchard in Stockton. That spring, Sara wrapped herself in the life of normalcy she had craved: cooking, cleaning, keeping a house. Even when Charlie and Coy were out working the orchard, she had Mary's company. The two women shared a quiet bond; they could work all day together in that house without the need of talk. Sara missed her home in Virginia and her children, but so did Mary, and what good was talking about it?

Sara was in love with the quiet of her life, with the ease, with the sameness of one day to another. And her celebrity was never a big hassle. She was known by name, and by voice, but not by face. So she could move through the shops and stores of downtown Stockton in complete anonymity. "Sara shunned any celebrity," says her niece Barbara Powell, who lived a mile down the road in Stockton. "She didn't enjoy it. She didn't want the publicity. She never boasted or tried to impress anyone. Some people like the limelight. Some don't."

Even Coy, who loved the glow of his wife's fame, learned to keep his lips buttoned about Sara's career. He could tease her mercilessly, pinch and coo and baby-talk, but he knew never to push her to perform, even when it was just family. In a way, the yin and yang of the relationship made it easier for Sara. Coy was naturally social, quick to draw attention to himself and away from Sara. "Her outlook was more pessimistic than optimistic," remembers Barbara Powell. "Not real positive. That was all the time I knew her. Coy was a jokester. I don't recall her ever telling a joke. She'd just sit in comfortable and enjoy the patter and conversation. She never came out as the life of a party. And it kind of perturbed her if you made her the center of attention and asked her to play.

And I never heard her listen to anybody on the radio. She never talked about [the music]. I think it was something she did to make money."

For so long, making music had meant making money for Sara, and the Charlotte radio show was more of the same. It also meant another separation from Coy. By the fall of 1942, the war production machine had swallowed up most of the country and Coy with it. Coy was working on a Ships for Victory crew at the port in Stockton. Even Charlie Bayes, at sixty-four, got hired on as a shipyard guard. The pay was too good for Coy to walk away. He was going to keep making the money while it lasted, and so was Sara. That fall, she got on a train and headed east for Charlotte. But she told herself that this was the last contract; she was going to take the money and run.

Maybelle and the girls were committed to Charlotte, because Eck was committed to their future out in the wide world. The Valley could drive Ezra crazy. "We come in from Bristol one time," Helen Carter remembered, "and Grandma Carter came across the hill, and she hollered, 'Whoa, Ezra! Ezra!' And Daddy said, 'What is it, Ma?' And she said, 'I just needed a little kindling and I come over and got me a little.' She'd burned up his curly maple, his redwood, and all this beautiful stuff he'd collected. He couldn't open his mouth."

What was worse, Eck was now watching his parents fail. Mollie had recently come over to Eck's house and grabbed Helen. "She said, 'Helen, I want to walk this mountain one time before I die,'" Helen remembered. "Said, 'Will you go with me? I'm sixty-seven years old. If I don't go soon, I won't go.' My cousin Juanita and I went with her. And of course we'd run way ahead and wait for her—and she would come and she'd take two steps up and fall back one. That's how the poor thing went up the mountain. But she made it all the way across that mountain down into Copper Creek where some folks she knew lived, and we spent time with them."

Pa Carter died first. Arthritis had crippled him and left him in pain he couldn't pray away. For a while near the end, Bob still got out on the circuit. He'd call out to Mollie, "I'm a-goin'," grab his cane, shoo his scrawny little shorthaired dog off his lap, and the two of them, Pa Carter and Hairpin, would go walking down the Valley road. But Pa Carter didn't stay gone long anymore. The visitor wasn't much up to visiting. For two long years, he just sat in his chair and stewed. Sometimes Mollie would sit at his feet with a bowl of hot water, dip a towel, and wring it over his swollen knees. That soothed the pain some, but never enough. Bob had always been high-strung and strong-willed, but after so long being housebound and hurting, he was becoming ill-tempered. "He was always yelling for Ma Carter to do this and do that," remembers his daughter-in-law Theda Carter. "And he needed it *right now*. One day he was yelling and carrying on and needed something, and Ma Carter was too slow and he got all worked up. And Ma Carter was crying. 'Childish' is what she called him. She said, 'I don't ever want to get like Bob if I live to be that old.' " Bob died in 1941, at age seventy-five, in the cabin Eck had built for him. Not long after, Mollie started to lose weight—and she didn't have much to give away. Sylvia was having a hard time nursing her ailing mother, and the family was talking about sending Fern to stay with her in the little cabin.

Death in a little cabin in Poor Valley was not what Eck had in mind for himself. And the truth was, it was hard to watch his mother slide. Ma Carter had understood his talents and his drive, and she'd nurtured them both. Sometimes there were even whispers of resentment among the other brothers, for while Eck had been allowed to go on to high school, they were stuck to the land. Eck didn't listen to that kind of talk. He was busy with the next generation, trying to push them to something better. When they got the radio offer from Charlotte, Eck bought a new accordion for Helen, a tenor guitar for June, and for Anita, the big bass fiddle.

When the Carters moved to Charlotte that fall, there wasn't a house or apartment to be rented, so A.P., Sara, Ezra, Maybelle, and the girls moved into the Roosevelt Hotel. Their radio show aired live, every morning as the farmers got up and got going, from 5:15 to 6:15. Monday through Saturday, the Carters wakened before dawn, fixed hot biscuits and gravy in the little kitchenette, and made their way to the station. "Anita never woke up at all," June wrote in *Among My Kledi-*

ments. "She hugged the bedpost while I put on her jeans. I steered her through the streets to the station and up the elevator into the studio." Steering Anita was a lot harder now that she had the bass fiddle. It was a lumbering five feet tall, a half foot higher than Anita's own self, and she had to stand on a chair just to play it. But she could play it. And she could sing.

In San Antonio, living above the girls at the boardinghouse, there had been a woman who taught opera, and every day she and her students would run the scales. Anita would sit at her window a floor below and sing along. "They'd sing as high as they could and when they'd stop, I could always go a little bit higher," Anita remembered. "She came and asked Mama if I could take lessons, and Mama said, 'I don't think so.' Mother didn't want us to sound like that." Mercifully, Eck was not in town when the offer came.

While they worked at WBT, Helen spent her mornings covering June's tracks. (For all the hours of performing, June's singing was not measurably improved.) After the morning show was over, Helen and June would take the Piedmont and Northern railroad out to Paw Creek High School. Helen had graduated from Hiltons High School the previous spring, just a few months before her sixteenth birthday, but she had nothing else to do all day long, so she went back to school. Like Eck, she loved books, and she had one advantage over her father. "Eck was pretty good in books," says Joe Carter. "He got into the mail-clerk business, and you have to be pretty smart to pass that test. But Eck's mind was no good for memorizing stuff. When he went into the Masons, he like to never learned his catechisms." Helen had a memory like that of Mandy Groves or Pa Carter or Eck's twin sister, Virgie. "She was our songbook, a walking songbook," said Anita. "Helen remembered everything. Daddy was always so proud of her mind. He always just looked at me and said, 'Shut up and sing.' I think he thought that was all I had going for me."

Helen and June were also getting older, old enough to sing a love song and know what it meant, old enough for girlish excitement over the handsome soldiers in their dress uniforms or their spit-shined paratrooper boots, and old enough to catch the boys' attention, too. Ezra even grunted ambivalent assents to a few young men who asked if they could take his daughters out on a date; but Eck agreed only when Helen and June double-dated, so that they could watch out for each other. That they could do. Four years of music work—the travel, the odd hours, the odd people, the teasing at school, the pressure to live up to the Carter name—had bound the girls in ways most sisters were not. The family was the one steadfast constant in the dizzying whirl of stage life. Even Anita, who was least interested in the life of an entertainer, could appreciate this blessing. "One thing we heard a lot wherever we were living was 'Time to go to work!' " Anita Carter once said. "But to me, that meant family time."

In March of 1943, when the Charlotte radio contract expired, the Original Carter Family disbanded for good. There was no big announcement, no valedictory radio show, no final good-bye. Sara simply headed west for California, leaving behind her old life forever. A.P. went back to Poor Valley, moving into the homeplace with Gladys and her family. For the rest of his life, he would try, fitfully, to reconstitute his musical family, but never with much success. His own once-driving ambition would pale by comparison to that of his younger, and always competitive, brother. Eck, Maybelle, and the girls headed back to Maces Springs in March of 1943, but Eck wasn't willing to let them sit there with Poor Valley dust gathering on their shoes. "When the children got up to where they could entertain, Eck wanted them to be out there, and he didn't really care if Sara and A.P. was there," says Stella Bayes. "When they got old enough and they could be on their own, Ezra wanted it that way." Sitting on the porch of Mollie's cabin one day, Eck turned to his mother and said, "Those girls will work if they have to go to South America."

The way June told it later, in the spring and summer of 1943 she had time to play basketball, drive across the mountain for a singing school, go with Fern to Breakneck Place, drive a logging truck, plow, sow, cut and shock fifty-four acres of wheat, and be saved, having "seen the tongues of fire as on the day of Pentecost" at a prayer meeting in Uncle Fland Bays's home. Maybelle provided a less evocative picture of that time, and one more in line with Eck's impatience. "We left Charlotte in March of 1943," she told Ed Kahn. "From there, me and the girls went to Richmond to work. [The Original Carter Family] disbanded in March and we went to work the first of June."

Maybelle did have one particularly vivid memory of that spring: the tryout at the radio station WRNL. "Helen, June, and Anita and I rode the bus from Bristol to Richmond for that audition," Maybelle told her friend Dixie Deen Hall in an interview in 1966. "We got there at two in the evening and we had to catch a bus back at six so that the girls would be home in time for school the following day."

"WRNL," Anita once said, "that was where we started. We went up and auditioned, and the manager of the station had this man in there with him who later became the announcer on our show, and he said, 'Hire them. They're corny as hell!' It was so bad. These little voices, you know. Corny as hell. And that's when we sang:

> *We're the Carter Sisters from the mountains*
> *And we're here to sing your favorite songs*
> *We hope you'll listen in this morning*
> *As we greet you with our songs*

For three years, "The Carter Sisters and Mother Maybelle" played WRNL, a dinky five-thousand-watt, strictly local station, recording shows for morning and afternoon, six days a week. In those days, the Carter Sisters and Mother Maybelle were best described as a "novelty act." None of the girls had their mother's instrumental chops. Eck hadn't helped matters when he saddled Helen with the forty-pound accordion and Anita with the big doghouse bass fiddle. In the beginning, in fact, Helen was befuddled by the accordion. She had to learn to play the basses with her right hand and the melody with her left. "This thing is just absolutely backwards to the piano," she'd complain. Still, under her father's insistent gaze, Helen kept at the awkward, heavy instrument. And it went a lot easier for her after a date the Carters played in Louisville, where she got some advice from the more studied eye of Pee Wee King. "Hey," he asked Helen, "did you know you've got that on upside down?"

On the radio show, fortunately, The Virginia Boys, Doc and Carl, were there to carry some of the load. Doc Addington, Maybelle's younger brother, and their cousin Carl McConnell had worked at the X-stations in Texas, and on the road with Maybelle and the girls. Having them to fill up airtime on the twice-a-day half-hour radio program took some of the pressure off the girls. Doc and Carl were able musicians, with an eye toward the jazzier musical tastes of the day. "Yes, indeed," the announcer would chime in, "Doc and Carl go to work first thing this morning with 'You've Two-Timed Me One Time Too Often.'"

June was gradually taking over as the marketing whiz. She could do the hard sell for any sponsor: "It's no job at all to talk about the wonderful summer clothes in Thalheimer's basement . . . a complete line of cotton peasant skirts in sizes twenty-four to thirty, and priced reasonably in their basement tradition at just $2.98. . . . There are floral spuns with full skirt in blue-with-white floral, and pink background with white floral. And there are three rows of thin rickrack trim at the bottom of the skirt, which is finished off with an attractive ruffle."

June was a born salesperson. She liked to be heard and had the instrument for it. One night at the dinner table, she proudly told the family that one of her teachers had praised the carrying qualities of her voice. "She said my voice had 'residence,'" June announced. "Resonance, June. *Resonance*," said Eck. "If your brain were in a bird, it would fly backwards." But sponsors such as *The Southern Planter* magazine were pleased to have June Carter's "resident" voice.

"Look, there's a towheaded farm boy posing with two beautiful sheep," she'd say to the WRNL announcer.

"That is a terrific cover, Junie, but it's the inside of this famous farm journal that means so much to our listeners."

"How very right you are, Ken. Tradition means very much to this great paper, but that doesn't keep it from being up to the minute on current farm needs and trends."

"It certainly doesn't, Junie. There's proof in the June issue of *The Southern Planter*, which carries on page six an all-important story on pasturage for poultry, written by Dr. Juhl, a world authority on poultry. . . ."

"I'm sure all our listeners will want to read it for themselves . . ."

". . . but right now it's music as Mother Maybelle sings 'So Long, Darling.' "

Though she was one of the best-loved performers in country music, Maybelle was most comfortable providing guitar backing for the girls. She'd get out front for a solo or two in each show, making sure to play the numbers her audience requested most: old Carter Family favorites, or the newer sentimental songs of wartime departures and returns. The girls also made a nod to tradition, always including a "hymn for the day." But meanwhile, they were always itching to move out beyond the old Carter Family stylings. Sometimes the girls could coax their announcer to work up piano arrangements of pop songs. "We sang 'Shoofly Pie and Apple Pan Dowdy,' " Anita said. "Makes your eyes light up and your stomach say howdy."

Despite the jazzy new sounds, the radio shows still brought teasing at their new schools. "We're the Korny Karter Sisters from the mountains," their friends would mock, although it never seemed mean-spirited. In Richmond, June was attending John Marshall High School, Anita a local grade school, and their new classmates were not the sort whose families encouraged music from the hollows. In fact, the Richmond public education was just the training Eck wanted for his girls. "A Richmond girl learns to cut a French-style green bean," June once wrote. "She learns to change the light, fluffy priscilla curtains from the heavy drapes in winter, to replace the straw mats with wool rugs, and to put on the linen slipcovers in the springtime." June went to a riding academy, sang in her school's girl's chorus and glee club, and acted as honored sponsor to the school's proud Cadet Corp. She managed to make herself part of the in crowd at John Marshall High, a crowd that was always welcome in Maybelle's home, no matter what they did. "They had this gang called the 'Hoodlums,' " Maybelle once told her friend Dixie Hall. "I know one night they came in and I had some eggs ready to fry. Well, one of them picked up an egg and threw it, and then eggs started flying all over the kitchen! Those youngsters were always up to some mischief. When I'd go to school to pick June up, they'd all climb on my car and weight it to the ground."

Even while she was running with these sophisticated city teenagers, June was hamming it up onstage as one of the most backward characters in country comedy, her own invention, "Aunt Polly Carter." Her Aunt Polly had a flat hat, pointed shoes, lacy pantaloonlike undergarments, and the same broad, unrefined sense of humor with which June had first invested her creation.

Aunt Polly was never invited to the radio show, but she was a big part of the Carters' traveling show. Their professional schedule wasn't confined to the radio-show recordings, or WRNL's wartime favorite *Canteen Woogie*. And their travel wasn't confined to Richmond's USO Parking Lot Canteen or McGuire General Hospital, where wounded country-boy soldiers were treated to a free show. Eck had taken an early retirement from the railroad, and he was booking dates nearby. Country acts on five-thousand-watt stations didn't get much in the way of salary in those days, but the radio shows were great for advertising upcoming concerts. As with so many other groups, the Carters' best source of income was gate receipts from personal appearances. So they worked the area, traveling constantly, performing for live audiences in the towns within range of their station's signal. The WRNL announcer kept folks apprised of the Carters' frantic schedule: "Very quickly, where the Carter Sisters and Doc and Carl can be seen in person: on Thursday, the thirtieth, at Reading, Pennsylvania, and Friday at Victoria Community House sponsored by Circle Number Five of the Victorian Methodist Church. And on Sunday, June the second, at Marius, Virginia, the Astor Theater. There will be three shows, five, seven, and nine P.M., that's on Sunday the second of June."

The Carter Sisters and Mother Maybelle played courthouses, schoolhouses, movie houses, the top of concession stands at drive-in movie theaters, even when wartime travel got difficult. Maybelle had a '41 Packard, the newest model available after the automobile maker quit turning out new cars and moved into war production. It was a big, commodious car, could handle the entire traveling troupe *and* the instruments . . . until Eck sold it. Eck was gung-ho about the war effort, leasing all the farmland he owned in Poor Valley for government wheat production. When Eck decided his patriotic operation needed a third truck, he traded in Maybelle's Packard. For a while, she had a '41 Cadillac. That car guzzled gas like it had a hole in the tank, and with wartime rationing in force, the Carters often had to beg or borrow gas stamps from friends and neighbors just so they could make dates. But the Caddy was big, sturdy, powerful, and roomy, which was good, because there were nights when Doc and Carl piled in with the girls, along with Maybelle's guitar, and Carl's and Helen's, and Doc's banjo and Helen's accordion and Anita's stand-up bass fiddle and June's autoharp and her guitar and maybe her room-and-board board for a trip to some town in North Carolina or West Virginia or Pennsylvania. The girls loved to play Newport News best. Between shows they'd have a chance to go to the beach, which was the closest thing they got to a day off.

Then, as Helen remembered, disaster struck: "Mama goes downtown and a blamed streetcar backed over her, just squashed our Cadillac." After that, it was everybody piled into Eck's '39 Packard roadster, which was designed more for a couple of buddies heading to the golf course than for a traveling troupe of musicians. Eck, Doc, and Maybelle took up the front seat; Anita and the instruments got the little cubby behind them. Carl, Helen, and June were stuck in the open-air rumble seat. "We had to tie skirts over our heads so our hair didn't fly away completely," said Helen.

When it was just Eck and Maybelle and the girls on the road, Maybelle usually took the wheel and ran the car like a demon through the hills. She could drive all night, through fog and foul weather, without complaint—and without incident. When Eck slid into the driver's seat, things seemed a little less secure, which the girls would do their best to forget. Holding tight in the backseat, they'd run through tried-and-true numbers such as "Engine 143" and "Old Joe Clark" or try out new numbers such as "Shoofly Pie" or "My Darling's Home at Last," or the Gene Autry songs that Helen loved. Anita had barely reached double digits and was full of twisting energy, so she had trouble in the long confinements of highway travel. Her amusement was pinching and clawing at her sisters, starting fights in the backseat. Helen and June were left to defend themselves as best they could. On one trip, Maybelle, from behind the steering wheel, begged her husband, "Eck, would you talk to Anita?" Eck whipped around in his seat. "Hello, Anita," he said sweetly, and turned back around.

The Carter Sisters and Mother Maybelle were a self-contained road show. Once they hit a town, they'd hook up their own public-address system, tune their instruments, take the tickets, and press their handmade clothes with a heated lightbulb. In the middle of wartime, somebody had given Maybelle a parachute, and she made silk dresses with black velvet ribbons for all three girls. "Mama ironed the fire out of everything," June says. "We never went onstage with a wrinkle or uncurled hair. And even though Mama might not have slept for two days, we always looked like we just stepped out of a bandbox." Keeping up appearances was a chore, especially when they'd play movie houses between pictures, sitting in the back of the audience until the movie neared conclusion, then stealing off to the basement dressing room (often under the stage next to the coal bin) and then clambering up a ladder onto the stage. There were times the Carter Sisters and Mother Maybelle would do five shows in a day, fix their own flat tires, and rehearse on the road in the Cadillac or one of the Packards. And some-times on those long drives, the old Carter Family songs would come on their car radio, and they'd all quiet down, bone-tired and aching, and just listen.

Even after her beautiful new Packard got sold out from under her, and her Cadillac got run over by the streetcar, no trip was too daunting for Maybelle. One time, she and the girls had to take a bus all the way to Kansas City to play a show. "And we had my bass fiddle on this bus!" Anita Carter said. "Can you imagine that?" When the fellow passengers saw the instruments and insisted on a performance, the Carters gave an impromptu middle-of-the-night show. Maybelle would have thought it rude to decline, especially with so many servicemen on board.

Maybelle approached life on the road with the same equanimity with which she faced life with her enervating husband; she was unflap-pable. Sometimes she and the girls would stay at boardinghouses, and sometimes they'd flop with relatives. If they had a date close enough, they'd stay with Maybelle's brother Bug and his family in Hiltons, in the basement under the Addington General Store. "That was a lot of people. They'd sleep anywhere, on the couch, on the floor," says Bug's daughter, Suzy. "They'd be too tired to not sleep." Maybelle and the girls rolled into Bug's house late one n ght and presented two-year-old Suzy Addington with a white dress trimmed in blue. "Maybelle had crocheted every bit of it herself," Suzy says. "And she must have been dead tired, but she would always do my hair. I don't remember much, but I do remember Maybelle made a point to wash out her undergarments *every night* no matter where she was."

Sometimes when they were playing near Maces Springs, the girls would catch a glimpse of A.P. standing at the back of the audience, a tall, lean specter who'd slip in and out without a word. "I really felt so sorry for him," Helen said. "He loved the business. He loved music. But his family at that time was so busted up that he didn't have anyone really to sing with. Janette wasn't singing at that time. She was married and her husband wouldn't let her sing It was really hard on him, and looking back, I can see where he might have come and worked with us, had we even thought about it at that time. But you know, when you're young, you don't see all these things at the time."

By the time the GIs straggled back from Europe and the Pacific to begin the work of remaking their nation, the various Carters were settling into new lives, too. A.P. Carter was back home in Maces Springs for good, living with the knowledge that his best times had passed. Sara Carter remained in California, in self-enforced exile, cut off from her music, from her home, and from the day-to-day pleasures and pains of her children and grandchildren. Maybelle Carter and her daughters, meanwhile, were full-time professional entertainers—which cut them off from home and extended family just as surely as did Sara's exile. For the next thirty years, Maybelle Carter would make her life on the road. She would remain a gentle, modest woman and a dedicated accompaniest— shy of the limelight, quick to push others out front. But she was also, underneath the quiet facade, a woman of remarkable force. Like those Poor Valley women of Mollie Carter's generation, Maybelle could work day and night, without expectation and without complaint. And it was Maybelle Carter's drive, her pride, and her prodigious talents that ensured the long, sweet sustain of Carter Family music.

The Carter Sisters and Mother Maybelle at work (Lorrie Davis Bennett)

Opposite: The Carters with Chet Atkins, circa 1950 ("The Carter Sisters and Mother Maybelle Song Folio No. 1") (Lorrie Davis Bennett)

... To Nashville

The Carter sisters' early career as professional entertainers was not without growing pains. Even June, who was the most committed to performing, had occasional second thoughts. Her successes among the sophisticated, urban daughters of Richmond's John Marshall High School had erased any doubts a tomboy country girl might have had about her femininity or her polish. When her graduation day came and those other girls were talking about the universities and colleges they would attend that fall, June cried because she would not be going off to college also. But that was a momentary hiccup. When a local newspaper reporter interviewed her, June insisted on her commitment to her craft. "Movies or stage?" she'd say. "I don't know. I guess I'll just follow whatever it drifts to."

It sounded so nonchalant . . . so unplanned . . . so natural. But the truth was, June was hardly drifting. By the time the nation turned away from war, June Carter was a vector, headed in a very specific direction, toward a very specific place, no matter the odds. In the late '40s, the

Carter Sisters and Mother Maybelle were one of thousands of country acts on literally hundreds of radio stations around the country. Even feeble five-thousand-watt radio stations in two-bit towns supported live shows. And if you shot those thousands of radio performers full of truth serum, nearly all would say the same thing: They dreamed of their ascension to "Hillbilly Heaven," in Nashville, Tennessee, on the stage of the Grand Ole Opry.

By the middle forties, the *Grand Ole Opry* was the dominant force in country music in the nation. WLS's *National Barn Dance*, the *Renfro Valley Barn Dance*, Shreveport's *Louisiana Hayride*—they all had big audiences and up-and-coming stars, but none drew numbers or talent like the *Opry* did. The *Opry* show aired live from seven-thirty to midnight every Saturday night, and it wasn't just for listeners within range of WSM's big fifty-thousand-watt signal. NBC had syndicated the show, so all over the country, every Saturday night at 7:30, folks from Boston to Los Angeles could get a half hour of the *Opry*, sponsored by Prince Albert Tobacco. The biggest stars were on that *Opry* stage, or on their way there. When the industry started toting up record sales on the new weekly *Billboard* charts in 1948, *Opry* acts dominated the country list. The Carters were no different from the other acts on minor-league radio. They dreamed of the *Opry*, too, even if they never dared speak of it. But even after they'd had a half dozen years on radio, the Carter sisters knew they weren't yet ready for the big time. As Maybelle would say, "The girls was just taking their feed on music."

Still, in 1946, they were heading in the right direction. Richmond's biggest station, WRVA, wanted the Carter Sisters and Mother Maybelle, so the group bolted the five-thousand-watt piker WRNL and moved to the jewel of Richmond's hillbilly music scene. In the summer of 1946, WRVA had spent loads of cash renovating an old theater called the Lyric. The newly christened WRVA Theater was at Ninth and Broad Streets, smack in the middle of downtown. The stage-door entrance faced the state capitol. For its debut season, the WRVA Theater booked a variety of shows: the *Ballet for America*, featuring exotic ballet stars Nana Gollner, Yurek Shabalevski, Kurek Lozowski, Tatiana Grantazeve, and Bettina Rosay; traveling productions of *Dear Ruth* and *Voice of the Turtle*, two of New York's most up-to-date comedies; the Richmond Musicians' Club, the Richmond Opera Group, and the Aladdin Players. But Saturday nights were given over entirely to hillbilly entertainment. The *Old Dominion Barn Dance* played twice a night, every Saturday, without fail.

The *Old Dominion Barn Dance* is where the Carters first learned that there was more at stake in the music business than ever before, and that the fight for the spoils would not always be friendly. That lesson came courtesy of the impresario of those Saturday events, an Iowa farm girl named Mary Arlene Workman. Mary Workman had started making music with her high-school sweetheart and husband-to-be, John "Sugarfoot" Workman, back in Keosauqua, Iowa. They'd made their way up from little Iowa stations to *The National Barn Dance* on WLS in Chicago, where Mary Workman inherited her stage name, sort of. One morning at the WLS studio, an emcee blanked on Workman's name. "When it was my time to go on," remembered Workman years later, "he looked at me and said, 'I don't know what your name is, little girl, but it ought to be Sunshine Sally.' The name stuck but had to be changed to Sue when another Sally proved to have a claim on the original name." As the emcee in Richmond, "Sunshine Sue" was a big draw for the rural folk who tramped downtown for the Saturday-night show. They tramped in such numbers, in fact, that the station had to open the box office at noon every Saturday so people didn't have to stand in line for hours waiting to buy tickets. And that was even when the comedy acts were so bad—Grandpa Jones complaining about the city slicker who sold him a tub, *with a hole in it!*—that some folks made it a point to get outside and have a smoke during breaks from the music.

Sunshine Sue proved a practiced hand at the accordion and a passable vocalist. She and Sugarfoot even made a charming rendition of "What Are Little Girls and Boys Made Of?"—sugar and spice and everything nice; snails and nails and puppy dog tails. She was a genial and enthusiastic mistress of ceremonies. "Take off your shoes, throw them in the aisles, and be ready for a party," she'd say as she stepped to the mike for her welcome song, "You Are My Sunshine." Her biggest fan was Virginia governor William Tuck. While in office,

Tuck had a private box reserved every Saturday night, where he delighted in entertaining visiting dignitaries and plenipotentiaries. By writ of official proclamation, Tuck christened Sunshine Sue "the Queen of the Hillbillies."

The Queen was also a skilled image maker who understood what her audience expected of a woman in the 1940s. Newspaper accounts of the day always noted Sunshine Sue's steadfastness in domestic chores. Despite her busy schedule on the radio and on the road, she found time to cook, to keep house, to get up at 5:30 on Monday mornings to do the wash. When reporters wanted to talk business, she'd demur. "John has the brains," she'd say of her husband, "and I have the big mouth." Beneath the act, Mary Workman was one heck of a businesswoman. She rarely saw a marketing opportunity that gave her pause. After her first son was born, she allowed a southern soft-drink company to put out mini-diapers that read, "Sunshine Sue says it's time for a change—to Dr Pepper."

When the Workmans incorporated Southland Shows, Mrs. was made president. Southland—that is, Sunshine Sue—brought to Richmond shows such as *Oklahoma, Annie, Get Your Gun*, and *Hollywood on Ice*, and stars such as Tex Ritter and Gene Autry. She also scouted and chose hillbilly performers, signed them to exclusive contracts, polished their acts, directed them, and sold them as a package to the WRVA barn-dance show. The *Old Dominion Barn Dance*, in effect, belonged to Sunshine Sue—which made problems for Maybelle Carter and her daughters. The Carters had a sort of side deal with WRVA. They had a nonexclusive contract with the station itself, and that contract allowed them to book their own show dates on days they weren't working the radio shows or the *Old Dominion Barn Dance*.

Sunshine Sue wasn't worried only about loss of control; she jealously guarded her standing in the Richmond radio world, so from the beginning, she was wary of the Carters and their big audience. When the Carters were on the radio show, or at the barn dance, Sunshine Sue let them know who was boss. Anita was getting to the age where she wanted to go to parties with her school friends or to high-school football games or dances, so she was always bumping heads with Sunshine Sue. Workman would tell Anita if she did a yodeling number she could get some time off. "I hated to yodel," said Anita, "but I'd do 'Freight Train Blues,' and *maybe* she'd give me a night off."

It didn't help matters any when Gene Autry, during a radio interview with Sunshine Sue, said his biggest thrill in Richmond was meeting Maybelle Carter. And it didn't help matters that June was acting as emcee of the morning show and drawing big numbers compared to Workman's own afternoon show. After just eighteen months at WRVA, things came to a head. Sunshine Sue wanted the Carters under the Southland Shows tent, full-time, earning for the company and letting her take a cut. The Carters wanted to maintain some independence. "[WRVA] wanted to speak to us," says June, "and I said, 'I know what they're going to ask us today. They're going to ask us to give up our park dates and would we just work for what everybody else works for, because they might be a little jealous of what was going on and they didn't want to say Sunshine Sue was jealous.' So I said [to the rest of the family], 'I would like us to just draw up a letter and have it typed and official, and we will all sign it and it's our resignation. We don't have to be at WRVA anymore. We want to do something else.' Mother said, 'You speak for us and we will do what you say. If you say stay, we'll stay. If you say go, we'll go.'

"So we typed up that letter and we got in that room and they said, 'Now, we think what you should do is just sign a contract with us, and us only.' And I said, 'Before you get any further in this—I'll just save you some time. We've all talked about this, and we would like to go home to southwestern Virginia. And then we feel we should be doing some other things.' And I gave them the letter. We'd already signed it. It was official, that was it. Then we went home to the Valley and had a chance to see all of our friends and to just stay in that part of the world."

That summer, in 1948, the Carters had no definite plan for the future, just a general sense that it would be grander than Sunshine Sue's *Old Dominion Barn Dance.* Their sudden reappearance in Maces Springs was a little awkward at first, because they had no place to live. Once the *Old Dominion Barn Dance* paychecks had started coming in, Eck had sold the homeplace to his brother Grant and Grant's wife, Theda, and bought a farm outside Richmond.

Fortunately, one of Maybelle's brothers had built a little cottage along the banks of the Holston. He'd practically grown up at Eck and Maybelle's house, so now, returning an old favor, he invited the Eck Carters to live with him, his wife, and their two daughters. Maybelle's brother had just enough room for a family of five, as long as the five were used to sleeping in cramped quarters—which, of course, they were. The metamorphosis from performers to farmers was a little more self-conscious than it had been in the past, but soon enough, they got the hang of it. Each morning at sunrise, Maybelle prepared biscuits and gravy with fried pork, hot cereal, juice, and coffee. At dinnertime (around noon) she set the table with truck-patch vegetables and, it seemed to June, "all the beef, pork, fish, or fowl that roamed the world." Finally, in the evening, with the tobacco wormed and the corn hoed, there was a small meal of milk and corn bread, with a few leftovers and a dessert of peach cobbler, or something like it—except for Eck, who always helped himself to a slice of cheddar cheese, topped with brown sugar.

Still, even among friends and family, living at a slow, safe, familiar routine, Eck and Maybelle, Helen and June knew they didn't belong to the Valley anymore. It simply couldn't hold them. It was as if they were getting up every morning and putting on clothes that didn't fit. Even while June helped her uncle with the farm chores, she was thinking mainly of the future, of the kind of entertainer she wanted to be—and of the kind she did not want to be. One day in the middle of that summer, she says, "I plumb killed Aunt Polly. I actually took her clothes and buried them in the yard."

Anita, meanwhile, was hoping to stay right where she was for a while. Now fifteen years old, she was ready to settle down a bit. She'd attended classes in Maces Springs, San Antonio, Hiltons, and Richmond, sometimes beginning the year in one school and ending in another. Besides, she was tired of the cornpone demands of radio and road-show work. There was newer music, western swing and jazz, for instance, that drew her. She didn't want to take some new job just to be another hillbilly act.

Often, when the family would convene for one of Maybelle's banquetlike luncheons, the radio would be tuned to WNOX out of

Knoxville, Tennessee. The signal was weak, but the noontime show, *Midday Merry-Go-Round*, was one of the most spirited country-music programs they had ever heard. Its impresario was Lowell Blanchard, who was busy making WNOX "the stepping-stone to the Grand Ole Opry." Roy Acuff, the Opry's biggest star, had been at WNOX. "We educate 'em," Blanchard would say with a trace of bitterness, "and Nashville gets 'em." But in Knoxville, Blanchard ruled; it was his bumptious, cornball sense of humor that set the tone for the midday show that included wacky skits and flashy hillbilly music.

So when Blanchard called and said he wanted the Carters on his show in Knoxville, Anita blanched. But Maybelle, who was not going to sit in the Valley much longer, convinced her youngest daughter that this would be a good move. Maybelle said she'd heard musicians at the Knoxville station who had no equal. They were young, fast, modern, and on the edge. Anita was not much cheered but had to knuckle under and go with her parents. By the end of the summer, the Carter Sisters and Mother Maybelle were in Knoxville, Tennessee, a town that was, notably, a hundred miles closer to Nashville than was Poor Valley.

The Carters moved into North Knoxville's Whittle Springs Hotel, a giant Tudor pile standing proudly on the brow of a hill, where the father of famed playwright Tennessee Williams was spending that summer in quiet splendor. "It looked like a country club," says June Carter, "with a swimming pool in front, and a golf course. Rich old ladies lived there, like Ma Sterchi [of the enormous Sterchi's Furniture fortune], and some rich older men, too." That summer, Knoxville was a town riding the wave of a postwar economic boom. Factories were rising along the banks of the Tennessee River. Roads were clogged with new cars and trucks and the John Deere tractors that were replacing the country mule on the smallest farms. The Tennessee Valley Authority was pushing electricity farther and farther outside the city limits; not even Senator Kenneth McKellar's warning that the TVA was "a hotbed of communism" could slow the juggernaut. After the lean years of depression and wartime rationing, people simply wanted *more*. A few had already climbed atop their roofs to place their own Brobdingnagian antennae, pulling the long wires through windows and into the backs of gleaming store-bought television sets. But even as those few invited friends and neighbors over to watch Milton Berle in lipstick and a dress, or the World Series, *live*, in their own living room, eggheads around the nation were debating whether television was the wave of the future or just a flash-in-the-pan gimmick. Radio, all agreed, still ruled the airwaves. News, both local and national, commodities prices, baseball games, weather, and entertainment—radio had them all. Folks couldn't afford not to have a radio. In Knoxville, the station to dial in was WNOX.

The WNOX studios were downtown on Gay Street, between Breezy Wynn's clothing factory and the Sterchi's Furniture outlet (the Sterchis had once owned WNOX). The station had only ten thousand watts, a local, minor-league affair, but its signature show, the *Midday Merry-Go-Round*, had attracted a stable of great musicians. One of the most talented was a skinny, shy, sad-faced guitar player up from Luttrell, Tennessee. And his was the first face the Carters saw upon entering the Gay Street studio. There he was, Chester "Chet" Atkins, sitting sullenly in a corner. He may have nodded a hello when the Carters entered, but he wouldn't have had much to say. Anita's high hopes must have wilted when she saw him that day, along with his band mates, a guitar-mandolin duo known as Homer and Jethro. These two were the perfect image of hillbilly, all floppy hats and overalls.

But Anita would never forget the first time she heard them play; it was just like her mother promised: Here was music unlike any she'd heard, a spectacular mix of country and jazz. "When I heard Chester and Homer and Jethro start playing, my mouth dropped about ten miles," Anita remembered, her voice rising with excitement a half century after the event. "There was no better group in the world. Jethro was such a great mandolin player, he just scared me. And they had Aitchee Burns, Jethro's brother, playing with them, the best bass player I ever heard." Anita intended to learn some things about playing a bass fiddle from "Dixie's fastest slapper of the bass," Aitchee. "We sat at their feet," says June. "Especially Chester's."

Chet Atkins did not immediately cleave to the Carters; he did not, at that time, cleave to anyone very quickly. In 1948 he was a young husband and a new father, wondering if he would ever make enough money from his music to support a family. Chet was born in 1924 in a hollow near Luttrell, and grew up there and in Georgia, splitting time between the homes of his divorced parents. He was a slight, introverted, asthma-stricken boy in a poor and broken family. The family was also, thank heaven, musical. His father pushed Chet to play the violin, but the boy didn't listen. "When I was eleven or twelve, I read in Daddy's *Etude* magazines about Heifetz and Albert Spalding and all those guys who started when they were seven years old. I thought, 'I'm too old to be a violinist.' So I played the guitar."

In the late '30s, Chet built himself a radio out of mail-order parts (he listened to the Carters on XERA) and his first electric guitar. In 1939, at age fifteen, he got work at the station WRBL in Columbus, Georgia. Three years later, he was hired at WNOX as a fiddle player, for three dollars a night. "It wasn't enough to live on, but I was in show business," he says, "and I loved it." Asthma kept Atkins out of the military, so he remained in Knoxville as part of the WNOX wartime parade of talented but oddball 4-Fs, which included Emory Martin, the one-armed banjo player, and Ray Meyer, who had no arms and played steel guitar with his feet. "We also had the Johnson Kids with us," said Chet. "They were, like, nine and eleven. Blanchard would give the little one a nickel every time he'd break wind. That little bastard could just go on and on."

One night, while driving home from an appearance, Lowell Blan-chard heard Atkins playing guitar in the backseat. Atkins's technique was his own variation of what is now known as "Travis picking." He plucked the muted bass strings in a quick thumping rhythm with his thumb; his fingers played the melody, creating intricate and beguiling melodies above the rhythmic bass. That night, in the car, Blanchard named Atkins the WNOX staff guitarist. "I had to learn country tunes, old standards, pop tunes, and once in a while, a new pop tune," said Chet. "And to learn new tunes, I had to learn new positions and how to play the melody and the rhythm at the same time." But Atkins's adven-turous streak quickly got the better of him. His liberal use of jazz chords and themes struck his Knoxville audience as a little peculiar, and it wasn't long before Blanchard was suggesting to Chet that he was ready for a more cosmopolitan market.

He went first to WLW in Cincinnati, then on to Nashville, Springfield, Denver. "I don't think they cared too much for what I did," Chet said of Cincinnatians. "I was there six months before they fired me. That's the way it went. I got fired all over the country." He finally circled back to Knoxville and, with Henry Haynes and Kenneth Burns (aka Homer and Jethro), began cooking up a home brew of jazz-infused country and country-infused jazz. When they took their show on the road in the late forties, Tennesseans still hadn't caught up with Chet and his buddies. "Hell," said Atkins, "we didn't even make gas money a lot of the time. We just didn't draw. I felt defeated."

Chet may not have been cheered by the goings-on around WNOX, either. Even after the war, the station retained some of its 4-F cast and feel. A rare photograph taken inside the WNOX studio shows the entire cast guffawing, as Blanchard presides over a boxing match between three-and-a-half-foot comedian Robert "Little Robert" Van Winkel and "Hot Shot Elmer," a half-wit character created by singer Bill Carlisle. In the middle of all the cornpone high jinks, the Carter girls' eager and unwavering enthusiasm for Chet's music began to win him over. But it was Eck Carter who really reeled him in.

By the time they got to Knoxville, Eck "Pop" Carter was Maybelle and the girls' full-time manager, arranging their out-of-town engagements, for which services he took his fifth of the money. He also helped out with the driving, but in this capacity he still required close supervision. "Now, Daddy," Maybelle would admonish as he climbed behind the wheel, "don't drive too fast." Within five minutes, he would be doing a hundred miles an hour while his daughters squealed at him from the backseat to please, please slow down. "Okay, okay," he'd grump, "since you don't really want to get there." Then he'd putter along at a crawl for a while, before gradually picking up the pace. Even after he finally gained a comfortable cruising speed, he still needed watching, because he sometimes dozed off in the driver's seat. "Somebody'd holler 'Daaadddeeee!' and he'd wake up," recalled guitarist Ray Edenton, who often filled in for Anita when she was in school. "They told me they had to do it all the time."

But Eck meant to earn his keep, and he took his role as manager seriously. And by himself, he came up with a brilliant idea. First he ran it past Maybelle, then their daughters. When all approved, he approached Atkins: How would Chet like to join the Carter Sisters and Mother Maybelle? They'd split the money evenly. He'd get a sixth just like the rest.

There are countless reasons why this experiment might have failed. Atkins's complex style of playing might have clashed with Maybelle's. He might have been overwhelmed by June's vivaciousness, sending him further into his shell. Even simple logistics were daunting; the addition of Chet meant *six* people crammed into a single Frasier automobile, along with the instruments, Chet's amplifier, and a brand-new, top-of-the-line RCA public-address system.

Maybe that's why they decided to leave Eck behind on the first road trip, assuring an inauspicious start to the partnership. It was raining hard, and somewhere on the road out of Knoxville, the Frasier began to limp. As the only male, Atkins was obliged to get out of the car and examine the tires; he found one punctured. "Flatter'n hell," he muttered, "and a car full of women." The women giggled at Chet's sudden, surprising volubility. Not entirely sure how to change a tire, Chet knelt in the mud and went to work. Periodically, a car would drive by and drench him, setting off a new round of ejaculatory curses—which, in turn, sent the Carter girls into new fits of giggles. For the rest of his life, he would refer to this as "the night I taught those girls how to cuss."

The road got smoother, fast, and the Carters soon found out that in Chet Atkins they'd got much more than a talented sideman. Though the Carter girls were already playing pop tunes, and had even injected a few jazzy numbers into their act on special occasions, it had never come as naturally to them as it did to Atkins. Songs they had sung all their lives were suddenly made fresh, as Chet's guitar painted them with unexpected flourish: to the mournful country ballad "In the Pines," he added stinging blues licks; for boot-stompers like "Stay a Little Longer," he played swing; and to his repertoire of solos, he added an instrumental version of "My Clinch Mountain Home" that was so fast and complicated, A.P. himself would scarcely have recognized it. What's more, a virtuoso such as Atkins makes everyone around him play better, and Helen's accordion, in particular, improved dramatically. She had always played melodies well enough, but now she developed a *chugga-chugga* rhythm to go along with Atkins's thumping thumb; and she, too, learned to swing out.

For the first time in his life, Atkins was making decent money, and his confidence increased day by day. The taciturn Chester was a perfect foil for June, who had buried Aunt Polly but had birthed a newer, sleeker, less cornpone hillbilly chatterbox, "Little Junie Carter." One of Little Junie's main missions was to get the clench-jawed guitar player to talk onstage. "I'd swing on the curtain way out over the audience, just so Chester would tell me to stop it," she later wrote. "Sometimes as he was playing his guitar, I'd run my nose up and down the frets—adding to or taking away from whatever he was playing at the time. He had a vibrato on his guitar that looked like a gear shift, and I'd throw him into high or low, whether he felt like it or not." When he finally did begin to talk onstage, there emerged an appealing "aw, shucks" young man that country people seemed to like. It had never occurred to Chet that anybody would like *him*. And for once he looked almost happy.

"I was spending more time in that Frasier than I was in bed," Atkins later wrote in his memoir, *Country Gentleman*. "But I loved every minute of it." On Saturday night, nearing midnight, after WNOX's *Tennessee Barn Dance* was behind them, the group would load the Frasier and hit the road, bound for somewhere as far-flung as the Pennsylvania fairgrounds. In the wee hours of the morning, they would stop at a sleepy relative's house in Poor Valley for breakfast, then continue on, as Chet put it, "like a bunch of zombies."

Right from the start, "The Carter Sisters and Mother Maybelle, Chet Atkins and His Famous Guitar" was a dynamic, and self-contained, road-show act. They'd even worked out a more efficient division of labor. Now everybody had assigned tasks: Maybelle tuned the instruments and Helen worked the door, while June and Chet set up the stage. Atkins, who loved tinkering with electronics, would try to adjust the controls on their new RCA sound system, but June would bark at him to keep his "blamed fingers" to himself. "I knew just where to put the little knobs," she'd say later. The sound system consisted of a single microphone and two large speakers, so even with a separate amplifier for Chet's guitar, stagecraft required subtle balancing. Four instruments and five separate voices had to share a single mike. "You had to play loud enough to be heard but quiet enough to hear the other people," says June. "It was complicated." There was rarely a time for a proper sound check to ensure that everything would be in balance; at best, there was only Eck, wandering around the audience, giving them the sign that everything was coming through okay.

Though the new act was moving toward improvisation, the shows had the same basic contours. After the theme song, "The Blue Ridge Mountains of Virginia," June would open the show with a toe-tapper such as "Goin' to Sugar Hill" or a novelty tune such as Felice and Boudleaux Bryant's "Plain Old Country Girl," which suited Little Junie Carter right down to the ground.

Next came a sentimental pop number, followed by Mother Maybelle singing a Carter Family standard such as "Gold Watch and Chain" or "Little Moses." If she sang one of the old duets, such as "Little Darlin' Pal of Mine" or "Jealous-Hearted Me," Helen would take Sara's part. Then Chet would play a solo on the guitar, which might be anything from an old Carter Family tune to "Liebestraum." Traveling and performing with the Carters had made Atkins much more aware of the audience; not just its size, but its prevailing tastes.

They'd be at a date in Pennsylvania, well outside of the WNOX range, and Chet would find himself in front of a crowd full of *Yankees*, and yet they seemed almost human. as though they had "the same problems and could identify with our songs just as quickly as the people who lived in the South," Atkins remembered. "It was the first time I ever took stock of the people to whom we were playing and of what our music was saying to them." The more he watched the audiences, the more able he was to read how he was going over. He was learning to change up, to go off the prescribed set, to shift his emphasis from country to jazz and back again—in short, to do whatever seemed to best suit the occasion.

After Chet's guitar solo, Anita would take over the mike and sing a love song in her clear, spine-shivering soprano. At fifteen, Anita had been a professional performer for eleven years, and she knew how to read an audience, too. Sometimes when the crowd got edgy, she would let fly with a song nobody expected, such as "That's How I Spell Ireland." After that, anything might happen. If the audience favored bluegrass, Chet would break out his fiddle and Maybelle her banjo. If it was a more somber, Sunday crowd, they would lean heavily on hymns and sacred songs while Helen's accordion sobbed like a church organ.

Maybelle, for her part, stuck to her knitting. She knew the foundation of the Carters' appeal was still the old original tunes, and she made sure every set had some. For the rest, she receded quietly into the background, pushing her daughters out front and toward new songs. Maybelle would hear a pop tune she liked and say to Helen or Anita, "I bet you could sing that." Sometimes, when one of the girls made a big success with a song, and the requests came again and again and again, until her daughter was simply sick of performing it, Maybelle would gently remind her, "Honey, you've got to give the people what they want."

After nearly a quarter century, pleasing the audience remained Maybelle's single focus. She never acted as if the effort deserved special reward; the way she saw it, it was her privilege to be given the chance to perform. But that effort was also physically demanding, requiring as many as five shows on a Sunday. At the end of a weekend full of shows, they'd all pile into the Frasier and run it like fury back to Knoxville to be ready for Monday's *Midday Merry-Go-Round.* And while that car raced through the dark highways toward "home," postperformance adrenaline often got the better of exhaustion. Who could sleep? New harmonies were discovered in the backseat of that Frasier, new songs learned. "We rehearsed so much that I could just look at Helen and Anita and know what notes they would sing," says June, "even though Helen sometimes sang above me, sometimes below me. People would send sheet music to the station, songs that nobody had ever heard before, and we sang them just like sacred-harp singing—you just took off, and everybody found a part." Sometimes in that car, new songs were written. Once when the big Frasier lurched, the giggling sisters decided it was high time to fit the word *lurch* into a song. "The Kneeling Drunkard's Prayer" ("I went down to the old country church, / and saw the drunkard stagger and lurch"), in fact, would be the first single the Carter Sisters and Mother

Maybelle recorded for RCA, in 1949. It didn't take long for Chet Atkins to discover that a carful of women has its advantages, especially when things finally got quiet. "I'd lay my head in one of 'em's lap and try to go to sleep," he said. "It wasn't all bad, I tell you."

By the time the car reached Knoxville, there was never much time before the five musicians had to get back to their regular day job at the radio station. The grinding schedule, and Eck's watchful eye, cut into the girls' social life. Sometimes they'd be invited to sing at fraternity houses at the University of Tennessee, where the college-age Carter sisters would stand around the piano, playing requests for the moon-faced boys in their blazers and ties. On rare occasions, they'd even go on dates with fraternity boys or football players, but this was as close to college life as June and her sisters would get. Maybelle, meanwhile, made friends with a WNOX singer named Bonnie Lou Moore. The two women shared the same professional and motherly concerns, would chat between shows or talk on the phone, but as June says, "There was no time for real friendship. We were so tied up in music—we were never *not* making music—and if we weren't, if Mother had any sense, she got into bed and went to sleep. We all did."

The Carters did have a smallish family reunion in Knoxville in 1948, when A.P. accepted a spot on the WNOX program. As far as the girls could see, their uncle Doc hadn't changed much. Some evenings, the entire family would gather at a diner across the street from WNOX. One night, as A.P. crossed Gay Street toward Regis' Restaurant, a pigeon relieved itself on his hat. "*Damn*-it," he said, pointing to his hat. "That pigeon took a shit on my head." Just then, out of the corner of his eye, he caught a lady passing. Instantly ashamed at his off-color language, A.P. tried to phum-pher out an apology. "No, he didn't, lady," he called after her. "No, he didn't." By the time he got to the table where the girls were waiting, the absurdity of his apology had struck him as funny, and as he sat down at the table, his shoulders were bouncing up and down, and hiccups of laughter were catching in his throat. "We all got to laughin'," said Helen, "and he laughed so hard that instead of cleaning up the mess, he got it stuck on his hat. And he ate his whole meal like that—with [pigeon droppings] sitting on his head."

In the WNOX studio, where there was tremendous curiosity about him, none of the musicians ever saw that informal, relaxed side of A.P. Carter. "A reserved, diginified sort of fellow" was how Chet Atkins described him, "a strange old duck. He'd stroll around all the time, wouldn't sit still."

"I heard of him all my life," says Ray Edenton. "I remembered him from the old records, and I'd always wondered why he'd wait so long to come in and sing." To Edenton, A.P. Carter just wasn't like the other musicians making their living at the Gay Street studio; it had been seven years since A.P. Carter had recorded, and five since he'd had a regular radio job, but he still had a following. All he seemed to want to do was make music and sell his new pamphlet, *Bible Questions and Answers*. "We were making thirty-five dollars a week from the station, but he said he didn't want no money," says Edenton, "just let him sell books. And I said, 'Man, that old man's gonna starve to death.' I didn't know what a following he had. He'd get up and do a couple of songs, then he'd sing bass with the Carter girls. And man, the mail! They brought it in by the basketload. Boy, he sold those books. They loved him, those country people." But A.P. didn't last long in Knoxville; he was anxious to get home to Maces Springs, where he had some ideas about building and presiding over his own summer stage.

The Carter sisters had always taken strength from one another. On-stage, sometimes, when Anita was bone-tired and maybe even a little sick of the road, she'd look over at Helen behind her accordion, or at June in her flat hat and comic pantaloons, and they'd smile at her and nod, and she felt at home, stronger, able to go on. But even before they'd been at Knoxville a year, there were signs that the Carter Sisters and Mother Maybelle were no longer a single, or single-minded, unit. The fault lines were not yet visible, but in the hurtling enclosed cocoon of the Frasier, each of the girls was beginning to form her own separate idea about what she wanted next.

June was an entertainer for life; she was happiest in front of an audience, and she knew she was good. So did the A&R man at RCA,

Steve Sholes. Sholes was a shrewd judge of artists, at least in terms of their commercial potential. He would ater gamble his own career by paying Sun Records what was then a preposterous sum—thirty-five thousand dollars, plus back royalties—to sign Elvis Presley. Sholes was a stickler for charisma; his artists had to have it. When he found somebody who had it, he grabbed him or her. So in early 1949, not long after the Carter Sisters and Mother Maybelle recorded a single for him, Sholes presented June with a solo contract and asked her to come to New York to record "Plain Old Country Girl" and some comic numbers with Homer and Jethro.

With Eck as chaperone, June took the train to New York for her first sessions outside the family. "Plain Old Country Girl" was a piece of cake; she could sing that material in her sleep. But Homer and Jethro had something a little more challenging in mind: a parody of "Baby, It's Cold Outside." The original, written by Frank Loesser, was a romantic duet featured in the Esther Williams aquatics film *Neptune's Daughter*. It had won the Academy Award for best song and had already been recorded by three famed duos: Dinah Shore and Buddy Clark; Margaret Whiting and Johnny Mercer; Ella Fitzgerald and Louis Jordan. The version Homer and Jethro cooked up was decidedly less reverent or romantic.

In the hillbilly version, June pays a visit to Homer and Jethro, who ply her with drinks and Eddy Arnold records. June tries to escape the house ("Pappy'll get the shotgun down!" she warns), but she's enjoying the moonshine ("maybe just a half jug more") and the men are telling her it's too cold to leave the house. Homer and Jethro liken her lips to bicycle pedals, moving in closer as Atkins's guitar swirls and Burns's mandolin trills.

Only after this over-the-top, and potentially embarrassing, version was recorded did it occur to Steve Sholes that Frank Loesser might find the parody offensive. Sholes had no interest in blindsiding one of the most popular songwriters in America, so he nervously sent Loesser a test pressing, along with a polite letter, asking his permission to release the cut. Loesser, it turned out, had a sense of humor and asked only that the label read, "with apologies to Frank Loesser." The single was released in

August of 1949 and began to climb both the country and the pop charts, rising to number nine and number twenty-two, respectively. That fall, news came that the Latin Quarter, one of New York City's toniest nightclubs, was anxious to have Homer and Jethro and June Carter for an extended engagement. June balked. Leaving the family for a few days to make a record was one thing, but leaving the Carter Sisters and Mother Maybelle for a long period was something else entirely. She knew she held the act together, and she wasn't going to risk its dissolution.

Neither of her sisters was as single-minded or as ambitious as June. Anita's one great ambition, as the fall of 1949 neared, was to convince her father to let her go back to Hiltons for her final year of high school. This would be her last chance to live like a normal teenage girl, chattering with her girlfriends, wading in the Holston River on hot days, and maybe even going to the prom. She told her father she could still work some of the weekend shows and it was only for a single school year. Finally he relented, and Anita moved in with her uncle Bug and aunt Florida to have a regular senior year. Helen was in a dicier position. There was a man she loved, someone who had been pursuing her for more than two years. Glenn Jones was handsome and dashing, a pilot with his own plane. He was also possessed of remarkable energy and enduring patience. But his patience was running out.

Glenn had met Helen in Richmond, not long after the war, and he was immediately, hopelessly, in love. "She wasn't loud," he says. "She didn't smoke, didn't drink. She wasn't wild like a lot of girls back then. Mother Maybelle kept a pretty tight rein on them. They were all good girls, like the girls I grew up with in the country." On the second date, he took Helen up in the plane, and even gave June (and her resonant voice) a ride. "June used to be up for almost anything," Glenn says. "I took her for what we call a 'buzz job' on my sister's house in the country. My sister swore she could hear June screamin'."

Glenn's biggest problem was Pop, though the younger man told himself it was nothing personal, that Eck's manner was meant to discourage *any* of his daughters' potential suitors. "If you went to the house," says Glenn, "he wouldn't talk to you. He'd just ignore you. Naturally, I tried to warm him up, because I knew it was important.

Eventually, he'd answer me in grunts and yeses or nos, but he made it clear that he didn't want any conversation."

Despite the silent treatment, Glenn didn't give up. When the family moved from Richmond back to Maces Springs for the summer of 1948, he cheerfully drove 350 miles to see Helen. Eck didn't scare him. At the time, Glenn was appearing in air shows in his new flip-wing Stearman airplane, performing spins, rolls, and other gut-bucking stunts. For his finale, he would swoop down to within eighteen inches of the ground to grab a handkerchief with his wingtip. "Looking back, I'd say it was a little knuckle-headed," he admitted years later. "But I was young and invincible, you know?" He was also a man whose vision of the future shimmered before him, and it always included Helen Carter. So even when the family moved farther away, to Knoxville, Glenn refused to give up.

But in the fall of 1949, in Glenn's cold war with Eck, the advantage took a definite turn toward the elder: The Carters got an offer from KWTO in Springfield, Missouri. Chet Atkins had worked at the station and, despite having been fired, had admiration for KWTO producer E. E. "Si" Siman. The family held an excited conference, noting the proximity to cities such as Kansas City, St. Louis, and Chicago. It was a step up, a step the family couldn't afford not to take. The lone dissenter was Anita, who was enjoying her standing at Hiltons High School. At sixteen, she had blossomed into a spectacular beauty, polite, ladylike, and wildly popular. To the Scott County crowd, she was a wealthy, glamorous figure. They were pleased and flattered that she seemed genuinely interested in their own lives. And then . . . she was gone. "All of a sudden we were moving to Missouri," Anita said. "I begged my daddy to let me stay, but he said, 'No, it's too important.'" Not only did Anita leave Hiltons High School, but she gave up school altogether. "I couldn't do all the work *and* go to school," she sighed, nearly fifty years after the fact. "My education had to come from different directions. Moving to Springfield was the right thing to do. But I wish I had finished." Glenn Jones, though not invited to the family conference, also dissented, sure that Pop Carter had orchestrated the entire affair, "moving Helen farther away, hoping to break us up," he says. "But he couldn't get her far enough."

In Springfield, Atkins installed his wife, Leona, and his daughter, Merle, in a modest rented cottage on Pacific Avenue, while the Carters moved into an elegant, three-story brick home on East Walnut Street. Then Eck traded the Frasier for a big, hulking Lincoln. "They spent money like there was no tomorrow," says Atkins. "Cars, clothes, anything they wanted." Each day, the Carters piloted the sleek new car down the sleepy streets of Springfield, Missouri, to KWTO ("Keep Watching the Ozarks"). The station itself was located in a onetime mortuary. ("All of the singing jingles were done in the embalming room," said Atkins, "because of its echo-chamber effect.") But by 1949 the large stone house held two separate studios running full-time, from which more than 150 live programs were broadcast each week. Performers were required to submit song lists twenty-four hours before their appearances to prevent repetition by other acts. KWTO was as country as country could be, with a schedule full of hill-billy music, agricultural and livestock reports, re-creations of St. Louis Cardinals baseball games—folks still had fond memories of farm boys Dizzy and Daffy Dean and their Gashouse Gang teammates—and even a farm-town soap opera, The Little Crossroads Store. But the down-home hayseed programming belied a solid, stainless-steel business plan drawn up by Si Siman. Siman and his partners had founded an operation called RadiOzark, a syndicate that recorded KWTO's best talent and aggressively sold it to station managers across the nation.

Not long after arriving in Springfield, the Carter Sisters and Mother Maybelle, Chet Atkins and His Famous Guitar was a featured attraction of RadiOzark's syndicated programs. The group recorded about forty separate fifteen-minute shows, in a process not dissimilar to the border-radio sessions. Magnetic tape was still a novelty, so the shows were transcribed on acetate disks. If somebody made a mistake, there was only one way to fix it: start the whole show over again. Sometimes it was Helen's nervous laughter or Anita's giggling that ruined a take, or sometimes Atkins simply called a halt to the proceedings. Where his playing was concerned, Chet was a perfectionist. Maybelle never complained, even when it took an hour to record a single fifteen-minute show. She was always happy for the chance to get it right.

The transcriptions, more than two hundred songs total, show a remarkable range of influences and abilities. The sisters' harmonies were tighter than ever and, at their best, reminiscent of the best of the Andrews Sisters. June did comic songs such as "Keep Them Cold, Icy Fingers Off of Me," "I Swear I'll Never Wear a Pair of Shoes," and "The Bald-Headed End of a Broom." Chet was already playing the songs he would be known for in later years, including "Dizzy Strings," "Canned Heat," and "There'll Be Some Changes Made." He even picked up his fiddle for vigorous renditions of "Whistlin' Rufus," "Dill Pickles Rag," and "Turkey in the Straw." His singing on sentimental numbers was nearly morose, but his shy charm came through on comic numbers such as "You Made Toothpicks of the Timber of My Heart" and "My Little Pup with the Patent-Leather Nose and the Wiggily-Waggily Tail." Anita's version of the Hank Williams hit "There'll Be No Teardrops Tonight" was heart-stopping, while her jazzy south-of-the-border torch song "Don Juan" ("There's a fella down in Mexico who's a señorita's dream, / As a buckaroo, he's a floparoo, but as a lover he's supreme") was pop-hit material. On bluegrass numbers, Maybelle even broke out her five-string banjo.

Moreover, the Carters were becoming a commercial success. Atkins was finally making real money, and the group's KWTO sponsor, Red Star Flour, was thrilled. June's long apprenticeship had paid off; on the radio or at a road show, she knew how to make a sale, and with panache. In the middle of a road show, Little Junie Carter would pluck from the audience a six- or seven-year-old girl and try to marry her off to Chet. Of course, June would admit to the little girl, Chester wasn't much to look at; was, in fact, ugly as fifteen miles of bad road. But still, he needed a wife, and since the girl was already seven years old and not yet married, she couldn't afford to be choosy. Problem was, June would say, Chester didn't know how to do anything except play the guitar, so they'd never have any money.

"He'll probably put you to work paying the bass," June would say, pointing to Anita. "You'll have to carry a big ole bass fiddle around, like that one there. Let's put it on your back and see if you can carry it. . . . No? . . . You don't think you can? Well, you *really* won't have any

money, then. You sure will have to get Red Star Flour [June always pronounced it 'flar'] and use it for a lotta things. You know, you can use it
on your face for powder; in fact, girl, you could use some on your face
right now. If Chester still don't like you the way you look, you can mix
up some of that *flar* with water in a little mug, and you've got a great
beauty mask, but you've gotta be sure it's Red Star Flour—the other
kind don't work."

Pretty soon, the Red Star sales team was inserting coupons in bags
of flour that could be presented for a discount to any Carter Sisters
show. Helen, who was still working the door at shows, was made even
more nervous by these gnarly fraction-laden transactions. "We didn't
have calculators back then," she said. "The people were entitled to double their coupon value at the door, so they might come in with thirty-
eight cents' worth of coupons and want five adults and six children, and
I had to do the math in my head. Can you imagine?" As the coupons
piled up, and Helen's sums became increasingly complicated, the
Carters realized they must be selling an awful lot of Red Star Flour.

Then, into the middle of this smooth, gliding success, came Glenn
Jones, to see Helen—and he presented her with something that
amounted to an ultimatum. He wanted Helen to marry him, but he
was done chasing. He'd come all the way to Missouri to see her, he
said, but he was drawing the line there. "If [Pop] takes you to California," he told her, "I can't go." Helen's response was surprising, and
one he never expected. She hated flying, she said, and she was afraid
to marry a pilot. When he told her, without a second's hesitation, that
he'd give up flying for good, Glenn had won his bride. Flying was the
one thing in the world he loved most, Helen knew—besides, evidently,
her. So Glenn and Helen agreed on one thing: Neither would force
the other to give up the things they loved best. "She knew I would have
liked her to have gone back to Richmond with me," Jones says, "but
she wanted to keep working with the family. So she told me she'd like
to try, and if it ever got to be a problem, she would quit and go back
with me wherever I went. I thought it would work, because I knew I
was going to do everything I could to make it work."

Glenn Jones also knew Pop Carter wouldn't like it, and he wasn't surprised at Eck's response when Glenn delivered the news. "I was wondering if you had any objections," he said to Eck.

"Would it make any difference if I did?"

"Not really, sir," Jones said. "But I wanted to show you the courtesy of asking."

Eck grunted something. Maybe it was consent, maybe it was surrender, Glenn couldn't tell.

Glenn was more surprised by Maybelle's reaction to the news. By the time Glenn got to her, Eck had already dropped the bombshell. Maybelle gave no hint of approval to Glenn, let alone any sign of joy. "She didn't say anything one way or another," remembers Jones. "Just matter-of-factly said that Pop had told her what we were planning."

"Glenn was okay," says June. "It was the fact that we were losing our sister. When Helen got to be pregnant, we knew she would go away and live with him."

Once they decided, Glenn and Helen wasted no time. They scheduled the wedding for a few weeks later, in a preacher's house not far from the Carters' home on Walnut Street. When the day arrived, Springfield was hit with a blizzard that shut off power to the entire city; the preacher never even removed his overcoat as he presided over the ceremony in a candlelit room. As Helen and Glenn took their vows, June began to sob. By the time the couple was pronounced man and wife, she was bawling. "It was as though I was cutting a sister out and handing her her life on a platter," says June, "with blood dripping from my hands." By the time the ceremony was over, Helen was weeping, too. Her honeymoon was short—just a week traveling through Tennessee and Virginia. She wasn't about to stay away longer; she was anxious to get back to the family, to reassure them that her marriage didn't mean the end of the group.

Pop Carter, meanwhile, was not as broken up as the girls might have expected. He was sitting on a big piece of news. The Martha White Flour Company had evidently taken note of Red Star's rising sales. The company wanted the Carter Sisters and Mother Maybelle as regulars on a segment they sponsored every Saturday night on WSM, in Nashville, Tennessee, at the Grand Ole Opry.

Mother Maybelle at the Opry (Lorrie Davis Bennett)

Opposite: The Carters with Hank Williams, Roy Acuff, and stewardess on a flight to New York (Lorrie Davis Bennett)

Mama Maybelle

Country performers rarely hesitated before accepting an offer from the Grand Ole Opry; a call from the Opry was like a call from the major leagues. Nobody turned it down. But Eck rejected the Opry's first overture in 1949 without even consulting his family, because the offer had come with a remarkable caveat: Chet Atkins wasn't welcome. To Pop, the reasons seemed confused—and confusing. There were already too many guitarists hanging around the Opry, he was told, so new ones could come in only under special circumstances. They had to be sponsored by another member of the musicians' union, and in any case, Atkins was not the "sort" of guitar player in demand there. As the explanation wound on, Eck began to get a whiff of the unmistakable scent of bullshit. The simple fact was, Nashville session musicians didn't want Chet Atkins taking work away from them. The whole thing was underhanded, unfair, and, since Chet was by now a member of the family, offensive to the Carters. So Eck told the Opry thanks just the same, but no deal.

Opry management did not seem to take Eck's refusal very seriously, because a few weeks later the offer was sweetened with a little extra cash and repeated with the same no-Atkins proviso. Again, Eck refused. A month later, another call; and still Eck refused. For six months or so, the offers would continue until finally Opry management began to understand that Pop was immovable. Discussions were apparently held with the union, and a sponsor was found for Atkins: Don Davis, who played steel guitar for Opry star George Morgan (both of whom had become close friends to the Carters while playing in Springfield). Opry management decided that the rules might be bent for Atkins after all, if the Carter Sisters and Mother Maybelle were worth the trouble. They were invited for a test performance—an audition, really, though no one called it that—to see if Opry audiences would take to them.

The Carters arrived at Nashville's Ryman Auditorium, home of the Grand Ole Opry, on a Saturday night in early 1950. The Ryman was not a comfortable place. Onstage, musicians in heavy spangled costumes endured sweltering heat caused by bright lights and a near total lack of ventilation. Audiences sat on hard oak pews; the color scheme of pale mint green, with gold, green, and brown accents, was not easy on the eyes. But the Ryman's churchlike architecture gave it an atmosphere of powerful solemnity and a sense of history in the making. "It was where everyone wanted to be," says June. "And we were like everyone."

The provenance of the hall itself was local legend: In 1885 Thomas Ryman was one of Nashville's wealthiest citizens. He'd made his fortune operating a fleet of riverboats that served as floating palaces of pleasure and sin. Each of his thirty-five paddle wheelers had saloons, gambling parlors, bad, bad women, and bulging cash registers. But that year a famed evangelist, Rev. Samuel Porter Jones, blew into town railing against the salacious riverboat trade and the men who profited from it. The preacher's sermonizing had an immediate and deleterious effect on Ryman's bottom line, so the tycoon went to one of Jones's revivals, hoping to catch the preacher afterward and reason with him. To do this, Ryman was compelled to sit through Jones's sermon. Though many of

Jones's doctrines seem absurd today (including his conviction that "there is nothing more corrupting this side of hell than baseball"), he was a riveting speaker. His simple slogan—"Quit Your Meanness!"— converted thousands, including, improbably, Thomas Ryman. So thankful was Ryman for his salvation that he eventually built an auditorium to give the Reverend Jones and other traveling men of God a suitable place to preach whenever they alighted in Nashville. The Ryman Auditorium was built for function, not elegance, with a brick exterior, an ample stage, long rows of pews, and arched windows all around to provide light while suggesting some sense of godliness. The Grand Ole Opry moved into the building in 1943, making the Ryman "the Mother Church of Country Music."

The thousands of country-music lovers who flocked there each week were something like pilgrims. Some would take the trouble to write ahead for reserved tickets, which cost sixty cents (federal tax included), but most did not. They drove an average of five hundred miles (the demographics had been well studied) from all over the South and Midwest. The crowd would begin to line up outside a little after noon, and by 7:30, when the show began, it was not unusual for five thousand people to be waiting in a line stretching past the Hazelwood Auto lot and around the block. Others would arrive over the course of the evening, because the Opry played on until midnight, with each half hour bought by a different sponsor. Only 2,400 unreserved seats were available, but many more half-price tickets would be sold each night, because not everyone stayed for the entire evening. The pews were punishing to the human fanny; there was no air-conditioning, except what could be created waving a cardboard fan or a program; and the worst seats, beneath the balcony—the "Confederate Gallery," which was added in 1897 to accommodate a gathering of Civil War veterans—could be especially trying. "If somebody spilled a Coke, it would leak on your head," Loretta Lynn once said. "At least, I hope it was Coke."

It was pretty much the same atmosphere in which the Carters had played their entire lives, only on a larger scale. Details of their first show were unrecorded, but according to June, they were so well received, "the roof came offa that building." The Carters had absolutely everything an Opry act of the period needed. They were venerable, wholesome, and traditional and, at the same time, young, beautiful, and contemporary. And they had remarkable energy. According to June, WSM hired them at $825 a week to play no fewer than four shows: a prime weekend slot on the *Opry* (8:00 P.M. on Saturday) sponsored by Martha White Flour; an evening show prior to the *Opry*, held for patients at Veterans' Hospital; a daytime show called *Noontime Neighbors;* and a Sunday-morning gospel program. Chet Atkins was forbidden from working with anyone but the Carters for a period of six months, but after that, he could do as he liked. In later years, he minced no words in expressing his gratitude. "I owe everything to the Carters," he said. "I don't know what the hell would have happened to me if I hadn't run into 'em."

Maybelle and her daughters could not have moved to Nashville at a better time. Commercial country music was entering its first golden age. Contemporaries of the Original Carter Family, the old-time artists who had achieved national fame in the '20s and '30s playing traditional numbers, hymns, and parlor tunes, were on their last legs. One of the few who lingered was Uncle Dave Macon, with his diamond-studded banjo. Macon knew more of the old songs and vaudeville numbers than anyone except the Carters; but by now he was a thoroughly nostalgic figure who had only a few more years to live.

"Who are you with, boy?" Macon would ask Chet Atkins night after night as they waited backstage for the show to begin.

"I play guitar with the Carter Sisters and Mother Maybelle, Uncle Dave."

"Oh, that's right," Macon would say. "Well, keep bringin' that thumb in, son, and you'll be just fine."

Few Opry-goers of 1950 came for Uncle Dave. They came to hear Roy Acuff belt out "The Great Speckled Bird," or Ernest Tubb croak "Walkin' the Floor Over You," or Minnie Pearl screech "Howwww-deee!" Country music was a $25 million *business*, and even judged against America's postwar economic boom, the industry's growth rate of nearly 25 percent a year was astonishing. Nineteen-fifty was the year "the whole country was taken with the Nashville muse," *Colliers* magazine gushed. "Sponsors are lined up five deep waiting for the first spot to open up on the [Opry] show." Red Foley's "Chattanooga Shoe Shine Boy" topped the pop charts in February, and Patti Page's "Tennessee Waltz" (penned by Pee Wee King and Redd Stewart) was the nation's number one song in December.

The Carters' Opry performances were similar to their RadiOzark shows, only more polished and, truth be told, less far-ranging or interesting. They plucked the most popular songs from their repertoire and performed them with regularity and predictability, because that was what the Opry wanted. June Carter thrived on this big-time showbiz stage, but more as a comedienne than as a musician. She was at least as funny as Minnie Pearl and a whole lot better-looking. In no time, it was an established rule that before the Carters played a song, June would do a comedy routine with the segment's emcee (each half hour of the Opry show was hosted by a different star). June would charge into the spotlight and tell Roy Acuff that she had been out at the local military base entertaining the troops, and while there, she had been forced to jump into "one o' them thar wolf holes." Roy would correct her: "Not a wolf hole, June. A fox hole." For a moment June would look confused, then she'd answer: "Well, a fox may a-dug it, but it was shore fulla wolves when I jumped in!" While the Opry audience laughed and clapped and stomped, she would strut over to where her family stood waiting, and lead them in one of her novelty numbers such as "It's My Lazy Day" or "Lookin' for Henry Lee." Later, Anita would sing "I'll Be All Smiles Tonight" or a similar love song. If prodded, she might sing "Freight Train Blues," a song that she still despised about as much as audiences loved it. It had a boogie-woogie beat (never her favorite), and each verse required her to yodel a little longer and a little higher, until, as one listener put it, "only the damn dogs could hear her."

Helen was much less forward than her sisters because, by the summer of 1950, she was pregnant. The specter of separation that had made her wedding day such a mournful occasion was at hand. But it turned out not to be as dreadful as had been feared. As Helen grew rounder, the Carters either made do without her (as they had often done without Anita when she was in school during their Knoxville days) or found a fill-in who could pick, sing, and look all right in a matching dress. In January of 1951, when Helen was delivering Pop and Maybelle's first grandchild, Glenn Daniel Jones, the family began to grudgingly admit that marriage had an upside even for a Carter sister.

The world of the Opry and its road shows was glorious for Maybelle, who happily chose to stay in the background and smile. She had always gotten far more pleasure from applause for her daughters than for herself, and now it was easier than ever to just let them have it. When she did step forward, it was to pick "Wildwood Flower" or sing a hymn, always to great acclaim, and occasionally eliciting tears. It was only on the Sunday gospel show that Maybelle took center stage, because she sang lead on so many of the hymns. Her voice was beginning to take on a hint of tremolo, and was growing deeper, in part because she had recently asked her daughters for permission to take up smoking again. "I wanted to set a good example for you girls," she said, "but I do enjoy a cigarette." It was not unusual for her to light one up before the Sunday program, because it could be surprisingly stressful.

"Oh, gosh," Maybelle would fret as she sped toward WSM's studio, still bleary-eyed from a Saturday-night show, "I hope Albert doesn't make it today." The girls would laugh, and then Maybelle would laugh a little, too. "Oh, goodness," she would go on, "Albert cannot sing. Can't sing at all. What am I going to do?"

When they arrived at the studio, the Jordanaires—soon to become famous as Elvis Presley's backup singers—would be finishing their early-morning show. And as the Carters unpacked their instruments, the leader of the quartet, Gordon Stoker, would always ask: "Mama Maybelle, would you play me just a little bit of that 'Cannonball Blues'?" Stoker could tell that Maybelle was tired and distracted, but he couldn't help himself, and he always made it a point to ask politely. "I just loved that song so much," he recalled much later. "And no matter how tired she was, she always played it for me."

The dreaded Albert—aka Tennessee senator Albert Gore Sr.— would usually walk in shortly after the show had commenced. Gore was a real country boy, a populist pol who understood where his audience would be on Sunday morning, and how to keep himself in their thoughts. He never asked permission or announced himself ahead of time, for a good politician, like a good traveling salesman, doesn't wait for an invitation. "Oh, Senator Gore," Mother Maybelle would say. "How nice to have you with us. If you know this song, you are welcome to sing along." Senator Gore wasn't shy. Whether he knew the song or not, he'd join in on a key of his own invention. In later years, the senator would sometimes bring along his little son, future vice president Albert Gore Jr., whom June recalls as "a nice, very well-mannered young fella who sat down and listened to the show and seemed to enjoy it very much."

If the early '50s was a time of wide-open opportunity for the Carters, they exploited it with mixed success. As a group, the Carter Sisters and Mother Maybelle recorded eighteen singles for RCA Victor and Columbia in four years. But they leaned too heavily toward mournful, even gloomy material: "Willow, Will You Weep for Me?," "Down on My Knees," and "Columbus, Georgia" (better known as "Columbus Stockade"). They never had anything close to a hit. In 1954 they recorded a catchy comic song called "He Went Slipping Around," and though it, too, failed to reach the charts, its mixture of good humor and musical chops suggests that a more upbeat repertoire might have been more successful. But "Slipping Around" turned out to be the group's last recording of the decade.

Meanwhile, June was going in the opposite direction with her solo career, recording the kind of comic and novelty songs that drew vigorous applause from Opry audiences. These included "Mommie's Real Peculiar," "Bashful Rascal," and "No Swallowing Place," a song that she wrote with Frank Loesser when he dropped by to say hello to the woman who had lampooned his "Baby It's Cold Outside." Helen recorded about ten singles, including two with Atkins, none of which attracted much attention. Anita had the greatest success—though not with any of the half-dozen solo disks she recorded in this period.

Anita's big break came partly as a result of Maybelle's emerging friendship with Minnie Snow, wife of Canadian singer Hank Snow, who had arrived at the Opry just about the same time as the Carters. Shortly after hitting town, Snow recorded his classic "I'm Movin' On" and became a national sensation. Maybelle and Minnie proved extremely compatible: Both were new in town; both were addicted to cardplaying; and both were content to putter around Maybelle's kitchen, scraping carrots and talking about their children. Min quickly became Maybelle's closest friend in Nashville. Whether it was this friendship, as Anita always modestly said, or her mesmerizing voice that brought her to the attention of Hank Snow, Anita was nonplussed when she received a telephone call from Snow, asking her in his deep, serious voice if she would record with him. "Sure," she said.

Anita was just seventeen at the time, and her teenage, devil-may-care attitude worried Steve Sholes, RCA's brilliant and ambitious producer. He had already come a cropper of Snow's short fuse and monstrous ego, and warned Anita to be on her best behavior in the studio. "For goodness sake, don't play with him, Anita," Sholes warned. "Hank doesn't play." And sure enough, shortly after the session began, Anita razzed Snow for singing the wrong harmony. "Hush, Hank," she told him, "you're singin' on my part!" Sholes held his breath, but Snow just burst out laughing. The record, "Bluebird Island" backed with "Down the Trail of Broken Hearts," went to number four on the country charts.

But for most country acts of that time, the big money was still in public appearances, not records. As "Stars of the Grand Ole Opry," the Carters were more in demand than ever and could charge more, too. They continued and even increased the pace they'd set for themselves in Knoxville and Springfield. Their schedule for the first week of January 1952 was typical, with road shows every day of the week: the Rex Theater in Galax, Virginia, on Monday; the Palace in Petersburg on Tuesday, followed by the Isis in Lynchburg; the State in Bluefield, West Virginia; and, on Friday, the Capitol in Elizabethon, Tennessee. They were paid about half of the gross receipts for every show, minus a 5 percent agent's fee, straight cash. By the time they arrived home for their Saturday Opry appearances, the banks were closed, so they'd stash huge wads of greenbacks in the blue roaster on Maybelle's kitchen shelf, where it would reside until Monday morning, when the banks reopened.

Weekends were devoted to the Opry. They made friends quickly in the Opry's cramped, unglamourous dressing rooms, but declined invitations to Mom's (later Tootsie's), the bar behind the theater frequented by musicians. Mom's was loud, boozy, and profane, a perfect microcosm of the Nashville music scene, which was a boy's club through and through. Most of the old-timers knew of the Original Carter Family, and they taught the youngsters how to treat Maybelle and her daughters with the requisite respect. Around Maybelle, they'd watch their manners *and* their language. "I don't care where they went, they were always treated with respect," says a woman who traveled with the Carters in the fifties. "And no one had to rise up and demand it. It was just taken for granted."

There were plenty of big stars playing the Opry in 1950, but the man who impressed the Carters more than any other was a tall, white, hunched skeleton of a man who smelled of liquor and hair tonic: twenty-seven-year-old Hank Williams. Hank was especially respectful of Maybelle and told the Carters that he had admired their RadiOzark shows out of Springfield. He had been struck by Anita's beautiful renditions of a few of his own songs, and perhaps that accounted for rumors about Hank lobbying hard to bring the family to the Opry.

There was pride in that, because Hank Williams was already a bona fide superstar. He'd once had six encores at the Ryman. By 1950 he'd charted with more than a dozen hits, mostly about being lonesome, lovesick, and just plain blue; he'd been on the charts almost constantly for two years. No one was more impressed with Hank than Eck. Pop would marvel as Williams crooned one of his poetic compositions such as "Teardrop on a Rose." "He's a genius," Pop would exclaim. "And no education!"

By the time the Carters were getting to know him in 1951, Hank Williams was Nashville's greatest artist, but he was also its most incorrigible drunk—caught in a vicious, though not uncommon, cycle. His drinking caused problems in his marriage, and his teetering marriage fed his alcoholism. When Hank's wife, Audrey, discovered she was pregnant again, she was not happy. The Williamses were already raising two children, Lycrecia Guy from Audrey's first marriage and Randall Hank, and Audrey didn't think they could handle another. Abortion was illegal, but Audrey procured one anyway, and the infection that followed landed her in the hospital. The story, as recorded by Colin Escott in *Hank Williams: The Biography*, goes that Hank went to visit his sick wife in the hospital. But when he leaned down to kiss her, Audrey shrank from him. "You sorry son of a bitch," she hissed, "it was you that caused me to suffer this." Hank went back home and sighed to his children's nanny that he was married to a woman with a "cold, cold heart."

A few months later, Williams stood on the Opry stage and sang a new masterpiece: "Why can't I free your doubtful mind and melt your cold, cold heart?" As he sang, Anita Carter stood transfixed, listening. By the time he got to the second verse, there were tears in her eyes, and before he finished the third, she was weeping openly. "I thought it was the saddest and most beautiful thing I'd ever heard," she said. She must have been quite a sight in the wings, eyes glistening with tears, lips trembling. Williams certainly noticed her, and asked her for a date.

He was at least a little drunk when he made the proposition, and Anita wasn't sure how to answer him. She'd never had liquor herself and didn't really understand its effect on people. Standing in front of Anita, Williams was so tall and gangly and three-sheets-to-the-wind that he swayed like a cobra. He scared her *and* he was married, but she made a counterproposal that really knocked him off balance: She'd be happy to go out with Hank, she said. In fact, her whole family would be happy to go out with him.

It wasn't what he'd had in mind—taking Eck, Maybelle, and their three daughters out for a meal—but the excursion helped cement a friendship. Hank became one of the first Opry stars to refer to Maybelle as "Mama," and before long, just about everyone was doing it. Some called her that because she was mama to the three girls, but Williams did so because she became a surrogate mother to him. He was a frequent visitor to Eck and Maybelle's house in suburban Nashville, where he'd load up on Maybelle's corn bread crumbled into a glass of cold milk, or biscuits and gravy. While he ate, he'd complain about Audrey—some of the time they were separated, some of the time together—or he'd sit and ogle Anita.

For the insecure, hard-lovin' Hank Williams, there was sustenance in Maybelle's kitchen that went beyond the food. Williams wasn't the first wounded soul who found himself drawn to Maybelle Carter, and he wouldn't be the last. The reason, according to Anita, was that she "never judged anyone." No matter how badly people acted, Maybelle simply wasn't scandalized. She would not be offended personally; she just helped as best she could. She rarely offered advice, but Maybelle had a genius for giving people a space where self-destruction and meanness didn't seem *inevitable*. She wasn't blind to Williams's desire for Anita, but she had faith that it would amount to nothing—and faith that her very presence was a hedge against lurid behavior. "Maybelle was the greatest woman, morally, I've ever known," Atkins explained. "People just never thought of doing or saying anything off-color when she was around." Men who were chastened by her always remembered how she did it, without ever uttering a word. She'd just fix those pale blue eyes on them. As the not-altogether-harmless Hank Snow once said, "Mama just whips us to death with those eyes."

When Williams complained about how Audrey cheated on him and treated herself to a new car every time the ashtrays filled up in the old one, Maybelle would gently urge him to try to think of a way to solve the problem, instead of working himself into another hopeless froth of rage. If he was overly harsh in his description of his wife, or if he gave vent to some violent fantasy about what he "oughtta do," she had only to give him the look, and he'd lower his head like a guilty dog.

The family's association with Williams was a mixed blessing for Anita. She didn't know what to make of his longing looks or the preposterously expensive gifts he offered her: a horse, a car, jewelry. She refused his gifts, but on at least one occasion she accepted his help. In April of 1952, the Carters were among the Opry stars invited to New York to appear on NBC's prime-time show *The Kate Smith Evening Hour*, and a segment was set aside for Anita. She was thrilled. Roy Acuff was not. Acuff had been an Opry star for nearly fifteen years, and he held sway as a sort of unofficial presiding officer of the Nashville boys' club. So when Roy wanted the slot for a protégé of his own, he had Anita bumped. Williams, however, came to her rescue, offering to let her sing with him. Their performance of "I Can't Help It If I'm Still in Love with You" was a stunning rebuke to any city slicker who regarded country music as dull and unsophisticated. Anita's perfect soprano took the biting edge off Williams's nasal delivery and turned the country lament into a complicated and powerful duet. The longing in Hank's eyes and Anita's bashful flirtation were surprisingly convincing, for reasons most viewers never could have imagined.

But there was always a price to pay for Hank's help, and Anita paid it. She had just celebrated her nineteenth birthday, and on the trip to New York, Williams presented her with a beautiful ring and an offer to take her anywhere her heart desired. She told him she wanted to see Peggy Lee at the Copacabana, and he arranged it. The Copa seemed to Anita a million miles from Nashville, to say nothing of Poor Valley, and she was enjoying herself immensely when, to her surprise, Lee launched into one of Williams's songs. Hank was so delighted, he invited Anita for a spin on the dance floor. Apparently, Williams had little experience in the kind of dancing that was appropriate in a New York nightclub. "I was embarrassed to death," Anita recalled. "His knees were coming up even with his ears. He was dancing like a Texas oilman. People just stopped and stared, until Peggy Lee announced who he was."

Anita recovered from her embarrassment, but for Hank Williams, everything grew worse. His jealous love for Audrey was driving him batty. It was bad enough when they were together; it was beyond bad when they were apart and Hank was left to wonder how she was spending her evenings. On top of that, he'd been given morphine for a back injury, and he was becoming addicted. He was also more dependent on the kind leeway shown him in the Carter household. At any time of the day or night, Anita's telephone might ring and there would be Williams, drunk or stoned or both, trying to pronounce her name: *Anita-wuh, zzHank.* Before many performances, Williams would be so drunk that the Carter women had to drop whatever they were doing and try to sober him up enough to go on. Sometimes he would come to Pop and Maybelle's for a meal and listen patiently while June encouraged him to forsake the demon alcohol. These sermons were not without effect, but that effect was short-lived. Chet Atkins recalled one of Williams's pathetic efforts to wean himself from booze during a road trip to Kansas City with the Carters: "I'd see him down at the newsstand, buying a whole bunch of comic books: Captain Marvel, Superman, and all that stuff. That was his reading material when he was trying to go straight. But he would call his wife at two o'clock in the morning and she would be out catting around. And that drove him to drink, of course. He never stopped loving Audrey. Men tend to fall in love with women they can't control. That's my opinion . . . and should be yours."

In 1952 Hank Williams was showing up for concerts too drunk to perform, or missing them altogether. The Opry was ready to fire him, and Audrey was heading for divorce court. Williams didn't let go easy, and his addictions fueled more jealous rages. On one occasion, as he drove to the Carters' home, he saw someone he thought was Audrey sitting next to June in a car. Exactly what went through his mind, no one ever found out, but he actually tried to run the car off the road. Fortunately, the screams made him realize his mistake before anyone was hurt or killed. This was the only time Maybelle ever upbraided him. Her jaw set, her outstretched finger trembling, she told him if he ever hurt one of her girls, he would regret it.

"But Mama," Williams began, trying to explain himself. Maybelle cut him off. "Don't you call me Mama," she said.

"That was the harshest thing I ever heard Mama say," Helen recalled years later. Williams, she added, shuddered as though he had been whipped.

Maybelle cooled toward Williams after that, but she never banned him from the house. And he turned to June for long, tearful conversations about Audrey and how miserable he was and how much he loved Anita. June listened with a mixture of sympathy and horror. The whole thing was a mess. Audrey, who was a friend of hers, "just didn't like Hank," and there was no question she was cheating on him.

"This is ridiculous, Hank," June would scold him. "This is just . . . ridiculous! And it's wrong, morally wrong." She would try to remind him that he was still legally married, and that married was married, and that union with Anita was forever out of the question. "I loved him for his talent and brilliance," she said, "but I never would have loved him for a brother-in-law. He was much too messed up, and always would be."

A few months after the escapade in the car, Hank showed up at Pop and Maybelle's house while Audrey was over for a visit. She saw him coming and made for the rear of the house, begging to be left undisturbed. Williams came in and had a perfunctory chat with Anita and then went to June for a private conversation. It was hard to tell exactly what mood he was in, but he said he wanted Audrey to come home for a talk. "I won't hurt her," he said.

"You promise, Hank?" asked June.

"I promise. I won't hurt her," he replied with a puppyish, repentant look.

"Well, of course you won't," said June. She went to the back of the house and told Audrey what Hank had said.

Audrey was wide-eyed. "Oh, no, you can't believe him," she whispered, shaking her head. "I'm not going home. He'll kill me before I even get there."

June offered to go home with Audrey, assuring her that Hank wouldn't do anything to hurt her. Then she sent Williams ahead, saying she and Audrey would come by soon. When the two women rolled up to the Williams house, Hank was waiting in the driveway. And he looked menacing. Audrey panicked and slid down in her seat, out of view.

Hank approached the car, talking through his clenched jaw: "I know she's in there. Tell 'er to get 'er ass up."

June didn't seem to grasp the danger. She got Audrey out of the car and walked her straight toward the house, talking to Hank like he was just a big troublesome child. But Hank bolted for Audrey, and Audrey bolted for the door. June got between them, pushing Williams in the chest. "You can't come in here like that."

"The hell I can't," he slurred. "It's my house."

Hank retreated to his car, and when he started back toward the house, he was carrying a pistol.

Now June was scared. "You cannot *do* this, Hank!" she yelled, and the two scuffled in the doorway. Then Williams took a step back, raised the gun, and squeezed the trigger.

The shot missed June by about six inches. The noise "rattled my head," she remembers. "I thought I'd never hear again." And then the absurdity of it finally occurred to her: *He's going to kill me . . . me, of all people.*

June screamed, gripped the doorway, and dropped to the ground as if she'd been shot. Hank stood frozen. "You've killed her!" Audrey screamed from inside the house. "You've killed June!"

Did Hank Williams throw down his gun, grasp June in his arms, and cry, "What have I done?" Did he run around the front lawn begging for help or forgiveness? Did he make up with Audrey long enough to enter the house and call an ambulance? He did not. Hank Williams sprinted to his car, gunned the motor, and took off.

"I began to look at him in another light," June later said dryly. "When he ran away, I realized he really was crazy."

More than a week passed before any of the Carters saw Hank Williams again. He finally showed up at one of their radio shows and meekly approached June. "I have to talk to you," he stammered. "I'm sorry. I'm . . . I'm desperately sorry." The apology hardly sufficed. "But," admits June, "I was inclined to forgive him. We knew he was going to die, and he was going to die soon."

In the final days of 1952, Hank Williams hired a college boy to drive him from Montgomery, Alabama, to a New Year's Eve concert in Charleston, West Virginia, and then on to a New Year's Day performance in Canton, Ohio. Once they got on the road, a snowstorm made it impossible to make the Charleston date, but he remained determined to make it to Canton. Williams spent much of the trip sprawled in the backseat, with chloral hydrate tablets, vodka, and whiskey for company. The booze probably didn't mix well with the morphine shots he got in Knoxville to alleviate his excruciating back pain, and as the driver sped the car toward Ohio, Hank Williams expired in that lonely backseat. He was pronounced dead at a hospital in Oak Hill, West Virginia, at seven o'clock in the morning on New Year's Day, 1953, at the age of twenty-nine.

Hank's death took a little of the strange heat off Anita, and she never seemed much interested in celebrity matches after that. "All the stars wanted to get something going with her," recalled Chet Atkins, "but she didn't go for stars." She preferred the company of regular guys, such as the brilliant fiddler Dale Potter. She'd met Potter through family friend Don Davis. Potter was handsome and courtly, and he could play any kind of music on the fiddle. It was like having three or four fiddlers playing at once, Chet Atkins used to say. Potter's musical talents entranced Anita, and she quickly developed a crush, which, in her inexperience, she mistook for love. She was also oblivious to a fact that would have made her shy from the relationship: Potter was a drinker. Unlike Hank Williams, he was fairly good at keeping his tendencies hidden. But he wasn't perfect. Maybelle once made the mistake of picking up his Coke and taking a sip. "Lord, Dale!" she sputtered. "What have you got in there?"

Anita was just nineteen when she decided to marry Potter, and she resolved to act before anybody could talk her out of it. "Mother Maybelle and Pop are up in the country, not home," says a friend of the Carters. "June was there, and Anita waltzed in and says, 'I'm gonna get married.' And June said, 'Mommy and Daddy are not here; wait until they're here.' And Anita said, 'No, I'm not gonna [wait].' I think they went to Franklin [Kentucky] that day and did it."

Before a week was out, Anita realized she'd made a terrible mistake. The marriage ended quickly, but in 1953 she married again—again hastily. This time to Don Davis.

June, meanwhile, had become one of the most popular stars in Nashville and had a long line of suitors. By the end of 1951, she had winnowed the list to three. One was a guy from the Valley, whom she would soon dump when he tried to become too intimate. Another was Carl Smith, a new arrival at the Opry who had recently released a smash hit, "Let Old Mother Nature Have Her Way." (The song became a favorite of Eck's, who liked to sing, "Let old Mother Maybelle have her way.") The third was steel-guitar whiz Frankie Kay, "the best-lookin' of 'em all," says June. Kay was anxious to please, and when he heard that the Carters were looking for someone to fill in for Helen, he suggested Becky Bowman.

Born and raised in Kansas City, Bowman had grown up with Carter Family music. Not only had her parents spun the old records, but during the war she'd performed on the same bill with the Carter Sisters and Mother Maybelle at Kansas City's Play-Mor Arena. She'd had an enjoyable round of girl talk with Helen and felt like she'd made a new friend "at a church picnic or something like that." By the time June contacted Becky in February of 1952, she had a steady gig playing bass with a western swing trio on radio station KRES, St. Joseph, Missouri. June asked if Becky would be interested in sitting in for Helen on the accordion, and Bowman agreed without hesitation. There was only one problem: Becky Bowman had never played the accordion in her life. So before packing herself, her sister Emily, and mother, Claudine "Mommy" Bowman, in an old green Kaiser automobile and heading out for Nashville, she stopped by Al Crocker's music store in Kansas City to buy one: "I felt that if I could just get an accordion I could fake it well enough and the other instruments I played—guitar, bass, and clarinet—would carry me."

The Bowmans drove through a snowstorm to get to Nashville, and June recalled Becky chugging up to Maybelle's house behind the wheel of the Kaiser, a long-billed cap on her head and a pipe in her mouth. Bowman says this is an exaggeration, that she didn't start the pipe until after she'd been in Nashville awhile (*Opry* sponsor Prince Albert tobacco used to give them out), and the cap she wore only on hot trips, with a damp washcloth underneath. But the two women agree that one of the first things she ever said to June was "I don't have enough hair to wad a shotgun."

"If you were to drive up to the Carters' house, the first thing Pop would say is 'Come on in. Have somethin' to eat. Stay all night,'" says Becky. "That's the way they were raised. They never treated anyone like a stranger. My dad used to love corn bread and milk, and that was the first real meal that we all sat down to eat in the Carters' home. Helen talked all the time—she was like a magpie—and she was telling some big story and she reached over and she gets this big glass of cold milk and this big hunk of corn bread, and I thought, 'Lord, I'm home.'" Becky was an immediate hit, personally and professionally, and she lived and traveled with the Carters most of the next four years.

"It was like one great big vacation," she says. "My first plane ride was in 1952 when the army flew a bunch of us from the Opry to Texas to play some of their bases. They put us on a C-119—Ernest Tubb, Lou Childre, a whole slug. They put parachutes on us, and Hank Williams looked like a big *H* with his legs hangin' down as thin as pool cues. That night, Ernest Tubb took us out for Mexican food."

For June Carter, especially, the Nashville ride continued to be bracing . . . and perilous. Carl Smith had established himself as one of the hottest stars of the moment and told June he wished to marry no one but her. Pop and Maybelle seemed to approve of him, but June was less sure. "He was a country boy from just about a hundred miles down the mountain from Poor Valley," says June. "He treated me with a lot of respect." Still, June had eyes. And she could see that women were drawn to Smith like bees to honey. "No way around am I gonna be marryin' you," June would tell him. Poor Carl swore it wasn't his fault. What could he do? Women just would not leave him in peace. For God's sake, even *Minnie Pearl* had propositioned him. It took some doing, but Smith finally convinced June that she was the one and only for him. They were married in July of 1952.

Professionally speaking, the partnership was a hit. They sang mush-song duets like "Love, Old Crazy Love," and June would parody Smith's hits. He'd sing "Wait 'Til I Get You Alone," and she would follow with "You Flopped When You Got Me Alone." They were the Opry's glamour couple, a feature in country-star magazines and tame gossip columns. "Their on-stage clowning doesn't hide the fact that they're just terribly in love," gushed *Hoedown* magazine. "Folks get a kick out of the way they flirt and carry on during the Opry perform-ance." They were also raking in money. One night at the Opry, June asked Becky and her mother to hold her billfold while she was onstage. "Mama just put it in her purse and never thought anything about it," says Becky. "A few days later, I wrote Mama a letter and said, 'Have you any idea how much money was in that billfold?' June had thirty-seven thousand dollars, and Mama was holding it for her!"

For the next three years, the Carters remained comfortably ensconced as country stars and road warriors—even with all three of the sisters mar-ried. Helen and June survived pregnancies, which were thought to be fatal to a woman's career. Adding Bowman had fixed that. Becky had been brought in to substitute for Helen, but when Helen was ready to rejoin her sisters, Eck suggested that Becky stay on so that she could sit in for whichever of the three Carter girls needed a night off.

It was a life of long, fast car rides, open-air theaters (or the occa-sional cotton field), hours of ironing clothes, hoping their wind-blown hair could be fixed in time for the show. Sometimes a husband would tag along for the ride. Nobody let Eck drive anymore, so he'd recline in the backseat singing—"Let Old Mother Maybelle have her way!"—while the rest of the crew tried to settle in around Anita's big bass fiddle. "You hear [musicians today] talk about the road and how terrible it is, and they're traveling in these big air-conditioned buses with bathrooms and beds and all the comforts of home," says Becky Bowman. "I feel like they have not trouped until, as Anita said, they've trouped with a bass fiddle beating 'em on the side of the head." For Maybelle, who was generally in the driver's seat, the life was pure joy, and she never lacked for strength or energy.

"I believe she so loved the business and the road and getting out and doing what she was born to do," says Becky Bowman. "She just drew from another source. One night Mother Maybelle was driving this great big huge Lincoln. And I'm driving the second car, Don and Anita's Mercury. I was going eighty miles an hour. And it's raining. And the blacktop is slick. And Mother Maybelle is leaving me back home in Indiana. I told Anita and Don, 'I'm not gonna *try* to keep up with her.'

"We left Mississippi one night. We were so tired, all of us. Anita and I and the bass fiddle climbed in the station wagon, and before our heads barely laid on that floor, Mother Maybelle was driving into the driveway in Nashville. I don't know how fast she was going. She had a lead foot. She drove like that all the time."

The performances themselves were easy, because they came naturally. Professional problems were hardly serious. At one show, for instance, somewhere in Pennsylvania, they were playing an outdoor venue that was built to resemble a front porch. ("It was coal country," Bowman remembers, "and there was coal dust on everything.") June had worked up a comedy routine in which, during one of her cackly, over-the-top country numbers, she would dance so exuberantly that she would kick one of her slippers into the audience. The coal porch must have been slippery that night, or June's aim was just bad. She flung the shoe sideways and it smacked her mother in the face, leaving a large black smudge on Maybelle's cheek. June and Becky were seized with giggles, and Anita laughed so hard she had to lean on her bass to keep from falling over. Maybelle played on, as if nothing had happened. "Never missed a note," Helen used to say. "But afterwards she got ahold of June, turned her upside down, and paddled her bottom. I'll tell you, June's pantaloons were a-flyin'."

Maybelle still had the girls out front, playing to the ever younger postwar crowds, but she made a point to play the best-remembered songs she'd done with Sara and A.P. "Mother Maybelle's idea was three-cornered harmony," says Becky. "You didn't put a lot of fancy variations in it. She used to say a 'plow-handle A.' And a 'three-cornered D.' She wanted things kept in the natural. But when I went to be a part of that program, I played clarinet. So June incorporated that into the act. I played clarinet and she would dance. That was fine with Mother Maybelle, but when it came to her music, she wanted it kept her way."

Pop wasn't spending much time on the road anymore. There was so much to do around home, like for instance spending the cash his family made. (Carl Smith was turning out to be just the sort of fellow he'd wanted for his favorite daughter: smart, successful, a moneymaking machine.) No one ever accused Ezra Carter of being a greedy man, but he was cursed with a tremendously active mind. And he fed it without stint. He began acquiring books, particularly on religious subjects, at a prodigious rate. He had always had a thing for farm equipment and had to have the latest and best. But now, with America's great industrial engine cranking away, stores were awash in new gizmos. Appliances, tools, and toys—Eck wanted them all. The only thing that seemed to please him more than a new gadget was *two* new gadgets. He rarely bought one of anything. When he grew bored with a purchase, which never seemed to take long, he'd abandon it without a thought. When he lost interest in a beautiful, expensive new Alice Chalmers bulldozer, he traded it to a neighbor for an old John Deere tractor worth half as much.

Friends and family recall Maybelle sitting at a table with her checkbook out, looking at the various bills that Pop had rung up, shaking her head, saying, "I'm not paying this. . . . I am not paying this." But she'd write check after check to cover her husband. More than one well-meaning relation took Pop aside and encouraged him to be conscious of how much things cost, so Pop adopted his own methods of *justifying* his purchases. They weren't toys. They were investments! "When he went out to buy a socket wrench," remembers his nephew Joe Carter, "he'd buy three, sayin' they'll be worth more money someday. Somewhere he run into a bucket of Wells Fargo belt buckles, and he bought a whole trunkload because he thought he'd found a real collector's item. What he had was a bunch of damn brass. Then there was a time he went down and bought a whole bunch of pickaxes; another time, it was pictures of Indians."

"He had this routine that he would do," recalls Eck's son-in-law Don Davis. "He'd say, 'Now, look. Here's the deal on this: I'm looking at a tractor.' Which he didn't need, of course, he didn't have a farm or nothin'. He just had a yard he wanted to plow up. 'And here's the deal; now, this is tentative.' Well, that was the giveaway word right there. When he said that word, that meant he'd already bought it. 'It's tentative, and here's the deal I can get on this thing. What do you think?' So I learned to just go ahead and tell him, 'Oh, did you get a deal on *that!*' I knew it was too late to tell him otherwise. That made him happy. He'd say, 'Well, great, I thought that'd be a good deal.' "

Some of Pop's purchases were meant to please his bride. He was constantly at work on home improvements, anxious for Maybelle to come off the road so that he could show what he'd done for her. One hot summer, he resolved to surprise her by buying and installing an air conditioner. He put it in their living room, which was a big, beautiful room with a cathedral ceiling and a large rock fireplace. But Pop was not fussy about appearances, so when he smashed a hole through the wall and installed the air conditioner, it was well off center. When Maybelle arrived home, Pop was all smiles. Maybelle looked at the air conditioner, and at Pop, and, according to Becky Bowman, just shook her head: *Well, Daddy.*

"That was it," swears Bowman. "That was the height of her anger. Another time, we all left to go on the road and came back a few days later. Maybelle says, 'Eck, did you get the utilities paid?' Well, he says, 'I went up there to pay them, and they had these deep-sea fishing reels on sale.' And he bought *two* of them. One for him and one for her. And there again: 'Well, Daddy.' " Maybelle responded the same way when he drilled unsightly locks onto the drawers of a beautiful and expensive antique desk he'd bought, and when he smashed a hole in another wall to install a safe in the house. On that occasion, according to Anita, Maybelle's response was a bit more caustic than usual: "I don't know why Daddy thinks we need a safe. We don't have nothin' left to put in it.' "

After nearly thirty years, her husband was predictable, but he was still a wonder to her. His obsession with rocks, for instance, could not be dimmed by time or age. "His greatest joy was digging all the rocks out of a yard," says Don Davis. "I could always tell when he was fixin' to trade. As soon as he got all the rocks dug up and dynamited out of the yard, he'd go on to a new place."

Through it all, Maybelle rarely complained, just as Pop didn't complain when his wife brought an entire square-dance team from Springfield, Missouri, to the house for dinner. And if he got the feeling he was headed for the doghouse, Eck would whip up a meal for Maybelle and the girls. "His biscuits were to die for," says Bowman. "You'd have to put your foot on 'em or they'd float away. He'd bake 'em on Monday and you could eat them a week later. They'd still be good. You'd take Mother Maybelle's tomato gravy on one of Pop's biscuits."

The few days a year when the Carters weren't on the road, life could be leisurely—in an unconventional sort of way. They'd rise at 4:30 in the morning and head for the WSM studios, traveling the still-dark Nashville streets, stopping at the same restaurant each day for a cinnamon roll and coffee to go. At the studio, they'd knock off two live fifteen-minute shows for the early-morning farm crowd. If they had a lot of road dates coming up, they would have to spend a day recording a week's, or even two weeks', worth of shows. "If you made a mistake, you had to start over," says Bowman. "You couldn't erase it. That meant, for every week, ten fifteen-minute programs, plus a thirty-minute Sunday-morning gospel. And you had to think ahead. Because you were recording on Monday, but you had to speak as if it were Wednesday or another day. You had to watch what you were doing. For *two* weeks, it would be ten times thirty. That's a lot of pressure. That's six hours counting the Sunday-morning gospel."

Sometimes the early-morning hours—or the grind of the long recording sessions—got the better of them. One marathon morning in the studio, they were down to the last song on the side: Mother Maybelle singing the maudlin "Weeping Willow Tree." While Maybelle sang, Anita made the rounds, whispering her new chorus into the ears of the others. *Why do you weep, dear Willy? Why do your britches hang low? Could it be you have a secret?* Becky was trying hard to stick to her accordion part, but she couldn't stop laughing . . . and then Anita lost it. Even Maybelle started to giggle, while the engineers tried in vain to calm them down. "We were so tired," says Becky, "blotto."

But when the morning sessions were done, and no road trip or local engagement loomed on the schedule, the day was theirs—and they usually spent it at the house Carl Smith had bought for June. "June had a lady who helped keep up the house, and her name was Evelyn," says Becky. "We would get back to the house and June would be the first one in. And as we came in the door, she would be handing out the dust cloth, the broom, the mop, the sweeper—to everybody. Even with Evelyn there, we still did that. And we'd get everything done and usually we'd go swimming, in 'the green plunge.' That's what they called them in the South. Not pools."

It was a happy moment in time, with comforts and ease, money and celebrity. But things in Nashville, and in popular music, were changing. Maybelle and her girls saw it happen. Early in 1955, the Carters were invited to join a package tour, headlined by Hank Snow and booked by a colorful promoter named Colonel Tom Parker. Other artists on the tour included the Louvin Brothers and country comic Whitey Ford, better known as "the Duke of Paducah." Anita heard a rumor that Bill "Rock Around the Clock" Haley might be added to the bill, and she liked the idea. But the mystery guest turned out to be an up-and-coming singer named Elvis Presley.

Of course, in early 1955, not so many people knew who—or what—Elvis Presley was. Sam Phillips, the Sun Records impresario who would make stars of Jerry Lee Lewis, Johnny Cash, and Carl Perkins, as well as Elvis, was hawking Presley records to any deejay who could be induced to play them. It wasn't an easy sell. Radio hadn't yet made up its mind about the well-mannered, spectacularly handsome twenty-year-old who, six months earlier, had released his first single, with his versions of a blues song by Arthur "Big Boy" Crudup ("That's All Right, Mama") on one side and a bluegrass song by Bill Monroe ("Blue Moon of Kentucky") on the other. The record, of course, was neither blues nor bluegrass—much too wild for most country radio stations, and way too cornpone for R&B outlets. In October of 1954, Elvis had achieved a lifelong dream of playing at the Opry, where

Phillips had avoided Monroe, worried that the father of bluegrass might be so appalled by Elvis's version of "Blue Moon" that he'd want to "break my jaw." But the audience, like Monroe himself, responded to the Elvis phenomenon with polite indifference. Away from the Ryman, Elvis found crowds who did respond to his wild-hipped stagecraft, and Colonel Parker—a man with genius but no discernible conscience— had signed him.

The Elvis whom the Carters met was nothing like the puffy, drug-addled caricature most of America remembers from his later years. "He was as good as gold, not at all messed up, and treated us all like ladies," said Helen. "He called his own mama every night." Even before he joined the package tour, Elvis knew all about the Carter Family in gen-eral, and Maybelle in particular. When he first met Maybelle, Elvis called her "ma'am," but soon after, he took to calling her "Mama" as everyone else did. And Maybelle brought him into the fold just as she had all the other young kids she'd toured with. Elvis was a special case, however, and on that 1955 tour, he required extra mothering. With all his gyrating onstage acrobatics, the new teen idol was constantly pop-ping the buttons off his shirts and trousers So Maybelle would remove buttons from her daughters' clothes and sew them onto Presley's. "We worked many a show with safety pins in our skirts," said Helen.

For all the unfettered sexuality Elvis unleashed on that tour, when he was offstage he seemed to the Carters a little nervous, even scared. And he probably had reason. Elvis incited all sorts of passions. Once in Midland, Texas, a group of teenage boys watched as the girls in town made a damn parade to Elvis's motel (his Caddy gave him away) and spent the day fawning poolside over the new star. So four local boys made a commando raid on Elvis's motel that night, held Presley down, and shaved off one of his precious sideburns.

In 1955 Elvis was not so far removed from Tupelo or Memphis, or the music he'd grown up on. Presley loved gospel music, and after most shows he'd sit down at the piano and harmonize with the Carter women. Their friendship grew closer, even as the tension was growing between Elvis and other members of the show. Hank Snow might have been headlining the tour, but Elvis was stealing every show. Audiences were getting younger and younger, more and more female. "When Elvis walked into the auditorium, [the crowds] wouldn't have seen him before. They wouldn't have known what he looked like, but they would be able to pick him out," remembers Bowman. "He'd be walking with his band and they could pick him out; they knew that *that* had to be Elvis. When he would be onstage, we'd peek through the curtain and people would be going nuts. And not just young women, either. There were women in their thirties, forties, and older who would have taken him home in a New York second."

Hank Snow soon realized—with some bitterness—that there was no following Elvis Presley, who riled up audiences, wore them out, and then riled them up some more. The catchy rumba rhythm that Snow had always depended on to get 'em dancing—"Rumba Boogie" and "The Golden Rocket"—sounded quaint and tepid after Elvis had torn through "Good Rockin' Tonight." The moody Ira Louvin of the Louvin Brothers, whose harmonizing Elvis worshiped, flew into a jealous rage one night, assaulting Elvis and calling him a "white nigger" who played "nigger trash."

"It was such a shock to him to be hurt by people he'd looked up to so much," said Anita. "He literally cried, and we sat there and cried with him." Over the next year and a half, as Elvis became a superstar, he continued to ask Parker to book the Carters. That suited the colonel fine. He got a kick out of Eck, and Maybelle became good friends with his wife, Marie. "Colonel Tom trusted us around Elvis," Anita said, "and Colonel Tom didn't trust everyone."

In retrospect the match may seem unnatural, but it was precisely the lack of similarity that saved the Carters. "It was hard to go on in front of Elvis Presley and not get booed off the stage," said Helen. "But we never did get booed off. You could tell at first the audience might be thinking, 'What are all these women doing out there?' But we did very well."

On one occasion, both Elvis and Rod Brasfield arrived late for a concert, so the Carter Sisters and Mother Maybelle were forced to hold the crowd until such time as reinforcements might arrive. They played for what seemed like hours, running through just about every song they knew. Becky Bowman pulled out her clarinet and tootled on that for a while, just to change things up. When Helen suggested they play a song called "Ricochet Romance," Anita began to panic a bit. They were reaching the far end of their repertoire. "It's a wonder they don't throw us off," she whispered to Helen. But just as the Carters launched into "Ricochet Romance," Elvis arrived backstage. When the song ended, Anita dashed to the edge of the stage.

"We'll do one more," she told Elvis as he gasped for breath, "and then we'll introduce you."

Elvis batted his eyelids like a lazy turtle. "I wanna watch y'all work for a while," he yawned.

Anita balled up her fists and explained the situation as quickly and calmly as she could.

"Well, I've got to get my clothes changed," he said.

He did so leisurely, wandered back to the wings, and sat down in a chair. Again, Anita conferred with him, and he smiled and repeated that he wanted to "hear you sing a couple." Now Anita knew she was being teased.

After a few minutes, Elvis rose and signaled his willingness to go on, and the Carters dragged themselves off. Not long into his set, Elvis busted a string on his guitar. Turning to the Carters, who still lingered offstage, he called for someone to "bring me Mama's guitar." Anita carried Maybelle's guitar onstage and handed it to him. But something about Elvis's sly grin provoked her. Elvis was sweating hard from his busy work onstage, so she ran her finger down his cheek; she licked her finger. Then, suddenly, she pretended to gag and rushed offstage with her hands over her mouth. Elvis's drummer, D. J. Fontana, laughed until he dropped his sticks.

"He'd never been so mad at me," Anita said later. "I'd ruined his image. But he'd put us through—pardon the expression—hell."

He didn't stay mad at her long. Elvis, predictably, was sweet on Anita. In 1955 Presley was already running women through his hotel room and his dressing room nightly. And the Carters were always getting tangled up in his love life. Elvis was driving a baby-blue Cadillac at the time; the Carters traveled in Helen's flashier red-and-white Caddy. But photographs and newsreels were mostly black-and-white in those days, so Elvis's gaggles of female admirers could hardly have been blamed for mistaking Helen's car for Presley's. With keys, fingernails, lipstick, or whatever else they could get their hands on, "the girls would scratch their phone numbers on my car," Helen laughed. "Elvis had it painted I don't know how many times." At the shows, crowds of girls would fight their way backstage, shoving one another out of the way in hopes of reaching the new pop god. "One time, this poor little girl got pushed clean back into our dressing room," said Helen. "We said, 'Now, honey, we'll let you out this way so you can go to your car.'" She said, "I can't! My mama's out there trying to kiss him!"

In the middle of it all, though, Elvis and Anita embarked on an extended flirtation. Presley's bodyguard Red West later wrote that Anita made Elvis act like "a kid with six pair of feet." Anita was already married to Don Davis, but Elvis was undeterred. He went to great lengths to get her attention, and she went to equally great lengths to show her indifference. One day, the two were in Elvis's Cadillac, driving through the streets of Nashville, when Anita started yelling at him. "It's Audie Murphy! Pull over, Elvis. It's Audie Murphy!"

"Well," said Elvis, "at least now I know what gets you excited."

When he used a "bad word" in Mother Maybelle's car (Maybelle was not present), Anita stopped the car and made him get out and hoof it. He retaliated after a packed concert at the Gator Bowl in February of 1956. The Carters had pulled their car close to the stage, and when Elvis finished his set, he headed right for them. Climbing into the car, he dropped limply into Anita's lap. He was out cold. He had been a little under the weather before he went on; his breathing was shallow. "I'd never seen a man do that before, so I started crying," Anita said. "In fact, I started screaming, 'He's going to die on me!'" A moment later, Colonel Parker turned up and tried to pull Elvis out of the car to sign autographs. When Anita screamed at him to stop, the colonel realized his meal ticket was in serious danger. A path was cleared and the car headed for a hospital, where Maybelle signed him in and took responsibility for the bill. The Carters went home that night worried sick. They had arranged to go deep-sea fishing with Presley the next day, but had no heart for it now and canceled the boat. The next morning Elvis walked into their hotel looking fit as could be. "We about killed him," Anita said. The whole thing, he later told West, had been an act to get Anita's attention.

The time finally came, of course, when Elvis wanted to talk seriously about their relationship. "If I married you," Elvis told her, "I'd feel comfortable, because I know you'd love me just as much if I still drove a truck." Anita, however, was not the type to have an affair, and she could not imagine herself as Mrs. Elvis.

"The thing is," he said, "I don't know anybody else like you and your sisters. Would you look for someone for me that's like you all?"

Anita shook her head. "I can't be the one to find someone for you."

"Well," he said with a sigh, "I guess I'm going to have to find one on my own and raise her to suit myself." Anita would often think of this years later, when she read about Elvis's relationship with his wife, Priscilla Beaulieu, whom he started "raising up" almost as soon as he met her, at the age of fourteen.

After he left for Hollywood in 1956, Anita and the rest of the family rarely saw Elvis. By then, though, Presley had helped usher in the age of rock and roll, an era in which the Carters' music would be subsumed. Sam Phillips's boys—Elvis, Carl Perkins, Jerry Lee Lewis, and Johnny Cash—were raised on gospel and country music. Prompted by the question "Y'all know 'Will the Circle Be Unbroken'?" the four had once sat in the Sun Records studio running through their favorite hymns. But their *hit* songs were the yearnings of the flesh. In fact, by the mid-fifties, everybody seemed to be singing about scratching the big itch, and Maybelle's more indirect and innocent songs of woodland cottages and myrtle, dewy roses and heavenly light, were starting to feel a little dusty.

The girls were splitting off again, too. Anita joined a pop ensemble with Rita Robbins and Ruby Wells (daughter of Kitty Wells) called Nita, Rita, and Ruby. By 1957 they were recording songs such as "You Came to the Prom Alone" for RCA. A solo record for Cadence, "Blue

Doll," won Anita an appearance on *American Bandstand*, but nothing much came of it. Before the end of the fifties, she and Don Davis left Nashville for the quieter shores of Mobile, Alabama.

June had decided to accept an offer from famed director Elia Kazan to study acting in New York. With her short marriage to Carl Smith more or less over and her finely tuned showbiz antenna telling her that country music was on the outs, she could hardly say no. Still, she did not leave the Opry altogether; she had a daughter now, Rebecca Carlene (named for Bowman and Smith), and was determined to maintain her independence and her income. She flew back and forth between New York and Nashville, writing commercials for Pet Milk, Kellogg's Cornflakes, and other Opry sponsors. Life in New York was a revelation. She became close friends with Robert Duvall (many years later, he would cast her as his mother in his acclaimed film *The Apostle*) and even dated James Dean. She appeared on television shows such as *The Tennessee Ernie Ford Show, Gunsmoke,* and *The Adventures of Jim Bowie;* she cohosted *The Mike Douglas Show.*

Maybelle rooted for her daughters, even while her own career ebbed. She continued to work the Opry, but the Ryman crowd was more interested in the Everly Brothers' "Wake Up Little Susie," and Marty Robbins's "A White Sport Coat (and a Pink Carnation)." Maybelle began to take whatever dates came her way. With Helen or Anita (Becky was now married and gone) and whoever else was available, she went on the road with the Duke of Paducah's traveling show. The Duke's program was the very antithesis of late-fifties cool. He was the ultimate hayseed and reveled in it. He would begin each show with his signature line: "These shoes are killin' me!" He would end each show with another tagline: "I'm goin' back to the wagon, boys. These shoes are killin' me!" In between, he would tell dozens of worn-out vaudeville groaners. (He is said to have sold his file of some four hundred thousand jokes to the producers of *Hee Haw*.) As audiences dwindled, the show pathetically began billing itself as a *Rock-and-Roll Revue.*

For the first time in Maybelle's career, touring was starting to feel like a chore. She'd always been content to be a small player in the big show, but now the show itself felt small. Even a trip to the Waffle House, once her favorite restaurant, brought Maybelle little cheer. Her income was falling. None of the Nashville companies wanted her to record, and royalties for the Original Carter Family songs had dried up completely. After more than thirty years in the music business, and nearing age fifty, Maybelle Carter found herself wondering if there was still a place for her.

Pleasant Carter, 1959 (Carter Family Museum)

Opposite: A.P. Carter Grocery (Carter Family Museum)

Pleasant on the Porch

Janette caught him at it a few times, his game with the chicken. There would be her daddy on the porch, just sitting, waiting . . . waiting for the chicken *to come to him*. He had a little method worked up: In his hand he held a string, which trembled along the length of it, to where it was fastened to the open door of a wire cage. He'd made a path of cornmeal from the yard to the porch and up the stairs, along the porch floor and right into the deepest corner of that cage. And when a chicken ate its way into that corner, Pleasant Carter was going to yank that string, and the door would slam shut, *whap!* Supper. Anybody else would just walk off the porch and grab a yard runner, the way Mollie Carter used to sail right out her front door, grab the first one she saw, break its neck with one quick swing, and have it plucked and cleaned inside ten minutes. Now, in the late fifties, on the cusp of the space age, anybody from the Valley could drive over to the grocery store in Gate City and a buy a fryer.

But A.P. Carter had a lot of time on his hands, so he could sit for hours, alone and daydreaming, waiting for his chicken. What made the enterprise doubly strange was how any other time you couldn't have made him sit still at gunpoint. But when he got a notion to do something—even if it required stillness—he still liked to give it a try, just to see if it could be done. Once when he was lying in wait, his three-year-old granddaughter came crashing out through the screen door, scaring away his prey. "I ought to turn you over my knee and spank you," he said, and the little girl saw a hard glint in his eyes. His anger passed, however, giving gave way to a simple resignation that he'd have to start over.

Pleasant Carter was an old man by then, with a farmer's coloring: dark in the face, neck, and hands, white as Gold Medal Flour everywhere else. There was a pinch of sadness at the corners of his watery blue eyes, and still the constant tremor in his hands, which hung palms back, passively, off his long arms. Pleasant had a thatch of gray hair, long on top and tousled, but close-cropped at the sides, just like he wore it back in the thirties. He didn't like to fuss over it much. A friend drove him to Weber City once to get him barbered. Pleasant sat hunched over and stock-still, grinning at the warm whir of clippers on the back of his neck, like a five-year-old in the chair for the first time, until he caught sight of the barber in the mirror, reaching for a bottle of hair tonic. Then he nearly jerked himself out of that chair.

"What's that?" A.P. demanded.

"Don't you want a little Vitalis?" the barber asked. "Top it off?"

There was a pause and then, loud enough for everyone in the shop to hear, A.P. boomed, "I'd just as soon have a stud horse leak all over my head."

The barber never even got the Vitalis opened. Stubborn, that was Pleasant Carter, still. "That Doc," people said, "you can't *change* his mind." And by now, A.P. Carter was well set in his ways.

Take his clothes, for instance. At first glance they were nothing special, straight out of the "Monkey Ward" catalog or Sears: cotton long-sleeve shirt with a soft collar, a tie that hadn't been in fashion since before World War II, and gray wool trousers held up by suspenders. Look closer and anybody could see the suspenders were busted at the hasp. But Pleasant was fond of them and didn't like to throw away comfortable things, so he salvaged them with a three-inch flathead nail that fastened through a belt loop of his pants. It's one of the few things his youngest grandson would remember about him. "You had to be careful when you sat on Papaw's lap," says Dale Jett.

Like as not, Pleasant had slept in those same clothes the night before, simply kicked off his brogans, pulled out the nail, and flopped down on one of the double beds he kept in the little room above his general store. He'd get up before dawn, slip on his shoes, and head out of the store and along the railroad tracks to the old homeplace, the house he'd bought for Sara. His daughter Gladys lived there still, with her husband, Milan. Gladys would get A.P. breakfast just like she had for the last quarter century. Gladys was an early riser, up and working before the sun—except on Sunday. Gladys liked to sleep in, Sundays. On Sundays, the old man would wear a path through the house, circling through the front room, stopping at ever-shortening intervals in front of the iron stove to give it a good, loud wake-up bang, until Gladys finally emerged from her bed to cook his eggs.

Or maybe he'd walk the hundred feet up Clinch Mountain to Janette's new house. Pleasant had built her the house after she broke up with Jimmy Jett and moved back from Bristol with two toddlers, Rita and Dale. Janette would get him breakfast, too, but she might also fuss at him to change his socks. So maybe he'd just walk back and forth along the tracks, *deciding* where to eat breakfast. Walking there in the earliest light of day, A.P. must have felt a special kinship with that old pair of iron runners disappearing off into the distance. They were more or less contemporaries, A.P. and those railroad tracks, having entered the Valley about the same time. He first knew the railroad as the deliverer of the outside world, daily dropping its loot at Poor Valley's front doorstep, which was Neal's Store. Only later came the dawning that those tracks didn't just lead in, they led out.

When he was growing up, and later as he was raising his own children, two or three passenger trains a day came roaring down those tracks. Of course, there were also the freights. Back in the day, a double-stack freight train would clang down off Duggan Hill, hitting the crossing in front of Neal's around first light, whistling awake the five hundred citizens of the Valley, and then, moving like time itself, without stopping, would continue toward its appointed destiny. Every morning, it left behind a plume of smoke black against the dawn, the conjoined aroma of burning coal and oil, and a chorus of roars and metallic screeches, all of which dissolved slowly, but so surely, and so finally, that the entire passing might have been an apparition. What remained, always, were the tracks, still leading away. While the tracks themselves could never reveal much about the world outside the Valley, they had once fevered Pleasant's boyhood dreams of what that world might be like, and encouraged the notion that he might have a place in it.

Looking back over his life, A.P. Carter could say he'd made it out, and that he'd made his place, but somehow his journey felt incomplete and, in its lack of defining finality, like another apparition dissolved. For like this broke-down railroad, pushed aside by interstate highways and cargo jets, A.P. Carter had been mostly forgotten.

Neighbors might see him walking back and forth alone, all six-foot-two of him, bent slightly forward as if walking into the wind, his hands still folded behind his back, his long legs still loping down the tracks. He wore a sly little grin, which was as steadfast and comfortable as the rest of his wardrobe. It was as though he was living in the line from one of his long-ago songs: *Do not disturb my waking dream.*

But nobody in the Valley knew precisely what all went on in that mind. Not that A.P. was another Poss Harris. Poss walked around with a little smile on his face all the time . . . never said a word. Somebody in Maces Springs would walk into his house and find Poss sitting in the living room, smiling, come for a visit. He'd not say a thing, just sit a while, then get up and leave. Poss could be a bit unnerving. But Pleasant, he just liked to live in his own head, and he'd long ago learned to keep his waking dreams to himself. So he was forever mumbling to himself, or humming, and then all of a sudden he'd sing out some lyric he'd worked up. Or maybe he'd start chuckling at some private joke. When he really got laughing, his shoulders bounced up and down, and it sounded like he might be choking. People around him might get caught up in the laughter, too even though they had no idea what he was laughing at.

Maybe he was laughing about something that had happened just a few hours ago. Or maybe he was laughing about something that happened years back and once again had struck him funny. The story of the two Tom Carters always got him going. There was Big Tom Carter, the preacher who lived across the Knob in the Little Valley, along Highway 58, and Little Tom Carter a farmer who had land a little farther down the highway. One night, Little Tom's wife called an ambulance for her ailing husband, and it came out of Holston Valley Hospital, wailing down 58. When the driver saw a mailbox that said Tom Carter, he pulled up along the wrong Tom's house. Well, Big Tom had been feeling poorly, and what did he know about these new doctors anyway, or how they monitored a body? Big Tom figured they must know something he didn't. So he laid down on the gurney and let them carry h m into the ambulance (all six and a half feet and 320 pounds of him) and off they went to the hospital. By then, Little Tom's wife was in a state, because her husband couldn't catch his breath at all and she had to call the emergency number *again,* and the ambulance driver and his partner came roaring back down 58, praying to their maker that this Tom Carter was not proportioned like the first.

Doc would also chuckle about the time one old farmer passed and his neighbors did what they always do in the Valley: They dug him a grave next to the wife. Problem was, the old man had had a busy life, and *three* wives, so by that afternoon there were three freshly dug graves and only one body. Or Pleasant might take off giggling about himself. There were plenty of stories. Pleasant and the cat. Pleasant and the mule. Pleasant and the Knoxville diner. Pleasant and the sawmill. Pleasant and the other mule. Pleasant and the other sawmill. There was a long list. In fact, from the tracks he could see a few of his follies: the too-small garage he'd made for Mr. Peer two decades before, a fair tobacco barn now; the long-unused sawmill boiler he and Milan had crowbarred off a truck—it landed on its side and they never did get it up and working. At least Milan had taken down the front gate for the fence A.P. never completed at the homeplace.

A.P. had built his store after the same fashion, not long after Sara left the music business for her new life in California. He'd started building it after the Second World War, across the road from Gladys's, on a two-acre parcel of land he owned north of the railroad. After he sank the posts and put in a subfloor, he framed out a door. For a long time, all that stood on the lot was a subfloor, and a front door in want of walls. Well, that was Doc for you. That's what his friends would say. Even after he got the walls up—along with a stylish double-peaked roof and a little porch—he didn't go about the business in an altogether businesslike fashion. In fact, he ran it to the beat of his own idiosyncratic rhythms. The store never really had regular hours, but opened when he felt like it. Pleasant might keep it shuttered all through the winter. Even in the height of summer, he never did a brisk trade in anything but soda pop, which he sold out of a big Coca-Cola cooler.

In the years after the war, trade in Maces Springs could barely support Neal's, much less A.P. Carter Grocery. But Pleasant was undeterred. What he liked most was that his store was a gathering place. Buddies such as Ernest Barker and Everett Parker and Clyde Gardner could come in and play checkers or have a visit, talk about the weather or the farming or what Preacher Tom had done lately. A.P. wasn't big on talk, but these men shared a history together, so there wasn't much talk required of him, though the storekeeper was much appreciated for his wry asides. One day the men heard a big new ambulance come screaming down the Valley road, splitting the silence of a perfectly quiet afternoon. Now, these were men who could remember the days when Doc Meade used to travel that road in a buggy, pitching himself forward off the seat, whipping his horse for speed. "It's getting so you can't afford to die," A.P. had said, shaking his head. And they all chuckled.

Pleasant was always good for a little entertainment, and the men got a kick out of aggravating him. They all knew he liked to go to bed early, so they might come into the store after dark and play checkers late into the night, see how late they could keep him up. But it hardly ever worked. When A.P. was of a mind, he simply retired to his loft bed above the store. "I'm a-goin' to bed," he'd say. "You all stay as late as you want."

Twice a year, a check would arrive at Gladys's house from Southern Music Publishing, and Flo would pedal her bicycle up the Valley road to the store to deliver the missive to her grandfather. Once, around 1950, Flo had presented an envelope to A.P., stood back while he opened it, and watched his face fall. "It was for ninety-six or ninety-eight dollars, less than a hundred anyway," Flo remembers. He just stared at it and said quietly, "Well, that's not too much anymore." In fact, through the fifties there were no re-releases of the Original Carter Family songs, even in the new postwar LP format. So there were small royalties from the Canadian Bluebird label and some small change from Carter songs that other artists recorded. Whenever a check arrived, no matter how small, A.P. dutifully calculated the three-way split, sent a third to Maybelle, a third to Sara, and kept his own portion. He'd still go out and do an occasional radio show, but not often, and rarely would he travel beyond Bristol or Kingsport. Sometimes fans would straggle into Maces Springs, but not many.

"I thought he was dead," says Bill Clifton, who was a college freshman at the University of Virginia and a budding bluegrass guitarist in 1949. "I had checked with an RCA rep in my area to see why there weren't any Carter Family LPs available. He said, 'The old man died,' so I presumed him dead. Then I was listening to Curly Lambert's radio show in the autumn of 1949 and heard him say, 'Don't turn that dial. Everybody is in for a real big surprise. You're not gonna believe who is here in the studio.'" Clifton stayed tuned, and after the break, Curly introduced his guest, "A.P. Carter, the man who started it all."

"He did 'Storms Are on the Ocean,'" says Clifton, "and then Curly says, 'Don't you be putting that overcoat on to go out. We want you to do another number.'"

The next spring, Bill drove 270 miles to Poor Valley to see if he could find the man who started it all. Off Highway 58 he followed an unfamiliar dirt road down to Maces Springs, where he saw a little store with a sign on it, A.P. CARTER GROCERY. It was a bright spring day, middle of business hours, so of course the store was closed. Two doors down, on the other side of the road, Clifton found a man out mowing his lawn and asked him where he might find A.P. Carter. Milan Millard pointed to the house, "He's sitting on the couch right over there." When Bill walked into the living room of the homeplace, he found A.P. Carter listening to the radio, and the two started talking about the music. "We just hit it off," says Clifton. "He liked that the younger generation had an interest in the Carter Family–style music."

When he could get free of his studies, Clifton started spending time in Maces with his new friend, A.P. Carter. Even at sixty, A.P. was a vital force. They'd be at the homeplace, or sitting around the store, and all of a sudden the old man would say, "Let's go up to the spring and get a drink of water." Then he'd take off up into the foothills of Clinch Mountain, with his long-legged strides eating up chunks of real estate while Clifton, forty years his junior, panted and struggled to keep up. Sometimes Clifton and banjo player Johnny Clark would form a trio with A.P. and play on WKIN, Kingsport. "If we had been out playing late, we would come back and sleep in one of the two double beds in the store," says Clifton. "We'd flop in one bed and he'd get in the other. And he didn't always take off his shoes. Seems like we'd hardly get started sleeping, then five A.M., he's up. 'Let's get up to the house and get breakfast.' He always walked to Gladys's house on the railroad tracks, never on the road."

The other thing that struck Bill was the old man's generosity. He had three tenant houses on the farm in Little Valley, and the renters were supposed to pay him half the earnings from their tobacco crops. Janette was sure they were stealing from him, but A.P. never fussed. In fact, those tenants would come to the store every week and run up charges they'd never pay off. A.P. never seemed to get bothered by that, either. When longtime fans came around asking for records or song sheets, he'd get them something. If he didn't have anything handy at the store, he'd go to Gladys's and check the cabinet of the old stand-up Victrola—the one the Peers had given him—to see if there were any 78s left in there. "He gave away anything," Clifton says. "And he gave away everything. If you could pay for it, he might wait until you offered. If you didn't, he'd just give it away for nothing. He'd be driving down the road around Mendota and see somebody walking, so he'd stop the car and say, 'Wanna ride, boy?' "

Sometimes Gladys and Milan's house was like a hotel. As a little girl, Flo was constantly being asked to wake up and give over her bed to somebody her grandfather brought home. They'd come for a night, or a week, or longer. The worst A.P. ever visited on them was a broke-down cowboy performer and trick-roper named Jimmy Riddle. "Jimmy Riddle lived with us the whole summer, and the only work he did was help Mom carry *one* tub of wash water up from the cellar," says Flo. "He'd chase down us kids and lasso us, or he'd knock a piece of paper out of our hands with a bullwhip. He was always knocking cigarettes out of somebody's mouth with his bullwhip."

A.P. didn't mind. Besides, Jimmy was an entertainer like he was, and that meant something. Even into the fifties, ten years after the Original Carter Family had broken apart, A.P. stubbornly guarded his sense of himself as a viable musician and a man of import. Those days, he got up every day and put on a necktie. A niece remembers seeing him on his tractor, *plowing*, with his tie on. "He was handsome," says his sister-in-law Theda Carter. "He walked straight and kept his head held high." Once in a while at revivals, in the middle of a hymn, out of nowhere, Pleasant Carter's voice would rise trembling above the entire gathering and take over a song. People would turn and watch.

Even when he wasn't making much music, A.P. always kept up with the entertainment business, listening daily to WKIN, Kingsport. One day, after hearing that the gospel harmony group out of Texas, the Chuck Wagon Gang, was to play a school in Kingsport, he asked Bill Clifton to drive him over to the show. A.P. thought he might be related to the Gang. They had the same last name, and he'd had a great-uncle move out of Scott County and go to Texas. A.P. figured they were cousins, somehow.

When Bill and A.P. got over to Kingsport that night, it was storming, so there they stood at the front entrance of the school, an unlikely pair. Clifton, a short and stocky twenty-four-year-old marine with his head shaved like a cue ball, and Pleasant, at sixty-three, still pushing six-two, rail thin, in an overcoat and a felt hat. Clifton tried to hurry the old man through the front door, with the rest of the crowd, but A.P. Carter wasn't going with the rest of the crowd.

"No," he said, "musicianers always go in the back."

The two men walked all the way around to the back of the auditorium, and Pleasant started tapping gingerly on the door, to no avail. He tapped again. Nothing. Nobody came. Clifton tugged at his sleeve, but A.P. Carter was not going through that front door. "Musicianers always go in the back," he repeated. Besides, he told Clifton, the promoter, Wally Fowler, would know him. And so he kept tapping on the stage door while the rain poured down, and his felt hat drooped around his ears. Clifton was completely soaked and agitating to go back around front. But Pleasant stood his ground. "They'll see us directly," he said. "Wally Fowler will let us in."

It was more than ten minutes before one of the musicians came to the door: "Can I help you, old-timer?"

"I want to see the head man," said A.P.

"Who should I tell him wants to see him?"

"You can tell him A.P. Carter. I reckon you've heared of the Original Carter Family." Clifton watched the guy's eyes grow big as saucers. And A.P. Carter walked proudly through the back door, like musicianers do.

"He always considered himself a professional," says Clifton. "And he always wanted to get back into music more." The continuing success of the Carter Sisters and Mother Maybelle kept him wondering what might have been if his own family had stayed together.

Pride and desire made him susceptible to certain questionable pitches. Clifford Spurlock, a fast-talking minister and businessman out of Kentucky, filled A.P. full of big ideas about what he could do for him. Spurlock would make new recordings, he said, and press them at his plant in Manchester, Kentucky, "one of the most complete and modern little manufacturing plants in the country." His Acme Records was going to get the Carter Family disks back into the Sears catalog, and sell them at revivals. "Spurlock was a jack-leg preacher and he had my dad hamstrung," says Joe Carter, "painting big beautiful pictures about what he was going to do. I said, 'Daddy, you better watch this guy.' And Daddy said, 'No, he's a good Christian man, a preacher.' I said, 'See if I ain't telling you right.' "

But A.P. was so excited that Joe had to go along. Besides, it meant reuniting the family. When Spurlock set up studio time in Bristol for the first new recordings early in 1952, Joe signed on, and Janette, and best of all, Sara agreed. Despite the distance. Sara did what she could to stay in her children's life. Christmastime, she'd send packages and letters. Every spring she and Coy would load up the camper and make their way across the country to spend a few months in Virginia. Most of the time, they stayed in Bristol. When Sara went to Maces Springs to visit, Coy stayed away, out of respect for A.P.

For A.P., Sara's returns were like the springtime bloom. "A.P. never stopped loving Sara," Theda Carter says. "He would hear that Sara was coming back into the Valley, and he couldn't be still. He'd fidget and he'd get up and walk back and forth, back and forth along the tracks, happy and a-laughin'."

The Spurlock manufacturing plant may not have been all it was cracked up to be, because the records that came out of the 1952 Bristol sessions were a technical mess. Still, A.P. was thrilled to have *his* family together, on record, for the first time ever. They'd done some old songs and some new, including a song Sara had written out west, "Railroading on the Great Divide." The next spring, A.P. decided to bring professional music to Clinch Mountain. So he carved a path from his general store up into the mountain, made a bandstand, and started booking acts. The night it opened, A.P.'s friend Bill Clifton played.

From the stage that night, Clifton looked out and saw a throng of people. A.P. was charging a dollar a head, but there was no box office, no fence, no usher. There was just A.P., in his glory, floating amiably through the crowd, collecting what money he might. "He ended up with about two hundred dollars with a crowd of a thousand," says Clifton.

"But he never cared. He just wanted the music out there. If I would have said I was hoping for more money, he would have come up with another hundred dollars. He would have collected it, or paid it out of his own pocket."

He was funny about money; he didn't much care if he had it or not, but he couldn't stand to be in arrears. "Pleasant still had some land, and he'd fool around with it, but he didn't make nothing," says Clyde Gardner. "He told me one time he wanted me to plow something for him up in the Little Valley, give me fifteen dollars. I said, 'I don't know if I've got time to do that or not.' He said, 'I'm going to give you this money. If you can do the job, you can. If you can't, you can give it back to me sometime. But if I don't give it to you now, I may not have it before you get to work.'

"Another time he wanted me to take a calf to Kingsport for him. He said, 'I don't owe but fifty dollars, and I want to take that calf and sell it and pay that off. And I won't owe nothing.' He bought a lot of land, but that fifty dollars was all he owed, he told me."

His only weakness was for land. If he did get a little windfall, Pleasant invested in more. By 1957 he had the 125-acre farm in Little Valley, a second 125-acre property nearby, some small acreage around his grocery store and summer stage, and another three acres just off Highway 58 a few miles west of Hiltons. "A.P. never had money but he had land," says Theda. "Anytime he got money he'd want to buy more land." Theda and her husband, A.P.'s youngest brother, Grant, had bought Eck and Maybelle's homeplace, and they owned it free and clear of any mortgage, so A.P. would sometimes ask Grant to cosign a note to buy more land. Like any young wife, Theda fretted over it, but Grant always said, "Doc's good for it. Don't worry."

Also by 1957, A.P. and his family had put out another round of songs for Spurlock's Acme Records. A.P. had even given away three dozen old song folios for Spurlock to sell. Spurlock was pushing the new Carter records through a few rabid fans, turning them into retail outlets around the world. "Now that we are giving a lot of time to promoting the Carter Family and other mountain music, thought I would try to get in touch with you again," Spurlock wrote to an avid Carter collector in March of 1958. "Before long we will have a new EP record with three songs to the side, both 78 and 45. We have Carters on different stations and they were on WCKY some time ago for a hitch. Of course a lot of our selling is still by mail and we have not sought big distributors. Do you still want to handle them in your part? If so, the singles are only 45 cents each, the multiple plays 60 cents to you. They should sell for 98 cents and 1.25. We still sell the 78s and 45s at 89 cents through the mail, but you should get more. The Carter Family Scrap Book put out not long ago is going good. You may have it for 60 cents each if you can use some and they retail at 1 dollar. Soon our whole works will be in Manchester where we are setting up beautiful new master studios and the pressing plant will be moved from Knoxville soon as a new building is ready for it. Thanks, and may the Lord bless you. P.S.: Freeman, Acme Records is just one affiliate of several different businesses now. We are also in the perfume manufacturing business, wood manufacturing, and electronic sales."

On paper, the operation looked great, under the bold letterhead:

Acme International Distributors
New York—Winnipeg—London—Cremorne
Home Office Greenville, Tennessee, U.S.A.

"Dear Friends " went one Spurlock mailing, "I wish to take this opportunity to thank all of you in the United States, Canada, England, Australia and New Zealand and in other countries, who have purchased or promoted our records and other items from time to time. Without you, our business could not have grown from an obscure, struggling firm to a world-wide organization. We are grateful to our Heavenly Master for His benediction as we have labored to preserve the worthwhile music of the past and present, and to keep our motto, 'Principle before Profit.' "

Where the Carters were concerned. the Acme motto was in full flower. While Spurlock was spectacularly low on principle, he showed absolutely *no* profit. The Carters never got a single royalty check from the preacher.

But by the late fifties, a new importance was beginning to attach itself to A.P. Carter and his music. In its way, it was as unsettling as the realization that Spurlock had taken him for a ride. About that time, earnest young college men started coming around, asking all kinds of strange questions. They wanted to know where he got this song or that, which lines he wrote, which he didn't, picking apart a song in a way he'd never even conceived. As far as A.P. was concerned, no matter where its parts came from, a song was all of a piece. What good could come in unraveling it? When letters came in asking him to parse the provenance of a particular song, he left them unanswered.

But there were other visitors whose feeling for the music was deep, and of the moment still, and when those people came to his doorstep, A.P. couldn't do enough for them. One summer day, Ed Romaniuk and his sister Elsie, two young kids from the Canadian coal camps who had copied out the Carter Family songs while listening to them on XERA, drove up to A.P.'s store in Maces Springs. They'd driven all the way from Alberta just to see the great man himself. They weren't disappointed. "A.P. is quite a remarkable man, very humble," Ed Romaniuk wrote to a friend. "We spent our time at his little store, but he is not keeping it running. The house was locked as Gladys was away with the keys. A.P. told us how they began recording and how he composed some of his songs. He asked us to sing for him so we got out our guitars and sang 'Gathering Flowers From the Hillside.' He remarked that we sounded just like they did and that he was mighty proud of us. Then A.P. told us . . . [when he] decided that he was going into the recording business, many people laughed at him. Others declared he was losing his mind. Then when Sara, Maybelle and A.P. recorded 'Little Darling Pal of Mine' people lined up by the blocks to buy it. It sold 2 and a half million copies. . . . A.P. told us of personal appearances they made and that they played at dances. He mentioned how Sara and Maybelle would be sleeping in the backseat of the car while he drove in the early hours of the morning after being up all night. It was a hard life, he said, but when a man's got music in his bones, he's got to get it out. A.P. told us that he would be recording again soon. He also showed us pictures, his contracts, lists of songs—350 of them." The following Christmas, A.P. sent a card to the Romaniuks. After years of writing cards and letters to him, it was the first they'd ever received from him. It was also the last.

As Pleasant Carter neared seventy and his heart started to weaken, the men who hung around his store didn't think much about it. "I've not been well all my life," he'd always told them. They never thought his health situation was dire, even when he quit minding the store and gave it over to Milan and Gladys to run. The Valley was beginning to look different. The roads were paved, the houses bricked. Every farmer had a tractor. In 1959 Neal's finally gave up the ghost, and without its post office, Maces Springs was no longer recognized as a town by the state of Virginia, or the Rand McNally mapmakers. A.P. must have sensed something, because around that time, he began to make known his final wishes, quietly, slyly, and at odd times. One afternoon on the porch he called to his granddaughter Rita Jett, who was not yet five. "There's something I want to tell you that I don't want you to ever forget," he said in earnest. Then after a long, pregnant pause, his granddaughter leaned in, waiting to get the wisdom of the ages. "Always vote Republican," he said.

He gave Janette advice about her youngest son, Dale Jett. The boy was only three, but A.P. already saw a lot of himself in Dale. Dale couldn't sit still, and though naturally gentle, he was also high-strung and hot-tempered. Dale was already something of a celebrity in the Valley for being able to hold his breath until he turned blue and passed out. "Watch out for him," A.P. told Janette, "for he has a high portion in nerves, and he will have a hard time in life."

A.P. Carter never was much for formal and legal documents, but in February of 1960 he was so weak he couldn't get out of bed, and his attorney suggested it was time to execute a will. "Pleasant got me and Everett Parker out [to Gladys's house], and he had the will read, the will he made," says Clyde Gardner. "He was in bed then. But his mind still seemed to be about as good as ever." By then A.P.'s hands trembled badly, and he didn't have the strength to make a good signature. All he could do was make his mark, an X, on the page.

A few weeks later, Gladys called Bill Clifton, distraught: "When can you come and see Daddy?"

"Maybe on the weekend."

"He'll not be here this weekend."

That day, Bill grabbed his wife, Sara Lee, and rushed over. When he got to Gladys's house, he found A.P. in bed, half delirious. For eight straight days, A.P. had refused to eat, and he was slowly wasting away. "Gladys had a bed set up in the living room," says Clifton, "and there was constant flow through there between the kitchen and the bathroom, so there was always somebody to stop and talk to A.P. They'd stop and talk to him. Gladys put a chair beside him, and people would sit with him all through the night. He told me, 'People say I'm gonna die. They had a lawyer up here to get me to write a will and had me to sign it.' He figured that was it; he was going to die."

But it seemed A.P. didn't want to walk that last valley alone. That night, he would waken from a deep sleep, sure he was in a radio show or a recording session, bassing in on a song. He'd announce a song and then say to Bill and Janette, who were sitting at his bedside, "You two get to singing." He kept at them to do a song called "Two Little Girls in Blue." Janette didn't even know the words, but she'd join in with Bill when he got to the chorus. When somebody would call across the room for Bill's wife, Sara, A.P. thought it was his own Sara come back to nurse him. Nearly thirty years since she'd left him, A.P. still kept Sara's long black ponytail, from when she cut her hair short with her girlfriends in the Valley. "His heart was broken," says Clifton. "He loved Sara to the end. He held on to the hope that she would come back."

The next morning, Bill was trying hard to bring his friend back to the here and now. "I said, 'A.P., you don't understand. We've got too much to do. We've got to rebuild that stage before summer. Somebody has to do that by June.' That was Thursday, and at lunchtime Gladys says, 'Daddy, can I get you something?' It'd been nine days without food now. And he says, 'I believe I'd like some of Myrtle Hensley's apple butter.' "

Gladys raced down to Myrtle's, who gave over all the apple butter she had. "If that's what's gonna keep him alive," said Myrtle, "I'll just have to make another batch."

Not even Myrtle's apple butter could keep him going much longer. A.P. made it through the summer, but by the fall of 1960, his failing heart landed him in the Holston Valley Community Hospital in Kingsport. The last time Clifton saw him, A.P. was flat on his back, under an oxygen tent, barely in the world. Bill was about to a make a Carter Family tribute record for a company called Starcay, but A.P. received this news without a glimmer of recognition.

On November 7, 1960, Janette went to visit her father and found him shading to blue. When she reached for him, his hand was cold and, for the first time she'd ever seen, still. "I took his hand and it wasn't shaking anymore," says Janette. "I ran out to the nurse, and I said, 'He's not shaking! You have to do something.' And she said, 'His nerves are dying. It'll not be long now.' " That evening, Janette went home to get some rest, to prepare for the death siege. But later that night, she saw a black hearse coming up the Valley road. She knew it must be carrying the body of her father. A.P. had asked to be taken back home, because he didn't want visitation in Kingsport.

His other wishes for his funeral were simple. He'd be buried near his parents, and his sister Ettaleen, in the cemetery behind Mount Vernon. He requested a wooden casket and said specifically, "I don't want no special singers over me. Just the Mount Vernon Quartet." In his funeral program, also according to his wishes, Sara Dougherty Carter was listed as his wife. All in all, the official remembrance of Alvin Pleasant Delaney Carter was a modest affair. Outside of family and near friends, his passing was barely marked. Short death notices ran in *Billboard*, the *Kingsport News*, and the *Kingsport Times*, but not in the nearest newspaper, the *Scott County News*. "For some reason," the

Scott County editor wrote to a folklorist who had requested a copy of the obituary, "we failed to carry the death of Mr. Carter."

A.P. Carter died as cash poor as he'd lived, but Ermine Carter, the only real workhorse among the Carter siblings, stoutly defended his oldest brother. "Well, I don't care what you say about Doc," he'd say. "He's the only one that left every young'un he had a house, and some land." Gladys got the 125-acre farm in Little Poor Valley and the homeplace. Janette got the 125 acres of land in Poor Valley, the general store, and the house her father built for her. Joe got a lot next to Janette, and the land near Highway 58, west of Hiltons. That legacy to his children was a point of pride for A.P. He had managed to reverse the losses of his old great-grandfather Dulaney Carter, who had drunk away two fortunes and left his heirs nothing but debt.

As was his way, A.P. left little debt to be settled. He owed $350 dollars on a note he'd taken in 1956 from the First National Bank in Gate City, and $230 in sundry small-time obligations. Even with $1,100 worth of hospital and funeral expenses piled on (he was right about how dear dying had become), A.P. Carter's worldly debts were cleared within ten months of his death. Sale of his livestock brought in $457.33, his household goods $45, and his last plat of tobacco $371.35. But the biggest check that winter came from Ralph Peer's company: $617.33 in royalties. The Kingston Trio had recently recorded a version of "Worried Man Blues," and both Columbia and RCA were re-releasing original Carter recordings as LP albums. Just three weeks after A.P.'s death, Elvis Presley recorded "Are You Lonesome Tonight?"

In fact, the growing royalties left room for the children to honor another of A.P.'s final wishes, to make a nod to heirs of a different sort, and to the boundless faith their father had in the staying power of Carter Family music. One day in the fall of 1961, having been duly instructed and paid, the Bill Begley Monument Company crew drove up the Valley road past Janette's house, then past the old homeplace, past Neal's boarded-up store and Eck's old house, before turning left onto a winding dirt path. The truck climbed slowly to Mount Vernon Methodist Church on the road that had been carved out of land donated long before by the old singing master, A.P.'s first musical mentor, Flanders Bays. At the cemetery, and without ceremony, the men placed a special marker on the grave of Alvin Pleasant Delaney Carter. It was like no other at Mount Vernon. Above his name and dates, carved in the smooth glassy sheen was the likeness of a 78 record, perfect in its roundness, and the words "Keep on the Sunny Side."

"Just before he died, A.P. told Gladys how he wanted to be remembered at Mount Vernon Cemetery," says Bill Clifton. "He had seen this pink marble in Texas that he really liked, and that was what he wanted for a marker. He wanted it to stand out. He said, 'Someday people will come to Mount Vernon and want to see where the Carter Family is buried.'"

June Carter and Johnny Cash, not long after they met (Stella Bayes)

Opposite: Maybelle, with Anita and June (Lorrie Davis Bennett)

On the Road Again

In Nashville, Eck must have been shaken by the lack of regard shown his brother; the performers at the Opry, the songwriters and producers and A&R men on Music Row, were more or less oblivious to A.P. Carter's death. This town was looking forward, not back. In the studios on Sixteenth Avenue, a new Nashville sound was being pioneered by Chet Atkins, now head of RCA's Nashville division, and Owen Bradley, who had a similar position at Decca. Atkins and Bradley wanted slick, uptown production, and big arrangements with lush string sections, drums, and smooth vocal backing—something that could compete with rock and roll for the millions of dollars at stake in the popular-music market. "Crossover" talents such as Jim Reeves, Don Gibson, and Patsy Cline were the sort of performers they were looking for—pop singers whose voices were better matched with piano than with banjo. And even at the Opry, management seemed more interested in expanding its audience than in pleasing the older, rural loyalists. Traditional country music couldn't be dispensed with altogether, and May-belle continued to do her weekly show at the Ryman, but little was done to promote her.

In the early sixties, it was harder than ever for Maybelle to get her daughters together on any stage. Anita was living in Mobile, Ala-bama, with her husband, Don Davis, and was in semiretirement. Anita had never stepped up to stardom, and it didn't seem likely she would now. Her firstborn baby was colicky, impossible on the road, and when her son Jay was diagnosed with autism, caring for him became her overriding priority. Helen had a houseful of boys and was beginning to see herself more as a songwriter than a performer, espe-cially after Ann-Margaret made a top-twenty hit of Helen's thor-oughly un-Carteresque pop tearjerker "What Am I Supposed to Do?" June, of course, was still onstage pitching away, just beginning to tour as a regular with the Johnny Cash road show. Maybelle still sup-plemented her show at the Opry with whatever road work she could get. But no label had much interest in putting out her records, so she was moonlighting as a practical nurse, sitting with the elderly and the infirm for a little extra cash.

Eck could see the writing on the wall: The Carter sisters had virtu-ally no future together, and Maybelle's career was sliding into obscurity. It must have been soon after A.P.'s death that he made the plan. He may have even mentioned it to Maybelle. Pop Carter had been thinking about it for a while, researching it in consumer magazines. He'd decided it was time to retire, and according to his research, New Port Richey, Florida, was the place to go; the little fishing village just north of Tampa was the best value the country offered. He found a bungalow there, on a crystal-clear freshwater river, a short boat ride away from the Gulf of Mexico. The fishing was great. Heck, he already had the deep-sea poles. So one night in 1961, Pop made his announcement. "Mom came in off the road, and he had decided that it was time for them to retire and go to Florida," says Becky Bowman. "And he had already bought a place and made two trips with his truck moving stuff down there!"

Maybelle nearly fainted. "Daddy, surely you didn't," she said. "Surely you didn't do that."

"Yes, I did," said Eck, and proud of it, too. He'd got a great deal on the house.

"Well, I'm not retiring."

Nobody was going to force Maybelle out, not Opry management, not Nashville record gurus. Making music was what she did, and she wasn't giving it up. Her resolve would pay off, partly because of a promising new movement building far away from Nashville's Music Row. It had begun in 1958, when the Kingston Trio had a smash hit with "Tom Dooley," a traditional ballad first recorded in 1929 by the near-blind fiddler G. B. Grayson. The champions of the "folk" music revival were mostly young Yankees, many of them intellectuals or liberals. A lot of them came out of academia, and some of its professors started writing Maybelle and asking if they could visit her in Tennessee. She never said no, and between semesters, college men would drive up to her house in suburban Nashville, pull out reel-to-reel tape recorders, and start asking her about the old days, the early recordings, Sara, and A.P. They'd quiz her on how she developed the Carter scratch, her autoharp technique, or where the family got its songs.

These strangers in his home drove Eck crazy. He'd say hello, maybe, and then get out of the house. Maybelle never seemed to be bothered. She was matter-of-fact and patient. They'd run through long lists of songs, and she'd tell them where they got each one. "A.P. found that one. . . . A.P. wrote that one. The eighth song we ever recorded was a song A.P. wrote . . . known all my life . . . known all my life . . . known that one a long time."

There was one guy who came all the way out from UCLA, who was going to be writing his dissertation on the Carter Family. He was getting a Ph.D. . . . in the Carters! "Did you have any notion you were setting a style that was going to be very important?" the doctoral candidate, Ed Kahn, wanted to know.

"I never thought it was important," she answered.

"But when were you first aware that the Carter Family had a distinctive style?"

"In fact, I hadn't thought too much about it in that way until the last few years, you know, when everybody started coming to me and telling me they would have never played the guitar if it hadn't been for our records. Lot of them tell me that. When they were kids, they listened to these records."

"You never had any idea your guitar was distinctive?"

At this, Maybelle let out a laugh. "No, I never did. I didn't even think about it. I just played the way I wanted to and that's it."

The new interest in Maybelle's old kind of music was not completely unheeded in Nashville. One of the first to understand the possibilities was Louise Scruggs. Louise was a famously shrewd and frosty woman, wife of Earl Scruggs and manager of the bluegrass band Flatt & Scruggs, named for her husband, and singer Lester Flatt. In January of 1961, she says, "Someone, I don't remember who, sent me 150 of the old Carter Family songs on reel-to-reel tapes. Earl was on tour with Johnny Cash. We'd had a big snow and I couldn't get out of the house. I was sitting there with nothing to do, so I put those tapes on and started listening to them." She sensed immediately the power of those songs, how they could be reinterpreted by a new generation without disturbing the emotional tug at the center. "By the time Earl came back in from the road," she says, "I was ready to tell him: 'You really should do a Carter Family album.'"

Her husband was delighted. Earl Scruggs had grown up on a farm in Shelby, North Carolina, and listened to the Carter Family's 1943 performances on WBT, Charlotte. "Maybelle just knocked me out," Scruggs said. "She and Merle Travis were my favorite guitar players." And Earl had been hearing around town "that Maybelle was settin' and nursin' with people instead of pickin' and singin'." So he asked her to sit in on the record, and she agreed, suggesting she'd like to play the autoharp. She'd been refining her technique over the past few years, she told him, and the instrument would give the sessions a Carter Family flavor distinct from other Flatt & Scruggs albums. Earl Scruggs figured he'd play the guitar when necessary, affecting Maybelle's style as best he could.

But once in the studio, Earl started to get frustrated. He had trouble reproducing Maybelle's unique tones and nuances, no matter how perfectly he copied her notes. He didn't lack for talent or confidence; he was, and is, widely regarded as the greatest banjo player in history. He figured he was having trouble matching up to Maybelle because the Gibson guitar she'd played for more than thirty years was so rare and well broken in. So Maybelle brought her Gibson into the studio . . . and Scruggs *still* couldn't get it right. "I never could find that pretty tone she got offa that guitar," he says. "I mean I picked all over it, but I just never could find it." The song that really drove Earl nuts was "You Are My Flower," with the Mexican-style licks Maybelle had first worked out back in Poor Valley, listening to border radio. The band had already recorded the song, and all that remained to complete the track was for Scruggs to overdub the guitar solo. After a few false starts, he asked Maybelle to play it, so he could study her more closely.

Maybelle took up the Gibson and played. "And as luck would have it," Scruggs said, "the producer had the mike open, and Maybelle played it in exactly the right tempo. So he just spliced it in, even though she didn't know that they were gonna put it on the record. There was very little splicin' done in those days, but it sounded fine."

To promote *Songs of the Famous Carter Family,* Flatt & Scruggs took Maybelle out on some local dates, small gatherings and shopping-center openings. "People swarmed around her like she was Elvis Presley," Scruggs remembered. Her own gigs were still rather sparse, and not all that lucrative, considering how far she had to travel to get to them. Not long after the Flatt & Scruggs recording, she released a little album of traditional songs called *Mother Maybelle Carter* on the tiny Briar label, and Carter Family songs began appearing on folk anthologies.

By the beginning of 1963, the folk revival was booming. Bob Dylan had recorded his first album, with a few traditional songs. He even did the Blind Lemon Jefferson song that A.P. had worked over, "See That My

Grave Is Kept Clean." Joan Baez, queen of the folk genre, had recorded "Wildwood Flower," "Little Darlin' Pal of Mine," and other songs plucked from obscurity by the Carters, but no composer's credit was given (the songs were listed on the album as "traditional"). ABC even had a weekly variety show featuring folk musicians—*Hootenanny.*

Maybelle hadn't been part of the new movement; it was not like her to get out front professionally. As famed producer and musician Jack Clement recalls, "If you wanted to cut across—that is, try something new—she'd go with you. But she wouldn't initiate it." Even as a bit player, Maybelle had grown comfortable in the commercial glamour of the Opry and its road shows. The folk scene, by comparison, felt like small potatoes. She'd played some of the festivals and clubs, but it wasn't until the spring of 1963 that she truly cut across, this time with the encouragement of a group called The New Lost City Ramblers. They were young enough to be her sons: Mike Seeger, John Cohen, and Tracy Schwarz. Seeger was the half brother of left-wing folksinger Pete Seeger; their father was a distinguished musicologist; Mike's mother was a classically trained modernist composer. Mike had grown up with old-timey and bluegrass music in the house. Family time was gathering friends and neighbors in their Washington, D.C., apartment, singing Carter songs such as "Worried Man Blues" or "East Virginia Blues." In 1961 Seeger had wanted Maybelle to guest on an anthology of auto-harp music, but her agent nixed the deal. "All we could offer was fifty bucks," says Seeger. "That's like $250 today; it still wasn't much, and her agent wouldn't even take her the offer." It was typical of the mixed signals flowing between the idealistic folk revivalists, who served the music with missionary zeal, and the country-music industry, for whom business was business.

Finally, in the spring of 1963, after a year of talking and planning, the New Lost City Ramblers were able to arrange a suitable business venture for Maybelle: a monthlong tour beginning at the Ash Grove in Hollywood. The club was a West Coast mecca for young folkies, the sort of place devotees would go even if they'd never heard of the head-liner. Beyond the Ramblers' love of Carter Family music, and their excitement about meeting Maybelle for the first time, Seeger and his band mates saw the engagement as an opportunity to bridge the unnatural chasm between the folk revival and country. A local country deejay named Hugh Cherry even asked the band to come on his show and promote Maybelle's appearance. "It was a new situation, country people coming to the Ash Grove," says John Cohen. "It was exciting." And then Maybelle got stuck on the East Coast, when she and the Carter Sisters were booked at the last minute on ABC's national *Hootenanny.* The Ramblers were certainly happy for her but it was hardly fair. They were two days into the engagement when they got the word: Maybelle Carter was on her way to L.A. She was taking the red-eye, flying through the night so that she'd be there in time for the third night.

When Seeger, Cohen, and Schwarz met her at LAX, the three musicians could barely contain themselves. Maybelle seemed oblivious to the historic possibilities of the Ash Grove dates. "For her," Seeger remembers, "it was just another gig." That was what struck them about Maybelle first: an ease, a calm, a nonchalance that bordered on a total lack of ego. They walked her over to baggage claim, where both Seeger and Cohen were horrified to see her guitar—"that beautiful, rare old Gibson"—come tumbling down the conveyor belt, in a plastic case, bumping against the American Touristers. "It was clear right away how down-home she was," Cohen says. "There was no star business about her."

The Ramblers weren't just excited, they were nervous. Maybelle's first Ash Grove appearance was that evening, and since the Ramblers had never played with her before, they were anxious to run through some numbers. So they raced from the airport to Seeger's apartment, got her settled in with her guitar, and started rehearsing songs. First an hour, then two, and Maybelle didn't say a word. Finally, she mentioned, almost in passing, that she hadn't really slept on the plane the night before: "I'm a bit tired," she said.

"I suddenly realized how inconsiderate we were being," says Seeger, "but she hadn't given us any sign until then. She was a trouper, and she took great pride in being a trouper."

The Ash Grove was a boxy storefront building in a commercial neighborhood on Melrose. Inside, the space was still pretty raw, a concrete floor, open ceiling rafters with lights hung over the stage. The room held no terror for Maybelle, and neither did the crowds. One night, a fan showed up in the dressing room with a stack of Carter Family 78s for her to sign. She signed them all, without complaint. The room was full every night, two hundred people or better. On Friday nights, there would be the young kids on their first dates; Saturdays were the more settled couples, marrieds, and live-ins. Weekdays and Sundays, the audience was packed with professional musicians and true aficionados. No matter the crowd, Maybelle made her music but had little to say. In thirty-five years of performing, Maybelle had rarely been a headlining solo act. She simply wasn't used to talking from the stage.

"It quickly became clear to me that she wasn't used to being alone," says Seeger.

"I will never forget standing up there onstage at the Ash Grove, in front of some two hundred people, and watching Maybelle," says Cohen. "The way she moved her hands in simple little elegant, graceful gestures, making this incredible sound come out of that Gibson. It reminded me of the way my grandmother used to crochet—she used the same skilled, graceful movements, repeated over and over. Everything about Maybelle was unpretentious and matter-of-fact."

From the Ash Grove, the tour went on to Tucson. Maybelle and the Ramblers loaded up a 1962 Studebaker Lark station wagon and started off on the dusty drive. By then, the guys thought Maybelle just wanted to be one of the boys. "We rigged up a platform in the back where she could sleep, because we had to drive all night," says Cohen. But Maybelle insisted on taking her turn at the wheel—and drove like a teamster. They did their best to draw her out, and she did her best to oblige. "We'd ask her about the old Carter Family schoolhouse gigs," says Seeger, "and she'd tell us, 'Well, A.P. would tell a story about where the song came from and then we'd sing and he'd tell a little bit more. Then maybe I'd put the riser on my guitar nut so I could play Hawaiian. And then we'd eat an apple.'" She even told them about one of A.P.'s innumerable flats, in which he was continually dusted by passing cars as he tried to change the tire. Every car went by, she told them, he'd yell: "Son of a bitch!"

"I think she felt she was being quite risqué with us boys," Seeger says, chuckling. At some point, she let it slip about her job nursing elderly patients. "I just couldn't conceive of how this could be," says Cohen. "She played the Opry. I'd assumed she was respected in Nashville. So why did she have to do this? I couldn't imagine it."

Perhaps the most important legacy of the tour, however, was that the Ramblers and others realized the importance of preserving Maybelle's style and her rich repertoire. Not just onstage but sitting around the dressing room, warming up before a show, or even fooling around after, Maybelle was always playing. "She played tunes we'd never heard before," says Seeger, " 'Red River Blues' and 'Liberty Dance.' Tracy Schwarz worked out how she played 'Victory Rag' and wrote it down."

It wasn't just the songs but the skill. Over time, Seeger came to appreciate a part of Maybelle she kept well beneath the surface. It was pride. She liked being the best—or the most distinctive—musician in the room. "I was wide-eyed," says Seeger. "She did B-flat [a difficult, hard-to-reach chord] so easily, so effortlessly. She liked to show off in her own quiet way."

That same year, the Ramblers took Maybelle to the Newport Folk Festival, where she was treated with an admixture of respect and awe. Both her autoharp style and her guitar techniques were presented at "workshops" by younger musicians who helped her explain, essentially, why her music was complex and interesting, despite involving very few chords. It was almost funny, the way these young people got so nervous around her. Trying to explain to an audience who Maybelle was and what she had done, A.P.'s old friend Bill Clifton had introduced her as "Maybelle Guitar." But Clifton quickly recovered. "I could call her that very easily, I think. . . . Maybelle Carter's guitar style has probably been the most unique, inventive method of guitar playing—flat-pick style as well as the finger-roll style—that has come out of the twenties, thirties, forties, in fact, to date." At the workshop she played the Carter scratch

on "Weeping Willow Tree" and what she called "the ole thumb and finger style" on "Cannonball Blues." ("A lot of people use two or three
fingers," she said, laughing, "but I've never been able to do that.")
Using a flat pick, she brought a touch of boogie to "Coal Miner's
Blues."

The autoharp workshop, in which she was assisted by Mike Seeger,
was a little more intimate. She played a tune for which she'd never had
a name—"the first tune that I ever heard on the autoharp, I guess, forty
years ago." And then she explained how she came to play melodies on
an instrument intended solely for accompaniment. "I just started messin'
around with it, and I thought: 'I know there oughtta be a way to get a
tune out of it.' So . . . it was when 'The San Antonio Rose' first came
out [and] that was the first one that I learned to play."

By the time she walked out on the main stage for her evening concert, the fresh-faced young crowd gave her a rousing ovation. The
applause and cheering for her performance of "Worried Man Blues"
was so enthusiastic and so sustained that even the unflappable Maybelle
Carter was visibly moved. "This is one of the greatest thrills of my life,"
she told the crowd. When she announced that "Wildwood Flower"
would be her last tune, there was an audible grumbling in the audience.
As Maybelle picked, the enthusiasm swelled, and her playing seemed to
feed from it. When the audience demanded an encore, the taciturn
Maybelle tried to communicate her deep pleasure: "You're real wonderful people, I'll tell ya" was all she could say.

In her fifth decade onstage, Maybelle Carter had never looked at the
performer-audience equation in any but one way: It was her job to entertain. The audience owed her nothing. "I never saw her give a bad performance," says Becky Bowman, who played with Maybelle throughout
the fifties. "There was something she was giving. I saw a group of people, an audience in Florida, in the offbeat cotton field. They were poor.
And I saw people come to that show—I can't remember now what they
charged—but they could have used that money to buy a loaf of bread.
But your physical food and spiritual food are different. This was something that was like medicine to them. They came and they left there with

a feeling of joy. I saw those people spend money to see a show. It wasn't bread that fed them. But they left feeling fed."

Maybelle left the Newport Folk Festival with her own sense of renewal. This wasn't about the Carter *Family* or her daughters or the Grand Ole Opry. This was about her, personally. After thirty-five years of blending in, of being the ultimate group musician, of mothering, of pushing others forward, Maybelle Carter was beginning to find her way toward her own spotlight. At later festivals, Mike Seeger started to see that maybe Maybelle *liked* being out front. She'd worked out a little stage patter; she'd even tell a story or two. But by the time that blossoming had begun, the Carter Family had been invaded by a man who would change everything for Maybelle and the others. For better, for worse, and forever.

John R. "Johnny" Cash left a wide wake wherever he went. Jimmy Dean once complained to Johnny that he was ruining Jimmy's tours: Jimmy and his band kept getting turned away from hotels Johnny had trashed. "I'm amused by him as a pet coon," Merle Travis once said. "I'm impressed with him like a snake behind glass. He's that unique to me. . . . Even though he's a kaleidoscope of a thousand different ideas, he's a straight line. There ain't no twilight and there ain't no dusk to Johnny Cash. He's like a sunny day, or he's completely dark."

Like the Carters, Johnny Cash had come up from the country. He grew up mainly in Dyess, Arkansas, where he and his brothers and sisters helped his father tend to a twenty-acre patch planted with cotton for cash and vegetables for their own table. The farm was government land, a Depression-era handout really, and its meager bounty afforded the Cash family little more than subsistence. They worked constantly for what little they got; the day after they buried Johnny's fourteen-year-old brother, Jack, who was killed in a farming accident, the family was back in the fields. Johnny graduated high school in Dyess, and joined the air force, which shipped him off to Germany. On his return to the States in 1954 he married his sweetheart, Vivian Liberto, of San Antonio,

Texas, moved to Memphis, and made himself a recording star for Sam Phillips's Sun Records. In 1956 his single "I Walk the Line" was a number one song, stayed on the *Billboard* charts for forty-three weeks, and earned $2 million. Between 1958 and 1960, he had twenty-five songs on the country-music charts.

But when Johnny Cash first came into the Carters' life in the early sixties, he seemed intent on throwing away both fame and fortune. He was popping vast quantities of painkillers, amphetamines, and downers, staying awake and wired for seventy-two hours straight, then sleeping for thirty. His drug habit had laid waste to his first marriage, and he rarely saw his four daughters. But even in the haze of drugs, Cash showed remarkable focus. He kept at writing songs, recording albums, and touring. The pills decimated his body, dropping his weight from 200 pounds to as little as 140, but he remained a man of thoroughgoing appetite. And he had decided that one thing he had to have . . . was June Carter.

He'd grown up listening to the Carter Family 78s and tuning in to their show on border radio. The way Johnny told it later, he'd first *seen* June in 1950, during Dyess High's senior-class trip to Nashville. The class went to the Opry, and Johnny sat gawking at the Carter Sisters and Mother Maybelle and at one Carter sister in particular. Five years later, he began playing at the Opry himself. At the time, both John and June were newlyweds. Still, he introduced himself to June with these words: "Hello, I'm Johnny Cash, and I'm going to marry you someday."

"Really?"

"Yeah."

"Well, good," June said. "I can't wait."

He didn't have much contact with her until December of 1961, at the Big D Jamboree in Dallas, Texas. Johnny's manager, Saul Hollif, had booked June on the show. Onstage that night, June's Huckleberry humor and wholesome sex appeal was a welcome counterpoint to Cash's macho, sneering "man in black." After the show that night, Johnny asked her to do some more shows. June said she didn't know, that Saul would have to make her a good offer. But in principle, she said, she'd love to. Saul came through.

In February of 1962, June Carter became a regular on the Cash road show and quickly convinced Cash and his manager to begin booking her mother and sisters, too. At the first date they all played together, in Des Moines, Iowa, June stopped by his dressing room before the show to say hello, saw his shirt was a wrinkled mess, and told him to take it off so she could press some respectability into the sorry thing. Just then, Maybelle walked in.

"What's going on here?" Maybelle asked, arching her eyebrows.

"Look at the shirt Johnny Cash *thinks* he's gonna wear onstage tonight!" June shouted.

Maybelle shook her head and clucked her tongue. "Get it off and let June iron it."

Johnny noted Maybelle's pronunciation of iron—"arn"—just the way his own mother would say it. "Boy," he grunted, "aren't we getting prissy tonight."

But he relented, stripping off his shirt and covering his chest with his hands. As June ironed, Maybelle sat chatting about her grandchildren. "Before I knew it," Johnny remembers, "I took my hands down from my chest. I felt better than I had in some time."

For reasons that he couldn't entirely explain at the time, Cash was more drawn to June than ever. June had recently married a former college football star named Edwin "Rip" Nix. But since they did so many shows together, June and Johnny saw a lot of each other. Johnny's marriage remained in purgatory. Vivian Cash wanted her husband to come off the road and settle down. "It was hopeless for her because I just *wasn't* going to do that," he wrote in his autobiography, "and it was hopeless for me because she'd sworn that I'd never be free from our marriage. She was a devout Catholic; she said she'd die before she'd give me a divorce."

Johnny had moved his wife and daughters to California in 1959, but now, when he came off the road, he just didn't bother going home.

Instead, he started hanging around Nashville, nearer the country-music business, and nearer June Carter. June was careful not to invite Johnny around the house she shared with Nix, but she began bringing him to Maybelle and Eck's house on Cude Lane.

They could all see Johnny Cash was a mess, but Eck and Maybelle told Cash he could come to Cude Lane to sleep over as often as he wanted. "They'd seen what happened to Hank Williams," Cash later speculated, "and I don't think they wanted it to happen to me." Johnny was happy to accept the offer, partly because it gave him the chance to make a friend of Pop Carter. Johnny was a smart man, and he understood the way to June was still through Eck.

Making friends with Eck paid off in unexpected ways. The more time Johnny Cash spent around the place, the more fascinated he was with Pop Carter. One of the first things he noticed about Pop was his obsession with rocks. "He'd be out there with a nine-pound sledgehammer, bustin' rocks in the heat of the summer," Cash says. "I just couldn't understand a man lovin' that kind of torture. I mean, he did it all day long, like a convict. Then he'd come in and cook supper."

Pop's obsession gave Cash an idea. Being a good deal more open-minded and eclectic than the average Nashville star, he had heard and admired the folksinging movement. "John Henry," the ballad of a hammer-wielding railroad man, was an increasingly popular traditional song. Johnny would see Eck out there busting his back, hammer ringing off ledge, and he couldn't get the song out of his head. Working with June, Cash arranged a nine-minute version of the song. Maybelle and the Carter sisters did the background vocals. It appeared on his 1962 album *Blood, Sweat & Tears*, which was most remarkable for a beautiful duet with Anita, "Another Man Done Gone."

While working on *Blood, Sweat & Tears*, Cash began to notice that Maybelle kept even stranger hours than he did, often rolling up to the house at four or five o'clock in the morning. At first, he assumed that she must be playing a lot of out-of-town gigs—until she told him she was "settin' with the elderly." Maybelle didn't go into much detail about her job as a practical nurse, except to assure him she liked it fine. Still, Johnny was shocked: "I thought, my God! This woman is staying up all night to sit with the elderly then getting a couple of hours of sleep before the breaking of the rocks starts. But she really loved those elderly people."

It made him anxious to get to know her better. But like everyone else, Cash found her difficult to draw out. "Maybelle was a very, very quiet southern woman," says Cash. "Like many quiet people, she knew more than most people, because she listened more. She was not introverted; she was happy and laughing whenever someone had something to say that was worth a laugh. But she gave nothing away, unless you asked for it. Nothing."

He began playing guitar and singing with her around the house as often as possible, but even then, talk was more about songs—where they came from, who she learned them from, who played them a little bit different—than anything about her own life. Cash found comfort in the ease of just *being* with her, without the need to work through *problems*. He felt no obligation to discuss, or to apologize for, the life he was leading. In the spaces of those silences, Maybelle became a reassuring figure: part mother, part mentor, part friend.

His association with the Carters also made Cash a more interesting artist. In 1963 he recorded "Ring of Fire," a song written by June and her distant cousin Merle Kilgore, and its success began to reestablish him as a big star. The song, about consuming passions that leave other people badly hurt, could have been about the painful A.P.-Sara-Coy triangle. It would also be remembered in the Carter-Cash household as the anthem of their own tortured courtship. June was eaten up by guilt; she was still married to Nix, but she had fallen deeply in love with Johnny. "I used to go to church about every day for a year," she said later. "I used to get out my Bible and look through it. I used to wear out my knees and pray."

And Johnny was crazy for June. On the road especially, she was the person who helped him wrestle with his drug addiction. She'd hide his pills, force food down his gullet, sweep up behind him when he wrecked hotel rooms or business relationships or friendships. June made Cash want to be a better man. For one thing, even if he could get free of Vivian, he knew June would never marry him until he got himself under control. By 1964, says their friend Dixie Deen Hall, "John had begun making his bid for June, but she was still keeping her distance on account of the pills. 'When he straightens up, yes, I'll marry him,' she used to say, 'but not now.' "

Johnny was working all the family angles. Time spent with Maybelle improved his manners immeasurably. "I began going fishing with her a great deal," recalls Cash. "And when I'm fishing, I'm always saying 'Shit!' if I lose a hook or something. But around Maybelle, I just couldn't do it. Nobody *ever* said one of those words around Maybelle. Not because she ever told anyone not to. She'd just say, 'Oh, John!' and then go back to her fishing. That was the worst she ever said to me: 'Oh, John!' "

Pop had spent most of his adult life watching men sniff around his daughters; he knew exactly what Johnny was after. The drug habit scared him a bit, but he liked Johnny Cash. He was country, and he came from a devout family. His mother, Carrie Cash, had baked scripture cakes, every ingredient from the Bible! More than that, he admired the younger man's talent, his success (both artistic and financial), and, when straight, his considerable charm. The two men shared a fascination with ancient history and an independent-minded attitude toward religion: Both were fervent Christians who rarely attended church. Cash professed awe at Eck's huge library of antique books, and Pop offered to lend Cash one.

The first loaner was a surprise to Cash. It was called *The Way of a Man with a Maid*, a work that has been described as both "erotica" and "pornography" by equally appreciative readers. "I read it all," says Cash, "and I enjoyed it." But when Pop asked Cash for an appraisal of the book, he knew exactly what to say: "I told him it was a filthy book, and I meant it. I was pretty close to telling him that I really, really liked his daughter, so it was important for me and him to share the idea that it was filthy. And after I told him what I thought, he said, 'Good, I thought so, too.' "

The next book Pop gave Cash was a considerably different volume by Flavius Josephus, whose writings on Roman Jewry fed Cash's interest in history and religion. When Johnny noticed that Eck's eyesight was failing, he found a version of the text with larger print and presented it to Pop so that they could discuss it more easily. On they went through the works of Pliny and Gibbon. "We spent hours and hours talking about those books," says Cash "We'd talk about the interesting things that took place in ancient times the very human things. We loved how, in Josephus, there's a passage where a Roman officer raises his garments and moons the Hebrews. I came to see Pop as a great teacher. On Sundays, we'd sit and talk about the Bible. I never asked him why he never went to church, and he never asked me. That was our church, right there—those books, those walls, those conversations. And it was very effective in sealing some very important things in my heart and soul."

From time to time, Pop would sit with June and discuss her relationship with Cash Eck admitted that he was "a little afraid of this." But the more time he spent with Johnny, the more he realized his gifts, and the more he came to believe the man was worth saving. If Cash could straighten himself out, he could be as popular, and as rich, as anyone in show business. And Pop suspected that if anyone could straighten out Cash, it was the Carter women. Pop had prayed on it, he told June, and he was convinced that "God had his hand on Johnny Cash." But he reminded her to be careful. "You're a smart girl, June. Just remember to be smart."

Maybelle wasn't giving much encouragement to the relationship; in fact, she and June never talked about it. "I know it sounds strange," June says, "but I used to try to tell what Mama felt by looking in her eyes. And as far as John was concerned, she always seemed sympathetic with anything I wanted to do." Johnny knew better than to press Maybelle on the question. "I knew she didn't want to [talk about it]. That's the old-fashioned country way. She did certain things—I can't really explain it—that said, 'We don't have to talk about this.'"

Unable to hold it in any longer, Cash finally declared his feelings to Pop one night over a mug of beer. "You know I'm in love with June," he blurted.

"Of course I know. What are you gonna do?"

"I want to marry her, obviously. But, ah, we're both in a very tight place and neither one of us can break free from the web."

"I hope you can work it out" is all Pop said.

Despite the drugs, Cash's road show stayed on the move, and Maybelle's association with the show, along with continued interest from the folk movement, had resulted in more work for her. Still, she didn't feel ready to give up the income from nursing, even when her life became a briar patch of scheduling conflicts. Opry management had little interest in promoting Mother Maybelle and scheduled her appearances to suit themselves. Dixie Deen Hall recalls Maybelle frantically trying to change an Opry date so that she could play a lucrative folk concert on the West Coast . . . to no avail. Maybelle's nursing agency was no more accommodating. The agency was run by a Mrs. Brooks, "a very caustic old bitch," says Dixie, "and very strict, as I'm sure she had to be. If you were on a case, you stayed on it. And that wore on Maybelle, because some of the cases went on and on." Dixie went to great lengths to get on Mrs. Brooks's good side so that she could substitute for Maybelle when the need arose. When she did sit in, Dixie would wonder how Maybelle could stand it, "especially for twelve dollars a night, which was what we were paid." Some of the cases were just sad. Red Foley's wife was one of her patients, though neither Maybelle nor Dixie could detect any sign of illness in her. "I think she just wanted somebody there," says Dixie, "for whatever reason." But some patients were cranky and tyrannical, and even abusive. "It made me very sad to see Maybelle in that position," Dixie says, "but she took it as a job. Maybe she shut it out, I'm not sure. She never seemed to find anything demeaning about it."

Johnny finally sat her down one day to have a talk about her life. "Maybelle, you're not going to work at the hospital anymore."

"Why's that?"

"Because I want you to go on the road with me."

"I'll go," she said, "but you know I don't *mind* working in the hospital."

Cash was silent for a minute and stared hard at her; he always did that when he wanted people to listen. Maybelle's concern for her patients was unquestionable, but Cash felt she had a greater responsibility. "Mother, don't you think your music's more important?"

"Of course I do."

Years later, Johnny would proudly recall that day. "She never worked at the hospital again. And I'll always remember that conversation."

Maybelle's makeover as a folk performer took another tiny step forward near the end of 1964, when she recorded a single for Smash Records called "Strummin' My Guitaro." Written by country song-spinner Harlan Howard, the tune was commissioned by the Oscar Schmidt Company, a guitar manufacturer anxious to promote its new, larger, mellower instrument to the folk crowd. Given its gimmicky purpose, Maybelle's vocal-instrumental rendition was a surprisingly moving track, with lyrics that suggested a traditional English ballad. But the single sold no better than the "Guitaro" itself, which quickly faded into obscurity.

In 1965 Columbia—not coincidentally, Cash's label—released *Best of the Carter Family*, featuring Maybelle and all three daughters. Though its title suggested a compilation of early Carter songs, it was actually a rather bland set of folk songs (chestnuts made popular by Peter, Paul and Mary, such as "If I Had a Hammer" and "Michael, Row the Boat Ashore") and country songs (Cash's "Big River"). Throughout the sixties, Johnny Cash rarely recorded a song without the Carters. On religious songs especially, the Carter women gave his earthbound growl a spiritual lift. Anita's backup vocals on "Were You There When They Crucified Our Lord" come as close to piercing through to heaven as anything on record. In those days, and later, Johnny heard whispers from performers, critics, and record executives that working with the Carter women was dragging him down. "Well, hogwash," he wrote in his 1997 autobiography. "I got to sing with the great Anita Carter not just once or twice or now and again in my career, but every night I walked on stage. I bet if you went around to the people who really *know*, the small number of musicians, singers and fans who have heard enough to make a judgment based on all the evidence . . . you'd find a fair number of them willing to endorse Anita Carter as the greatest female country singer of them all."

It wasn't just Johnny who fell for the Carters. Session men found Maybelle a welcome presence in the studio. She wasn't just an accomplished musician, she was also an enthusiastic cardplayer who didn't mind risking a buck or two. She often brought food to the sessions, too, as did Pop, who showed up periodically with a steaming pot of his Sons-a-bitchin' Stew and homemade biscuits.

Toward the end of 1965, Columbia—probably at Cash's urging, though he resolutely denies it—decided to record a solo album featuring Maybelle. Don Law and his assistant Frank Jones assembled Nashville's "A-team," a skilled but overused set of session musicians. Grady Martin and Harold Bradley switched off on lead guitar; Ray Edenton (an old friend from Knoxville days who had occasionally substituted for Anita on bass) played rhythm guitar; Junior Huskey played bass, and Buddy Harman, drums. The songs for the album were a good mix: several down-home dance tunes featuring Maybelle's virtuosity (including the barn burner "Black Mountain Rag," which she played on autoharp) and a few little-remembered Carter Family songs such as "Let's Be Lovers Again." There were also some original tunes, such as "Letter from Home," a maudlin cowboy ballad that Maybelle and Dixie had written together, and "I Told Them What You're Fighting For." "I Told Them" was what might be called a reactionary protest song—a flag-waving condemnation of people who questioned the war in Vietnam. It was written by Dixie's future husband, an ex-marine named Tom T. Hall. The album, titled *Living Legend*, was overproduced, and Maybelle's virtuosity got swallowed up by the big band around her. It didn't sell.

While Maybelle was working on *Living Legend* in December of 1965, she got a package from Angel's Camp, California. Coy Bayes had bought a tape recorder, and he and Sara had used it to send Christmas greetings to their Nashville relations. Sara even sent along new music recordings she was making on Coy's reel-to-reel. One was a gospel song called "Farther On," which she dedicated to Cash. She hinted it would be perfect for him to record: "Johnny Cash could sing under the floor, he's got such a low voice," she said. "I can't sing it myself. I'm getting on in years and just con't have the breath anymore."

Johnny got other ideas and began agitating at Columbia to bring Sara out of retirement, to record an album with Maybelle. And in June of 1966, the label brought Sara and Maybelle into a Nashville studio to record a reunion album. Joe Carter stood in for A.P. "I don't know why they asked me," Joe says thirty-five years later. "I'd never done any records before, but I always did sing my daddy's parts."

With Sara in the room, Maybelle quietly stepped back and allowed her cousin to sing lead on every song. It was like old times. Almost all the selections were either mournful or religious; the tracks were streamlined, stripped of the A-team session men, back to guitar, autoharp, and voices. But to Joe Carter, the studio itself seemed excessive. "They had us all three separated," he grumbles. "When you're close together, the harmony is better, 'cause you get the feeling." Still, *Historic Reunion* was a stylistic success, lean and evocative. Maybelle coaxed Sara out to play a series of concerts and TV shows to promote it. She even brought her cousin to meet her new audience at the Newport Folk Festival. The album, however, did not sell.

Maybelle was still appearing regularly at the Opry, but with albums to promote, folk festivals to play, and the open invitation with the Cash road show, she was back to her familiar rhythms of life on the road. "If we had a thousand mile car ride coming up, something we really weren't looking forward to," Johnny wrote, "her approach was 'Well, let's get on the road.' That was her way of dealing with difficult things: 'Let's do it.'"

With Maybelle gone so much, Pop began spending more and more time at the house he'd bought in New Port Richey. What the heck, *he* was retired. He was also a bit lonely. Though Eck was never a naturally outgoing man, he was learning to make new friends. In fact, to this day, his Florida friends remember an Eck Carter quite different from the one his Poor Valley neighbors recall. "He never met a stranger, and isn't that a wonderful way to be?" says Mickey Little, who got to know Eck with her husband, Des, in the sixties. If he stayed around the house, he'd be by himself, so Pop spent mornings wandering his neighborhood, in a ramble reminiscent of his father's back in Poor Valley, getting the news and spreading it. "He'd stop at a house and talk to someone for a minute," says neighbor Jo Korman, "and the next thing you knew he was inside having coffee."

Social life in New Port Richey happened at the "fishing camps," which were little wooden shacks built on stilts in the shallows of the Gulf. Pop spent much of his time at Des Little's camp, on the north side of the channel marker, second one in. Of course, Eck went to work improving the place. He built a wind generator that provided enough electricity to power a radio and a percolator. Pretty soon, fishing boats were stopping by for a spot of java and the latest news, all courtesy of Eck Carter.

Living among the fishermen, Pop had to have a boat of his own, so he bought one, then another, then another. Alas, Eck was not a terribly skillful mariner; he got lost at sea so often that he was soon on a first-name basis with the Coast Guard crew who was repeatedly ordered out to find him. On the road, Maybelle might get word that her husband was lost, had been for a few days, but she never worried. "Oh, that's Eck," she'd say. Her children and grandchildren might have been upset by this apparent lack of concern for her husband's well-being, if they didn't sometimes overhear Pop and Maybelle on the phone, actually using the word *love*, whispering it like it was a secret.

In a way, it was a secret; something they shared between themselves, apart from the rest of the world. Nobody else really got inside it, but Anita thought she understood it a little: "There was a feeling that flowed between them that the other one could do anything—could accomplish anything—they wanted to." Somehow, Maybelle always figured, Eck would take care of himself.

Every few weeks when he was in Florida, Eck would get a check from Maybelle. He'd take it straightaway to the Gulf State Bank, where Jo Korman would cash it for him. "It was his allowance, I guess," says

Korman. "I think it was about a hundred dollars." That Eck could hold
to an allowance was laughable to anybody who knew him. In New Port
Richey, he'd already made friends with fellows who shared his passion
for gadgets. He spent hours at the Kormans' boat landing where Jo's
father-in-law, Ward, would show him the very latest electric fishing reel
or a jazzy new camper or something else that made Pop drool. "It got to
be like a competition," says Jo. "They had to have the same toys. Pop
would buy whatever and charge it all to Maybelle's bill. And sometimes
Maybelle got a little upset because he spent too much. She'd send down
a note that would say, 'I don't know why he needs these things, it has to
stop.' And I'd say, 'Pop, you gotta slow down. Maybelle's gettin' mad.'
But he'd say, 'That's all right! If she don't pay for it, Junie will.' "

"He loved to trade things, too," says Eck's friend Ann Zetner.
"He'd try to trade stuff with my husband, Tommy. It would tickle
Tommy 'til his eyes filled up with tears. It's been more than thirty years
now, but I've still got a little Evinrude engine that Pop traded towards a
boat that Tommy had. And when Pop would get in money trouble he'd
say, 'Send it to Maybelle!' or 'Send it to June! Junie'll take care of me.
She can squeeze a nickel 'til the buffalo yells.' "

"As far as I can remember," says Korman, "it was always Maybelle
who paid."

Home in Nashville wasn't much different. Of course, tighter family finances didn't seem to rein in Pop. Dixie came home one day to
find him unwrapping a portable dishwasher. "May's comin' in," Pop
said excitedly, apparently thinking his wife would be pleased with the
surprise he had in store. He hooked up the contraption and got it
going, but it began making odd noises and something was clearly
wrong. Just then, Maybelle drove up in her Cadillac. "She opened the
door," recalls Dixie, "and there was this dishwasher, jumping around
at the end of a hose, with Pop just standing there, scratching his head
and looking at it."

Maybelle stood silently for a moment, watching her husband.

"Lord, Daddy. What have you gone and done now?"

At least at home in Nashville, Eck had company. Sometimes more
than he wanted, since they had a houseful living with them. They'd

more or less adopted Dixie Deen, who wasn't much younger than their own daughters. She'd grown up in the English countryside, fallen in love with country music, and moved to Nashville to be a songwriter. In the meantime, she worked at press and publicity connected to the music industry. Pop and Maybelle had taken to her instantly, and invited her to live with them at the house, maybe help out where help was needed. Despite the difference in their ages, she became Maybelle's closest companion outside Minnie Snow.

It was an unconventional household. Dixie stayed in a room at the end of the hall; across from her was a room reserved for Cash, whenever he might choose to appear. The next room down was Pop and Maybelle's. "They had space for a bed and that was about all," says Dixie. "That and some shelves, which Pop nailed to the wall and filled with dusty, musty books." Most evenings, after cooking himself dinner, Dixie says, "Pop would get in his pajamas and spread out in the middle of the bed, wallowing like a big old whale, with all these books spread out around him, opened at different places. Maybelle would come in and she'd just stand there and say: 'Lord, Daddy.' That was her favorite expression."

On a typical evening, when Maybelle was free of work, she would pick up Minnie Snow (Minnie didn't drive) and bring her to the house. Then Maybelle, Dixie, and Pop would put on their bathrobes. The four of them would then play canasta or a board game called Don't Get Mad. These contests could be ferociously competitive. Maybelle loved to accuse Minnie of cheating, with mock seriousness. And Pop would get so wrought up, he was forced to invent his own swear word, which he repeated throughout the night whenever his luck turned bad: *SHTUH!*

But a lot of those games would end suddenly when Johnny Cash arrived, sweating and pale, his eyes wide as flapjacks, knees trembling and arms jerking. "He would pace the floor higher than a kite," remembers Dixie, "while Maybelle patiently tried to talk him into going to bed." Eck just kept assuring the room that everything was going to be all right. "The Lord's got his hand on Johnny Cash and nothing's going to happen to him," Pop would say. "The Lord's got greater things for him to do."

In those days, it wasn't the Lord's hard John R. Cash had to worry about, but his own. It looked like he was trying to kill himself. In 1965 he'd started to slide badly. His official address in those days was a one-bedroom hovel in the Fountain Bleu apartments on the outskirts of Nashville. In one of a series of bad decisions, he'd invited a young singer from Texas named Waylon Jennings to share the place. "I was on dope," Waylon once told an interviewer about that time. "John and I were big dummies. We were going through a time when we felt uncommonly sorry for ourselves in the process of trying to get rid of one wife while trying to hang on to another woman, and neither one of them understood us."

There were painkillers, amphetamines, and barbiturates hidden throughout the apartment. For all the pills in the house, they could be surprisingly hard to find. Occasionally, June would come in and confiscate what she could; sometimes Johnny would simply forget where he'd hidden a cache. When he needed drugs and couldn't find them, he'd stalk through the place like a caged animal. Once he tore the glove compartment out of Waylon's new Cadillac. "There was a carpenter who we kept working a lot," Waylon said. "Putting the hinges back on our door because we was always locking each other out. Kicking the door in."

During a performance at the Opry one night, Johnny decided it might be fun to smash all the footlights with his mike stand. "You don't have to come back anymore," the Opry manager told him on the way out the door. "We can't use you." Then Johnny talked June out of her car keys—against her better judgment—drove off alone, and wrapped her Cadillac around a utility pole. The car was totaled, and so was his face; he had a broken nose and four missing teeth. And he was afraid to call June to tell her.

She always got the calls eventually: when he accidentally burned down 508 acres of national forest in California; when he got arrested crossing the Mexican border with 688 Dexedrine tablets and 475 Equanil concealed—badly—in a guitar. He spent the night in an El Paso jail cell, whence he was marched handcuffed and teary-eyed past snapping photographers. Not long after, a Ku Klux Klan offshoot published a leaflet claiming that his wife, Vivian, was "a Negress" (she had a dark Mediterranean complexion and a flat nose), which, to their way of thinking, made his children "mongrelized." Cash hied himself to Maybelle's house, probably looking for June, weeping with rage and despair. "My babies," he sobbed. "They're talking about my babies!" Of course his daughters were in California, and there wasn't much comfort he could give them. Guilt about his lousy performance as a father ("I just wasn't there," he said in later years) drove him further than ever toward self-destruction. Meanwhile, the pill-induced paranoia made him think the Klan was after him. He armed himself with guns and tear-gas pencils, and began watching over his shoulder constantly.

June's daughter Rosie Nix recalls bumping into him in Maybelle's darkened hallway one night while a police cruiser waited outside. He looked like a ghost, his eyes bulging, as he pressed his finger to his lips and begged her to stop screaming. "I was always sick," says Cash, "and Maybelle was always trying to take care of me. She saw me at my very worst and never pointed it out to me except to say loving things like 'I hope you'll take care of yourself because we really need you.' She did *everything* with love, even coming into the bedroom at night to tuck me in. She'd shake her finger at me sometimes without a word, but always with a smile, as if to say, 'You stay there, now!' And she and Eck always had a big meal for me the next morning."

Even at Maybelle's, Cash could not control his temper. If he got there late at night and found the house locked up, he'd kick in a door or pry off a window to get himself in. "He always fixed everything he tore up," Maybelle once said. "You know when he'd come to the house, he'd come starved. I'd always see he got something to eat, and if his clothes needed washing, I'd see to that, because John did a lot for me. We had to stick by him. His people weren't here. He was alone."

Cash tried to take the stress off his friends in 1966, when he bought a mansion in Hendersonville, Tennessee, just outside Nashville, and moved in by himself. Maybelle and June spent hours traipsing from room to room, looking for the stashes of pills they knew he'd hidden. Sometimes Rosie Nix would figure out what they were doing and join in. "It was like an Easter egg hunt," says Rosie.

Finally, in October of 1967, Cash was arrested for the seventh time, in Lafayette, Georgia. The local sheriff, Ralph Jones, not only released him but offered to give him back his drugs. "Go on, take 'em and get out of here. My wife and I have every record you've ever made, and it broke my heart when they brought you in here," the sheriff told him. "You've got free will: Kill yourself or save your life." Johnny went back to Nashville, drove a tractor into the lake by his home, then crawled into a cave, hoping to get lost and die. He didn't get lost, and he didn't die. And when he came out, he told June he wanted to kick. She summoned psychiatrist Nat Winston, then Tennessee's commissioner of mental health, and John went off the pills, cold turkey.

Maybelle, Pop, and June moved into the Hendersonville mansion, formed a circle around John Cash's bed, and began to pray. When he fell asleep, they left him, but they never stopped praying or bringing him food that he wouldn't eat and whispering comfort that he wouldn't hear. For weeks, Cash had horrendous nightmares and unbearable stomach cramps. When he woke, he would tear his room apart looking for pills, then try to break open his locked bedroom door. It took about a month to go through withdrawal, but he made it. June and her parents had stuck it out with Johnny through the worst of times, and when he emerged from his addiction, she was ready to marry him. June and Rip had split up. Vivian had finally given Johnny a divorce.

Just three months after beating his habit, Cash recorded a live album at Folsom Prison that is widely regarded as one of his finest. A few weeks later, he proposed to June, onstage in London, Ontario, in front of five thousand people. They were married in Franklin, Kentucky, on March 1, 1968. Of course, Pop and Maybelle were on hand for the huge reception that followed at Cash's Hendersonville home. Eck, who had done all that was seemly to promote the match, beamed with triumph. It was hard to say exactly what Maybelle felt, but Anita interpreted the look on her face as "something like relief."

It might have been fatigue. Nearly seven years of vigilant, around-the-clock watch over Cash had taken its toll on Maybelle. Once, when it was all over, she confessed to one of the New Lost City Ramblers: "I don't think I could do it again."

At Eck's urging, Maybelle started to spend more time at their bungalow in New Port Richey. The Florida Gulf weather didn't necessarily agree with her, if for no other reason than it curled her hair something terrible. "As soon as she'd get there, Maybelle would start sweating because of the humidity," remembers Cash, "and then she'd start complaining about the way it made her look."

But gradually, the place began to win her over. The fishing was glorious, and Maybelle, who had always loved to fish, now became a fanatic. There were freshwater catches in the Pithlachascotee River, which flowed just a few hundred feet in front of the house, and the Gulf of Mexico was just a short boat ride away. With a huge sun hat on her head, dark sunglasses, and a long-sleeve flannel shirt to protect her from sunburn, she would head out with Eck to the Littles' fishing camp. She could fish for hours without growing bored, hauling in trout, redfish, and snook all day long. In the evening, she'd sit in a lounge chair and play cards with all comers. At certain times of the year, she loved to watch the "water fires"—effervescent reflections of moonlight. Some nights, a porpoise would jump, silvery in the light. In the end, she had to admit that buying a place in New Port Richey was not the worst brainstorm Pop had ever had. "When everybody else wanted to go in, Maybelle wanted to stay out on the Gulf," says Cash. "Almost every day, she and Pop would have a big fish fry with potatoes."

She was popular with local ladies, who would buzz about Maybelle's beautiful complexion. "I owe it to Pond's," she'd say.

"She'd sit and tell how, in the old days, they used to drive around in an old model T," says neighbor Ruth Obenreder. "They'd do afternoon performances and wear heavy makeup and take it off with Pond's. Then they'd do evening performances and get their faces plastered again with heavy makeup. So she said, 'We used Pond's several times a day. Thank goodness, we could afford it; not everybody could.' "

New Port Richey was also a great place for Maybelle to get to know her grandchildren, and to spoil them. In Florida, Eck and Maybelle did not deny themselves or anyone else small pleasures. The kids were allowed to sit in on Don't Get Mad games, and often well past bedtime. Years later, the grandchildren would remember the leeway they got in that house: a warm drag from Maybelle's cigarette, or a little nip from Eck's wineglass. Even before they had licenses, the kids were allowed to drive one of Pop's cars around the block, so long as they promised not to drive too fast or mention it to their parents. And they were all encouraged to play music. Maybelle taught them each her scratch, but the lessons ended there. She never liked to teach particular songs, even to her daughters: "You play it like *you* feel it," she'd tell them. June's oldest, Carlene, had a cover-girl beauty and a bell-like voice; her sister, Rosie, sang with power, more like Bessie Smith than any of the Carters. Anita's daughter Lorrie had the same pure tones as her mother, and all of Helen's sons could sing and play. But Helen's Kenny was the prodigy. He played guitar and trumpet, sang beautifully, and loved to write songs. He wrote snatches of songs everywhere, on the back of his hand, on paper bags, even on his bedroom wall while he was laid up sick. By 1969, at sixteen, he was obviously headed for a life in music. Monument Records released his first single, a dark, Dylanesque antiwar protest song called "Is This the Way of the Free?"

"Kenny was more like Maybelle than anyone I ever knew," says Johnny Cash. "He was quiet and laid-back and very effective in what he did. When he did say something, it was worth hearing. At sixteen it was like he was twice as old. And Maybelle loved him more like a son than a grandson. She thought he hung the moon."

In February of that year, Maybelle, Helen, June, and Anita were in California to play a Johnny Cash show at the Oakland Coliseum; the promoter gave Cash a five-thousand-dollar bonus, in cash, for selling out the stadium. Then came the call, to Helen. Kenny had been hurt in a car accident; his injuries were life-threatening. "Helen was distraught," remembers the promoter, Lou Robin. "I mean they all were, and they used the money to charter a plane to get her back to Nashville." Kenny and four friends had climbed into a sports car built for two. When the car flew off the road, the driver suffered only light injuries, but none of his passengers survived. Kenny Jones died on March 8, 1969.

Maybelle was destroyed. For the first time in her life, she simply collapsed. Her neighbors Les and Dot Leverett could scarcely believe what they saw at her house in suburban Nashville. Dot made a casserole and waited in the car while Les (who was the Opry's official photographer and had known the Carters almost twenty years) walked up to the house to deliver it. He was met at the door by Sara, who had come from California to look after her cousin. Sara led Leverett to the living room where Maybelle lay on a sofa, staring silently up at the ceiling as tears poured from her eyes. "I got on my knees and loved her a little bit," says Leverett, "but she was inconsolable."

Sara had little to say as she took care of Maybelle, and Maybelle said even less. If she ever articulated her grief, nobody heard it. She mourned until the weight of her sorrow was bearable, then she got on with her life as best she could.

What else could she do? There was work to do. Johnny needed her. That spring he was preparing a weekly variety show for ABC television. Clean and sober, Johnny Cash was among the hottest entertainers in America. His *Johnny Cash at Folsom Prison* album went gold in a hurry, selling a quarter million copies every month. He was outselling the Beatles. The front room of Cash's Hendersonville mansion was one of the most important creative centers in popular music. The Cashes began holding "guitar pulls" there. Singer-songwriters would sit together in a circle and try out new songs. "The most memorable night," Cash recalls, "was when Kris Kristofferson sang 'Me and Bobby McGee,' Bob Dylan sang 'Lay, Lady, Lay,' Joni Mitchell sang 'Both Sides Now,' Graham Nash sang 'Marrakesh Express,' and Shel Silverstein sang 'A Boy Named Sue'—all in the same night." A few weeks later, Cash himself performed 'A Boy Named Sue' for the album *Live at San Quentin*, which also went gold.

ABC was hoping to mine a little of that Cash magic, but they didn't want to make much of an investment. The network expected a run-of-the-mill "summer replacement" program: Flavor-of-the-month singers would sing their current hits, and mediocre comedians would do routine routines. *The Johnny Cash Show* would not raise the comedy bar much, but the music mattered to Johnny. From the beginning, Cash himself selected the performers, often to the dismay of ABC execs. According to Cash, ABC was not at all happy about making a showcase for leftist protest singers such as Pete Seeger and Arlo Guthrie. But Johnny held his ground. "I told 'em, it's either my way or the highway," he says. The first program featured Bob Dylan, Joni Mitchell, and rowdy Cajun fiddler Doug Kershaw. The show closed with a gospel number, in which Cash was backed by both the Carters and the Statler Brothers: "Daddy Sang Bass," a Carl Perkins song, which broke from its melody in each chorus for a line of "Will the Circle Be Unbroken." What began as a summer replacement became one of America's top-rated weekly TV shows.

The show also gave Cash another way to repay a debt; he meant to reintroduce Maybelle Carter to the entire nation. In the beginning, Maybelle faded into the background of the show. In fact, says Cash, "It seemed like that was all she wanted to do, sing backup with her daughters." So Cash began featuring her on the show from time to time, teasing out of her the story of 1927, when she and A.P. and Sara made their way to Bristol and changed popular music forever. This must have caused some uneasy stirring in the country-music industry. The Country Music Hall of Fame had been established in 1961, with Jimmie Rodgers as its first inductee. Since that time, fifteen more inductees had been selected, including Uncle Dave Macon, Jim Reeves, and even promoter J. L. Frank, while the Carter Family was passed over. Finally, on October 14, 1970, the Original Carter Family was inducted. At the ceremony at the Ryman, Maybelle and Sara spoke briefly. Cash said a few words about A.P.: "I never knew Doc Carter, but I know his music. He discovered and wrote over three hundred songs which form the foundation for my music and yours."

With the TV show, and the honors, Maybelle was becoming positively expansive. She loved backing her son-in-law on humorous songs such as "Everybody Loves a Nut" and "Dirty Old Egg-Suckin' Dog." When some of the other cast members started calling her "Mother Mothballs," she wore the moniker proudly. She even started making sly little asides. She and the Statler Brothers developed a ritual that followed every finale. "Great show, Maybelle," one of the Statlers would say. "Coulda been," she'd reply, "but June ruint it."

The Cash show went off the air in 1971, but Maybelle still wasn't ready to retire. When she got a call about joining a recording session with a group called The Nitty Gritty Dirt Band, she told them she was pleased to be included. Maybelle might not have known much about the Dirt Band, but they knew all about her.

Bill and John McEuen were young Southern Californians, fanatical fans of folk and bluegrass music. John, a guitar player and banjo picker, owned a cherished copy of Flatt & Scruggs's 1961 album *Songs of the Famous Carter Family*. Earl Scruggs was his hero, and Maybelle, he knew, was Earl's. One day in 1965, when the McEuens' father mentioned that he needed a truckload of diesel equipment dropped off somewhere in the Midwest, John and Bill volunteered to make the run. "Unknown to Daddy," says John, "the Grand Ole Opry was really our primary destination."

They arrived in Nashville on a rainy Saturday night and found the show sold out. They could just hear the tinkle of instruments and the rustle of applause inside the Ryman, and it was almost too much to bear. So they crept through the alley on the north side of the building, and John, a tall man, stood on his tiptoes to peer through a window and onto the stage. "We were just in time," he remembers, "to hear Lester Flatt announce, 'We're gonna bring Mama Maybelle Carter out here to do the "Wildwood Flower." ' Seeing Maybelle walk out on that stage to do that song was one of the most powerful moments of my life. And I said to myself, someday I'm going to play with that woman."

Six years later, at the age of twenty-five, John McEuen was a star and Bill was his manager. Their Nitty Gritty Dirt Band, a conglomeration of folk musicians adept at rock, blues, and country, had already scored a huge hit with "Mr. Bojangles." In June of 1971, John cornered Earl Scruggs in a hotel room in Boulder, Colorado. Scruggs had previously complimented McEuen's banjo playing, and this gave McEuen the courage to ask him to record with the Dirt Band. When Scruggs agreed without hesitation, Bill McEuen suggested expanding the project. "Let's do something really special," he said. They asked guitarist Doc Watson to record, and he, too, agreed It wasn't easy to persuade Liberty Records that there was anything commercial in the idea. "I don't see what you boys see," a company executive told the McEuens, "but I'll put up the money, because you seem to believe in it." Besides, it was only twenty-two thousand dollars, a small price to pay to keep the artists happy.

Scruggs recruited some other country heavyweights for the session: Merle Travis, Jimmy Martin, and even the hyperconservative Roy Acuff agreed to participate, but only after making Scruggs promise to play lead guitar for him. Bill Monroe was the lone musician to decline. And, of course, the McEuens specifically asked for Maybelle Carter. Maybelle betrayed not a hint of excitement at rehearsals, which lasted only a couple of hours. "We didn't want to wear her out." says John McEuen. At sixty-two, she seemed like a very old woman to the Dirt Band. A few days later, when she arrived at Woodland Studio 3 to record, the McEuens' adrenaline was running high. They were bordering on stage fright. The term *generation gap* was still in use in those days, and all the musicians seemed aware of it. Acuff remarked on it to reporter Jack Hurst: "You're supposed to know a man by the character of his face, but if you have got your face all covered up with [hair], well . . .' He admitted that the Dirt Band seemed like "very nice young boys," though he couldn't help adding, "To be honest with you, I couldn't tell whether they were young boys or old men . . . but they certainly knew what they were doing."

The problem wasn't really generational. The problem was that Acuff was acting like a jerk. In fact, there was no such tension when Maybelle took her seat. All the musicians, young and old, treated her with the respect due a beloved grandparent. John McEuen was fascinated by the idiosyncrasies in her style—the way she tuned her guitar low and added unusual notes to simple chords, usually by playing an open string.

"Maybelle," he asked her, "are you gonna stay tuned like that for all the songs we do?"

"Well, I may do 'Wildwood Flower' on the autoharp," she said demurely, then added, "if you all don't mind?"

McEuen bit his tongue. "I wanted to say, 'What the f— do you mean, 'If we all don't mind?' To me it was exactly like Jimi Hendrix saying, 'I'd like to play "Foxey Lady" in E with a flatted thirteenth, if you all don't mind.' I was thinking, 'Just line us up and tell us how to do it!' She was a person who'd created this tremendous art and had accomplished so much. But now I saw she was also just a sweet, gentle lady who, instead of making pies or quilts, made music."

Maybelle played "Keep on the Sunny Side," "Wildwood Flower," and "I'm Thinking Tonight of My Blue Eyes." It was while recording this last tune that she showed her only hint of dissatisfaction. Fiddler Vasser Clements, a musician who liked jazzy improvisation, was a little too free on his solo, and Maybelle smiled at him sweetly: "Vasser, how about if you just play the melody and quit that foolin' around?"

"She was joshing him a little," says McEuen, "but she meant it, too."

The sessions marked the first time Maybelle was successfully recorded with the accompaniment of a large band. And the recordings still serve as a fresh introduction to the Carters' music, more accessible to the modern ear than the harsher recordings of the 1920s and 1930s. In all, the Dirt Band and their guests recorded nearly forty songs, from the fiddle tune "Soldier's Joy" to Hank Williams's "Honky Tonkin' " to Joni Mitchell's "Both Sides Now." For the session finale, the Dirt Band chose "Will the Circle Be Unbroken," hoping to make the point that young musicians like themselves—even if they did have long hair— were able to carry on the folk-music tradition and pass it down in turn.

"That was just the right style for me," Maybelle told Helen after Will the Circle Be Unbroken hit the stores. The guest stars' names were listed on the album cover, with "Mother Maybelle Carter" at the top of the bill. It was a triple album, which meant that it was expensive, and sold a little slowly at first. But great reviews and word of mouth gradually convinced people to risk their money. Many who did so had never bought a country record in their lives; Bruce Springsteen was one, and he later told the Dirt Band's Jeff Hanna that the album was one of his favorites. Newspapers and magazines everywhere began referring to Maybelle Carter as a *legend* and an icon. "She was just awestruck by that," laughed Chet Atkins. "She'd get out clippings and show me. 'Isn't that amazing? . . . How can that be?' "

"Two years past the *Circle* album, the Dirt Band ends up on shows with who else but Doc Watson," says John McEuen. "I mean, one week we play with Aerosmith and Johnny Winter, and the next day we're doing a show with Maybelle Carter. Because here's 'Bojangles' on the radio, but the *Circle* album's effects are starting to sink in. The festivals are starting to pick up, and here we are with Maybelle and standing onstage with her during a sound check, and she says, 'It's really good to see you, John. Boy, it's just wonderful how that album's being accepted.' "

Not long after, McEuen showed up at Maybelle's house in Nashville with a memento he wanted her to have. The *Circle* album had been certified gold, May 23, 1973. "I co remember going to Nashville and going out to her house and giving it to her, and saying, 'I hope you have a place for this.' She goes, 'That's the first time I ever got one of those.' Because her music hadn't been tracked. The gold-record thing didn't *exist* at the zenith of her career."

Soon after the release of *Circle*, offers poured in, mostly from colleges and summer festivals. So Maybelle hit the road with a newly constituted Carter Family: Helen, Anita, and a flotilla of grandchildren, beginning with Carlene Carter, Danny Jones, and Lorrie Davis. Later, the group would be joined, at intervals, by David and Kevin Jones and Rosie Nix. On these shows, Maybelle was the headliner.

One of her first concerts after the *Circle* album's release was in Morgantown, West Virginia, where the Carters opened for the Dirt Band. Carlene was sixteen and nervous; she was to perform "Country Roads" on the piano, first time ever. "There were ten thousand kids sitting in the audience," she says, "and I realize they're smoking pot! Marijuana was just wafting up onto the stage. And my grandma walked onstage in her little dress with her guitar. The audience stood up, applauding, and they would not *stop* applauding. That's when it dawned on me, wow, my grandma's really big!"

At one festival, Anita was walking through the crowd with her daughter Lorrie and heard some longhairs say, "Oh, here come two chicks." Anita just kept walking, but she heard another say, "Shut up, you fool, those are Maybelle's girls."

"At all these festivals the audiences were mostly young people, half-stoned out of their heads," Helen said. "As we made our way through the crowds, we could hear them saying, 'Look, look, it's Mother Maybelle!' and they'd make a path for her." Anyone who failed to show proper respect was brought up short. At another festival in Warrenton, Virginia, John McEuen happened to see Maybelle standing by herself in the summer heat. He immediately stomped up to the promoter: "See that woman? She's responsible for a huge percentage of the music that brought people to this show. You've got her standing in a foot and a half of garbage, in the hot sun, with no water. Think you can fix that?" A moment later, Maybelle was standing under an umbrella, sipping a cool drink.

Thus was Maybelle Carter treated for the remainder of her life, though she never fully adjusted to it. In 1973 the updated Carter Family received an award for "Favorite Country Group," and according to Anita, her mother, who had been passed over for this sort of thing for more than twenty years, almost "fell out of bed." The following year, she received the Tex Ritter Award at Nashville's Fan Fair, and the year after, an award from the Smithsonian.

When she recorded her last great work, a double album of instrumentals for Columbia titled *Mother Maybelle Carter*, she was once again backed by a collection of elite Nashville session musicians, including drummer Buddy Harman, who had played on *Living Legend*. But this time, producer Larry Butler ordered the musicians to take their cues from Maybelle. (One only has to compare her free and lively performance of "Black Mountain Rag" on *Mother Maybelle Carter* with her careful, plodding performance of the same tune on *Living Legend* to appreciate the benefit of letting Mama Maybelle have her way.) In intervals between the songs, she can be heard chatting comfortably with the musicians and telling the familiar stories about recording in Bristol and backing up Jimmie Rodgers. But why, some wondered, did she play autoharp on every single song? She was, after all, widely advertised as a master of the guitar.

Truth was, arthritis was taking its toll. Not only did it make guitar playing a painful chore, but it increased the possibility of errors, which Maybelle could never abide. It is not known how long she may have been suffering; her daughters learned of it only when it became too much for Maybelle to bear. One afternoon, before a show, she sat them down and told them that, henceforth, Helen would play the guitar part on "Wildwood Flower." Her pain must have been considerable, because she rarely let that sort of thing interfere with what she did. Around the same time, says Rosie Nix, "I remember her having three molars pulled out one afternoon and going onstage that night, singing with a mouthful of cotton."

Nothing was going to stop Maybelle from getting out there now. She was most pleased that a third generation was taking up the family business, which, of course, increased "family time." Owing greatly to Maybelle's long efforts, the Carter Family's legacy was now an established fact and would carry on indefinitely. What's more, her own success—and that of her fabulously wealthy son-in-law—put most of her financial worries to rest. Eck may have been a spendthrift for a family with an ordinary income, but in a rich one, his fascination with gadgets, antique books, and farming and fishing equipment could be easily absorbed. He treated himself to everything now, including one of the first available microwave ovens. Anxious to try it out, he immediately invited the Carter Family Fan Club president, Peggy Marsheck, to lunch. In the kitchen, he held aloft a frozen chicken, promising her it would be ready in three minutes. "He didn't realize you have to thaw the food first," says Peggy, "so we had to eat something else."

Maybelle, meanwhile, who had always enjoyed a low-stakes game of bingo or cards, began to indulge her taste for gambling more freely. Her bets remained modest, but she started frequenting the dog tracks and, whenever her itinerary brought her near Nevada, the slot machines. On one such trip, Carlene recalls waking at four in the morning, with her grandmother standing over her. She wanted Carlene to go down to the casino with her.

"Grandma! It's four."

"Come on, honey, I'm lonely. It's all right, you'll be with me. I've got a bunch of quarters. Now, you come on."

They played until dawn.

Life with the younger generation loosened her up considerably, made her more and more like that game young mother hosting teenage parties back in Maces Springs. She still insisted on wearing a girdle onstage, every performance, but it had become difficult for her to get into it, so she made donning it a community event. She'd pull it up as far as she could on her own, then shout to any available daughters or granddaughters, "Hoist me up!"

"There'd be three of us," remembers Rosie. "We'd grab hold of that girdle and pull, and she'd jump up and down. Then, always, she'd start to get tickled and she'd laugh and she'd laugh." In return for the hard work on the girdle, Maybelle would try her hand at off-color jokes. "Problem was, Grandma could never tell any joke that had the word *shit* in it," says Carlene. "She could never finish because she'd get to laughing so hard. I'd say, 'Grandma, tell us the parrot joke.' And she'd try to tell it, but she'd just start giggling so hard. . . . I don't think I ever heard the end of that joke."

In the cars or in the hotel rooms, Maybelle let the grandchildren tune the radio to the stations they wanted to hear, and got to be quite fond of a particular gospel song they were playing in those days: "One Toe Over the Line." She was anxious to learn it, she said. When her grandkids explained that the song was actually called "One *Toke* Over the Line," she had no idea what that meant. When they explained it, she wouldn't stop laughing.

As she had in Eck's Essex or A.P.'s Chevrolet or the big wartime Packard or the smooth, big-finned fifties Cadillac, Maybelle was still hurtling from gig to gig behind the steering wheel of a car. The band traveled in *two* cars now—Maybelle's black Cadillac and Helen's black Lincoln—and each had a trailer full of luggage and instruments. "We'd drive forty hours to play thirty minutes," says Carlene, "and Grandma drove *fast*, hoo-boy!" One night, a Virginia state trooper pulled over both speeding cars and gruffly demanded of David Jones, who was driving the Lincoln, what in hell he thought he was doing. The young man sheepishly pointed to the big Cadillac, which moments before had been barreling down the Virginia highway ahead of him: "Just trying to keep up with Grandma."

Sara Carter Bayes (Carter Family Museum)

Opposite: Sara and her daughter Gladys (Carter Family Museum)

Mother of Mine

When her daughter asked her, Sara couldn't say no. Janette was making musical programs at A.P.'s old store, and she wanted her mother to perform at a special event in August of 1975: the "First A.P. Carter Memorial Day Festival and Crafts Show." "Good Music, Good Food" was how Janette was billing the show, and she wanted Sara and Maybelle to headline. It had been eight years since Sara and Maybelle performed onstage together, and nine since they'd recorded their reunion album. Janette was shy to ask. She'd expected her mother to put up some resistance.

Even Sara's best friend in California would have bet against Sara's coming out of retirement again, even for Janette. Gladys Greiner had been Sara's friend for almost thirty years; she knew just how Sara felt about the music business. The two women had remained friends for so long precisely because Gladys never seemed to care much about Sara's celebrity, and never tried to make Sara talk about her old life. When they first met at the Zenith store in Angel's Camp, California, Gladys didn't even recognize Sara Carter, star of record and radio. She was just a lady who staggered into the store one day, exhausted.

"Can I help you?" Gladys said.

"I want to sit in that chair that you're sitting in," Sara said. She was always direct.

"What in the world happened to you?"

"I have bad legs. I have to sit down every once't in a while," Sara told her. Apparently, she found the chair comfortable. "Would you mind, anytime I'm in town, if I come and sit in your chair?"

"Of course not."

After that, Coy and Sara would drive to town once or twice a week. As maintenance man at the Calaveras County fairgrounds (home to Mark Twain's jumping frog), Coy always had a little shopping to do and a lot of free time. So while he poked around in the stores and visited with friends, Sara put her feet up at Gladys's desk and the two women would talk for hours. Of course, Sara never said much about herself, so it was a long time before Gladys understood her new friend had been one of the Original Carter Family. They'd talk about neighbors or friends or what Sara *really* wanted to talk about: her children and her grandchildren. Gladys's new friend was so casual, it was hard to imagine she'd been a celebrity. Sara dressed for comfort: open-toed, sling-back sandals, light sweaters or sleeveless shirts, a scarf tied around her neck—even in the heat—and slacks, always. "Don't you ever wear a dress?" Gladys finally asked her. "Not if I can help it," Sara said.

But there was formality to Sara also, a constant awareness of her appearance that belied ease. Every morning—before *anybody* saw her—she'd take time with her makeup, her manicure, her outfit. She was perfumed in her fragrance of choice, White Shoulders, and her permanent was recent. Her silver hair was colored to a rich and youthful auburn. Even in quiet repose, Sara had a bearing that set her beyond anybody Gladys had ever known. There were times when Sara simply intimidated people, made them think she didn't like them. It was a long time before she'd let down in front of anybody, but then, all of a sudden, something would tickle her, and she'd burst into a long, satisfying release of laughter. And as the chuckles trailed off, she'd exclaim, "Oh, law," sit back in her chair, and put her hands under her breasts and lift them, as if the even had so discombobulated them they needed to be reset to their proper position.

But most of the time, Sara was hard to read. Her directness could be unsettling, even cutting. "She was—how can I say it?—the opposite of having a velvet glove," says Gladys. "On the outside she had a work glove. And inside she was wearing a velvet glove, because she was so sweet. When she spoke to you, you didn't know whether she was reprimanding you or not. And yet it wasn't that at all, she was just saying what she felt and she loved you inside. And I know; she told me she loved me many, many times."

But even after Gladys understood how Sara felt about her, she knew to steer clear of certain topics. It was long after she'd first met Sara, and after she and her husband and Coy and Sara started making a little music together in the trailer, that Gladys Greiner finally asked her point-blank: "Sara, why don't you ever want to talk about your past career?"

"I was so tired of that career that I don't even want to have to *think* about it," Sara told her. "I'm living a different life now."

It wasn't always easy for Sara to escape the past. From the time she walked away from the music business, people had been straggling up to the trailer where Coy and Sara lived, wanting to talk to her. In 1948 a young writer working on a story about Highway 49 happened upon the Bayeses at a motor court they were running at the time in Altaville, California. Sara invited the young man and his wife to breakfast the next morning. Still, he wouldn't even have known who Sara was, except that there was another woman at breakfast who was driving everyone crazy, making a big to-do about her daughter, the opera singer, who had just made a *record.* Sara, put off by the woman's big mouth, finally piped up. "I've made some records," she said.

"How many records have *you* made?" the woman said, a bit too condescendingly for Sara's liking.

Apparently hoping to awe the woman into silence, Sara silently toted up her recordings *and* her transcriptions, and said, for effect, "About six hundred."

This did silence the woman, but opened up a whole new line of questioning from the writer, who eventually came back with a recorder to get her on tape. After that, visitors would sometimes show up with wire recorders or reel-to-reel tape recorders and ask her to tell them about the old days: about the first recordings in Bristol, about where the Carters got all their songs, about how she learned to play, about Mr. Peer. One man wanted to take color photographs of her quilts and crocheting. Often as not, visitors finally got around to asking her to sing. Sometimes she would relent, especially if Coy was there to help with the persuading. (Coy was always eager to see how the latest recording gadgets worked.) But sometimes she simply refused. "I don't feel in the mood," she'd say. She meant to be gentle about it, but in her deep, smoky voice, things didn't always come out as soft as she intended.

The visitors she liked the best were the professionals she thought could help her. When the New Lost City Ramblers came to record her in the early sixties, Sara sang "Railroading on the Great Divide," a tune she'd written herself. "Boys, I'd really like for you to use that song," she told them when she was done. Royalties were always welcome. The new folkies could say what they wanted about the innocence and naivete of the recording pioneers who came out of the sticks, but Sara Carter had always understood that this was a business. She made a point to copyright every song she wrote. And she stayed in constant contact with Ralph Peer's company, whose annual payouts to Sara were climbing toward $10,000 a year. Gladys Greiner typed a stream of correspondence from Sara to Southern Music Publishing, Inc., but these were hardly love letters. Sara could do the math. If her third of the royalties was that high, Southern was minting money. "We made Peer *millions*," she told the New Lost City Ramblers, with more than a pinch of bitterness.

Many of the people who made their way to Sara were the sort of lonely hearts who had always been deeply affected by Carter Family music. For these pilgrims, an actual visit with Sara was like entry into some hallowed chamber. Those who had gained an audience had a way of finding one another, writing letters back and forth, describing their visits with Sara, the songs she'd played for them ("The Wabash Cannonball," with a new verse!), the stories she'd revealed (Jimmie Rodgers took dope in the arm and was a heavy drinker), the records she'd requested ("We Shall Rise"), the gifts she might like. Correspondence often took the form of not-so-subtle one-upmanship. "I'm going to send [Sara] a Christmas present from now on," wrote a Canadian fan and record collector named Keith, in 1959. "I think that someone should show Sara how much the people appreciate her wonderful music." The next year Keith reported that he had sent Sara a bottle of French perfume for her birthday. What with the loot, Sara tolerated these minimal intrusions without great distress. She never let her fans go away hungry, even if all she could offer was corn bread and beans.

Historians and folklorists, though, had a tough go with Sara; academics were generally left to their own devices. Back in 1961, one desperate folklorist was forced to send two of Sara's cousins into Uncle Mil and Aunt Nick's house to see if there was anything of note. When they emerged, they wrote to him at his college: "The old house . . . is now vacant with the exception of hay in the living room and an old trunk in one of the bedrooms. The trunk was unlocked so we rummaged. We found some of Sara's correspondence with her record manager, also some with an attorney in regard to her divorce. These were dated from 1933 to 1936. We also found a bundle of ballads tied up with a piece of cloth. These were various handwritings and on all sorts of paper. I presume that various people had sent these to her. Since they were unsigned, there is no background to any of them. In the lot we found an early picture of Sara, and a cousin, Madge Addington, now deceased, a sister to Maybelle. Sara in that picture had a banjo." Well, if somebody wanted to go rummaging through her long-forgotten trunks, go ahead, but Sara wasn't going to let anybody drag her back to that time. When Barbara Powell would try to quiz her aunt Sara about her family, the older woman never had much to say, except that she didn't really remember her own mother. "She didn't have a sentimental bone in her body," says Barbara. "She sold her spinning wheel, which had been in her family for generations, to Stella's second husband, Louie. She said, 'Louie, I need forty dollars. Will you give me forty dollars for it?' "

Still, Sara Carter took pride in what she'd been, and if somebody was going to make sufficient fuss about the Original Carter Family, she'd make an appearance. She had played alongside Maybelle at the Newport Folk Festival in 1967. Standing in the wings, Coy was so happy that he put his arm around Mike Seeger and the two men watched in silent awe. She'd recorded the *Historic Reunion* album with Maybelle. She'd loaned her autoharp for display at the Country Music Hall of Fame, and even traveled to Nashville in 1970 for induction into the Hall. In August of 1971 she'd come back to State Street in Bristol for the unveiling of a plaque commemorating the first recordings of the Carter Family and Jimmie Rodgers. In public that day, Sara was nonchalant: "None of us had any idea what would result from that day in 1927 in Bristol." In private she was a bit more jaundiced: "Well, I expect this is the last thing they'll ever do for the Carter Family." Onstage, she was the same as always. When her world-famous nephew-in-law, Johnny Cash, brought her up to sing at a benefit in Gate City (right where she'd performed with Uncle Fland's choir at singing conventions), she gave no quarter. Johnny and his musicians led into a song and Sara stopped them in their tracks: "You've got to lower that pitch," she told them. "I can't reach up there anymore."

By the seventies, a lifetime of smoking had drastically deepened Sara's voice. The smoking was also a constant threat to her health. A trip across the length of the trailer left Sara weary and panting. It drove Coy crazy that she wouldn't quit smoking, and there were times he'd go right at her. "I'm going to divorce you if you don't stop smoking!" he'd tell her. "I can't live with you, seeing you dying bit by bit." He even enlisted Gladys Greiner to talk to Sara. It took some doing, but Gladys screwed up her courage and went at her friend head-on: "It's not fair to your children and it's not fair to Coy. He is tearing himself to pieces, trying to get you to stop smoking."

"You can talk, Gladys, 'til Doomsday, and I'm still gonna keep on smoking," Sara said. "In the hospital they always tell me I can't smoke; I smoke just the same. I can't give it up. I don't know why I can't, but I can't give it up."

By 1975, when Janette asked her mother about the festival, Gladys Greiner didn't think Sara was up to performing. "She didn't like to do anything or go anywhere at that stage of the game," Gladys says. "She wasn't really feeling well at any time. I think she had arthritis, but she couldn't breathe good, either." But Sara could not say no to Janette. So preparations began.

One day that spring, Sara found out the man who ran the fairgrounds was on his way to Stockton: "So, you're taking us with you," she told him, "me and Gladys." The man almost fell over. Sara never even cracked a smile, but Gladys could see her eyes sparkle. So the man drove them to Stockton, and Sara asked to be let out at the corner of Main and San Joaquin, in the downtown shopping area. "When do we pick you up again?" asked the driver.

"Well, I'd like you to be back here in about two hours," she said. Now, Gladys knew Sara was after a dress for Janette's festival. And as anybody who ever shopped with Sara knew, two hours probably wasn't going to be enough time, even for just one dress. The problem with Sara was never indecision; she always knew *exactly* what she wanted. The problem was finding it. Her friends and nieces might take her shopping all day, to every shoe store in town, until she found the right open-toed, flat-soled, sling-back sandals. Gladys knew she might be in for a long day, but as she says, "You didn't say no to Sara. You did what she said." Gladys was in luck that day. In the first store, they found a high-necked dress, pink, with a filmy see-through chiffon coverlet.

When Sara put it on, Gladys could see her friend was instantly, uncharacteristically, unsure of herself. "She said, 'You like it? Does it look okay on me? Are you sure?'" Gladys remembers, and twenty years later, she tears up. "I said, 'You are a lovely floating vision going by.' And Sara said, 'Hoooooo!'"

Janette barely got through the introduction at the first festival that day in August. "I tell you, you don't know how proud I am of them. And I just hope I can keep from falling apart up here. . . . I tell you what I want you all to do: While they're coming on the stage, I want you to give the best applause that ever was applauded to anybody. And I want you to meet the two prettiest, the two most wonderful women in the world, my mother and my aunt Maybelle. . . . I'm just so thrilled that they're here. If they don't sing a note, it'll be all right with me. They don't feel good. It's hot. It really is. And we're going to let 'em do just exactly what they want to do."

Even under the canopy of the outdoor stage, the sun was menacing. Men in the crowd shielded their balding heads with seed caps; teenage girls were stripped down to shorts and halter tops. It was too hot to smoke a cigarette. Somebody had to take Maybelle by the elbow and walk her up the few steps to the stage, which stood four feet above the gently sloping hillside. Wearing a pair of tortoiseshell sunglasses, Maybelle stooped forward, leaning in to the stairs, unable to carry her autoharp. She was only sixty-seven years old, but the arthritis had stripped her of her natural confidence. Playing the guitar, even for friends and family in Poor Valley, was beyond her. If she could not be *great*, she would not try.

Sara's legs were weaker than ever, but she insisted on walking onto that stage without aid. As she made her way across, with a shy wave to the smallish crowd, a breeze gently fanned her gauzy coverlet. "You wanna stand up, Sara?" Maybelle asked. "You wanna sit down?"

"I'll sit."

"Well, you have to sing on mike, though, see," Maybelle said, then she turned to the crowd. Her sunglasses were off now. It would have been rude to hide her eyes from the audience. "I don't know, but we haven't done this in a long time but we're going to do what we can. They's neither one of us got any business up here trying to sing."

"Oh, I don't know," Sara said from her chair, where she sat stiff-necked, with her chin raised ever so slightly. While the techies placed her mike, Sara raised her right hand to give an inquiring pat to her fresh permanent. She'd been to Kingsport that morning, where the family's professional beautician, Theda Carter, had given her a new perm *and* color. It was Theda's professional policy to do these separate treatments on separate days. Forty-eight hours was what she needed to do the job right. But Sara always wanted them done the same day, and Theda knew enough not to argue.

Sara and Maybelle actually did two shows that day, one in the afternoon and one in the evening. It wasn't like the early days, when they'd get behind those kerosene lanterns on the old plank stages and go for hours. Now Joe and Helen—and even Helen's son, Kevin—had to fill in the gaps while the ladies caught their breath. Through both shows, Maybelle kept making apologies for her playing ("My hands don't work like they used to") and their inability to play their old songs on request. ("We haven't sang together in so long that we've just got a very few tunes that we kind of run over a little bit.")

Out beyond the audience, the two women could just see the now-quiet path where the trains used to roll through Maces Springs. "You know they got a chain on this track up here anymore," Maybelle told the audience. "We used to ride the train up and down this railroad track many years ago . . . but we're going to do a song about a train." There was a long pause. "This is 'Lonesome Pine Special.' . . . Couldn't think of the name."

Sara sang lead on the songs they'd run through earlier: "Lonesome Pine Special" and "Happiest Days of All." But when she had a request to do "No More Goodbyes," she shook her head. "I can't sing it," she said to Maybelle.

"That one's too hard to sing," Maybelle told the crowd. "I tell you what we're gonna do. We're gonna do 'Anchored in Love.' How about that? Okay?"

Again Sara took the lead, and she sang with all she had, pausing to steal a breath, or cutting short a phrase to save one. Through both shows, Sara did all she could. But she would not apologize for what she could not.

From the stage that day, Sara and Maybelle were treated to a performance meant just for them. Janette had rounded up the grandchildren and great-grandchildren to make a dance for the two singers. At first, the oldest grandson demurred. "You can, honey, I know," Janette said to her son, but Don Jett was nearing thirty-five and beyond doing what his mother told him to do. Then Sara leaned in to her microphone: "C'mon, Don, dance for your Mommy Jake," she said. And he did.

But it was over too fast. The shows, the festival, even the visit to Poor Valley. Pretty soon, Coy and Sara had the trailer packed for the long drive back to California.

She'd been living as an exile from Poor Valley for nearly forty years. Even A.P.'s death in 1960 didn't really change things. The only difference was Sara didn't have to worry about hurting her ex-husband, so Coy didn't have to stay behind in Bristol when she went to visit in Maces Springs. Coy liked it fine in the Valley; he had plenty of family, plenty of friends. But he was usually anxious to get on the road headed back to California. That was home to Coy.

As far as anybody in California could tell, it was Sara's home, too. She never really kicked; never complained. She bore her exile from Virginia like it was justice served, a sentence she deserved. She did like the simple life they led in Angel's Camp, where Coy tended the fairgrounds. Coy and Sara had what they needed and no more. They had the trailer, which was just one bedroom, one bath, a kitchen, and a tiny eating area. But when they could, they'd eat outside on the campgrounds. Later Coy put a little addition on the outside of the trailer and that made a nice comfy living room, even if it did leak a bit where it hadn't been properly sealed to the trailer itself. Sara could be in there most of the day. She'd smoke, read magazines, smoke, work on a bedspread or a tablecloth she was crocheting for one of the children, smoke, read a magazine, smoke, do a little housework, smoke. She still cooked the same simple foods she'd always made: corn bread and soup beans, biscuits and gravy, tomato gravy, ham, maybe fried mustard greens, or a green salad. Of course, her oil and vinegar was still mixed to its perfect proportion, always. And the corn bread, as her niece says, "was down to a gnat's eyebrow." She never *invited* anybody for a meal, but if somebody came to visit, she'd feed them. "Well, if you'll stay, we'll have a dirty little bite," she'd tell them, as she got down the Guardian Cookware flat pans to go to work on corn bread and beans. When she was in the mood, Sara might do a song or two. "She'd sing 'My Blue Eyes' and she'd always grin at Coy and he'd grin at her," says Gladys Greiner. Sometimes Sara would take visitors out and show them the peacocks she raised on the grounds. "They jump on my back sometimes," she'd say. "Sometimes I have to hit 'em with a hoe." But as she got older, Sara didn't get outdoors much.

When she and Coy had first moved to California, she was always up for outdoor adventure. "Sara was a good sport," says Coy's sister Stella. "When they went hunting, Sara would put on her hunting clothes and go with them. [Coy] always wanted her with him."

"She was a real good shot," says Barbara Powell. "She used to go deer hunting with them all the time, until she shot the deer. And that was the end of that. She cried. I was at the house. And she sat there and she just cried. She said, 'That big buck, those eyes just looking at me.' So after that she never went hunting again."

Sara was funny that way. She could surprise people. She rarely wanted to listen to music, and never talked about it, but sometimes Barbara would be in the house while Sara was dusting the furniture or washing the dishes at the kitchen sink, and she'd hear her singing, quietly, to herself: "Carry me back, to ole Virginny, / Back to my Clinch Mountain home."

Sometimes if Coy was out on a motorcycle or up in the airplane Sara's royalties had bought him, Barbara would watch Sara wear a path through that trailer. "Anytime he would go anyplace, she would worry," Barbara says. "She'd pace and smoke and worry, pace and smoke and worry." Sara's husband gave her reason to worry. Once, when he was nearly seventy years old, Coy had spun out on a motorcycle and broken his leg. They had to put him in the back of a pickup truck and carry him to the hospital. "It was such a bad break, and because of his age it never healed," says Barbara. "It like to worried her to death. She just went crazy. She was so upset." Sara worried because Coy was a drinker, and a fearless one, too. Almost every family gathering, for years, somebody would say, "Coy's in his back." When she was little, Barbara thought her uncle had some kind of back problem. The real problem was he didn't know when to quit drinking. "He drank.

Sara worried. She smoked. Coy worried," Barbara says. "They'd both promise to quit, and then Sara would go out and sneak a cigarette, and Coy would go out and sneak the bottle."

What scared Sara most was when Coy would get loaded and go up in the airplane. Sara finally sold it off, had somebody haul it away before Coy knew what happened. When he was sober, Coy was still the same attentive good-time Charlie he'd always been. For a while, he'd even wanted to perform onstage with Sara; he said he could do his imitation of a train whistle. But the first time he'd tried it in front of an audience, he opened his mouth . . . and not a single sound sallied forth. And Sara loved him and his pranks, even when she had to call the neighbors to apologize for his dropping toilet paper into their trees from his airplane. But as she got older, his drinking wore on her. There were times when she'd confide to a friend she wished she'd never married Coy: "That was the worst mistake I ever made."

But of all the regrets Sara silently bore, the biggest regret was the separation from her children. There were times when Joe lived in California, but he'd always go back home to Virginia. Her daughter Gladys and her husband, Milan, were perfectly content in the homeplace in Maces Springs, where Janette's front door was a two-minute walk. Packages went back and forth from California to Clinch Mountain. Gladys would send clothes she'd made for her mother; Sara sent her crocheting. Janette would send a plaster shoe for decoration in the trailer; Sara would send Christmas packages with reel-to-reel tapes of greetings and stories for all the family. But those tapes were just another reminder of the physical separation. At Christmastime, when her children and their families gathered at Clinch Mountain, Sara was in California with Coy's family.

There was one Christmas, in 1959, when Gladys and Milan decided to drive their new car across the country to spend the holiday with Sara. They took Janette and her two youngest, Rita and Dale. The trip turned out to be something of a misery. For three thousand miles, Dale and Rita wrestled with carsickness and squabbled with each other. In California, the family crowded in with Coy and Sara, who listened to the children cry for snow, for Santa Claus, for home. But it was only after the short visit was over and the Virginia crew was headed back east that Sara sat in the emptiness of her trailer, alone, and cried for missing them.

By 1977 Janette's musical program was a going concern. Joe had helped construct a big new building that seated hundreds, and fans were coming from all over the country for the festival. That year was the fiftieth anniversary of the Carter Family's first recordings in Bristol, and Sara and Maybelle both made the show in gold-colored dresses. They were in Sara's style, floor-length and high-necked, but Maybelle went along. The morning of the show, Sara was supposed to go to Theda's early for her perm-and-color treatment but she couldn't get out of bed. When she finally made it, Theda had to help her up onto the short porch and into the house. Sara's blood circulation was so bad, there were times when her legs went numb.

When the festival was over and it came time for Sara to go home, Theda wondered f she'd ever see her friend again. Sara's oldest granddaughter, Flo, was a mess the day Sara left for California. It should have been old hat: Sara and Flo's leave-takings had been happening for forty years, since Sara said good-bye to her weeks-old granddaughter for that first trip to Del Rio, Texas. How many times had Flo stood in front of the homeplace while Sara came back for one last bit of "sugar" from her first grandchild? But this time. Theda saw, was different. Flo was crying so hard that Sara had to come back to console her. "Don't cry, honey," Sara said. "I'll be back one way or another."

The Valley had a way of drawing people back. In 1974 some of Eck's nieces noticed he was spending time in Maces Springs again. Actually, it was a little odd to see him there. Eck Carter had got out of Poor Valley as fast as he could, and he hadn't come back often. But that summer he was shuttling back and forth from Tennessee, and it looked like he was fixing up Bob and Mollie's old cabin for comfortable living. Actually, he didn't seem healthy. One of the nieces wondered if he was coming home for his final days.

One day that summer, when Eck was home in Madison, Peggy Marsheck, president of the Carter Family Fan Club, dropped by for a game of chess. (He'd bought a collection of expensive chess sets on a whim, and it was his new favorite game.) They played for a while, and then Pop took Peggy outside to show off his garden. As he led her up a hill, Peggy noticed he was sweating badly, but it *was* hot, she noted, and he *was* wearing long pants and a long-sleeve shirt. Peggy was overheated, too, and Pop kept chattering about his tomatoes, and his future produce plans. But he looked unsteady, and Peggy finally asked him if he was okay.

He took out his handkerchief, but instead of wiping his own brow, he handed it to her.

"Why don't we sit down for a minute?" she suggested.

"I have more to show you," he told her, but sat down anyway. He kept talking, and when he felt a bit better, he took her to a shed and showed her the new gristmill he'd installed. Before she left, Peggy made him promise to get some rest. That night, he had a heart attack. Maybelle had just come in from the road and got him quickly to Madison Hospital. He spent the next several months shuttling from a hospital bed set up at home to a bed at the hospital.

"Maybelle felt she needed to be at his side every minute," says Johnny Cash. "At the same time, we were very busy with concerts, and she was a part of them. . . . There was kind of a silent understanding that she'd come with us whenever she could. And she did."

Everyone hoped the work would help take Maybelle's mind off Eck's failing health, at least for a while. But she was always worried, talked about her husband all the time, and kept saying she had to get back to him. "The truth is, I never thought of them as being all that close," says Cash. "They never really spent that much time together. But when he got sick, you saw how close they really were."

Eck's heart didn't get better, and then he had a stroke, which left him mute. He lingered for months, wasting away to one hundred pounds. After all Maybelle had endured with Kenny's sudden death and Johnny's drug addiction, Eck's long, slow dying diminished her. By the time she saw his coffin into the ground, she was drawn and skeletal, her eyes bulging in their sockets.

"She didn't have the same energy," says June. "We waited for it to come back, but we were afraid it might never." Maybelle roused herself for one last record with her children and grandchildren, *Country's First Family*, but she didn't seem to enjoy playing much anymore. The final straw, according to June, came at a TV taping in which she fumbled a couple of notes and asked for a retake. "They told her no, that it was fine," says June, "and that really upset her. To Mama, if it wasn't perfect, it wasn't fine at all." Only after her daughters raised a commotion was Maybelle allowed another take.

A few weeks later, just before a show with Cash, Maybelle called her three daughters together and told them she was done; she couldn't play anymore. Her stunned daughters left and shipped Johnny Cash in to reason with her. Sitting alone in the dressing room, she looked smaller than ever to her son-in-law.

"Mother," he said softly, "we got a show coming up, and if you'd just come out with us, the people would love you."

"John," she said, "I can't play anymore."

"But Mother, you don't understand. They're expecting you. They know you've got a problem."

She seemed surprised to hear it. "Do they?" she asked.

"Well, I, uh, I don't know," Johnny stammered. "But people are saying that you may not have long to play. You know that."

Still, Maybelle wouldn't budge. "I can't go on that stage thinking I might embarrass myself or my girls or you."

And Johnny wouldn't give up. "But, Mother, it don't matter *what* you do when you go on that stage. They're going to give you a standing ovation, just like they've been doing."

She was silent but trembling. "I cannot do it, John," she said finally. "I cannot play anymore."

"After that, she pretty much gave up," said Chet Atkins, who visited her shortly after her retirement. "She took me around the house and showed me all of her guitars. She said, 'I'm going to give this one to

Helen, and this one to June, and Anita will get this one.' I said, 'Maybelle, hell, you're going to be around a long time; don't talk like that.' But she just said, 'Well, I don't know.'"

Mother Maybelle quit performing, but she didn't quit living. In fact, she did finally have the retirement Pop had planned for her—thanks in no small part to Peggy Knight. Peggy was Maybelle's constant companion. The women had met at the VFW bingo hall in 1968. Peggy had simply walked up and said, "Aren't you Maybelle Carter?" and Maybelle invited the young woman to sit in with her and Minnie Snow. Pretty soon, Peggy was part of the family, though officially an employee. Having Peggy around had taken some pressure off Maybelle. She was a natural cook and could imitate perfectly all of Maybelle's recipes—from dressed quail to stack cake. For a while, she and Maybelle even formed half of "the Rebel Housewives," a game but not particularly fearsome team in one of Nashville's weekday bowling leagues.

After Eck died, Peggy would take Maybelle to the bungalow in New Port Richey. There was a bicycle there for Peggy, and she bought Maybelle a silver three-wheeler—it was basically an oversize tricycle—with an Indian's head emblazoned on the front, and a basket on the back. Morning and evening, they would set off on their wheels, tracing the circuit Eck used to make, checking in on the friends they had shared there. People would see Maybelle coming on the trike, wearing her big floppy sun hat. She never got far before somebody stopped for a little chat. She'd dab her brow with her handkerchief and remark on the weather: "Isn't it pretty?"

She seemed more relaxed than anyone could remember, but she didn't seem well. Even at the leisurely pace she chose, pedaling the tricycle was hard work for her. At the Obenreders' house, Ruth's husband would urge her to go inside and talk to Ruth while he pumped up the tires and fed the chain a little WD-40. And if, while chatting with a neighbor, Maybelle sniffed something savory coming from the kitchen, she would ask what it was, knowing the question alone would get her an invitation to a meal. At night, she and Peggy played canasta or watched television. When Johnny made a guest appearance on *Columbo*, she went over to a friend's house to watch, but she could never take Johnny's acting seriously. "She'd sit on the couch and have hysterics," remembers Ruth Obenreder.

What Maybelle loved best, though was gambling. She and Peggy would visit a track in Tampa with the Littles and sit in the clubhouse, betting ten or twenty dollars, while people around them bet thousands. One day they shared a table with Pete Rose and another ballplayer, who laid out their money in stacks. Maybelle's gambling did cause a little discomfort for June and Johnny when they had their friends Billy Graham and his wife, Ruth, to New Port Richey for a visit. June carefully hid all the cards she could find, fearing her preacher friend would disapprove. But when the subject came up, Graham urged June to "let them play." His own father, Graham said, enjoyed a visit to the track as much as anyone.

At home in Tennessee, Maybelle and Peggy played bingo almost every night, or they drove across the border to Arkansas, to the dog track. Whenever the Cash show played in Nevada, Maybelle went along for the ride. In Reno one night, Johnny saw Maybelle at the slots. And she was so animated, he thought, that she could do anything.

"Whew, she loved to play the slot machines!" he says. "And I loved to stand next to her and play the one beside her, because she was a trip. She would run them coins through there in record time—exactly the way she drove. She was a slot-machine *machine.* And she seemed so energetic, I said to her, 'These are your people here tonight. How about going onstage with me?' But she said, 'John, I'm not going to do it.' So I said, 'Allll right, have a good night and enjoy yourself.' "

Mother Maybelle did. Even when her health began to deteriorate, she grabbed her fun whenever she felt able. "When she started to get a bad back, I had to carry her back and forth from her room to the slot machines," says Peggy. "One time, it was about two in the morning and she asked me to carry her back up [to her room]. I went back down again after I put her to bed, and an hour later, I was talking to this chicken farmer from Mississippi, and I look up and there's Maybelle. She came back down on her own, and we played until six in the morning."

By the summer of 1978, her physical complaints began to multiply: There were thyroid problems, circulatory problems, bladder problems.

By September, Maybelle had such a tangle of ailments it was difficult to diagnose exactly what was wrong, even for the esteemed doctors at the Mayo Clinic. Various rare syndromes were suggested, but the only thing doctors really agreed on was that she was not likely to live to the end of the year. Her daughters decided not to tell her.

The afternoon of October 22, 1978, was Indian summer in Tennessee, perfect for a cookout. Maybelle asked Peggy to put some steaks out on the grill, and they spent a few hours putting up fruit. Then it was time for bingo. When Peggy suggested that perhaps they should skip it, Maybelle wouldn't hear of it. She went, and she won. Other nights, she'd always been content to let her bingo winnings be brought to her, but that night, she told Peggy she wanted to walk up to the podium and collect her fifty dollars herself. She never even put the money in her purse, but carried it all the way home, crumpled in her fist.

When they got home, there was a *Bonanza* rerun on TV, and Hoyt Axton was guest-starring. Maybelle insisted they watch; she'd known Axton forever. Hoyt's mother, Mae, had written "Heartbreak Hotel" for Elvis! And Maybelle loved Hoyt. She asked Peggy for a steak sandwich with plenty of ketchup but declined her bladder pill.

"I'll take it in the morning," she said.

After the show, Peggy took Maybelle's glasses and walked her to bed. When she went in to wake her the next morning, she found that Maybelle had died sometime in the night, apparently in the manner she lived, with ease and grace. Peggy Knight would always remember Maybelle's last words to her, when she'd tucked her in the night before: "Good night," she'd said. "I love you."

Four days later, Maybelle's nieces, nephews, grandchildren, daughters, and sons-in-law convened at her graveside to bid her good-bye with an a capella version of "Will the Circle Be Unbroken." Her passing was national news, noted by *Time, Newsweek, The New York Times,* and scores of other publications. The most eloquent remembrance appeared in the youthful and rockin' *Rolling Stone* magazine, where writer Chet Flippo recalled the Nitty Gritty Dirt Band's 1971 *Will the Circle Be Unbroken* album. There were Scruggs and Watson and Travis and Acuff—but it was Mother Maybelle who topped them all. "One of the most moving performances on record," Flippo wrote. "Hers was a voice out of a vanished past." Flippo had been present at the recording sessions back in 1971. And as they were readying the final track—the title track—the writer had been shanghaied to join in the chorus. Everybody in the room—musicians, friends, family, even reporters—was invited. Flippo demurred. He was a writer, after all, really wasn't much of a singer. "Don't worry, son," Maybelle told him. "Just sing it from the heart, and you'll be all right."

Maybelle Carter never said much so when she did, people paid attention—and remembered. More than twenty years after her death, the Nitty Gritty Dirt Band's John McEuen recalled asking Maybelle what she did in a big auditorium or stadium with that little autoharp. "We were in Knoxville, in the Coliseum, of course, and I was concerned about her getting the sound out there. She goes, 'Well, like I tell the girls, if you have trouble with the mike, just smile real loud.' "

Stella Bayes heard about Maybelle's death on her car radio, and she drove straight to Sara's to break the news. She didn't want Sara to hear it from some announcer voice. At the trailer, Stella found Sara sitting on the couch, with her head in her hands, feeling lousy as always. Stella stood in front of her sister-in-law, worried about Sara's bad heart, hoping to be gentle: "Honey, I heard something on the news," Stella told her. "I'm not sure if it's true, but it must be. . . . They said Maybelle died." Sara's reaction was immediate, without time for filter. She went pale, drew in a breath, then gasped, while swallowing a sob. "Oh, my little Maybelle," she cried. "My Maybelle." And then she wept. It lasted only a minute; that's all she allowed. But she let Stella put her arms around her, and they held each other.

The news of Maybelle's death struck Sara hard, because it was a blow she hadn't expected. She'd seen her friend and partner earlier that year, when Maybelle stopped in California after tagging along to a Johnny Cash show at Lake Tahoe. The two women had a few days of visiting at Coy and Sara's trailer, talking over old times, laughing like they always could, or just sitting in comfortable silence. When it was time for Maybelle to go, they'd both been emotional. As she was getting in the car to go into the airport, Maybelle said to Stella, "I'll never see Sara again." When Stella went back to the trailer, Sara had said, "I'll never see Maybelle again."

But everybody, Sara included, thought Sara would be the first to go. She'd had been in and out of the hospital for more than a year, fighting circulatory and respiratory complications. And within weeks of Maybelle's death, in December of 1978, she was back in. Sara had no worries left for herself, but she worried constantly about what would become of Coy. One day after visiting Sara at the hospital, Gladys Greiner stopped by Coy's mother's house. When she got there, Mary Bayes had something to tell Gladys.

"Gladys, Sara just called me from the hospital."

"Oh, is she better?" Gladys asked.

"I don't think she's any better," said Mary. "She just said to tell you this . . . and I told her you wouldn't do it."

"What is it, Mama?" Gladys asked.

"She said to me, 'Coy has been dying to go to Alaska for a long time. I want Gladys to go to Alaska with Coy.' "

"I can't go," Gladys protested. "I'm not married to him or anything, I can't go to Alaska." Gladys understood immediately what Sara was asking. Gladys had lost her husband; Coy was about to be widowed. Sara wanted Gladys to marry Coy after she was gone.

"Well, she wants you to go," said Mary Bayes, "because she wants him to go to Alaska, and you're the only one that she trusts. And you'd take good care of him on the trip if he wasn't well or something."

That night, Mary Bayes told Sara that Gladys Greiner had refused. "Well, someday," Sara said, "she's going to take him to Alaska."

When Barbara Powell visited her aunt Sara in the hospital that winter, she found the room full of floral arrangements, and she told Sara she wanted to bring flowers but a new vase would only add clutter. "Sara said, 'Would you do something for me?' " Barbara recalls. " 'Would you get me some perfume?' And she wanted White Shoulders. But she never got well. She never came out of the hospital. I don't know if she used it."

Sara Carter died January 8, 1979, six months after her eightieth birthday. Her death was the final event of a long tug-of-war between Sara's husband and her children. "About a year or two before she died, she said she wanted to be brought back here and buried," remembers Janette Carter. "Coy didn't want to bring her at first. The last time I was out there, he talked to me. He said, 'Now I want her here.' And I said, 'Well, I guess you do, but whatever she wants is what needs to be fulfilled. She wanted to go back to the Valley. And I'm not gonna say you can put her out here. Whatever she wants, why that's the way it should be.'"

Even by airplane, Sara's final trip to the Valley took a day and a half. Coy flew with the body from Sacramento to San Francisco to Atlanta, and then into the Tri-Cities Airport serving Bristol, Kingsport, and Johnson City. On one stop, Coy sat in the terminal watching the casket being off-loaded onto a tarmac for removal to a connecting flight. Two days before the funeral in Maces Springs, as the ground was being readied at the Mount Vernon cemetery, Coy talked to a reporter from a local newspaper: "My home is in California now, and we have a special burial plot there with space for her beside my parents. But I loved her enough to grant her request. She belonged to the world, and the world loved her, too. This is where I found her, and this is where I'll leave her. We've had a good, long, and happy life together, but she'll be laid to rest by my brother Dewey, who passed away in 1931."

Sara wanted her funeral services at the Carter Fold (the six-hundred-seat indoor arena Janette had had built for music programs), to hold the crowd she expected. The day of the funeral, Friday, January 12, 1979, dawned dank and cold, and it only got worse. But as the big coal stove began to warm the Fold, family, friends, and fans filed slowly through the doors, filling the building beyond its full capacity. Sara's body rested on the stage in a gold-colored casket, surrounded by floral sprays and guitar- and harp-shaped flower arrangements. When all had settled into the bleacherlike seating, Mount Vernon's preacher read the outlines of her life: her birth, the death of her mother, her baptism, her marriage to A.P. Carter, the singing career, the marriage to Coy and removal to California, her frequent trips back to Virginia. Johnny Cash talked about Sara's talent, her professionalism, her lasting mark on the world of music. "She touched the lives of countless millions of people. . . . Sara's voice continues to inspire artists." Flanders Bays's children sang a hymn, "Hallelujah, We Shall Rise."

There was no sermon proper, but there was a reading of the thirty-first chapter of Proverbs: "Who can find a virtuous woman? For her price is far above rubies. . . . She seeketh wool and flax, and worketh willingly with her hands. . . . She girdeth her loins with strength, and strengtheneth her arms. . . . Strength and honour *are* her clothing; and she shall *rejoice* in time to come. . . . Her children arise up, and call her blessed; her husband *also*, and he praiseth her. Many daughters have done virtuously, but thou excellest them all."

There was also plenty of witnessing by those willing to stand up and testify. "When someone was down, she always had something good to say to that person. To make them feel better. We loved her dearly."

"My father used to say, 'If heaven has music like the Carter Family sings, I don't want to miss it.' "

"She was a wonderful wife and a wonderful mother."

The service was a tribute partly to the person Sara had actually been, and partly to the Sara others needed her to be or wished her to be. This last was true of the scores of people in attendance who knew her only through her singing, and it was no less true of the blood of her blood and the bone of her bone. Janette started crying at the beginning of the service, and she could not stop. For years there had been a half silence between them; there were so many things they would never talk about. Janette had never been able to feel as close to her mother as she had to her father, but that didn't make the last good-bye any easier. "I always thought that nothing would hurt me like giving up my daddy," she said many years later. "And I thought, well, it won't hurt like that when my mother's gone, but I couldn't tell you what the difference was. One hurt just as bad as the other. It hurt just as bad as the other."

Her mother's death, Janette says, was like losing her twice. She was mourning not simply the loss of her mother but the relationship they'd lost so long ago, when her mother left home. Near the end of the service, the Mount Vernon preacher read a Rudyard Kipling poem the family requested, "which attempts to express the love between Sara Carter Bayes and her family."

> *If I were hanged on the highest hill,*
> *I know whose love would follow me still;*
> *If I were drowned in the deepest sea,*
> *I know whose tears would come down to me;*
> *If I were damned in body and soul*
> *I know whose prayers would make me whole;*
> *Mother of mine! Mother of mine! Mother of mine!*

That's when Janette lost any Carter reserve she had left, and as she was taken up to the open casket for the last look at her mother, she could no longer control her sobbing. *Mommy,* she cried out, for something beyond that body in the casket. *Mommy. Mommy.*

An icy rain beat down on the funeral procession as it headed up the Valley road and toward the Mount Vernon cemetery. Behind the hearse and the family car were three trucks carrying the flowers from the Fold to the graveside. A hundred and fifty people climbed through the sleet to the hilltop cemetery, where the Red Clay Ramblers sang "Anchored in Love" over Sara's grave. After the mourners dispersed, Sara Carter Bayes was lowered into the ground in the foothills of Clinch Mountain, into the grave dug next to Dewey's, two rows away from A.P.'s. But even then, the Bill Begley Monument Company was readying the tombstone. It would be like only one other at Mount Vernon, hewn of red granite. Above Sara's name and dates, carved in the smooth glassy sheen, would be the likeness of a 78 record, perfect in its roundness, and the words "Keep on the Sunny Side."

Maybelle and Sara at the Carter Fold (Gladys Greiner)

Index

ABC, 340, 341, 364–65
Acme Records, 325–28
Acuff, Roy, 122, 265, 283, 286, 287, 294, 367, 392
Adams family (Buchanan County, Va.), 117, 142
Addington, Charles Cromwell, 68
Addington, Dewey, 68, 69–70
Addington, D.J. "Deejer," 68
Addington, Duke, 184
Addington, Ezra, 37–38, 47, 68, 70
Addington, Florida, 276
Addington, Henry, 68
Addington, Hugh Jack, 45–46, 65, 67–69, 74, 189
Addington, Hugh Jack, Jr. ("Doc"), 68, 252, 254, 255
Addington, Linnie Myrl, 68
Addington, Madge, 40–41, 42, 45, 68, 101, 189, 379
Addington, Margaret Elizabeth Kilgore, 45, 65, 67–71, 122, 128, 184, 197, 215, 226
Addington, Maybelle, see Carter, Maybelle Addington
Addington, Milburn B. "Toobe," 68, 189–90
Addington, Norma, 68
Addington, Suzy, 257
Addington, Warren M. "Bug," 68, 189–90, 256–57, 276
Addington, William, 68
Addington, Willie B. "Sawcat," 68
Addington Frame Church, 45, 72–74
Ake, George, 92

Allison, Dexter, 88
American Bandstand, 312
American Medical Association (AMA), 207, 212
American Recording Company (ARC), 176–77
Among My Klediments (June Carter), 192, 248–49
"Anchored in Love," 108, 383, 397
Ann-Margret, 336
"Another Man Done Gone," 348
Appalachia:
  culture of, 13–16
  musical traditions of, 10, 41–45, 101
  song transmission in, 41–42, 43–44, 70–71
Appalachian Power Company, 195
"Are You Lonesome Tonight?", 332
Armstrong, Louis, 83, 84
Ash Grove (Hollywood), 340–42
Atkins, Chester "Chet," 6, 235, 266–74, 277, 289, 293, 295, 298, 335, 369
  audience awareness of, 271
  background of, 266–68
  guitar playing of, 267, 269–70
  June's comic routines and, 270, 279–80
  on Maybelle's final days, 389–90
  Opry offer and, 283–84, 286
  perfectionism of, 278
  playing with Carters, 259, 266, 268–74, 278–80, 283–84, 286
Atkins, Leona, 278
Atkins, Merle, 278

Autry, Gene, 83, 255, 262, 263
Axton, Hoyt, 392

"Baby, It's Cold Outside," 275, 289
Baez, Joan, 4, 109, 340
"Bald-Headed End of a Broom, The,"
    279
"Barbara Allen," 117, 119
Barker, Ernest, 320
Barn Dances, 7
"Bashful Rascal," 289
Baxter, Dode, 230
Baxter, Don, 230, 233, 236
Bays, Alma (later Bayes), 55, *145,* 149,
    151, 152, 160, 218–19
Bays, Bobby, 165
Bays, Charlie (later Bayes), *12,* 24, 30,
    55–56, 149–55, 158, 242, 246,
    247
    business ventures of, 149–50
    children of, stricken with tuberculosis,
        101, 151–55, 160, 180, 220–21
    family taken west by, 160, 218–21
    inadvertent name change and, 219
Bays, Charmie (later Bayes), 55,
    149–55, 160, 161, 180,
    218–21
Bays, Coy (later Bayes), 55, *145,* 149,
    151, 152–53, 155, *201,* 217–23,
    232, 247, 325, 354–55, 376–78,
    380, 384–87, 393
    drinking of, 385–86
    flying as pastime of, 158
    move west of, 160–61, 179–80,
        218–21
    personality and demeanor of, 158–59
    Sara reunited with, 217–18, 222
    Sara's affair with, 158–61, 163, 164,
        179–80, 186, 217–18, 221–22
    Sara's death and, 394, 395
    Sara's marriage to, 222, 225–26
    Sara's relationship with, 221–23,
        237–38, 246, 385–86
Bays, Dewey, *12,* 55, *144,* 149–55,
    160, 227, 395, 397

Bays, Eliza Morgan, 21–22
Bays, Elva, 55, 149, 152, 154, 218–19
Bays, Fiddlin' Billy, 150
Bays, Flanders, 30, 34, 47, 52, 56, 72,
    101, 104, 123, 154, 250, 333,
    396
    as A.P.'s mentor, 31–33
    Carter Family's song gathering and,
        107, 108
    choir of, 31, 62, 380
    as farmer, 31–32, 195
    singing school of, 32–33, 37, 70
Bays, F.M., Jr., 118, 158, 195
Bays, Gordon, 66
Bays, Mary Smith (later Bayes), *12,* 55,
    144, 149–55, 242, 246, 394
    children of, stricken with tuberculosis,
        151–55, 160, 180, 220–21
    family taken west by, 160–61, 218–21
    Sara and Coy's affair and, 160–61,
        221, 222
Bays, Mollie, *see* Carter, Mollie Bays
Bays, Myrtle, 118, 123, 124
Bays, Stanley (later Bayes), 55, *145,*
    149, 151–53, 155, 158, 160,
    180, 218–21
Bays, Stella (later Bayes), 55, 67, *145,*
    149, 153, 157, 250, 385
    ailing siblings and, 151, 152, 154,
        220–21
    on Coy and Sara's relationship, 159,
        222–23
    on life at Eck and Maybelle's house,
        155–56
    marriage of, 219
    Maybelle's death and, 393, 394
    move west of, 160–61, 218–20
Bays, Vernon, 17–18, 32, 56, 57, 154,
    158, 195, 241
Bays, Will, *12,* 30, 124
Bays, William Anderson, 20
Bays, William H., 21–22, 24
Bean, Roy, 197
"Bear Creek Blues," 242
Bear Family Records, 4

Benet, Stephen Vincent, 89
Berliner, Emile, 85
Best of the Carter Family, 353
Bible Questions and Answers, 274
Billboard charts, 260
"Birds Were Singing of You, The," 133
Bisbee, Jasper E., 38
"Black Mountain Rag," 354, 370
black musicians:
    A.P. and, 127–29, 131–38
    Peer and, 83, 84, 87
    Pentecostalism and, 133–36
Blanchard, Lowell, 265, 267
Blood, Sweat & Tears, 348
Bluebird, 321
"Bluebird Island " 290
"Blue Doll," 311–12
"Blue Moon of Kentucky," 306, 307
"Blue Ridge Mountains of Virginia,
    The," 271
blues, 127–28, 132–33, 137–38, 184,
    241–42
"Blue Yodel," 140
Boggs, Dock, 139
Bond, L. H., 180
Borglum, Gutzon, 234
Bourne, Sol, 176
Bowman, Becky, 299–306, 308, 309,
    312, 336, 344–45
    as fill-in for Carter Sisters, 299–300,
    301
Bowman, Claudine "Mommy," 299
Bowman, Emily, 299
"Boy Named Sue, A," 364
Bradford, Perry, 84
Bradley, Harold, 354
Bradley, Owen, 335
Brasfield, Rod, 308
Briar, 339
Bright, Lindsay, 189
Brinkley, "Doctor" John Romulus, 1–4,
    5, 10, 197–213, 200, 215, 241
    background of, 201–3, 207
    border-radio station of, 3–4, 197,
    209–18

gubernatorial campaign of, 3, 208–9
home of, 198–99, 222
impotence treatments of, 2, 203–8,
    210–13
investigations into, 206–7, 212, 213
radio broadcasts of, 203–12
success of, 206–7
Brinkley, Johnny Boy, 212, 213
Brinkley, Minnie, 204, 210
Bristol News Bulletin, 80, 94
Brockman, Polk, 89–90, 92, 139
Brunswick, 76–77
Bryant, Boudleaux, 271
Bryant, Felice, 271
"Buddies in the Saddle," 241
Burns, Aitchee, 266
Burns, Kenneth, 268
Bush, Ethyl, 40

Cadence, 311
"Canned Heat," 279
"Cannonball, The," 132
"Cannonball Blues," 288, 344
Canteen Woogie, 254
Carson, Fiddlin' John, 75, 87–90, 92
Carson, Gerald, 199
Carter, Alvin Pleasant Delaney (A.P.),
    25–36, 46–53, 57–63, 76–79,
    95–250, 269
    bandstand built by, 325–26, 330
    birth of, 25
    after Carter Family breakup, 9, 250,
    315–33
    Carter Sisters and Mother Maybelle
    and, 257, 273–74
    childhood of, 16–17, 18, 26–33
    as church singer, 30, 31, 37–38
    courtship and wedding of, 35–36, 38,
    46–49, 50
    death and burial of, 331–33, 335,
    384, 397
    divorce of, 180–81
    employment of, 28, 33–36, 57–59,
    76
    family history of, 19–22

Carter, A.P. (*cont.*)
  as farmer, 33, 34, 47, 124–25, 156,
    172–73
  as father, 147, 171
  final days of, 329–33
  generosity of, 322–23
  grocery store of, *315*, 320–21, 322,
    328, 329, 332
  guitar playing attempted by, 146
  homes of, 47–48, 51–53, 110–12,
    125, 156, 174, 240, 241, 317,
    319
  Janette's marriage and, 238–40
  land bought by, 240, 326
  musical abilities of, 29–30, 31,
    37–38
  music seen as way to make money by,
    62–63, 76–79, 103
  old songs valued by, 77
  onstage presence of, 114, 115
  personality and demeanor of, 27–29,
    38, 103, 146–47, 187–88, 316,
    318–19, 322–23, 326
  photographs of, *xiv, 12,* 48–49, *50,*
    107, 126, 127, 244, 245, *314*
  physical appearance of, 316–17, 323
  return to music attempted by, 324–28
  Sara's extramarital affair and,
    158–59, 163, 221
  Sara's first meeting with, 35–36
  Sara's relationship with, 62, 145–48,
    157, 163–64, 170, 180, 185–86,
    225, 232–33, 325, 330
  Sara's remarriage and, 225–26
  Sara's separation from, 163–68,
    170–71, 177–81
  slackening in song production of, 186
  as solo vocalist, 132, 242
  song-hunting expeditions of, 5,
    107–8, 111, 118–22, 127–38,
    145–46, 148–49, 159, 165,
    175, 177
  as songwriter, 34, 107, 120, 133,
    174, 175, 177, 186
  tremor of, 27, 29–30, 187, 316, 330

  voice and singing style of, 5, 29–30,
    31, 47, 99–100, 109, 115, 147,
    232, 242
  wandering nature of, 57, 58–59, 99,
    115
  see also Original Carter Family
Carter, Anita (Maybelle's daughter),
    167, 179, 186, 187, 190–91,
    194, 195–96, 242, 361, 390
  birth of, 190
  first Texas trip of, 197, 199–200,
    215, 216, 226
  marriages of, 298–99
  musical training of, 226–27
  on parents' relationship, 356
  as performer, 215, 226–30, 232, 233,
    236–37, 247–313, 369, 370
  personality and demeanor of, 228
  photographs of, *183, 224, 245, 283,*
    335
  Presley and, 308, 309–11
  reluctant to continue performing, 264,
    265, 336
  schooling of, 253, 264, 276, 277,
    288
  singing with Original Carter Family,
    215, 226, 232, 233, 236–37
  social life of, 273
  solo career of, 289–90, 311–12
  as songwriter, 236–37
  voice of, 271–72, 353–54
  Williams and, 291–96, 298
  yodeling of, 262–63, 287
  see also Carter Sisters and Mother
    Maybelle
"Carter, Aunt Polly" (character), 254,
    270
Carter, Big Tom (A.P.'s cousin), 73–74,
    118–19, 123, 319, 320
Carter, Carlene (Maybelle's grand-
    daughter), 363, 369–73
Carter, Dale (A.P.'s cousin), 73, 119
Carter, Dulaney (A.P.'s great-grandfather),
    19, 332
Carter, E. T., 181

Carter, Elisha "Lish" (A.P.'s uncle), *12*, 20, 30, 34, 66, 78, 101, 108
Carter, Ermine (A.P.'s brother), 25–26, 46, 52, 75, 173, 332
Carter, Ettaleen (A.P.'s sister), *12*, 25, 101–2, 227, 331
Carter, Ezra "Eck" ("Pop") (A.P.'s brother; Maybelle's husband), 77, 78, 108, 112, 116, 166–67, 187–97, 299, 308, 354, 355–58
  Bayses aided by, 152, 153
  birth of, 25
  books of, 249, 303, 350–51, 358
  cars and driving of, 57, 62, 78, 100, 123, 188, 268, 278
  Carter Family's audition and, 78, 104
  Carter Sisters managed by, 268–69, 271, 273, 283–84, 301
  Cash and, 348, 350–52, 358, 360, 361
  childhood of, 26–27, 28
  competitiveness of, 188–89
  cooking of, 196–97, 305
  courtship and wedding of, 65–67
  daughters' musical careers and, 226–27, 229, 248, 250–51, 254, 255, 275–77, 335, 336
  daughters' suitors and, 249–50, 273, 276–77, 280–81, 300
  drinking of, 191–92
  as farmer, 194
  as father, 188, 190–91, 226–27, 228–29, 249–50, 253, 255–56, 300
  final days of, 387–89
  Florida life of, 336–37, 355–57, 362–63, 390
  generosity of, 193–95, 196
  as grandfather, 362–63
  homes of, 75, 124, 155–56, 157, 179, 186, 189–91, 194–96, 263–64, 304, 326, 336–37, 356
  Maybelle's relationship with, 74–76, 187, 190, 192, 303, 304–5, 338
  motorcycle riding of, 74–75, 188
  Opry offer and, 283–84
  parents' deaths and, 247, 248
  personality and demeanor of, 26, 66, 187–89, 191, 193–96, 355–56
  photographs of, *xv*, *12*, *182*
  as railway mail clerk, 27, 56–57, 67, 155, 189, 191, 249, 254
  religion and, 74, 192–94
  retirement plans of, 336–37, 390
  rock clearing of, 194, 304–5, 348
  spending habits of, 56–57, 75, 124, 156, 189, 195–96, 278, 303–4, 357, 371
  war effort and, 254–55
  Williams and, 291, 295
Carter, Fern, *see* Salyers, Fern Carter
Carter, Gladys Ettaleen (later Mrs. Milan Millard) (A.P. and Sara's daughter), 47–48, 60, 62, 76, 108, 111, 112, 142, 147, 148, 174, 240, 250, 317, 321, 322, 323, 328, 386
  A.P.'s final days and, 329–31, 333
  A.P.'s legacy to, 332
  on A.P.'s songwriting, 120, 121
  birth of, 59
  at Carter Family's audition, 78, 97–99
  courtship and wedding of, 179, 214, 227
  family homeplace deeded to, 241
  household duties of, 167
  as mother, 214
  New York trip of, 167–70
  parents' separation and, 164, 166, 167, 171, 179
  photographs of, 97, *163*, *375*
Carter, Grant (A.P.'s brother), 25, 192, 263, 326
Carter, Helen (later Mrs. Glenn Jones) (Maybelle's daughter), 155, 167, 179, 181, 186, 187, 190, 192, 194, 196, 197, 215, 363, 368, 390
  accordion playing of, 251, 270
  birth of, 104

Carter, Helen (cont.)
  Bowman as fill-in for, 299–300, 301
  childbearing of, 281, 287–88, 301
  courtship and wedding of, 276–77,
    280–81
  first Texas trip of, 229, 231–32, 233,
    236, 237
  on Ma Carter, 227–28
  musical training of, 226–27
  as performer, 226–27, 229–30, 232,
    233, 236–37, 247–313, 369–71,
    383
  personality and demeanor of, 227
  photographs of, 183, 224, 245, 283
  schooling of, 231, 249
  singing with Original Carter Family,
    232, 233, 236–37
  social life of, 273
  solo career of, 289
  as songwriter, 336
  see also Carter Sisters and Mother
    Maybelle
Carter, Janette (later Mrs. Jimmy Jett)
    (A.P. and Sara's daughter),
    60–61, 76, 78, 103, 108,
    110–11, 118, 121, 124, 147,
    148, 174, 186, 196, 214, 315,
    317, 322, 325, 329–32, 386
  A.P.'s legacy to, 332
  birth of, 59
  festivals organized by, 375, 380–84,
    387, 395
  first Texas trip of, 230–32, 233–34
  marriage of, 238–40
  parents' separation and, 163–66,
    170–71, 179
  as performer, 115–16, 229, 230,
    233–36, 238, 240, 257
  photographs of, 97, 163
  Sara's death and, 395, 396–97
  schooling of, 231
  songs gathered by, 236
Carter, Jim (A.P.'s brother), 12, 25, 29,
    129

Carter, Joe (A.P. and Sara's son), 46,
    58, 74, 76, 103, 108, 142,
    145–46, 167, 174, 200, 214,
    225, 241, 303, 325, 386
  A.P.'s legacy to, 332
  birth of, 60
  at Carter Family's audition, 78,
    97–99
  farm work and, 172–73
  first Texas trip of, 230–32, 234, 236
  parents' separation and, 164–66,
    170, 171, 179
  as performer, 234, 355, 383
  photographs of, 97, 163, 334
  schooling of, 231
  streaking of, 147–48
Carter, June (later Mrs. Johnny Cash)
    (Maybelle's daughter), 31, 115,
    155, 161, 167, 179, 186, 188,
    190, 192, 193, 195, 196, 197,
    215, 357, 389, 390, 391
  as actress, 312
  Cash's courtship of and wedding to,
    346–52, 361
  Cash's drug habit and, 349, 359–61
  childbearing of, 301
  as comic, 232, 242–43, 254, 270,
    279–80, 287, 302
  first Texas trip of, 229–34, 236
  on Maybelle's guitar playing, 71
  musical training of, 226–27
  as performer, 6, 7, 226–27, 229–30,
    232, 233, 236–37, 242–43,
    247–313
  personality and demeanor of, 228–29
  photographs of, 183, 224, 245, 283,
    334, 335
  as salesperson, 252–53, 279–80,
    312
  schooling of, 249, 253, 259
  singing with Original Carter Family,
    232, 233, 236–37
  Smith's courtship of and marriage to,
    299, 300–301, 312

social life of, 273
solo career of, 274–75, 289, 312, 336
sound systems and, 270–71
Williams and, 295, 296–97
see also Carter Sisters and Mother Maybelle
"Carter, Little June" (character), 270, 271, 279
Carter, Little Tom, 319
Carter, Lois (A.P.'s niece), *see* Hensley, Lois Carter
Carter, Martha Bays (A.P.'s aunt), 30
Carter, Maybelle Addington, 5, 7, 33, 65–79, 95–313, 335–73
academics' interest in, 337–38
arthritis suffered by, 371, 382
audience as focus of, 184, 272, 344
autoharp playing of, 344
awards received by, 370
Bayses' move west and, 160, 161, 179
birth of, 67
cars and driving of, 254–55, 256, 301–2, 372–73
Cash and, 6, 347–53, 355, 358, 360–62, 364–66, 371, 388–91
childbearing of, 76, 78, 79, 97, 104, 190
childhood of, 45, 68–70
churchgoing of, 71–74, 192–93
cooking of, 196–97
courtship and wedding of, 65–67
death and burial of, 392–94
decline in career of (1950s), 312–13, 335–37
Eck's death and, 388–89
Eck's relationship with, 74–76, 187, 190, 192, 303, 304–5, 356, 388
family history of, 67–69
final days of, 388–92
Florida life of, 336–37, 362–63, 390–91
folk music revival and, 337–45, 353

gambling enjoyed by, 371–72, 391
as grandmother, 362–64
guitars and guitar-playing style of, 63, 70, 71, 108, 109–10, 184–85, 187, 233, 338–39, 341, 343–44, 367, 371, 382, 390
homes of, 75, 124, 155–56, 157, 179, 186, 189–91, 194–96, 263–64, 304, 326, 356
housekeeping of, 196–97
life on the road and, 254–57, 301–2
"Mama" moniker for, 292–93
as mother, 276, 300
musical abilities of, 5, 45, 70–71, 132–33, 184–85
musicians' respect for, 6–7, 288, 291, 292–93, 343, 354, 367, 370
New Lost City Ramblers tour with, 340–43
Nitty Gritty Dirt Band's recording with, 366–69, 392–93
as nurse, 343, 348–49, 352–53
Opry stars' treatment of, 291, 292–93
perfectionism of, 183–84, 278
personality and demeanor of, 70, 76, 183–84, 190, 293, 341, 349
photographs of, xiv, xv, 64, 65, 107, 126, 127, 183, 282, 283, 335, 398
physical appearance of, 67, 70
Presley and, 307
retirement of, 389, 391
Sara and A.P.'s marital difficulties and, 185–86
Sara's relationship with, 76
Sara's reunion album and performances with, 354–55, 375, 380–84, 387
smoking of, 288
solo albums of, 354, 370–71
solo career of, 335–45, 352–58, 364–69, 370–71
as songwriter, 186–87, 241–42

Carter, Maybelle Addington (*cont.*)
    television appearances of, 365
    unable to read music, 122
    Williams and, 292–93, 295–96
    see also Carter Sisters and Mother
      Maybelle; Original Carter Family
Carter, Mollie Bays (A.P.'s mother), *12,*
    13, 16–31, 33, 34, 39, 52, 59–60,
    66, 67, 76, 77, 116, 171, 190,
    214, 231, 250, 315, 331, 387
    churchgoing of, 30–31, 192
    Dewey's illness and death and, 153,
      154–55, 227
    Eck's drinking and, 192
    Ettaleen's death and, 102, 227
    family history of, 21–22
    final days of, 247, 248
    household run by, 22–24
    personality and demeanor of, 227–28
    pregnancies and childbearing of, 25,
      27, 28, 29
    singing of, 24–25, 31
Carter, Nancy (A.P.'s grandmother),
    19–20
Carter, Ora (A.P.'s sister-in-law), 52, 61,
    116, 173
Carter, Preacher R. T., 240
Carter, Rebecca Smith (A.P.'s great-
    grandmother), 19
Carter, Robert (A.P.'s father), *12,*
    17–20, 23, 24, 26, 29, 33, 59,
    66–67, 73, 76, 77, 119, 153,
    193, 194, 249, 331, 387
    churchgoing of, 30–31
    death of, 247–48
    family history of, 19–20, 22
Carter, Sara Dougherty (later Mrs. Coy
    Bayes), 5, 37–53, 59–63, 76–79,
    95–250, 364
    academics' interest in, 379
    A.P.'s death and, 331
    A.P.'s first meeting with, 35–36
    A.P.'s relationship with, 62, 145–48,
      157, 163–64, 170, 180, 185–86,
      225, 232–33, 325, 330

    A.P.'s separation from, 163–68,
      170–71, 177–81
    autoharp played by, 40, 62
    California life of, 375–80, 384–87
    after Carter Family breakup, 257,
      375–87
    celebrity shunned by, 246–47
    childbearing of, 59
    childhood of, 38–41, 67, 101, 164
    coming out of retirement, 354–55,
      375, 380–84, 387
    courtship and wedding of, 35–36, 38,
      46–49, *50*
    Coy reunited with, 217–18, 222
    Coy's affair with, 158–61, 163, 164,
      179–80, 186, 217–18, 221–22
    Coy's marriage to, 222, 225–26
    Coy's relationship with, 221–23,
      237–38, 246, 385–86
    death and burial of, 395–97
    divorce of, 180–81
    final days of, 393–95
    as grandmother, 214, 387
    homes of, 47–48, 51–53, 110–12,
      125, 156, 174, 246, 384
    household run by, 59–60, 103–4,
      145–46, 147–49
    liberation of, 61–62
    Maybelle's death and, 393–94
    Maybelle's relationship with, 76
    Maybelle's reunion album and perfor-
      mances with, 354–55, 375,
      380–84, 387
    as mother, 146–47, 148, 164–65,
      170–71, 179, 257, 325, 386–87,
      396–97
    musical abilities of, 35, 40–41, 62–63
    performing for live audience disliked
      by, 145
    personality and demeanor of, 38,
      59–62, 76, 103, 179, 246,
      376–77
    photographs of, *xiv, 36, 37, 48–49,*
      50, 107, 126, 127, 145, 162,
      201, 374, 375, 398

physical appearance of, 5, 48, 60,
179, 376
retirement of, 246–47, 250
Rich Valley musical traditions and,
41–45
smoking of, 61, 380, 386
as songwriter, 133, 178, 214–15,
241, 242, 325, 378
unable to read music, 122
voice of, 5, 35, 62, 99, 100, 109, 380
work ethic of, 59–60
see also Original Carter Family
Carter, Sylvia (A.P.'s sister), 25, 102,
145, 161, 172, 193, 197, 248
Carter, Theda (A.P.'s sister-in-law), 57,
102, 191, 248, 263, 323, 324,
326, 382, 387
Carter, Vangie (A.P.'s sister-in-law), 61,
116
Carter, Virgie (A.P.'s sister), *12*, 25, 26,
34, 66, 97, 98, 119, 120, 249
Carter, William (A.P.'s cousin), 20
Carter Family (original), *see* Original
Carter Family
Carter Family (1970s), 369–73, 389
Carter Family Scrap Book, 327
Carter Family Songbook, *126*
Carter Fold, 395
A.P. Carter Grocery, *315*, 320–21, 322,
328, 329, 332
Carter scratch, 71, 109–10, 343–44
Carter Sisters and Mother Maybelle, 7,
250–313, 324, 341
A.P.'s performances with, 273–74
Atkins's performances with, *259*,
266, 268–74, 278–80, 283–84,
286
Carter Family standards played by,
253, 271, 272, 302
Cash and, 5, 347, 348, 353–54,
363, 365
decline of interest in, 312–13,
335–36
disbanding of, 336
earnings of, 284, 290–91, 301

Eck as manager of, 268–69, 271,
273, 283–84, 301
Eck's ambitions and, 250–51
at Grand Ole Opry, 281, 282,
283–89, 291, 301–2, 312, 346
harmonies of, 272, 279, 302–3
June's comic routines and, 254, 270,
279–80, 287, 302
Knoxville radio broadcasts of, 273–74
Maybelle's tendency to stay in background of, 253, 288
Nashville radio broadcasts of, 281,
285–89, 305–6
photographs of, *258*, *259*, *282*, *283*,
335
playing short-handed or with fill-ins,
276, 288, 299–300, 301
recordings of, 289, 348, 353
Richmond radio broadcasts of,
251–53, 254, 260–63
road shows of, 254–57, 268–73,
290–91, 301–2, 306–11
sisters' solo careers and, 274–76,
289–90, 311–12
Springfield radio broadcasts of,
277–80
television appearances of, 294
on tour with Presley, 306–11
Williams and, 291–98
Caruso, Enrico, 92, 93
Cash, Carrie, 350
Cash, Jack, 345
Cash, John R. "Johnny," 4, 6, 109, 235,
306, 311, 336, 338, 345–55,
363, 371, 380, 388, 390–91,
393, 396
background of, 345–46
drug habit of, 346, 349, 350, 352,
358–61, 388
June courted by and wed to, 346–52,
361
Maybelle's retirement and, 389, 391
self-destructive days of, 358–61
television shows of, 364–66
Cash, June Carter, *see* Carter, June

Cash, Vivian Liberto, 345–46, 347, 349, 360, 361
Chandler, Harry, 203
Cherry, Hugh, 341
"Chewing Gum," 44–45, 109
Childre, Lou, 216, 300
"Chime Bells," 236
"Chinese Breakdown," 233
Chuck Wagon Gang, 323–24
church-house music, 71–73, 133–38
    African-American sacred songs and, 133–37
    Holiness revivals and, 71–72, 110, 133, 136, 186, 242
    Pentecostalism and, 133–36
    shape-note singing and, 32
Civil War, 20, 21, 41–43, 72, 130, 285
    party affiliation and, 238–39
Clark, Johnny, 322
Clement, Jack, 340
Clements, Vasser, 368
Clifton, Bill, 321–26, 343
    A.P. sought out by, 321–22
    on A.P.'s final days, 330, 331, 333
    on A.P.'s generosity, 322–23
    playing at A.P.'s bandstand, 325–26
Clifton, Sara Lee, 330
Clinch Mountain, 13
Cline, Patsy, 109, 335
"Coal Miner's Blues," 344
Cohen, John, 340–43
Colliers, 287
Columbia, 85–86, 87, 90–91, 332, 353, 354, 370
Columbo, 390
"Columbus, Georgia," or "Columbus Stockade," 289
Como, Perry, 110
Consolidated Drug Trade Products, 246
Consolidated Royal Chemical Corporation, 197, 216, 217, 226, 230, 246
copyrights, 93, 107, 113, 123, 157, 171, 175–76, 378

Country Gentleman (Atkins), 270
Country Music Hall of Fame, 365, 380
country-music industry, 286–87, 340
"Country Roads," 369
Country's First Family, 389
cowboy songs, 233, 237, 241, 354
"Cowboy's Wild Song to His Herd," 235
Crawford, Henry "Coonie," 213
Crocker, Al, 299
Crudup, Arthur "Big Boy," 306
Curtis, James P., 15
"Cyclone of Rye Cove, The," 101

Dalhart, Vernon, 75, 92, 108, 122, 185
dancing and dance music, 45–46, 69–70
"Dark-Haired True Lover," 178, 233
Davis, Blind Willie, 137
Davis, Don, 284, 298, 299, 302, 304, 305, 310, 312, 336
Davis, Gussie, 130, 232
Davis, Jay, 336
Davis, Lorrie, 363, 369, 370
Deacon, Wise, 89
Dean, James, 312, 345
Decca, 181, 186
Denison, Daddy, 125
Depression, Great, 1, 2, 5, 9, 142, 145, 194, 196, 210, 265
    Carter Family music and, 7–8, 157, 235
    Carter Family's earnings and, 171, 189, 241
    record industry and, 87, 138–39, 156, 171–72
Derting, Bud, 111, 119, 120, 124, 146
Dingus, Leonidas Reuben, 14
"Dixie Darling," 233
"Dizzy Strings," 279
"Don Juan," 279
"Don't Forget This Song," 123
Dougherty, Bob, 37, 38
Dougherty, Elizabeth Kilgore, 38, 67, 164, 379
Dougherty, Nathan, 37, 38

Dougherty, Sara, *see* Carter, Sara
  Dougherty
Dougherty, Sevier, 38, 39, 164
Dougherty, Stephen, 37 38
Dougherty, Thursa Mae, *see* Hartsock,
  Thursa Mae Dougherty
"Down on My Knees," 289
"Down the Trail of Broken Hearts," 290
Dunford, Eck, 94
Duvall, Robert, 312
Dylan, Bob, 4, 109, 339–40, 364, 365

Easterling, A. B., 210
Easterling, Albert, 44
Easterling, Mary Bell, 69
Eastman Kodak, 55, 46
"East Virginia Blues," 340
Edenton, Ray, 268, 274, 354
Edison (company), 85–86, 87
Edison, Thomas, 85, 88
electricity, 56, 195–95, 265
"Engine 143," 7, 35 123, 233, 255
"English" songs, 24–25
Escott, Colin, 292
Essie and Kay (Prairie Sweethearts), 216
Evans, John, 127
event songs, 91–92, 101, 186

"Farewell, Nellie," 178
"Farther On," 355
"Fate of Dewey Lee, The," 186
Federal Radio Commission, 203, 207, 209
Ferera, Frank (Palaziko Ferreira), 108,
  185
Fergus, John, 92
fiddle contests, 88–90
"Fifty Miles of Elbow Room," 242
"First A.P. Carter Memorial Day Festival
  and Crafts Show," 375
Flatt, Lester, 338, 366
Flatt & Scruggs, 109, 338–39, 366
Flippo, Chet. 392–93
"Floyd Collins Trapped in a Cave,"
  91–92
Foley, Mrs. Red, 352

Foley, Red, 287
folk music revival, 337–45, 348, 353,
  368
Fontana, D. J., 309
Ford, Henry, 88
Ford, Whitey, 306, 312
Forrester, Fita, 225
"Forsaken Love," 108
Fowler, Wally, 324
"Freight Train Blues," 263, 287
"Funny When You Feel That Way," 181,
  233

Gardner, Clyde, 60, 124, 143, 196,
  320, 326, 329–30
Gardner, Willie, 188–89
Gary, Pauline, 136–37
"Gathering Flowers on the Hillside," 178
General Phonograph Corporation, 86
Gibson, Don, 335
"Goin' to Sugar Hill," 271
"Gold Watch and Chain," 168, 271
Good Neighbor Get-Together, The, 7,
  216–17, 222, 230, 232–36
Gore, Albert, Jr., 289
Gore, Albert. Sr., 288, 289
Graham, Billy, 391
Graham, Ruth, 391
Grand Ole Opry, 75, 242, 260, 265,
  306–7, 312, 340, 366
  Atkins proviso and, 283–84, 286
  audience at, 285
  Carter Sisters and Mother Maybelle
    at, 281, 282, 283–89, 291,
    301–2, 312, 346
  Cash fired by, 359
  change of taste at, 335–36
  Maybelle's solo appearances at, 352,
    355
  Ryman Auditorium as home of,
    284–85
Grand Ole Opry, 7, 235, 260, 281, 286
"Grave on the Green Hillside, The,"
  119, 123
Grayson, G. B., 337

"Great Speckled Bird," 122
Greiner, Gladys, 375–77, 378, 380–81,
    385, 394
Groves, Abraham, 18, 159
Groves, Amanda, *12*, 18, 20, 73,
    119–20, 249
Guild, Brother Bill, 230, 233, 242
Guthrie, Arlo, 365
Guthrie, Woody, 4, 132, 137–38, 177

Haley, Bill, 306
Hall, Dixie Deen, 65, 195, 253,
    349–50, 352, 354, 357–58
Hall, Tom T., 7, 235, 354
Hanna, Jeff, 369
"Happiest Days of All," 383
Harman, Buddy, 354, 370
Harrell, Kelly, 92
Harris, Ap, 40, 70, 122
Harris, Charles K., 130–31
Harris, Emmylou, 4, 109, 168
Harris, Poss, 318
Hartsock, Beecher, 189
Hartsock, Paul, 165
Hartsock, Thursa Mae Dougherty, *37*,
    39, 40, 47, 48, 62–63, 164
Hartsock, William Joseph "Buff," 47, 48,
    62–63
Haucke, Frank, 209
Havana Treaty, 213
Hawaiian-style playing, 108, 110, 185
Hawkins, Nanny, 118
Haynes, Henry, 268
Hayrides, 7
Hays, William Shakespeare, 131
"Hello Stranger," 181
Hensley, Chester, 118, 159, 188–89
Hensley, Lois Carter, 7, 26, 103, 116,
    125, 130, 179, 227, 228
Hensley, Myrtle, 61, 116, 147, 331
Hensley, Ruth, 196
"He Went Slipping Around," 289
hillbilly records, 83, 84, 87–95
    birth of genre, 90
Historic Reunion, 355, 380

Holiness revivals and music, 71–72, 110,
    133, 136, 186, 242
Hollif, Saul, 346–47
"Home by the Sea," 168
Homer and Jethro, 266, 268, 275–76
Hootenanny, 340, 341
Al Hopkins and the Hill Billies, 90
"Hot Time in the Old Town Tonight,"
    141–42
Howard, Harlan, 353
Hurst, Jack, 367
Hurt, Mississippi John, 132
Huskey, Junior, 354

"I Ain't Goin' to Work Tomorrow," 108
"I Can't Help It If I'm Still in Love with
    You," 294
"I Found You Among the Roses," 242
"I'll Be All Smiles Tonight," 287
"I'll Twine 'Mid the Ringlets," 43–44
"I Loved You Better Than You Knew,"
    168
"I'm Movin' On," 290
"I'm Thinking Tonight of My Blue
    Eyes," 122, 177, 184–85,
    217–18, 222, 368, 384–85
"I'm Working on a Building," 137
"I Never Will Marry," 168
Internal Revenue Service (IRS), 212, 213
"In the Pines," 269
I Remember Daddy (Gladys Carter), 168
Irving, Maud, 43
"I Swear I'll Never Wear a Pair of
    Shoes," 279
"It'll Aggravate Your Soul," 174
"I Told Them What You're Fighting
    For," 354
"It's My Lazy Day," 287
"It Wasn't God Who Made Honky-Tonk
    Angels," 122
Ives, Burl, 119

"Jealous-Hearted Me," 271
Jefferson, Blind Lemon, 127, 128, 132,
    177, 339

Jenkins, Andrew "Blind Andy," 91–92
Jennings, Waylon, 6–7, 235, 359
Jett, Dale, 317, 329, 386–87
Jett, Don, 383
Jett, Janette Carter, *see* Carter, Janette
Jett, Jimmy, 238, 240, 257, 317
    family background of, 238–40
Jett, Rita, 317, 329, 386–87
jig music, 24
"Jimmy Brown, the Paper Boy," 131
"John Hardy Was a Desperate Little
    Man," 4, 109
"John Henry," 128, 348
Johnny Cash at Folsom Prison, 361,
    364
Johnny Cash Show, The, 364–66
Jones, Danny, 369
Jones, David, 369, 373
Jones, Frank, 354
Jones, Glenn (father), 276–77, 280–81
Jones, Glenn Daniel (son), 288
Jones, Helen, *see* Carter, Helen
Jones, Kenny, 363–64, 388
Jones, Kevin, 369, 383
Jones, Ralph, 361
Jones, Rev. Samuel Forter, 284–85
Jordanaires, 288

Kahn, Ed, 77, 78, 184, 209, 226, 233,
    251, 337–38
Kate Smith Evening Hour, The, 294
Kay, Frankie, 299
Kazan, Elia, 312
"Keep on the Firing Line," 242
"Keep on the Sunny Side," 7, 108, 117,
    177, 216, 230, 333, 368, 397
"Keep Them Cold, Icy Fingers Off of
    Me," 279
Kephart, Horace, 13–14
Kershaw, Doug, 365
KFKB, 203–7, 209
Kilgore, Arnett, 45
Kilgore, Merle, 349
Kilgore, Steve, 69–70
King, Pee Wee, 251

Kingsport, Tenn., 54–56, 123
    black musicians in, 127–28
Kingston Trio, 332, 337
Kipling, Rudyard, 397
"Kneeling Drunkard's Prayer, The,"
    272–73
Knight, Peggy, 390, 391, 392
Korman, Jo, 356–57
Kristofferson, Kris, 364
Ku Klux Klan, 136, 359–60
KWTO, 277–80

Lambert, Curly, 321
Langston, Tony, 84
Larkey, Garn, 191
Larkey, Haven, 125
Latin Quarter (New York), 276
Law, Don, 354
Lee, Peggy, 294
"Let's Be Lovers Again," 354
"Letter from Home," 354
"Let the Church Roll On," 137
Leverett, Dot, 364
Leverett, Les, 364
Lewis, Furry, 132
Lewis, Jerry Lee, 306, 311
Liberty Records, 367
Life, 242, 243
Little, Des, 356, 362, 391
Little, Mickey, 356, 362, 391
"Little Black Train," 186
"Little Buckaroo," 215, 226
"Little Darlin' Pal of Mine," 107, 108,
    177, 185, 271, 328, 340
"Little Log Hut in the Lane," 131
"Little Moses," 118, 123, 271
Live at San Quentin, 364
Living Legend, 354, 370
Living with Memories (Janette Carter),
    59, 78, 103, 165
Llewellyn, "Uncle John," 89
Loesser, Frank, 275, 289
Lomax, Alan, 137, 138
"Lonesome for You," 133
"Lonesome Homesick Blues," 241–42

"Lonesome Pine Special," 383
Lonesome Pine Specials, 130
"Lonesome Road Blues," 138
"Lonesome Valley," 232
Long, Huey, 202
Look Homeward Angel (Wolfe), 102
"Lookin' for Henry Lee," 287
Louisiana Hayride, 260
Louvin Brothers, 306, 308
"Love, Old Crazy Love," 301
"Lover's Lane," 178
Lynn, Loretta, 109, 285
Lyons, John Henry, 128

Maces Springs School, 63, 65
Macon, Dave, 286
Mann, Manfred, 109
"March Winds Goin' to Blow My Blues
    All Away," 175
Marsheck, Peggy, 371, 388
Martha White Flour Company, 281, 286
Martin, Ed, 127, 128
Martin, Grady, 354
Martin, Jimmy, 367
McConnell, Carl, 252, 254, 255
McConnell, Daphne, 68
McConnell, Ford, 189–90, 194
McConnell, Jack, 189–90
McEuen, Bill, 366–69
McEuen, John, 184–85, 366–69, 370,
    393
McGhee, Brownie, 127–28
McGhee, George "Duff," 127
McGhee, Sticks, 127
McKellar, Kenneth, 265
McLister, Cecil, 58, 75, 77, 93, 104,
    105, 124
McMurray family (Poor Valley, Va.), 159
Meade, Doc, 59, 123, 190, 320
Medical Question Box, 206
"Meet Me by the Moonlight, Alone,"
    108, 122
Mexican-style playing, 187, 339
Midday Merry-Go-Round, 265, 266,
    272

Middlebrook, J. R., 213
"Mid the Green Fields of Virginia," 131
Millard, Flo, 214, 321, 323, 387
Millard, Gladys Carter, *see* Carter,
    Gladys Ettaleen
Millard, Milan, 179, 214, 227, 240,
    241, 317, 319, 322, 323, 329,
    386
Mitchell, Joni, 364, 368
"Mommie's Real Peculiar," 289
Monroe, Bill, 306, 307, 367
Monument Records, 363
Moore, Bonnie Lou, 273
Morgan, George, 284
"Motherless Children Sees a Hard
    Time," 128
Mother Maybelle Carter, 339, 370–71
Mount Vernon Methodist Church,
    30–31, 72, 73, 125, 154,
    192–93
  cemetery at, 155, 331–33, 395, 397
"My Clinch Mountain Home," 34, 120,
    122–23, 141, 170–71, 177, 269
"My Darling's Home at Last," 255
"My Little Pup with the Patent-Leather
    Nose and the Wiggily-Waggily
    Tail," 279
"My Virginia Rose Is Blooming," 178

Nash, Graham, 364
National Barn Dance, 235, 260
National Public Radio, 109
NBC, 260, 294
Neal, Beverly, 155
Neal, John, 23, 52
Neal, Leonard, 52, 53, 112, 155, 174
Neal, Vivian, 155
Neal's Store, 23, 26–27, 52–53, 174,
    190, 196, 239, 317, 320, 329
Nelson, Willie, 6–7
New Lost City Ramblers, 340–43, 378
Newport Folk Festival, 343–45, 355, 380
New York Times, 9–10
Nickels, Melinda (Aunt Nick), 39–40,
    47–48, 65, 164, 165, 178, 379

Nickels, Milburn (Uncle Mil), 35,
39–40, 46, 65, 122, 164, 165,
178, 379
Nickels, Susie, 35
Nita, Rita, and Ruby, 311
Nitty Gritty Dirt Band, 4, 366–69,
392–93
Nix, Edwin "Rip," 347, 348, 349
Nix, Rosie, 360, 363, 369, 371, 372
"No More Goodbyes," 383
Noontime Neighbors, 286
"No Swallowing Place," 289

Obenreder, Ruth, 362, 390, 391
Oberstein, Eli, 175, 176
Okeh, 86–92, 93, 95, 139, 157, 175
Old Dominion Barn Dance, 261–63
"Old Joe Clark," 255
"Old Texas Trail, The," 6
"On a Hill Lone and Gray," 137
O'Neill, Harry, 197, 217, 226, 230,
246
O'Neill, Henrietta "Hattie" Nickels,
129, 130
O'Neill, Kate, 130, 172
O'Neill, William, 129–30
"One Little Word," 232
"One Toke Over the Line," 372
"On My Way to Canaan's Land," 137
"On the Sea of Galilee," 168
Original Carter Family, 5, 76–250, 256,
299, 354, 355
auditions of, 76–78, 95, 97–101,
103
beginnings of, 62–63, 65, 76–79, 95,
97–105
border-radio broadcasts of, 4, 5–9,
10–11, 197, 213–18, 222,
225–26, 229–30, 232–38, 241,
242, 245–46, 267, 328
Carter children performing with,
115–16, 215, 226–27, 229–30,
232–34, 236–37, 247, 248–50
celebrity of, 6, 8, 10, 104, 142–43,
145, 241, 245, 246

Charlotte radio broadcasts of, 246,
247, 248–50
contracts of, 110, 156–57, 175–76
disbanding of, 9, 226, 246–47,
250–51
earnings of, 105, 107, 110, 123–24,
156–57, 171, 176–77, 181, 214,
230, 313, 321, 332, 378
entertainments (live shows) of, *106*,
113–16, *114*, 145, 172, 185, 237
harmonies of, 5, 6, 108, 109
inducted into Country Music Hall of
Fame, 365, 380
Janette's festivals and, 375, 380–84,
387
legacy of, 4–7, 9–10, 109, 371
"lining out" of songs for, 120–22, 131
loyal audience of, 117
Maybelle as most musically adventurous of, 184–85
New York trip of, 167–70
personal pain as subject matter of, 7,
10, 101–2
photographs of, *xiv*, *107*, 111, *126*,
127, 242
privacy maintained by, 8–9
recording sessions of, 98–101, 104–5,
107–10, 112–13, 116–23, 139,
141–42, 156, 157, 159, 166–68,
171–72, 174–77, 181, 183–84,
241–42
rehearsals of, 108, 118, 183, 186
re-release of recordings by, 332
reunion album of, 355
reunion performances of, 375,
380–84, 387
revival of interest in (late 1950s),
328–29, 333, 337–45
Sara and A.P.'s separation and,
165–68, 170, 177, 178, 180,
181
songs gathered for, 5, 107–8, 111,
118–22, 127–38, 145–46,
148–49, 159, 165, 175, 177,
186–87, 328, 337

Original Carter Family (*cont.*)
  standards of, played by Carter Sisters
    and Mother Maybelle, 253, 271,
    272, 302
  translating melodies of, into sheet-
    music notes, 113
  see also Carter, Alvin Pleasant Delaney;
    Carter, Maybelle Addington;
    Carter, Sara Dougherty
"Orphan Child, The," 236
Our Southern Highlanders (Kephart), 14
Owens, Buck, 236
Owens, Price, 63, 101

Page, Patti, 287
Parham, Charles Fox, 134
Parker, Colonel Tom, 306, 307, 308,
  310
Parker, Everett, 320, 329
Parker, Jerry, 241
Parker, Marie, 308
Parker, Ruby, 31, 33, 61, 62, 109, 193,
  196
parlor songs, 130–31
Pearl, Minnie, 242–43, 286, 287, 300
Peer, Abraham, 86
Peer, Anita Glander, *81*, 98, 99, 112,
  166, 169, 322
Peer, Ralph Sylvester, 8, *81*, 81–95,
  111, 127, 169, 186, 214, 322,
  332, 378
  A.P. and Sara's marital difficulties
    and, 166, 180, 181
  background and early career of,
    86–93
  black musicians and, 83, 84, 87
  Carter Family's audition for, 77–78,
    95, 98–101, 103
  Carter Family's contracts with, 110,
    156–57, 175–76
  Carter Family's recording sessions
    with, 98–101, 104–5, 107–10,
    112–13, 116–23, 139, 141–42,
    156, 157, 159, 166–68, 171–72,
    174–77, 181, 183–84

Carter home visited by, 112–13, 319
copyright and royalty arrangements of,
  93, 94, 107, 113, 157, 175–76
hillbilly music and, 83, 84, 87–95
personality and demeanor of, 81–83
RCA Victor's conflict with, 175–76
Rodgers and, 113, 139–42, 174
scouting expeditions of, 77–78,
  81–82, 93–95, 98–101, 113
Pentecostalism, 133–36, 177–78
Perkins, Carl, 306, 311, 365
Persley, George, 120
Peter, Paul and Mary, 353
Phillips, Bud, 235
Phillips, Sam, 306, 307, 311, 346
phonograph technology, 85–86, 93
Pickard Family, 4, 216
"Plain Old Country Girl," 271,
  275–76
Poole, Charlie, 132
"Poor Orphan Child," 104
Poor Valley, Va., 6, 39, *51*
  churchgoing in, 30–31
  competitiveness of men in, 188–89
  economic opportunities outside of,
    54–57
  heating fuel in, 51–52
  party affiliation in, 238–39
  railroad tracks in, 51–52, 317–18
  water in, 52
  women of, 22–23, 60–61
Porter, Myrtle, 43
Porterfield, Nolan, 139, 142
Potter, Dale, 298–99
Powell, Barbara, 48, 219, 222, 246–47,
  379, 385, 394
Prairie Sweethearts (Essie and Kay),
  216
Presley, Elvis, 4, 275, 288, 306–11,
  332, 392
  attracted to Anita, 309–11
  female admirers of, 307–8, 309–10
  personality and demeanor of, 307, 308
Presley, Priscilla Beaulieu, 311
"Prisoner's Song," 122

radio, 87
   border stations and, 187, 245–46; see
      also XERA
   live audiences and, 235
   power of, 2–3, 234, 266
   recording technology and, 230, 278
Radio City Music Hal., 167, 168, 169
RadiOzark, 278, 287, 291
"Railroading on the Great Divide," 325,
      378
RCA, 273, 274–75, 290, 311, 321,
      332, 335
RCA Victor, 157, 171–72, 241, 289
   Peer's arrangements with, 157,
      175–76
records and record business:
   early days of, 85–86
   ethnic markets and, 87
   race music and, 83, 84, 87
   southern mountain music and, 87–95
   three-minute maximum and, 108
Red Clay Ramblers, 397
Red Star Flour, 279–80, 281
Reeves, Jim, 335
Renfro Valley Barn Dance, 260
Rich Valley, Va., 39
   musical traditions in, 41–45
   social life in, 45–46
"Ricochet Romance," 309
Riddle, Jimmy, 323
Riddle, Lesley "Esley," 146, 171, 175,
      240, 241
   A.P.'s song-hunting expeditions with,
      128–33, 136–38
   blues as viewed by, 137
   Maybelle's guitar playing and, 184
Rinehart, Cowboy Slim, 4, 7, 216, 233
"Ring of Fire," 349
Ritter, Tex, 262
Tex Ritter Award, 370
"River of Jordan," 109, 121, 177
Roach, Hal, 157
Robbins, Rita, 311
Robin, Lou, 363
"Rock of Ages," 137

Rodgers, Jimmie, 83–84, 113, *127*,
      139–42, 153, 174, 365, 371,
      379, 380
   Carter Family's recording with, 139,
      41–42, 156
Rolling Stone, 392–93
Romaniuk, Ed, 213–14, 328–29
Romaniuk, Elsie, 213–14, 328–29
Ronstadt, Linda, 4
Rose, Pete, 391
Rouncer, 4
royalties, 94, 105, 123, 156, 157, 181,
      313, 321, 328, 332, 378
   Peer's deals and, 93, 94, 107, 113,
      175–76, 214
Ryman, Thomas, 284–85
Ryman Auditorium, 284–85

"Sad and Lonesome Day," 177
Salyers, Fern Carter, 121, 173, 179,
      197, 228, 243, 248, 250
"San Antonio Rose, The," 344
Oscar Schmidt Company, 353
Schwarz, Tracy, 340–43
Scruggs, Earl, 4, 338–39, 366–67, 392
Scruggs, Louise, 338
Seeger, Mike, 71, 128, 132, 133, 185,
      340–45, 380
Seeger, Pete, 340, 365
"See That My Grave Is Kept Clean,"
      177, 339–40
Seymour, William Joseph, 134–36
shape-note singing, 32
sheet-music business, 41, 130–31
Shilkret, Nat, 93
shivarees, 67
Sholes, Steve, 275, 290
"Shoofly Pie and Apple Pan Dowdy,"
      253, 255
Silverstein, Shel, 364
Siman, E. E. "Si," 277, 278
singing conventions, 62
"Single Girl, Married Girl," 25, 100,
      105, 174, 177
Skeens, Mutt, 165, 172, 240

Smash Records, 353
Smith, Carl, 299, 300, 301, 303, 306,
    312
Smith, John "Dutch," 19, 33
Smith, Rebecca Carlene, 312
Smithsonian Institution, 370
Snow, Hank, 290, 293, 306, 307, 308
Snow, Minnie, 290, 358, 390
Songs of the Famous Carter Family,
    338–39, 366
song transmission, 41–42, 43–44,
    70–71, 184
"Sourwood Mountain," 119
Southern Music Publishing Company,
    157, 175, 176, 321, 378
Southern Planter, 252–53
Southland Shows, 262, 263
Springsteen, Bruce, 368–69
Spurlock, Clifford, 324–28
Stalcup, William, 89
Stapleton, Daphne Kilgore, 33, 46, 72,
    74, 178
Starday, 331
Statler Brothers, 365, 366
"Stay a Little Longer," 269
Steele, Harry, 216, 217, 226
Stephens, "Uncle Bunt," 88
Stoker, Gordon, 288
Stokes, Marcus Lowe, 89
Stoneman, Ernest V. "Pop," 78, 90–94,
    139
Stoneman, Hattie, 94, 139
"Storms Are on the Ocean, The," 105,
    321
"Strummin' My Guitaro," 353
Sun Records, 275, 306, 311, 346
"Sunshine in the Shadows," 177
"Sweet Bird," 120
"Sweet Fern," 120, 123
"Sweet Heaven in My View," 186

Tarter, Steve, 127, 128
Taylor, "Hi," 89
"Tell Me That You Loved Me," 157
Tennessee Barn Dance, 270

Tennessee Valley Authority (TVA), 196,
    265
"That's How I Spell Ireland," 272
"There'll Be No Distinction There," 242
"There'll Be No Teardrops Tonight,"
    279
"There's No One Like Mother to Me,"
    186
"There's Something Got Ahold of Me,"
    242
"This Land Is Your Land," 137
Thomas, Brown, 148–49, 191
Thomas, Dicey, 60–61, 116, 148
"Tom Dooley," 337
Travis, Merle, 338, 345, 367, 392
Travis picking, 267
Tubb, Ernest, 286, 300
Tuck, William, 261–62
"Turkey in the Straw," 279
"Two Little Girls in Blue," 330

Vaughan, James D., 32
Vermillion, Cleo, 63
Vicars, Worley, 112
Victor, 5, 77–78, 87, 92–101, 105,
    113, 116–17, 139, 157
    Carter Family's audition for, 77–78,
        95, 97–101, 103
    Peer's first field-recording sessions for,
        93–95, 98–101
    see also RCA Victor
Virginia Boys, 252, 254, 255

"Wait 'Til I Get You Alone," 301
"Wandering Boy, The," 62, 100, 104,
    114
Waterman, Mrs. Lem, 89
Watson, Doc, 109, 110, 367, 369, 392
Watts, Stubbins, 88–89
"Wayfaring Stranger, The," 119
WBT, 246, 247, 248–50, 338
WCKY, 327
"Weeping Willow Tree," 305–6, 344
Welch, J. P., 43
Wells, Kitty, 109, 122, 311

Wells, Ruby, 311
"Were You There When They Crucified Our Lord," 353
"We Shall Rise," 379
West, Red, 310, 311
Westendorf, Thomas P., 120, 130
"What Am I Supposed to Do?", 336
"What's It?", 140
"When the Roses Bloom in Dixieland," 110
"When the Roses Come Home Again," 168
"When the World's on Fire," 137, 185
Whitter, Henry, 83, 90
"Why Do You Cry, Little Darling?", 241
"Wildwood Flower," 4 108–9, 117, 177, 288, 340, 344, 366, 368, 371
Williams, Audrey, 292–97
Williams, Hank, 279, 283, 291–98, 300, 348, 368
    Anita courted by, 292–96, 298
    death of, 297–98
    drinking and drug use of, 292, 294–95
    shooting incident and, 296–97
Williams, Lucinda, 4, 109
Williams, Tennessee, 265
"Willow, Will You Weep for Me?", 289
Will the Circle Be Unbroken, 366–69, 392–93
"Will the Circle Be Unbroken," 4, 168, 172, 177–78, 311, 365, 368, 392
"Will You Miss Me When I'm Gone?", 96, 102, 108, 109
Winston, Nat, 361
WKIN, 322, 323
WLS, 260, 261
WNOX, 264–68, 270, 273–74

Wolfe, Charles, 43, 120
Wolfe, Ernest, 123
Wolfe, Flo, 6
Wolfe, Thomas, 102
"Wonderful City, The," 141
Woodring, Harry, 209
Workman, John "Sugarfoot," 261, 262
Workman, Mary Arlene "Sunshine Sue," 261–63
World's Fair (1933), 195–96
World War II, 245, 254–55, 265
"Worried Man Blues," 4, 138, 332, 340, 344
"Wreck of Old 97, The," 75, 108, 185
WRNL, 25 –53, 254, 260
WRVA, 260–63
WSM, 260 281, 286, 305

XEG, 187, 213
XELO, 187, 213, 237
XEPN, 213
XERA, 3–4, 187, 197, 201, 210–18, 225
    Carter Family's broadcasts on, 4, 7, 197, 213–18, 222, 225–26, 229–30, 232–38, 245, 267, 328
    closure of, 213, 245
    founding of, 209–10
XERB, 213
XET, 230

"You Are My Flower," 184, 186–87, 339
"You Flopped When You Got Me Alone," 301
"You Made Toothpicks of the Timber of My Heart," 279
"You've Been a Friend to Me," 131

Zetner, Ann, 357
Zetner, Tammy, 357